Human Variation

FOURTH EDITION

Human Variation

Races, Types, and Ethnic Groups

STEPHEN MOLNAR

Washington University

PRENTICE HALL, Upper Saddle River, New Jersey 07458

Library of Congress Cataloging-in-Publication Data

MOLNAR, STEPHEN
    Human variation: races, types, and ethnic groups/Stephen
Molnar.—4th ed.
        p. cm.
    Includes bibliographical references and index.
    ISBN 0-13-269523-5
    1. Physical anthropology. 2. Race. I. Title.
GN62.8.M63 1997
599.9—dc21   97-1104
                                              CIP

Editor-in-chief: Nancy Roberts
Sociology editor: Stephen T. Jordan
Associate editor: Sharon Chambliss
Editorial/production supervision and interior design: Rob DeGeorge
Copyeditor: Virginia Rubens
Buyer: Mary Ann Gloriande
Line art coordinator: Michele Giusti
Line art studio: Tech-Graphics
Photo researcher: Rona Tuccillo

This book was set in 10/12 Baskerville by DM Cradle Associates
and was printed and bound by Courier Companies, Inc.
The cover was printed by Phoenix Color Corp.

© 1998, 1992, 1983, 1975 by Prentice-Hall, Inc.
Simon & Schuster/A Viacom Company
Upper Saddle River, New Jersey 07458

Printed in the United States of America

10 9 8 7 6 5 4 3 2 1

ISBN 0-13-269523-5

PRENTICE-HALL INTERNATIONAL (UK) LIMITED, *London*
PRENTICE-HALL OF AUSTRALIA PTY. LIMITED, *Sydney*
PRENTICE-HALL CANADA INC., *Toronto*
PRENTICE-HALL HISPANOAMERICANA, S.A., *Mexico*
PRENTICE-HALL OF INDIA PRIVATE LIMITED, *New Delhi*
PRENTICE-HALL OF JAPAN, INC., *Tokyo*
SIMON & SCHUSTER ASIA PTE. LTD., *Singapore*
EDITORA PRENTICE-HALL DO BRASIL, LTDA., *Rio de Janeiro*

TO IVA
who worked so hard to make this book possible

Contents

7   Human Variability and Behavior   279

8   Changing Dimensions of the Human Species   318

TABLES

FIGURES

Preface

Almost daily we are informed of a newly discovered gene for a disease, behavior, or physical characteristic. The implication is that individuals are what they are because of a particular code in our genome; a DNA sequence supposedly determines alcoholism, homosexuality, intelligence, several types of cancers, diabetes, and heart disease, for example. Cause and effect are more implied than real; what is actually reported is the discovery of a higher frequency of a genetic marker in some family lineages with a history of a certain disease. Nevertheless, these frequent reports support a confidence that the mysteries of human biological diversity have been solved and that our variability and origins have been clearly described. Unfortunately, this is not true. The range of human genetic diversity and its causes have yet to be fully explored, though progress is being made. Also, there remain many unanswered questions regarding human origins.

Confronting the nature of human diversity and its meaning still presents a problem. What I said in the preface to the third edition still applies to this edition six years later. There continues to be a dependence on the race concept, and biological determinism is often a central theme in discussions of social problems. Race and class are commingled, and the heritability of numerous behavioral attributes is offered as an explanation for the major social issues confronting the world today. This mixing of sociopolitical issues with biological explanations continues despite the advances that have been made in the mapping of the human genome. In fact, it is the very growth of knowledge about our genome that has, in some ways, supported a confidence in biological determinism. In this edition, as in previous editions, I shall continue to explore the scope of our knowledge of human diversity and criticize the reliance on racial labels. The mass of new data on genetic markers underscores the weaknesses of these "classic" race divisions. I shall try to guide the reader past the major pitfalls of nineteenth-century thinking as the recent data on gene geography is discussed.

Much of this edition has been reorganized to incorporate the newer records of DNA polymorphisms and to place these data in a frame of reference that does not depend on race categories. This has meant some expansion of Chapter 2, "The Biological Basis for Human Variation," and the addition of a new Chapter 4 on hemoglobin variants and DNA markers. Chapter 3, "Human Biology 1: Traits of Simple Inheritance," has been similarly revised and updated. The major changes in this edition, however, have involved a reorganization to bring the discussion of natural selection together with the listing of the various genetic markers. Solid evidence linking population gene frequencies to the influences of natural selection in *Homo sapiens* is still not as extensive as we might wish, but the link is explained wherever possible. The selective forces of disease acting on the blood groups, hemoglobins, and various enzymes are described. Environmental factors affecting complex traits of body form, size, and skin color are also discussed. Chapter 8, the final chapter, has been revised to include all the current demographic data. It has also been expanded to incorporate information on the return of the "old" diseases as modern threats to human survival. Disproportionate growth of regional populations continues as it has for the last twenty-five years, straining national and ethnic boundaries and interrelationships.

The revision of Chapter 7 continues to outline and criticize the misunderstanding of heritability and the misuse of racial taxons. Several recent books, published since the last edition, illustrate how far some authors will go in an attempt to support the old dogma of inherited inequality of presumed racial divisions. The study of human diversity continues to be hampered by such attempts, which are no more than an extension of nineteenth-century beliefs. It is disappointing to have to continue to cover new variants of these same arguments in each edition. It is essential, however, to relate these new publications to their old intellectual foundations. Their authors still offer measures of IQ by standardized tests as indicators of inherited ability of class and race despite the vast amount of genetic and behavioral data to the contrary.

As in previous editions, the reviewers' comments, as well as comments from friends and colleagues, are gratefully acknowledged. The following individuals reviewed the manuscript for the fourth edition: James H. Mielke, University of Kansas–Lawrence; David P. Tracer, University of Washington; and Trudy Turner, University of Wisconsin–Milwaukee. I would also like to thank the editorial staff of Prentice Hall for their help in guiding this revision through all of the steps leading to publication. A special note of appreciation goes to my wife, Iva, who has continued in her support and encouragement. As always, she has been a partner in all phases of the research and writing.

1

Racial Variation and the Perception of Human Differences

HOW DO HUMANS VARY?
AN INTRODUCTION TO THE RACE CONCEPT

There is no doubt about the fact of human biological diversity. Traditional racial divisions, however, are based on a faulty perception of human differences and a lack of understanding of the causes and meanings of these differences. Like our ancestors in previous centuries, we rely on a simple visual appraisal of appearances related to size, form, and color to identify distinctions between various groups. Some of the biggest differences seem to exist in skin color, because degrees of pigmentation extend from a very pale color among northern Europeans to an extremely dark brown among, for example, the peoples of the African Congo or New Guinea. In addition, human body size varies widely—from the $4^1/2$-foot-tall pygmies in Africa and Oceania to the $6^1/2$-foot-tall Nilotic peoples of East Africa. Europeans themselves vary from short (in southern Europe) to tall (in northwestern Europe). Body shape ranges from a thin and linear build to a shorter and heavier one, as seen in the contrast between several arctic peoples and native Australians. Face form and head shape are other distinguishing characteristics that may differentiate between populations. Hair form, another trait that has attracted a great deal of attention, varies from straight and long to short and spiral-shaped. All of these features have led, or I should say, misled writers to draw conclusions about the relationships between groups. Lookalikes have been considered to be closely related by common descent, while dissimilar appearances have been taken as evidence of fixed racial boundaries.

The development of twentieth-century medical technology with all its sophisticated laboratory methods has revealed many more distinctions among humans. Such distinctions are inherited traits not easily determined but require special techniques for their detection. The blood types, enzymes, and numerous biochemical factors began to be discovered early in this century and showed a range of frequencies among the various groups studied. The list of these traits is increasing rapidly as newer and more efficient methods are employed. The most important addition has been the discovery of deoxyribonucleic acid (DNA). In the last two decades, major strides have been made in techniques that permit quantities of measurements to be made of this "code of life." These measurements have uncovered human diversity at a new level. Certain regions of DNA fragments show so much variability that differentiations may be made between populations or between families or even at the personal level, as in DNA "fingerprinting." With a combination of the new methods of biochemical and DNA analysis, a whole new dimension of study has been opened up. Studies can now be made at the subgenetic level.

This newly acquired ability to study biological diversity forces us to reject perceptions of superficial human differences, many of which are due to factors of nutrition and child growth. But even a simple appraisal suggests that *Homo sapiens* consists of many diverse population groups whose range of physical variability is enormous. Such variety causes one to ponder the composition of our species and casts doubt on any scheme that attempts to divide humanity into a few definite races or ethnic groups. Just why is *Homo sapiens* such a polymorphic, polytypic species? That is, how can we explain the individual variability within a population (polymorphic) or the distinctions among the human groups we frequently call races (polytypic)? Why are characteristics of skin, hair, body size, blood factors, or DNA fragment types distributed among the world's peoples in the way they are?

Biological variability today appears to result from the combined influence of human behavior and natural forces that have been at work throughout human prehistory. The size of populations, their isolation, and their adaptation to environmental stresses contribute to or detract from the survival of individuals or of the entire group. Each population grouping also reflects, to some degree, the experiences of its ancestors and gives evidence of elements in its environment that have been shaping it through time. This modification over the course of generations is still proceeding and may contribute to future population diversity. No matter how we may define or classify clusters of populations today, their composition will undoubtedly change over future generations as a result of major alterations in evolutionary forces through human adaptation and because of continuing migrations and inter-breeding. These and other factors cause the extensive changes in boundaries between peoples.

With the rapid increase in population diversity that has occurred within the Western world as immigration has accelerated in the last few decades, we have all tended to become students of human variation to some degree. National population composition—that is, the percentages of minorities—is quite different from that of previous generations and is continuing to change, both here in the United States as well as in western Europe. This change has frequently been noted in the popular press under headlines heralding "The Changing Face of America" or "The Browning of America." Such articles, with or without implied value judgments about socioeconomic or cultural differences, outline some of the sources of the change. Little is contributed to the understanding of biological diversity, however. All too often, traditional racial classification is revived along with a version of nineteenth-century racism. In this book I will describe the major components of the biological diversity of our species and will attempt to examine its various causes.

HUMAN VARIATION AND ITS CLASSIFICATION

How have we become conscious of the varieties of *Homo sapiens* and their place among the living organisms in the world? This awareness developed gradually as a result of extensive explorations of the world by Europeans during recent centuries. Explorers brought back specimens of plants and animals unknown in Europe, and these, together with encounters with peoples of the new lands, demonstrated the diversity in the living world—and challenged many of the Europeans' long-established beliefs. The idea that humans descended from an original pair was especially hard to cling to after the discovery of populations differing as much as Africans, Malaysians, and Native Americans. A revival of Aristotle's worldview of idealized living forms scaled to fit within eleven grades of development became the most useful scheme to reconcile such diversity. As expressed by Lamarck (1744–1829), the famous French naturalist whose ideas on the evolution of life forms predated Darwin's, "man represents the type of highest perfection of nature and the more an animal organization approaches that of man the more perfect it is" (quoted in Mayr, 1982:353). With such graded categories, natural scientists were able to reconcile the discoveries of these new peoples with current religious dogma through an arrangement of all living creatures in a scale from lower to higher categories, from inanimate to animate, with humans at the top. This "Great Chain of Being" concept greatly simplified the study of human variability. Europeans were placed at the top of an ascending order, with newly discovered peoples arranged below—an idea that remained popular throughout the nineteenth century.

The "chain" concept fostered the belief that no two varieties of humans could occupy the same developmental level. Later, in the latter half of the nineteenth century, as Darwin's evolutionary theories were gaining acceptance, the human varieties were thought to represent several past stages of development. But even before Darwin, there was a firmly held belief that many ancestral human pairs had been created, each differing externally and internally in a way that suited them for a particular environment. These arrangements of our species into varieties were frequently complicated by the scientists' personal biases. Many believed that certain groups had been retarded in their progress toward civilization by environmental conditions. Naturally, these schemes placed Europeans as the superior group and as being thousands of years ahead of other races. This idea of the superiority of one race over another persisted well into this century, as illustrated in Carleton Coon's *Origin of Races*: "As far as we know now, the Congoid (Negroid) line started on the same evolutionary level as the Eurasiatic ones in the Early Middle Pleistocene and then stood still for a half a million years, after which Negroes and Pygmies appear as if out of nowhere" (1962:659). It is, perhaps, ironic, that thirty-five years later a reverse order is generally accepted. The new laboratory techniques that compare mitochondrial DNA polymorphisms offer strong evidence for Africa as the homeland of the earliest populations of *Homo sapiens.*

These issues of racial origins and rates of development were secondary to the major problem confronting scientists two hundred years ago: what to do with the overwhelming quantities of data accumulating from the discoveries in the recently explored world. Their problem was not whether humans varied in their biological makeup; they could see that with their own eyes, although the variation was not always what they supposed it to be because of the impressionistic means used to perceive human differences. But what were the boundaries of these differences, and how might these boundaries relate to humans' past and to human survival?

The modern systematic study of human diversity begins with an attempt to place populations in a classification system. Most classifications depend on the system established by the Swedish botanist Carolus Linnaeus (1707–1778). Linnaeus based his classification system on the assumption, current in his day, that species had been of a fixed type and number since creation. Species were seen as units of organisms that could interbreed only among themselves; an earlier description noted that "a species could not spring from the seed of another, different species." This sharp distinction between species would assist the process of classification. Further, Linnaeus and other natural scientists believed that the number of species was limited, fixed, and unchanging. All one had to do was to collect and classify samples of the various life forms. But, as it turned out, Linnaeus was confronted with growing evidence of the variety of organisms, and the categories had to be expanded and modified with each new edition of his *Systema Naturae,* first published in 1735. This was especially true when human populations from other continents were discovered. Explorers, including Columbus, brought back a few of these exotic people encountered during their travels to display before curious European audiences. The differences in appearance, language, and customs of these exotic human "specimens" increased the questions about the classification of humankind.

The discovery of monkeys and apes in Africa and Southeast Asia presented a special challenge. Where should these new humanlike animals be placed? After much consideration, apes, monkeys, and humans were given a shared classification in an order of mammals, the primates. Monkeys and apes were separated into different divisions (superfamilies); apes and humans shared *Hominoidea*, while monkeys were placed in the superfamily *Cercopithecoidea*. Though recognizing similarities between humans and apes, Linnaeus ignored the evolutionary implications of his classifications throughout several editions of his work and continued to maintain that species were fixed in number. However, overwhelmed by the increasing evidence of nature's diversity, he gradually altered his position and allowed that certain varieties were unstable—a conclusion that suggested evolutionary change. Today, of course, biologists no longer consider special creation or the fixity of species but instead consider the fossil record and the natural diversity of biological organisms as evidence of evolutionary change—that contributes to the formation of new species or to species extinction. Not only do we view species as dynamic units of the natural world, but we consider each species in its environmental context, as shown in this definition by Mayr (1982:273): "A species is a reproductive community of populations (reproductively isolated from others) that occupies a specific niche in nature." However, population groups within a species are another matter and can change rapidly even within a single generation, since they can freely interbreed. This interbreeding can lead to wideranging diversity, resulting in further classification into subspecies.

Linnaeus dealt with the classification of human diversity by using subspecies categories he called human varieties, listed in Table 1-1, which

TABLE 1-1 Early Racial Classifications

LINNAEUS (1735)	BUFFON (1749)	BLUMENBACH[a] (1781)	CUVIER (1790)
American (Reddish)	Laplander	Caucasoid	Caucasoid
European (White)	Tartar	Mongoloid	Mongoloid
Asiatic (Yellow)	South Asiatic	American Indian	Negroid
Negro (Black)	European	Ethiopian	
	Ethiopian	Malay	
	American		

[a]This scheme for racial division was an expansion of Blumenbach's earlier one (1770). As he described the problem: "Formerly in the first edition of this work I divided all mankind into four varieties but after I had more accurately investigated the different nations of Eastern Asia and America, and, so to speak, looked at them more closely, I was compelled to give up that division, and to place in its stead the following five varieties as more consonant to nature."

Source: From Blumenbach, J. F., *Readings in Early Anthropology*, ed. J. S. Slotkin, 1965. Copyright © by Viking Fund Publications. Reprinted by permission of the publisher.

includes some of the classifications offered by other eighteenth-century naturalists as well. These early classifications, later called *races*, were determined by
comparisons of skin color, face form, and skull shape. Measuring the form
and size of the skull was an especially popular method for racial studies,
because ancient populations could be studied and supposed racial affinities
could be determined from their skeletal remains. Often, stature, hair form,
and shape of the nose were used. Frequently these traits were used in combination in an effort to precisely distinguish among populations. However, a
large subjective component present in each of these classifications led some
early workers to suggest that racial classification was unimportant. Also, the
fact that all races could freely interbreed made it clear that no group could be
very far removed from the original form of the species, and that all shared
close common ancestors.

Though the boundaries for these racial divisions were established as
much on the basis of geographical distribution as on biological differences,
behavioral attributes of language and social customs were often associated
with biological criteria. Linnaeus attributed behavioral as well as biological
characteristics to each group. He defined *Homo Europeaus* as fickle, sanguine,
blue-eyed, gentle, and governed by laws; he described *Homo afer* as choleric,
obstinate, contented, and regulated by customs; and he characterized *Homo
asiaticus* as grave, dignified, avaricious, and ruled by opinion. These personality profiles that Linnaeus offered together with physical traits are illustrations of biodeterminism: the attribution of certain types of behavior to certain
racial groups. Although this practice may have been understandable in the
eighteenth century, given the primitive state of biology and psychology of the
day, such confusion of cultural features with biological traits is inexcusable
today. Though there has been little or no evidence to support correlations
between behavior, character, and skin color since those offered by earlier writers on human diversity, we still read descriptions that claim to demonstrate
correlations between race and a whole range of "native" abilities.

Following Linnaeus, other natural scientists turned their attention to
classifications of human varieties. A German physician, Johann Friedrich Blumenbach (1752–1840), the reputed "Father of Physical Anthropology," gave
us several of the racial terms in wide use today. He classified humanity into five
races: *Caucasoid, Mongoloid, American, Ethiopian,* and *Malayan.* To the usual criterion of skin color Blumenbach added hair form and facial characteristics,
with special attention to the shape of the skull. Skull shape was supposed to
be a significant racial trait and was regarded as a trait highly resistant to environmental influences. Blumenbach amassed a large collection of human
skulls from all over the world for study and, in keeping with the eighteenth-
century belief in ideal types, he searched for and found one that represented
his ideal of beauty, a perfect specimen. The skull that came closest to fitting
this image of perfection was one that had been recovered from the Caucasus
Mountains, in an area near Mount Ararat. *Caucasoid* eventually became a term

applied to a major category that encompassed the European, North African, and Middle Eastern populations.

During this period of studies of human variety, our affinity to the lower primates did not go unnoticed. Peter Simon Pallas (1741–1811), a German naturalist and a student of Linnaeus, provided the first family-tree diagram used in biology. In a communication with Blumenbach, Pallas described a diagram depicting degrees of morphological affinity between several animal groups. This tree, or "biological pedigree," depicted what may have been Pallas's belief in organic evolution (see McCown and Kennedy, 1972). Its arrangement indicated a close affinity between *Homo sapiens* and the lower primates—a relationship, based on anatomical similarities, that was considered as a possibility by other naturalists; Buffon, a French naturalist (1707–1788), noted a greater resemblance between humans and orangutans than between humans and baboons. His conservatism, however, prevented him from accepting human and primate affinities. Despite the similarity in anatomy between our species and other primates, humans were set apart by Buffon on the grounds that only *Homo sapiens* had a soul.

Blumenbach, Buffon, Linnaeus, and others in the eighteenth century were handicapped in their attempts to work out a classification more reflective of the actual nature of human variability. They lacked the insights possessed by later generations of scientists who had additional evidence and a clearer understanding of evolution. In addition, Blumenbach and his contemporaries assumed that the taxonomic groups of humanity were fixed and unchanging, as they believed species to be. There were distinct boundaries between races, established at the creation, and any biological diversity was presumed to be a variation around an ideal racial type. The characteristics of a European, whose features and skull shape differed from the ideal Caucasoid type, were explained as the result of climate, diet, or even social class. Such concepts and beliefs in racial types and diversity provided a foundation for modern studies of human diversity throughout the nineteenth and most of this century.

As descriptions of additional human populations were offered, explanations of the origins of their diversity were sought. Climate was most often described as a significant influence (the Ethiopian, blackened by the sun, was the usual example offered), but this oversimplification ignored the influence of heredity. As far back as the sixteenth century, Leonardo da Vinci had observed that the black races of Ethiopia could not be the product of the sun's effects, because black parents produce offspring who are black (Slotkin, 1965:91). "Domestication of mankind," a process that supposedly accompanied the development of civilization, was presumed to be another influence on race formation and was described by James Cowles Prichard (1786–1848) in *Researches into the Physical History of Man* (1813). However, in the second edition, published in 1826, Prichard rejected this domestication theory and described the environmental influences and the close correlations between climate and physical type.

In addition to the question of origins or causes of racial variation, the classification of races itself was called into question. Prichard recognized early the problems imposed by dividing humanity into only a few fixed species, and he rejected attempts to divide the human species into "principal families," which was a common practice when divisions were made on the basis of skull shape. "It is by no means evidence that all those nations who resemble each other in shape of their skulls, or in any other peculiarity, are of one race, or more nearly allied by kindred to each other than to tribes who differ from them in the same particulars" (Prichard, 1826:28). Though he did reject such divisions, Prichard described major types of *Homo sapiens* based on head form and coloration. He argued that this was done only to facilitate comparisons independently of any design to ascribe common origins. He suggested that there was no such thing as a Negro race in the customary sense: "Among those swarthy nations of Africa which we ideally represent under the term negro, there was perhaps not one single nation in which all the characters ascribed to the negro are found in the highest degree" (Stocking, 1973:48). This insight, though strikingly modern, is seldom recalled today.

This lack of association between traits and boundaries when several traits are used to distinguish between groups of populations renders any search for racial purity a futile and often silly exercise. Nevertheless, attempts are repeatedly made to work with idealized forms when racial divisions are attempted. The concept of an ideal type persisted into modern times, as illustrated by the fact that Otto Ammon (1842–1911), a German anthropologist who had measured thousands of human heads and had frequently discussed Nordic and Alpine types of Europeans, could not produce a "perfect" specimen of either type. He confessed that he was not able to find a specimen perfect in all details (in Montagu, 1974:454).

ANTHROPOMETRY: THE MEASURES OF HUMAN VARIATION

During the nineteenth century, numerous attempts were made to introduce scientific method into the analysis of measures of human diversity. For example, statistical methods were applied to the interpretation of variation in size, and the concept "average man" was introduced as a "scientific" way of establishing types. Such "ideal types" or averages work well for sorting out widely differing species, but matters become more difficult when investigators are dealing with closely related organisms, and "type" becomes a mere abstraction for comparisons of subspecies (or races). This difficulty increases when we search for forms that match notions of the ideal specimen, a factor that has caused many problems in studies of human evolution. Often the investigator had in mind an image of what the type specimen should look like and then searched until it was found, neglecting the deviations from this image. Such a simplified view of the natural world has been applied many times well into this century. For example, Kretschmer (1888–1964), who studied human body form (constitutional types), emphasized in 1930 that this typological system was based on the most beautiful specimens, the rare and happy finds.

Such subjective imagery impedes the understanding of the scope of human variation and serves only to contribute to the number of stereotypes. Rather than acknowledge the variations of traits in populations, many natural scientists were content to view the human species as consisting of a few original "types" despite the accumulation of data on human diversity by the end of the nineteenth century. These types could, in turn, be used to divide our species into a few "basic" races that actually masked the ranges of individual diversities. Any group, large or small, could be said to vary around some ideal or average, and as more knowledge was gained more reference points or types could be used to establish new divisions.

There was a further development of anthropometry—the physical measurement of human body form—with special description of several cranial features. The major reason that the size and shape of the skull was given so much attention in anthropometric studies was the assumption that skull form was the feature of the anatomy most resistant to change and, hence, cranial form was considered a good measure of one's ancestry. In addition, because the skull housed the brain, the head's shape and contours were supposed to be indicative of the brain's characteristics and even a measure of its quality. The belief that a person's character and intelligence were indicated by the morphology of his or her head has a long history. The study of these supposed interrelationships expanded and developed into a "science" at the beginning of the last century through the efforts of two German physicians, Franz Joseph Gall (1758–1828) and Johann Kaspar Spurzheim (1776–1832). Their work provided the basis for phrenology, a widely popular pseudoscience of the nineteenth century that examined and recorded the skull's contours, which were thought to provide a map or diagram of an individual's latent abilities and talents.

Later, in 1842, Anders Retzius (1769–1860) added a new index to cranial studies that described the general shape of the cranial vault. Retzius divided the maximum breadth of the skull by its maximum length, which gave a ratio known as the *cephalic index* (see Figure 1-1). This index became an important element in cranial studies and was widely used after Retzius reported that European populations could be divided into three types based on their head shapes: *dolichocephalic* (long, narrow head), *mesocephalic* (intermediate shape), and *brachycephalic* (round-headed or short and broad-shaped). The cephalic index, together with the two types of face form, *orthognathic* (straight-faced) and *prognathic* (lower face projecting), provided another set of criteria for racial studies. Face form together with cephalic index provided Retzius with a means to divide European populations into four possible groups. Comparing cephalic indices between populations, Retzius reported differences between the skulls of Finnish and Swedish populations. The round-headed Finns were

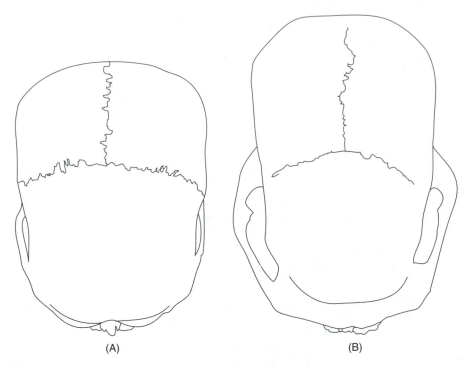

FIGURE 1-1 Representative Skull Shapes Viewed from Above. The broader skull (A) is classed as *brachycephalic* in contrast to the long and narrow shape of the *dolichocephalic* skull (B).

considered an indigenous race, whereas the long-headed Swedes had supposedly descended from Indo-European Aryans who invaded Europe thousands
of years ago from western Asia. Overall, the cephalic index has been popular
for a long time, and it was widely applied in studies of human variation even
up to the mid-twentieth century.

One of the leading scientists of the day who took a keen interest in Retzius's work was Pierre Paul Broca (1824–1880), a famous French neurosur-
geon and founder of the first anthropological society in Europe (1859). Broca
applied his training and experience in comparative studies of craniology to
provide further support to those who endeavored to relate human behavior
to a particular head form. He was convinced that the measured shape of the
skull was the best indicator of the quality of the brain. The concern with brain
contents, and hence craniology as Broca developed it, was based on an interest in racial differences that he believed to be primordial. Broca assumed that
because racial differences also find their expression in behavior, the brain had
something to do with race (a false assumption still very much with us today—
see Chapter 7). Broca worked with great care and treated his measurements
with a fine precision. He did not stop with a mere numerical descriptive system but deduced from his measurements the racial history or even the social
status of the group under study. He translated skull dimensions into a series

of mathematical indices and then deduced the personality and social attitudes of the long-dead individuals, together with their supposed biological affinities. However, after years of such efforts Broca admitted that no single criterion was sufficient to separate the races of humanity.

Though he contributed much to neuroanatomy and anthropology in the mid-nineteenth century and introduced several new techniques of analysis, his achievements have been overshadowed by the erroneous generalizations he made about social class and intelligence—that were very similar to the imaginative speculations of the phrenologists. His attempt to associate lumps or prominences on the skull with various activity centers of the brain may be understood within the intellectual perspectives of nineteenth-century neuroscience. However, the correlation of character, race, and social class to skull form is more difficult to understand, especially since Broca admitted that several organic diseases contracted during childhood could cause deformation of the skull. Despite the efforts of Broca and many others, phrenology passed from scientific acceptability by the end of the nineteenth century. As one author writes, "Phrenology died a pauper's death in the late nineteenth century, victimized by the vicious ostracism of the period's most reputable anthropologists" (Haller, 1971:17). Though this pseudoscience disappeared quietly, the racial classifications begun or supported by phrenologists, which relegated Mongolians, Malayans, Indians, and Ethiopians to inferior positions below Caucasians, were seldom criticized or attacked.

While Retzius, Gall, and Broca were developing theories of craniology, several scientists in America were occupied with similar studies. Samuel Morton (1799–1851), a famous physician of his day, is best remembered for the thousands of skulls he collected; many were from Native American remains but a sizable number came from other parts of the world. Morton believed, as did his European colleagues, that skull shape and size indicated race and character. They equated size of skull with intelligence and often reported smaller average cranial volumes for non-Europeans. Morton showed by his measurements that Native Americans had a much smaller cranial volume than did the Caucasoid skulls in his collection. Typological concepts and skeletal samples influenced his conclusions.[1]

Because the European skulls in his collection had the largest cranial capacity, Morton concluded that Caucasoids were the most intelligent of the races—a contention brought up repeatedly in the century following Morton's studies. Therefore, the discovery of skulls of reportedly Caucasoid type in several of the large earth mounds located in the Ohio and Mississippi valleys of the midwestern United States were taken as proof that a vanished race of ancient Caucasian people was responsible for the construction of the vast and

---

[1]Recent reexamination of Morton's measurements and his use of arithmetic means by Gould (1978 and 1983) showed that there were, in fact, insignificant differences between the racial groups. The large differences reported by Morton could be demonstrated only if there had been a bias in the selection of the measurements and skull samples.

impressive earthworks rather than the Native Americans who were seen by the earliest European colonists in the eighteenth century.

Morton's work influenced many others, notably George Gliddon (1809–1857), a famous Egyptologist of his day. Gliddon eagerly and uncritically applied Morton's methods to cranial studies of the skeletal remains he recovered from Egypt to prove that the pharaoh and the pyramid builders were, in fact, members of the Caucasoid race. This conclusion lent added support to the conviction held by scholars of the day that only the Caucasoids were capable of building higher civilizations. The large mounds and urban centers in the midwestern United States, the Mayan pyramids of Guatemala and Mexico, and the highly developed civilizations of the Andes and Thailand were all presumed to be a result of Caucasoid influence. This is a myth that will not die but keeps reappearing, as for example in the recent arguments over the "racial origins" of the ancient Egyptians. These kinds of studies intermingling ancient history and biology continued for many years through the early part of this century. Though now thoroughly discredited, this misuse of craniology was once accepted as "scientific proof" of the racial composition of ancient populations.

Throughout the development of anthropometry there has been the belief that if only enough measurements were taken, facts would emerge that would clear up the mysteries surrounding human origins and variations. Numerous select groups were measured throughout Europe, with schoolchildren and military personnel the most frequent subjects. Given the vast number of measurements made during the course of anthropometric studies, a means of analysis had to be devised, and several mathematicians developed statistical methods. Foremost among these early statisticians was Lambert Quetelet (1796–1874), an astronomer and mathematician interested in social statistics. He gathered anthropometric measurements from a large number of military conscripts, university students, and prison convicts, and comparisons were made with a broader sample of European populations. Statistically significant differences of height, weight, and several body proportions were reported between the samples—differences that were attributed to environment or heredity. Most important, these studies established the concept of the "average man" that continues to influence our perspective on human diversity (Stigler 1986:170).

Especially influential were the measurements of Belgian army conscripts and convicts, which provided the raw data for many of the correlations of behavior with body form Quetelet described. These materials permitted the application of probability statistics to predictions of behavior, a method that became widely accepted in both Europe and North America. The statistical methods provided a seemingly scientific basis for investigators who attempted to identify criminal types from a few physical characteristics. Further, Quetelet's statistical work and his descriptions of the "average man" lent support to those searching for the ideal of beauty and perfection in humans and seeking broader meanings in anthropometric dimensions. The use of such standards or types as predictors of behavior or intelligence was not, however, without its critics, as illustrated by Ambrose Bierce (1842–1914), an American journalist known for his wit and sarcastic pen. "Physiognomy," he wrote, "is the art of determining the character of another by resemblances and differences between his face and our own, which is the standard of excellence" (see Bierce, 1978).

Among the major effects of Quetelet's work on population averages and "types" was his influence on the work of groups like the "Sanitary Commission," organized during the United States Civil War. This group of physicians, clergymen, and women nursing volunteers was originally established to inspect camps and hospitals, to advise on the living facilities for the rapidly growing army, and to aid in the treatment of the sick and wounded. From this early beginning, the group went on to establish hospitals, convalescent homes, and organize an ambulance service. As the Civil War continued, the Sanitary Commission's role expanded to include collection of statistical data and there was a special concern with the health and fitness of recruits.

The Sanitary Commission examined and measured thousands of people, including many recently freed slaves and Native Americans inducted into the army during the Civil War. The results provided an unparalleled opportunity for comparing anthropometric traits of the males of these three groups. Though the stated purpose of these examinations was the practical goal of determining fitness of individuals for army duty, the commission's efforts provided a major study of human variability and was perhaps one of the earliest applications of anthropological theory to practical problems relating physique and endurance to job performance. Generally, the thrust of the study was to determine which physical "types" or "races" were most suitable for military service, and for which job. However, as is often the case with military establishments, qualifications and aptitudes meant little in practice. Practical military goals aside, the commission did generate large amounts of anthropometric data collected from a variety of ethnic groups.

Though the anthropometric data collected by the Sanitary Commission is scarcely remembered today, it convinced scientists of the usefulness of such racial variation studies. Joseph Le Conte (1823–1901) wrote in *Man's Place in Nature* (1878) that scientists held the keys to proper race relations in America: "The scientist's methods and his understanding of evolution provided the basis for sorting mankind into a hierarchy of abilities" (Haller, 1971:35). These and many similar statements were merely a reaffirmation of beliefs held by the general public based on simple personal experience—prejudices that accumulated for generations on both sides of the Atlantic. From such works, inspired by "what everyone knows about race," there developed firm beliefs in "racial purity" and a solid conviction that a nation's strength depended on the maintenance of its pure stock (read "Caucasian"). But, though supposedly based on a firm "scientific" foundation, such beliefs were seriously challenged by the end of the nineteenth century as new data were accumulated and a clearer understanding was gained of the mechanisms of inheritance and evolutionary processes.

Race differences were not the only focuses of nineteenth-century anthropometry. With the expansion of measurement techniques to include many features of the living human form, anthropometry was used for standard identification techniques in criminology. As individual anthropometric traits accumulated, comparative studies of the physiques of convicted criminals were inevitable. The increase in crime during the urbanization of Europe spurred the search for specific answers to many of the social problems of the day. The newly accumulated data on a particular segment of society led to the assumption that many crimes were committed by biologically inferior persons. This school of thought was founded on several comparative studies, principally the work of an Italian physician, Cesare Lombroso (1836–1909), who expounded the theory of the "born criminal." He was convinced that the presence of certain physical traits that deviated significantly from the general population norm were atavistic remnants of our "ape" past and that these traits were indicators of a "savage" form of behavior. Through his extensive publications Lombroso cited a long list of "abnormalities"— such conditions as receding forehead, large ears, square and projecting chin, broad cheekbones, left-handedness, deficient olfactory and taste organs, and exhibitionism evidenced by addiction to decorating the body with tattoos. Persons displaying five or more of these conditions, according to Lombroso, could be considered a type with a hereditary propensity towards sociopathological acts.

For a time this new school of "criminal anthropometry" enjoyed a wide popularity because of its seemingly quick and simple answers to what ailed society. Moreover, it reinforced popular perceptions about family lineages and inherited abilities. Studies were expanded to include more of the general population, and large numbers of people were studied in an attempt to establish a relationship between behavior and physique—an early form of *somatology*. This concept of biologically determined "criminal tendencies" tends to linger on, and from time to time there is a resurgence of interest when identification of "pre-delinquents" by their body types are proposed as a solution to the reduction of crime. Though simple causes for complex social problems were often sought, there was no evidence to support Lombroso's basic assumptions and there is still none today. Lombroso himself began to express doubts about the significance of his findings and eventually allowed that only 40 percent of crimes were committed by persons with these atavistic traits. Criminal anthropometry was dealt a severe blow by the publication of Charles Goring's *The English Convict: A Statistical Study* (1919), which refuted many of Lombroso's conclusions. Goring stated that if there were any associations between physical character and crime they were likely to be too microscopic to be revealed. Goring argued instead that criminality was not restricted to particular stocks or sections of the community. Nevertheless, the idea of a section or "stock" in society with peculiar tendencies was one of the guiding influences within the Galton Laboratory for National Eugenics.

The founder of and major contributor of the work that led to the establishment of this laboratory was Francis Galton (1822–1911). As a mathematician, Galton was keenly impressed with the ideas of Quetelet and applied them to develop the field of biometrics. Standardized measurements were collected from thousands of British citizens, and these measurements were presented in mathematical form to identify the norm and distributions of traits within population samples. A graphic depiction of the norm and distribution is given by the Gaussian, or "bell-shaped" curve, with the most frequently occurring measurements clustered in the middle portion, or highest point of the curve. For example, there was a calculated norm of body height for the male population of London, and the majority, or approximately 85 percent, clustered about this central point, while shorter or taller individuals were fewer and fell below or above this norm. These were distributed along the smaller, trailing edges of the curve, some distance from the norm, or arithmetic mean. Through this work, testing procedures for comparing individuals or samples from entire populations were established.

Galton and his students expanded the scope of their studies and sought hereditary influences through analysis of certain traits in twins and their families. The investigators attempted to demonstrate through measurements and testing procedures the degree to which inheritance or environment influenced a person's physique, mental ability, and behavior. If parents passed on traits or abilities to their offspring, each family lineage would contain a group or pattern of numerous physical and mental traits of their earlier ancestors. The mass of collected data and genealogies showing that traits seemed to "run" in families began to be understood with rediscovery of the particulate inheritance of Mendelian genetics (see Chapter 2). What today would be considered broad, sweeping conclusions were reached concerning every type of human trait from health and body size to education and achievement in the social hierarchy.

EUGENICS

What was of particular interest to researchers of the era was a search for evidence of innate behavioral differences among social classes, especially mental ability. Galton outlined a hereditarian position in detail in his influential book *Hereditary Genius* (1869). In it he traced the genealogies of many of Britain's leading families and noted the frequencies of individuals in each lineage who had distinguished themselves as scientists, lawyers, members of Parliament, literary figures, and so on. The book played a prominent role in the concept of the biological inequality of races and nations for nearly the next half century (see Stepan, 1982). In any consideration of the relative influences of environment (nurture) and heredity (nature) on the determination of mental ability, Galton would be placed on the nature side of the nature–nurture argument.

Deeply embedded in this book as well as in his other writing is the theme that the progress of civilization was threatened by high reproduction rates among the poor, weak, or sick, who, he claimed, were allowed to live and reproduce rather than being eliminated in the struggle for survival. Such a theme was not too different from the beliefs held by many of Galton's contemporaries. Most notable was Herbert Spencer, called the "distorter" of Darwinian evolution theory (Stepan, 1982). Spencer misapplied the concepts "struggle for existence" and "natural selection" to the social issues confronting Victorian England. The growing gap in education, health, and behavior between the classes could be explained, he said, in biological terms. Put bluntly: People in a social hierarchy rise to the top because of superior heredity, while people less well endowed fall behind.

Galton stated firmly that given the scientific fact that intelligence was inherited, the only remedy was to alter the relative fertility of the good and bad stocks in the community. Galton's solution for overcoming this misperceived threat to the nation was to found an organization dedicated to working toward ending the haphazard marriage customs that allowed or encouraged the reproduction of those deemed unfit. He named his organization the Eugenics Society, after the Greek word *eugenes*, meaning good birth. He proposed that the organization encourage the mating of talented men with talented women, a plan that he concluded would increase the number of eminent men more than tenfold and improve the race. Though Galton planted the idea of eugenics, which gained wide acceptance in the United States and western Europe, it was left to his famous student and later colleague Karl Pearson (1857–1936) to carry on the work attempting to demonstrate hereditary influences on a wide range of behaviors. With the convening of eugenics congresses (the first one held in 1912) and prolific publication in periodicals such as the *Eugenics Review* and *Biometrica*, Pearson expanded the work of the Galton laboratory. These publications, and the guiding philosophy behind them, had, and continue to have, a profound influence.

The eugenics movement grew worldwide during the early decades of this century but most rapidly in the United States, where the leading advocate, Charles Davenport (1866–1944), established the Station for Experimental Evolution at Cold Spring Harbor, Long Island in 1904. At first this laboratory was concerned with studies of nonhuman species, but by 1910 a second division was organized to do eugenics research. This Eugenics Record office, as it was called, directed its efforts to gathering census and family data of many types. Davenport, a zoologist, was most interested in applications of Mendel's laws of inheritance to human physical, behavioral, and emotional traits. His reasoning, as well as that of other scientists at the time, was that if blood types and certain metabolic defects were inherited, then Mendelian inheritance could be applied to other human traits as well. Anthropometric traits of size and shape were considered fixed by the genes and were listed in endless detail. Because of interest in eugenics, most work focused on behavioral attributes. Family pedigrees were combed for evidence of criminality, alcoholism, feeblemindedness, and moral degeneracy, but most attention was directed toward mental ability, aided by the newly introduced intelligence tests (from about 1912). It was but a simple step from this level of family studies to an expansion encompassing whole national groups and races. Family "bloodlines" and races were seen as predestined for certain roles in life or for certain limitations. Though acceptable to most, this effort to demonstrate a range of unchanging, immutable family attributes did not go unchallenged.

The major handicap to Davenport's studies, as well as to those of other eugenicists of the day, was a lack of understanding of genetic and environmental mechanisms. The careless and vague use of the race concept was another problem in the research into human variation. These weaknesses were pointed out early in this century by Franz Boas (1858–1942), one of the founders of American anthropology, who stated:

> If the defenders of race theories prove that a certain kind of behavior is hereditary and wish to explain in this way that it belongs to a racial type they would have to prove that the particular kind of behavior is characteristic of all the genetic lines composing the race. (Boas, 1911:253)

Unfortunately for social science research over the next five decades, this observation was ignored.

An additional problem was that many physical traits were treated as if they were permanent and unchanging throughout generations. Boas, in a series of studies of children and adults of immigrant populations, showed the plasticity or changeable nature of these supposed permanent characteristics, such as head or body form. He observed that the many constitutional types of which a race (or ethnic group) is composed cannot be considered absolutely permanent. His *Report on Changes of the Bodily Form of Descendants of Immigrants* (1911) stands as a landmark study of interactions between environments and inheritance. This report compared body form and size of children of immigrants with their parents. Children who were born in America significantly differed from their foreign-born parents in body size and form. They were larger and heavier than their parents—changes that were attributed to improved living conditions, especially nutritional (Boas, 1940). Interestingly, head shape was one of the more changeable traits: American-born children had longer, narrower heads compared with their parents, hence raising serious doubts about the use of this trait as a "racial" characteristic.

The concept of eugenics was even more strongly attacked. Alfred Kroeber (1876–1960), one of the most brilliant of Boas's students, wrote early in his distinguished career that "If social phenomena are only or mainly organic, eugenics is right, and there is nothing more to be said. If social is something more than the organic, eugenics is an error of unclear thought" (Kroeber, 1917:175). He hurled a further challenge at those who argue for heredity as a "mainspring" of civilization. "The reason why mental heredity has so little if anything to do with civilization is that civilization is not a mental action but a body or a stream of products of mental exercise. Mentality relates to the individual. The social or cultural, on the other hand, is in its essence non individual. Civilization, as such, begins only where the individual ends." (Kroeber, 1917:180). Considering such observations, it is impossible now, as it was then, to evaluate nation, state, and race on the basis of heredity.

In sum, ignorance about environmental influences on mental attributes and on body form led to many misconceptions about human diversity and its origins and meaning. In addition to the grievous social costs stemming from the misunderstanding of human diversity, one of the greatest errors has been made in various schemes of classification. These schemes err when they (1) expect all characteristics to be shared by all members of the same group; and (2) mix unrelated characteristics, as did Lombroso in describing his criminal types. Such "types" are no more real than the "average man." However, simple visual appraisals of human populations other than our own often involve this sort of error. These distinctions, based on limited information, lead us to make faulty groupings of humans and faulty assumptions about the "worth" of these groups. The criteria we may use are not as interrelated as we imagine. Nose form and head shape or stature, for example, have small correlations with one another, and the skin color of the world's peoples has its own special relationship to the environment. Measures or scales of group behaviors are even less meaningful and offer no heredity correlations.

An outstanding development of the twentieth century has been the replacement of typological and racist thinking with a populationist approach that takes into account the range of variability of our species and avoids a simple reliance on averages or means (see Mayr, 1988). A consideration of variability and intermediates (the populationist approach) avoids much of the confusion generated when primary or secondary races are defined to set boundaries of geographic population clusters.

RACIAL BOUNDARIES: FACT OR FICTION?

Archaeological and historical records indicate many contacts among peoples in all areas of the world. The frequent and free interbreeding of these populations, whether European with African, African with Native American, or Polynesian with Chinese, to mention a few examples, is a matter of record. Such evidence has long established that we all belong to the same species and has destroyed many of the racist myths of the last two centuries. This fluidity of breeding boundaries has probably existed ever since ancestral humans' mobility overcame geographical barriers. Despite this evidence, confusion still occasionally arises over what races are and how racial boundaries, if they exist, can be established.

The term *race* was applied to varieties of *Homo sapiens* in the middle of the eighteenth century by Buffon, the French naturalist mentioned earlier. Prior to this time, *race* described breeds of domestic animals, their group membership or descent from a common ancestor. Since then, the term has been used in numerous social and biological contexts and has become encumbered with contradictory and imprecise meanings. Many people take it for granted that they know what race means and assume that scientific investigation has long ago proven the significance and reality of racial classification. Each time the term is applied, however, a definition must be provided so that the reader will know what concept it represents. Does the term refer to the "Chinese race" as opposed to a "Malayan race," or "Hispanic race," the "human race," or the "sturdy British race," a famous phrase used often by Winston Churchill. There is even confusion over the number of divisions that should be identified: As few as three and as many as thirty-seven races have been described. Two carefully argued papers published in 1950 listed six and thirty races respectively (Boyd, 1950; Coon, Garn, and Birdsell, 1950).

The number of races and their boundaries, especially the boundaries, remains a subject of dispute partially because of the lack of agreement on which traits identify a person's race. Further, just what constitutes a race is a hard question to answer because one's classification system depends on the purpose of the classification; various approaches to the science of classification (taxonomy) have a built-in bias, especially when applied to humans. It is usually assumed that there is an actual structure or collection of organisms in the natural world awaiting classification—the concept of real, natural unit (race concept). The samples of definitions that follow give some idea of the vagueness surrounding the race concept over the past fifty years in biology as well as anthropology.

Definitions of Race

DOBZHANSKY:	Races are defined as populations differing in the incidence of certain genes, but actually exchanging or potentially able to exchange genes across whatever boundaries (usually geographic) separate them. (1944:52)
	Race differences are objectively ascertainable facts; the number of races we choose to recognize is a matter of convenience. (1962:266)
HULSE:	. . . races are populations which can be readily distinguished from one another on genetic grounds alone. (1963:262)
BOYD:	We may define a human race as a population which differs significantly from other human populations in regard to the frequency of one or more of the genes it possesses. It is an arbitrary matter

which, and how many, gene loci we choose to consider as a significant "constellation" . . . (1950:207)

GARN: At the present time there is general agreement that a race is a breeding population, largely if not entirely isolated reproductively from other breeding populations. The measure of race is thus reproductive isolation, arising commonly but not exclusively from geographical isolation. (1960:7)

MAYR: A subspecies is an aggregate of local populations of a species, inhabiting a geographic subdivision of the range of the species, and differing taxonomically from other populations of the species. It is a unit of convenience for the taxonomist, but not a unit of evolution. (1982:289)

BAKER: It is concluded that race may be defined as a rough measure of genetic distance in human populations and as such may function as an informational construct in the multidisciplinary area of research in human biology. (1967:21)

BRUES: A race is: a division of a species which differs from other divisions by the frequency with which certain hereditary traits appear among its members. Among these traits are features of external appearance that make it possible to recognize members of different populations by visual inspection with greater or less accuracy. Members of such a division of a species share ancestry with one another to a greater degree than they share it with individuals of other races. Finally, races are usually associated with particular geographic areas. (1977:1–2)

VOGEL and MOTULSKY: A race is a large population of individuals who have a significant fraction of their genes in common and can be distinguished from other races by their common gene pool. (1986:534)

Because of the prejudice surrounding the concept of human races and the misunderstanding of human biological diversity, the following definition, which substitutes the term *ethnic group* for the term *race*, was offered:

MONTAGU: An ethnic group represents one of a number of populations, comprising the single species *Homo sapiens,* which individually maintain their differences, physical and cultural, by means of isolating mechanisms such as geographic and social barriers. These differences will vary as the power of the geographic and social barriers acting upon the original genetic differences varies. (1964:317)

This broader, more descriptive attempt to define human groupings on an objective basis without regard to the biases of the day was a reminder of an earlier effort to treat human diversity and its allied social problems from the scientific basis of degree of genetic differences:

HUXLEY and HADDON: Populations differed from one another, Huxley
                       and Haddon stressed, only in the relative pro-
                       portions of genes for given characters that they
                       possessed. "For existing populations," they main-
                       tained, "the word race should be banished, and
                       the descriptive and non-committal term *ethnic
                       groups* should be substituted." (quoted in Kevles,
                       1985:133)

These definitions, though they may appear quite diverse, emphasize certain common factors. The first is an assumption about the role of geographic
distribution in race formation. Primarily, the divisions are based on the sharing of a common territory or space and on the assumption that geography
played some role in establishing boundaries until recent times (Figure 1-2).
The second factor is that all agree on the importance of breeding populations

**FIGURE 1-2   Polar-Projection Map of the World Showing the Limits of Nine Geographical Races
Described by Garn (1961).** Geographical barriers set off the race collections (From Garn, S. M., *Human
Races*, 1961. Copyright © 1961 by Charles C Thomas, Publisher, Springfield, Illinois. Reprinted by permission
of the publisher.)

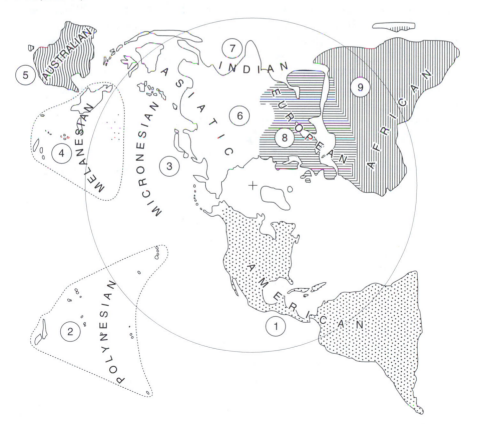

that possess a collection of traits that sets the group apart. Beyond these two factors, there seems to be little agreement in terms of boundaries or groupings. There is some belief that dividing humanity into racial groups distorts the facts and forces the investigator into erroneous channels of thinking, and that the purpose for classification is unclear. As emphasized by Dobzhansky (1968:166), "The reliability and usefulness of racial classification have often been exaggerated." But regardless of the numerous ways of looking at human diversity or the evaluation of the utility of race groupings, the fact remains that many biological differences are real and cannot be described or explained away by simple statements. The concept of race is not merely a taxonomic problem about which group of populations fits together within a certain classification. It is a problem about the ways in which one views *Homo sapiens* in the perspective of time and space. In short, our perceptions of biological diversity and its origins have been changing and are often faulty.

Our perceptions of biological diversity are ever changing as new data are gained from populations around the world. The more we learn about the variability of population groups, the more difficult it is to fix boundaries between them. The numbers of races and local types of *Homo sapiens* have simply been increased to encompass this expanded knowledge. This may be illustrated by the way in which European populations showed an increased number of contrasts with more thorough study. From southern to northern Europe and from eastern to western Europe, body form and size were seen to differ significantly, as did hair and even skin coloration. In order to encompass this newly recognized diversity, several authors simply added new racial subdivisions. For example, Ripley determined that European populations consisted of three races: Nordic, Alpine, and Mediterranean. The Nordics were tall, fair-skinned people with large dolichocephalic heads who made up the majority of the northwestern European population. The southern European Mediterranean race were short, brachycephalic people with dark complexions in stark contrast to the Nordics. The Alpine race, the majority of occupants of central and eastern Europe, possessed average head size and shapes intermediate between the two. Unfortunately for the study of race, individuals as well as whole population groups possessed mixtures of these traits and could easily be classified into one or another of the races of Europe. Also, recall the changing of head shape with environments as noted above. This concern with the identification of groups continued into the middle of the present century, when concern shifted toward the question of what race actually is and what the purpose of the classification was. The following description of classifications shows this changing concern.

Earnest Hooton in *Up From the Ape* (1946) defined race as a group whose members present individually identical combinations of specific physical characters that they owe to their common descent. He divided *Homo sapiens* into three main physical groups or main races and subdivided these into an array of subcategories. His sorting criteria were primarily skin color, hair color, eye color, and hair form. Similarly, Coon, Garn, and Birdsell in *Races* (1950) used several subdivisions to encompass an expanding knowledge of diversity as they described race as a population that differs phenotypically from all others. They distinguished six groups or "stocks" which grouped together thirty races. These races were determined on the basis of evolutionary status as reflected in certain features of the skull and body and special surface features, such as dark skin and face form, that appear as special adaptations to the environment. In 1960 Garn offered a classification differing somewhat from that constructed in his work with Birdsell and Coon. He described nine races, which were geographically delimited collections of local races. The local races were defined as breeding populations, the numbers of which in any geographical race were very large. A sample of thirty local races was listed as representative (Tables 1-2a, 1-2b). Both the 1950 and 1960 publications emphasized that race divisions were not static.

Boyd, in *Genetics and the Races of Man* (1950), defined six races on the basis of certain blood-type frequencies. By 1963 the distribution of the different blood types throughout the world became better known, causing Boyd to increase his original six races to thirteen. The major increase was in the European group, from two to five. This expansion of the number of categories was

TABLE 1-2a   A Racial Classification[a]

1. Murraylan	16. Hindu
2. Aniu	17. Mediterranean
3. Alpine	18. Nordic
4. N. W. European	19. N. American Colored
4a. N. W. European Prototype	20. S. African Colored
5. N. E. European	21. Classic Mongoloid
6. Lapp	22. N. Chinese
7. Forest Negro	23. S. E. Asiatic
8. Melanesian	24. Tibeto-Indonesian Mongoloid
9. Negrito	25. Turkic
10. Bushman	26. Am. Indian Marginal
11. Bantu	27. Am. Indian Central
12. Sudanese	28. Landino
13. Carpentarian	29. Polynesian
14. Dravidian	30. Neo-Hawaiian
15. Hamite	

[a]The authors described this classification as a tentative list. They stated: "The foregoing list of 30 'races' might have been ten or 50; the line of discrimination in many cases is arbitrary. In some cases we have nearly adequate data on which to base descriptions, in others almost none at all. . . . If this list does nothing else, we hope that it will bring home to the student the realization that race is not a static thing at all, but that new races are constantly being formed through the mechanisms described earlier in this Lecture, and that a new race such as the 'Neo-Hawaiian' (#30) is just as real as an old one such as the Mediterranean (#17) or the Negrito (#9). History, in the biological as well as the cultural sense, is always in motion."

TABLE 1-2b   Major Racial Stocks

1. *Negroid:* All peoples showing special adaptation to bright light and intense heat, wherever found.
2. *Mongoloid:* The same for adaptation to intense cold.
3. *White:* Peoples of the Old World, excluding Australia and the southeastern fringe of Asia, who possess neither of those two kinds of adaptation. Overseas settlers of the same origin, and similar phenotypical form.
4. *Australoid:* The native inhabitants of Australia, whom one of us (Birdsell) has shown to belong to two distinct races and to include one other type, Veddas of Ceylon, and possibly some other remnant populations in Malaysia.
5. *American Indian:* The descendants of the pre-Columbian inhabitants of North, Central, and South America.
6. *Polynesian:* The inhabitants of the outer islands of the Pacific, from New Zealand to Hawaii to Easter Island. While moderately variable, they show resemblances to Mongoloids, white Australoids, and possibly Negroids.

Source: After Coon, Garn, and Birdsell, 1950: 140. Copyright © 1950 by Charles C. Thomas, Publisher. Reprinted by permission of the publisher.

clearly a result of the increased knowledge about blood types of the world's peoples (see Table 1-3).

    Another author, Carleton Coon, combined the paleontological record with classifications of living *Homo sapiens.* By using a mixed criteria of morphological traits, blood types, and skin color, he divided our species into five races. The Causcasoid, Mongoloid, and Australoid races were no different than those divisions used many times before. But the peoples of Africa were separated into a Congoid race, which included a majority of populations of sub-Saharan Africa, and a Capoid race, consisting of the Khoisan in the southern Africa (including groups formerly called Bushman and Hottentot). According to Coon, these five races were modern descendants of ancient lin-

TABLE 1-3   Racial Taxonomy of *Homo sapiens*

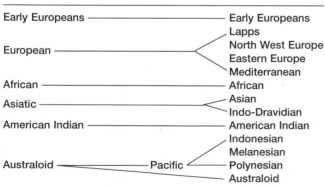

Source: Based on the frequencies of blood types in major groups of *Homo sapiens*; from Boyd, 1950, 1963a.

eages that could be traced back to ancestors hundreds of thousands of years old and were represented in the fossil record. These lineages evolved separately and at different rates, with the Eurasian lineage of the Caucasoid reaching the level of modern *Homo sapiens* earliest while the others arrived later at the sapiens level of development, implying an inferiority of races. His attempt at intermingling fossil and living evidence was roundly criticized for misinterpretation of the fossil record and for the racist implications of his conclusions. His descriptions of the living did, however, recognize the difficulties of human classification. These "racial stocks" contained local races of considerable diversity, as in the case of the Capoids and the pygmoid people, who did not quite fit the general category label (Table 1-4).

RACES, POPULATIONS, AND SOME CAUSES OF VARIABILITY

Races or subspecies are collections of populations, and each population is constantly changing as individuals are added through birth or lost through death. This creates a dynamic situation as numbers of people, composition of age groups, and sex ratios change over time. Because of the nature of human reproduction, an individual inherits a unique combination of traits, but in every population, individuals share many of these traits, as in the case of family lineages. Since the breeding population (the collection of individuals forming a reproductive unit) is regionally defined, these characteristic traits will appear as clusters in space; and certain of these clusters, be they skin color, body form, or gene types, have often been used as the basis for racial typologies. However, because the "typical" or "average" individual is an abstraction, a majority of a population covers a wide range of variation that may overlap with nearby groups, causing a gradient or cline of variation to be distributed over a wide area. One such cline, skin pigmentation, has been plotted worldwide (see Figure 1-3). Even in this seemingly smooth distribution of human skin color there are populations that do not conform—the darker pigmentation of people in the Canadian Arctic in contrast to the very

TABLE 1-4 Classification of Modern Races

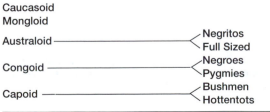

Caucasoid
Mongloid
Australoid ——————————< Negritos / Full Sized
Congoid ————————————< Negroes / Pygmies
Capoid ——————————————< Bushmen / Hottentots

Source: After Coon, 1962, 1965.

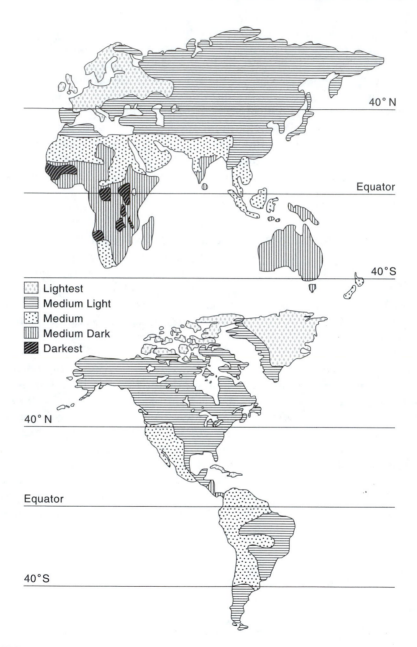

FIGURE 1-3   Distribution of Human Skin Color. (From Frisancho, A. R., *Human Adaptation*, 1979, St. Louis: The C. V. Mosby Co.; modified from Brace, C. L., and A. Montagu, *Man's Evolution*, 1965, New York: Macmillan.)

pale skin of the Laplanders of Scandinavia, for example. These and other exceptions pose many difficulties in the use of types, especially above the population level. The concept of racial types has no significance in itself, and only under certain specified conditions are racial taxonomies useful to the zoologist or anthropologist.

The collections or concentrations of characteristics that we see today in certain regionally defined populations are probably the result of an ordering of genetic variability in response to the selective forces present in past environments. Various diets, diseases, and climates are among those factors that influence survival and may differentiate between individuals depending on certain characteristics they possess. Also, the very dynamic nature of population itself is a determiner of biological diversity. Due to expansions or contractions in size or to interbreeding, the history of populations is, of course, of significance since it involves migrations and the merging or separating of groups during the last centuries or millenia. It is especially important to know the degree of contact between population groups and the length of time they have occupied a given environment. Equally important is the time elapsed since the populations shared a common ancestoral group, either recent migrants in the last few generations, or derived from an ancient separation hundreds of thousands of years ago from the earliest, archaic form of *Homo sapiens.* In other words, it is helpful to consider the origins and evolution of what may be referred to as "geographic races." This interest in divergence from common ancestors has been revived today with the controversy over the time and place of modern *Homo sapiens'* origin, an updated concern with the antiquity of races.

Race, Geography, and Origins

For the origin and evolution of human diversity we can turn to the fossil evidence of our species' past, but it is not sufficiently complete to fill out an adequate record. Neither are the total fossil remains capable of establishing a line of evolution leading to any one of the modern groups. We can say with confidence, however, that the earliest fossils, some four to five million years ago, that establish an origin of our ancestral lineage have been found in Africa. This lineage can be traced to a period of anatomical transition to *Homo erectus,* near human but not quite. By this point, about a million years ago, these early hunters and users of fire leave evidence of their occupation in Africa and Southeast Asia, then in China, and finally in Europe. Following this point, the pace of human evolution accelerated, leaving a more complete archaeological record, and by 200,000 years ago, *Homo sapiens* were established in much of the world (Western Hemisphere excepted). It is within this period that some paleoanthropologists have tried to identify origins of the geographical races recognized today. Carlton Coon, mentioned above, argued that the lineages of modern races (his group of five) could be traced back through about

500,000 years of time. But, he contended, the earliest to advance to the level of modern *Homo sapiens* were the ancestral Caucasoids in the Mideast and Europe, some 200,000 years before the other lineages.

The wealth of additional fossil evidence discovered over the last thirty years has not supported these hypotheses about regions of origins and rates of evolution. What the more recently discovered fossils have done is extend the antiquity of the human genus, *Homo*, back in time to nearly four million years ago. It has also identified Africa as the homeland of these earliest ancestors and this record underscores Africa's broadly diverse environment as encouraging a range of variation within this lineage. This time depth of evolution and the diversity that it generated has become something of a mixed blessing for students of human paleontology and biological variation. Numerous controversies have erupted over the place in the human lineage of each new discovery. The arguments and disagreements among human paleontologists have focused on which fossil could be the earliest *Homo sapiens*. What has unfolded within this past decade has been a complete re-evaluation of the record of the more recent fossils of genus *Homo*, that is, those from about 100–200,000 years ago that are anatomically nearly modern.

The earliest skeletal evidence for the arrival of *Homo sapiens* is believed to be found in Africa, a complete reversal of the theories of human origins advanced up until thirty years ago, theories that claimed the Middle East as a homeland for modern humans. This new, "out of Africa" theory has relegated many of the hominid fossils, including the later ones from Europe, Asia, and even the Middle East, to an evolutionary side branch. The Neandertals, Australoids, and *Homo erectus* outside of Africa have been discarded from the mainstream of human evolution. While these groups were ranging over subarctic steppes, through tropical grasslands, or living in caves under arctic-like conditions 200,000 years ago, *Homo sapiens* is said to have evolved in Africa and then migrated to other regions, replacing or interbreeding with the less evolved forms to estabish the foundations of modern populations. This is an over-simplified summary, of course, and the time estimates of these migrations have varied (from 100,000 to 200,000 years). The major point is not that reconstructions of human racial origins have shifted geographic locations but that such reconstructions are still attempted after all the years of genetic research and all the criticisms of the basis for racial taxonomy. Besides the necessity for returning to the typological methods (a certain skull form and size, for example) that were discarded a generation ago, it is puzzling that the issue of population extinction by a "superior group," in this case African instead of Middle Eastern, should be raised anew. The advocates of the "out of Africa theory" have modified their earlier position and have allowed that the newly arrived *Homo sapiens* could have interbred with some of the Neandertal survivors.

The twists and turns of the various interpretations of hominid fossil remains have a long history of controversy too intricate and detailed to enter into here. The reader should consult some of the major review articles or recent books for a full and balanced coverage (see Stringer, 1993; Wolpoff, 1996; and Frayer et al., 1993). It should be noted that the revival of the extinction or "hominid catastrophy" theory coincided with the introduction of a technique to analyze extranuclear DNA of the mitochondria, which I will explain in the next chapter. Also, the long and continued rejection of the European Neandertals as ancestors of modern humans has had its influence. The fact that they did not look quite like us (if one seeks only ideal types), nor like their supposed replacements, has often been seen as justification for removal of more archaic forms from the modern human lineage. The urge to apply a new and sophisticated laboratory method to an old question of human fossil interpretation has proven too much for some writers. They have rushed to criticize interpretations of the fossil evidence for human evolution while at the same time relying on these very fossils for data to calibrate rates of genetic change.

Counter to what could be called a migration–extinction model or an "out of Africa" theory of *Homo sapiens* evolution, a multiregional hypothesis offers an alternative explanation that includes all of the fossils of genus *Homo* from the several regions of the inhabited world. It argues that geographical varieties have existed since about 1,000,000 years ago, at least. Basically, the multiregional hypothesis posits that hominids (*Homo erectus*) left Africa at an early stage and occupied broad regions of the Old World. In Asia, the Middle East, and in Europe, they became the founders of lineages that evolved, each contributing to modern *Homo sapiens* descendants (Wolpoff, 1996). Rather than a parallel evolution of separated lineages, migrations and intermingling of populations were most probable. Similarities, that is, common traits, were maintained by gene flow between groups and all retained the same species identity. The more isolated populations would have developed some collection of unique traits as we see in living people today due to multiple causes discussed in Chapter Two. What might be called incipient races would expand or contract over time because of the harshness of the environment, their small population sizes, and the degree of gene flow among them.

Rates of evolution appear to have been maintained across these regional population groups and none were more or less advanced than others. This multiregional theory appears to be not too different from Carleton Coon's reconstruction of human evolution offered in his 1962 book, without the implied racial inequality, of course. Both the multiregional theorist and Coon acknowledged Franz Weidenreich as the originator of the concept; the hominid fossil record, at any one time, showed no distinctions above the subspecies (race) level. However, the fossil record is often used too selectively and human paleontologists frequently ignore Franz Weidenreich's warning, "Any theory of origin of *Homo sapiens* has to be based on paleontological facts and only on them. It is a contradiction to logic and scientific reasoning to eliminate first all recovered fossil hominids from the line of man's ancestry and then give play to one's fantasy to build this line again by free invention of new forms." (Weidenreich, 1947:148). This caution applies especially to those who use limited genetic samples of the living, and then examine fossil evidence of hominid evolution in light of this genetically derived reconstruction.

Given the wide dispersal over many diverse environments since the time of early *Homo erectus,* from Africa to Asia and to Europe, it is not surprising to find diverse morphological traits in these and more recent fossils of ancestral *Homo sapiens,* just as there are many differences seen today. If morphological characteristics of living humans are examined as they are in human fossils, then we would find not four or five geographic lineages but many, and even these change over the generations for the many reasons described in the balance of the book. The over-interpretation of these data, that is, the reading of too much into morphological differences in fossil ancestors or in ourselves, leads to major errors in classification.

CONFUSIONS AND CONTRADICTIONS
OF HUMAN CLASSIFICATION

> No argument has ever been advanced by any reasonable man against the fact of
> differences among men. The whole argument is about what differences exist
> and how they are to be gauged. (Jacques Barzun, 1965:201)

Biological and cultural diversity are often confused when classification is attempted; group identity, whether labeled racial or ethnic, is frequently defined using a mix of behavioral, linguistic, and biological traits. In the eighteenth and nineteenth centuries, physical traits were often confused with cultural habits of dress or language, or with technological adaptations such as hunting, farming, or pastoralism. A classic example is the term *Aryan,* which originally was applied to a group of languages (Indo-European) related to Sanskrit, the language of ancient populations of northern India. Many writers persisted in using the term as if it described a biological unit, even though *Aryan* used as a linguistic term by Mueller included groups as diverse as Iranians, Europeans, and the Singhalese of Ceylon (Sri Lanka). Terms like *Celtic, Teutonic,* or *Slavic* are also frequently used to describe a biological unit, though these terms more accurately distinguish between language groupings. Another example of the misapplication of a cultural attribute is the classification Europeans used to distinguish between some southern African populations of the Khoisan group. Those people herding cattle were labeled "Hottentot" and the hunting nomads were called "Bushmen" without regard to the fact that the two groups were closely related and would shift from one economy to another as environmental resources changed. Similar distinctions were also made between eastern African groups, and, in fact, are still being made. Witness the confusion over Tutsi and Hutu in Ruanda and Burundi today.

Even though these groupings are just as real to the observer as any based on genetic traits, explanations of biological variability should not be offered on the basis of these classifications. Nevertheless, racial divisions are often described by such popularized terms as European, Negro, Indian, Hispanic, or Jewish; each includes many populations of numerous diverse characteristics. This mixing of units—the confusion between biological and social traits—posed a major problem for anthropologists and still adds confusion today. This is in large part because race studies are, at least partially, grounded in the assumption that certain basic units of humanity are of great antiquity.

Today, cultural differences are still confused with biological diversity in group labeling. Social behavior and linguistic ability are used to identify groups, as in the example of Mexico. In most of Latin America, differences between "Indio" (a person of Indian ancestry) and "Mestizo"(a person of mixed European–Indian ancestry) are a simple matter of language and clothing. But a person may be identified as Mestizo in Mexico if he or she speaks Spanish and wears shoes, ignoring the degree of Indian or European ancestry. In the United States, recent Latin American immigrants as well as U.S. citizens who are descendants of colonists in the Southwest and California are lumped into the Hispanic category. This is without regard to a complex genetic heritage. Likewise, persons from several of the other Latin American countries are lumped together in the Hispanic category over the objection of Brazilians. The term *Hispanic* is derived from a sharing of the Spanish language, but that does not apply to Brazilians, who speak Portuguese. Such casual uses of classification obscures the diversity while not revealing much about population ancestry.

We use such labels so commonly and carelessly in our daily lives that we have come to assume that they are meaningful in the biological sense. To some degree classifications can have a biological component: Many Jamaicans are dark-skinned, unless, of course, their ancestry is more European than African. Likewise, a migrant from Mexico is expected to have certain facial features and relatively small body size, unless the person has several Spanish ancestors in his or her ancestry. These illustrations could be extended to include contrasts among Europeans as well—the distinctions between northern and southern Europeans, or eastern and western Europeans, for example.

For social or political purposes, the race–ethnic identification may serve a purpose, but these identities can often confuse the question of genetic differences. The difficulty encountered by the U.S. government in collecting vital statistics, especially data on disease incidence, illustrates this confusion. To record race or ethnic group for the purpose of collecting infant mortality statistics, infants of "mixed" parents are classified by these rules: "(1) if one parent is white, the fetus or infant is assigned to the other parent's race; (2) when neither parent is white, the fetus or infant is assigned to the father's race." The exception is that if the mother is Hawaiian the infant is classified Hawaiian (see *Monthly Vital Statistics,* supplement 1989). This follows a long tradition that has treated children of ethnically mixed marriages as if they possess traits, especially behavioral traits, of the parent who is from a socially disadvantaged ethnic group.

The term *race* originally applied to populations who shared close common ancestry and certain unique traits, but the traits list has changed, and doubts about origins and common ancestry have mounted. The term has been so overworked and its applications so broad and general that it has become nearly useless; it now is often replaced by the term *ethnic group.* But classifications by race or ethnic group still appear and were used in the 1990 census (see Figure 1-4). Each respondent to the census is asked to choose a category from among those that are the traditional race types and from several national or ethnic groups (Native Americans, Hispanics, Pacific Islanders, Asians, et al.). The results of this self-classification may be useful for political or economic purposes, but the identification itself will reveal little about the actual range of human biological variation. Realizing this problem, the classifications will be further revised and expanded for the year 2000 census form. Additional options will be offered (De Vita, 1996).

In sum, these examples and contrasts between group labels show that we should not take for granted the categories into which we put people. The

FIGURE 1-4   Racial Classifications According to U.S. Census of 1990

Item four on the census form requests a self-identification of each member of the household and attempts to include all groups commonly thought of as "race, tribe, or ethnic group." There is some problem with even these broad categories since they do not allow for residents of several islands or regions (such as Hawaii, Samoa, Guam, Vietnam, or Korea). Blank spaces are available for "other race" and other "Asian or Pacific Islander." Source: Extracted from Census Bureau form; U.S. Department of Commerce.

Race
FILL ONE circle for the race that the person considers himself/herself to be.
   If **Indian (Amer.),** print the name of the enrolled or principal tribe. ⟶

If **Other Asian or Pacific Islander (API),** print one group, for example: Hmong, Fijian, Laotian, Thai, Tongan, Pakistani, Cambodian, and so on. ⟶

If **Other race,** print race. ⟶

○ White
○ Black
○ Indian (Amer.) (Print the name of the enrolled or principal tribe.)

○ Eskimo
○ Aleut
            Asian or Pacific Islander (API)
○ Chinese   ○ Japanese
○ Filipino   ○ Asian Indian
○ Hawaiian   ○ Samoan
○ Korean   ○ Guamanian
○ Vietnamese   ○ Other API

○ Other race (Print race)

expansion of the number of options for self-identification in the next census will be no more meaningful in the biological sense and will not contribute to our understanding of human diversity. We can not consider the old or newer categories as a reality of nature but should recognize them for what they are: a construct, a means of grouping data describing a portion of our species.

I shall remind the reader of these problems throughout the book, and I shall use, where necessary, the term *race* to mean a group or *complex* of breeding populations sharing a number of traits. When it is necessary to refer to a broader range of peoples, such as inhabitants of continents, then race will be used in a geographical sense, i.e., the "African" or "European." But, whatever the application, the intent will be clear—to identify a major segment of *Homo sapiens* that differs in some ways from other such groups.

What, then, is the reality of human diversity and what are its origins? If race or subspecies is an artificial construct—a device of convenience to enable the human mind to organize information from the natural world—then origins cease to be an important consideration. Rather our concern should be with (1) possible biological responses to the environment, (2) our behavior directing gene flow between generations, and (3) population size or isolation as factors influencing variation between generations and among populations. With these factors in mind, we shall attempt to sort out the different influences on *Homo sapiens*. The term *race*, or *population*, is used to refer to that geographically and culturally determined collection of individuals who share a common gene pool. *Ethnic group* has some special meanings due to its various political and social applications and may or may not affect genetic variability, as I shall discuss.

2

The Biological Basis for Human Variation

Humans share similar modes of reproduction with most of the other mammals, and inheritance mechanisms are the same—the combination of certain material in the germ cells of male and female parent to produce a fertilized egg. These mechanisms of inheritance are the source of much of the vast diversity seen in the biological world. Though the variety may seem to be extremely random and unlimited, there are, in fact, limits to the extent and degree of variation in each species. *Homo sapiens*, the species with which we are most concerned, contains as much or perhaps more variation than any other mammalian group, but its diversity is also limited by certain processes. For many centuries, natural scientists had sought to comprehend and explain the processes of reproduction and the transmission of traits between generations. The explanations varied from a description of a "blending" of parental bloodlines, favored by animal husbandry, to a theory of "preformism," the idea that the individual, in miniature form, existed in either the ovum or sperm awaiting stimulation by fertilization to begin its development. None of these explanations could account for the ranges of individual similarities or differences among offspring and their parents. A thorough understanding of the mechanisms of inheritance was slowly gained through the accumulated work of many investigators from the nineteenth century into the middle of this century. A significant—and perhaps the initial—advance was made in the middle of the last century by a botanist experimenting with plant hybridization. The discovery of the laws of biological inheritance by Mendel eventually led to the understanding of these mechanisms and provided the answer to a crucial question—the source of individual variation, a question that had plagued Charles Darwin.

PRINCIPLES OF INHERITANCE

Johann Gregor Mendel (1822–1884), often described as the founder of the science of genetics, spent most of his life as a member of the Augustinian order in a monastery in Brunn, Czechoslovakia. He had been an excellent student but had been forced to discontinue his studies because of ill health and poverty. On entering the priesthood he was able to continue his education, in part as preparation for teaching in the local secondary schools. Mendel studied in Vienna under leading natural scientists of the period, and far from being an isolated, obscure, ill-trained monk as has been described, he was well educated for the period. Most important for the future of genetics, Mendel came under the influence of Franz Unger, a botanist whose theory on the importance of varieties in natural populations probably was the stimulus that caused Mendel to begin work on the problem of inheritance (see Mayr 1982).

Whatever the influence, Mendel spent years studying plant hybridization, and he is best known for his extensive experiments on cross-pollination of common varieties of garden pea (*Lathyrus*). Mendel was fortunate in his choice of characteristics because they happened to be traits of simple inheritance: The plants bred true without intermediate traits—that is, each succeeding generation possessed traits like the parental generation. He cross-pollinated these plants for color, shape, size, and form of seed pod. Analysis of these multiple crosses led Mendel to derive the hypothesis that an organism's characteristics were inherited as discrete units or elements and not through a blending of parental traits, as was assumed in Mendel's day.

In some of his earliest experiments Mendel crossed plants that had violet-red blossoms with plants that had white (colorless) blossoms and produced hybrids that all had violet-red blossoms. But when these hybrids were crossed they produced a mixture of white and violet-red (Figure 2-1). Also, plants of different stem length were crossed (tall with dwarf), and the F_1 (first filial) generation were all of the tall variety. Crossbreeding of plants of this hybrid generation (the F_2) produced a mixture of tall and short plants. Mendel sought to explain these results by hypothesizing that these traits were determined by a pair of elements. One of the elements, or heredity particles, was dominant over the other, and they segregated independently in each generation—the *Law of Independent Segregation*. Mendel continued these kinds of experiments many times, and his results were close to a certain ratio of traits in the F_2 generation as diagrammed in Figure 2-1. The relative frequency of these traits is known as the *Mendelian ratio*.

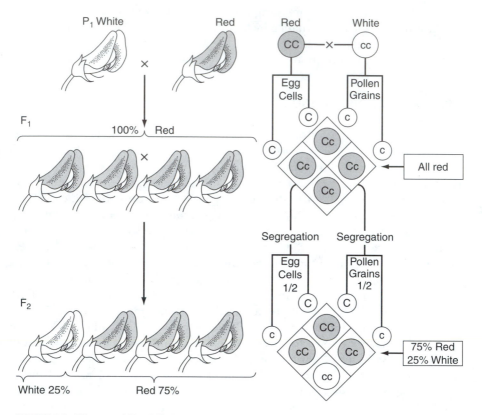

FIGURE 2-1   Diagram of Mendel's Experiments and the Results.

Experiments crossing plants selected for a difference of two traits produced dihybrids with a certain ratio of these traits among the F$_2$ generation,
as was the case with crosses of single traits. These results demonstrated that
traits such as seed shape and color were determined by paired elements that
independently assorted in ovule and pollen (diagram in Figure 2-2). The repetition of such experiments produced results that could be predicted because
they always fell within close range of the expected, establishing the *Law of
Independent Assortment.* Thousands of experimental crosses of plants, selecting
for single or paired traits, proved the correctness of Mendel's hypothesis and
demonstrated the mechanisms of inheritance.

Mendel's work remained unappreciated during his lifetime, partly
because cellular structures and their functions were just being discovered and
partly because of a choice of traits that just happened to have a simple mode
of inheritance. It was not until 1900 that particulate inheritance was recognized as the mode of transmission of characteristics between generations.
Three botanical researchers (de Vries, Correns, and Tschermak), working
independently on plant hybridization, provided experimental support. Within

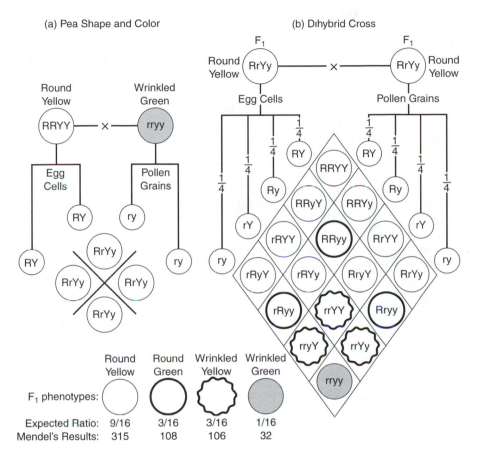

FIGURE 2-2 Independent Assortment: Mendel's Second Law.

When Mendel crossed plants, selecting for two characteristics at a time, he found that the paired factors for each character assorted independently. Diagram A shows the cross of plants to produce a "dihybrid" generation that, when crossed, produces four different characteristics, shown in diagram B.

less than a decade other scientists showed that inheritance of traits in animals also followed Mendel's laws. These studies and the thousands of experiments that followed during the early decades of this century established the foundations of modern genetics.

The Gene

In 1909, the element described by Mendel became known as the *gene,* a unit of inheritance—a term derived from the Greek root *gen* (to become or to grow out of). Each species has a specific quantity of genes numbering in the thousands or tens of thousands. It is estimated that our species, for example, has between 50,000 and 100,000 genes. Geneticists recognized early that genes segregated just as did chromosomes, the darkly staining, threadlike bodies in a cell's nucleus. Groups of these genes are arranged lineally along the chromosomes. The locus, or position, of each gene in this linear sequence has a special significance for determination of a trait. For example, the reproduction of dihybrids for color and seed shape, as in Mendel's experiments, suggested that the locus for seed color is on a different chromosome than the locus that carries the gene for seed shape. In addition, there may be more than one form of gene for each locus—for example, one that determines that the seed is green or one that determines that the seed is yellow. These alternate forms of the gene for a particular characteristic were called *allelomorphs*, from which the term *allele* is derived as used today to describe the variety of gene forms of a trait. Again, in reference to Mendel's study, we see that some alleles are dominant to others, as was the case with plant color shown in Figure 2-1. The paired combination of alleles, one carried at a locus on each of the chromosomes of the pair, is called the *genotype*. Hence, the genotype, or heredity type, for color may be CC, Cc, or cc. The trait that is the result of the genotype combination is the *phenotype* (the visible type or trait).

Chromosomes and Cell Division

Each cell of an organism contains several pairs of chromosomes within its nucleus. When the cell grows and eventually divides, as in cell reproduction, these chromosomes undergo several changes that alter their shapes prior to division. They reorganize from the irregular threadlike bodies of darkly staining material to form shorter, thicker structures. The chromosomes are recognized as independent bodies at this stage and each appears as two joined strands. These strands are called *chromatids* and are held together at a point along their length called the *centromere*. During cell division, or *mitosis*, the chromatids of each chromosome are pulled apart and each is attracted to opposite poles of the cell, which become the center for the formation of the daughter cells (see Figure 2-3). The end result of mitosis is to double the number of cells with an even distribution of chromosome materials between the daughter cells. During the interphase, or resting stage, the missing halves of chromosomes (the chromatids) are duplicated from materials in the cells' cytoplasm, and the chromosomes are then completed and will be ready for the next cell division. The splitting of each chromosome in half and the movement of the chromatids into the daughter cell ensures that each cell has a full and identical complement of genes. Such a process allows tissues to grow and still maintain their identity and special functions.

The number and sizes of chromosomes of the body's cells, or *diploid* number, is fixed for each species. For example, this distinctive array, or karyotype, in *Homo sapiens* has forty-six, whereas the chimp and gorilla have forty-eight and the gibbon forty-four. The forty-six chromosomes in our species are arranged as twenty-three pairs, of which twenty-two are known as *auto-*

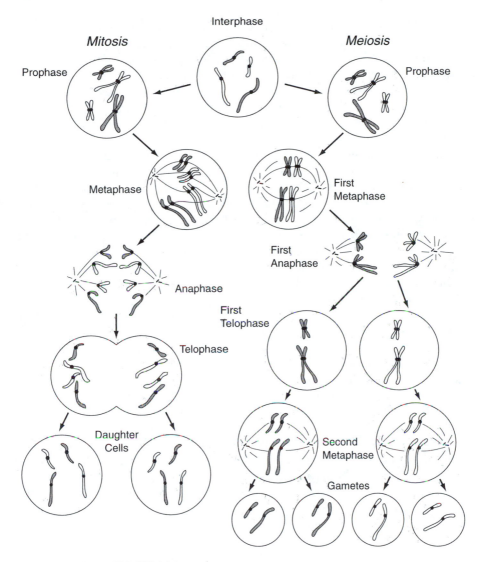

FIGURE 2-3   Stages of Cell Division.

These diagrams show the major steps that occur in cell division. A comparison between *mitosis* and *meiosis* illustrates the organization of the chromosomes at each stage.

Mitosis: This simple cell division starts with chromosomes as pairs of chromatids joined at some point along their length by a centromere. Through metaphase and anaphase stages the chromosomes are arranged in the equatorial plane of the dividing cell and, finally, the chromatids are pulled apart by the end of the anaphase. Telophase is the stage during which the cell membrane grows and eventually separates into two daughter cells.

Meiosis: The major distinction of meiosis is that through a process of reduction and division, daughter cells are produced that have one-half of the chromosomes of the parent cell. The chromosomes are aligned side by side along the equatorial plane in the first metaphase rather than end to end as in mitosis. By the end of the first anaphase the pairs have been separated into cells at a telophase stage, but these cells continue to divide. The second metaphase separates the chromatids into the germ cells called *gametes*.

somes and one pair, the sex chromosomes, are responsible for initiating sex determination. The sizes of the chromosomes of the same pair are identical, and, though there is some similarity between certain pairs, the structural uniqueness of each pair of autosomes sets them apart and prevents the combining of chromosomes from different pairs, though occasionally a fragment from one chromosome will attach to a chromosome of another pair (nonhomologous). This *translocation* frequently causes severe disruption of the cellular functions, which almost always leads to destruction of the cell. If abnormal chromosome form or number occurs, the *zygote* (fertilized ovum) will not grow and divide beyond a few divisions, and only rarely will it reach the embryo stage. There are, however, occasional abnormal combinations of chromosomes. The best-known example is *Down syndrome,* formerly called Mongolism.[1] An individual with this affliction has forty-seven chromosomes instead of forty-six because of an extra chromosome at the twenty-first pair, or *trisomy.* Down syndrome includes a group of abnormal physical traits in addition to a varying degree of mental retardation. Several other syndromes, described below, are due to abnormal numbers of sex chromosomes.

Because the number of chromosomes is critical and must remain constant from one generation to the next, a basic problem of sexual reproduction is how to ensure that an equal number of chromosomes are passed on to the next generation. Because sexual reproduction involves a combination of materials from two individuals in order to produce the offspring, this problem of the maintenance of the species' chromosome number is solved by a process of cellular reduction and division known as *meiosis.* Meiosis is, to a certain extent, comparable to mitosis of somatic cell division, with several important exceptions (see Figure 2-3). A major distinction is one of chromosome number: The dividing cell separates the homologous chromosomes shortly before division. The cells, now with only twenty-three chromosomes or one from each pair, continue to divide and, during the second metaphase, the chromatids are pulled apart. The final stage produces cells, the *gametes,* with one half the number of chromosomes, the *haploid* number.

The germ cells, whose major function is production of the gametes (eggs in the case of a female or sperm in the case of a male), are formed in specialized tissues found in the gonads. These cells undergo *meiosis,* which divides the chromosome pairs to form a gamete able to combine with a gamete of the opposite sex in order to form the fertilized egg or *zygote.* This fertilized egg pairs up chromosomes from each parent in order to duplicate the proper number of chromosomes for the species. This process of sexual

---

[1]Langdon Down, a nineteenth-century London physician, described patients with a particular type of congenital mental deficiency as "typical mongols." These individuals, because of their general appearance of a broad, flattened face, epicanthic eye folds, and other features, were likened to the Mongoloid race.

reproduction is one of the most fundamental and important factors in the introduction of new varieties because it combines materials from two individuals. During meiosis each chromosome segregates independently from all of the others. Therefore, chromosomes that were provided to the individual at conception by the gamete from the male or female parent are often separated, so it is highly improbable that a person's gametes will contain an even distribution of the chromosomes that were inherited from each of the parents. Of the twenty-three individual chromosomes contained in a particular gamete, for example, fifteen may have been derived from those inherited from one parent and the remaining eight from the other parent. This independent assortment of chromosomes during meiosis is one kind of *recombination* that occurs during meiosis and contributes to diverse combinations of genes in each gamete. The mixing of proportions of one's maternal and paternal chromosomes during meiosis generates a variety of gametes; the total number of gamete types that can be produced by humans is 2^{23} or over eight million.

Another type of recombination, and one that is of primary importance in its influence on gamete diversity, is *crossover* during an early stage of meiosis. Crossover refers to an exchange of parts of non-sister chromatids of homologous chromosomes. The homologous chromosomes align in pairs, or *synapsis*. The chromatids of the pair of chromosomes are closely bound into a tetrad bundle, and when they begin to separate to opposite poles of the dividing cells there is a swapping of parts of the non-sister chromatids, as illustrated in Figure 2-4. This breakage and rejoining after an exchange of corresponding parts is called *chiasma*, which causes a realignment of the linear arrangement of genes along each chromosome, and the frequency of this occurrence or the chance that it will happen depends on the distance between gene loci (Figure 2-4).

Neither type of recombination adds new genetic information into the population. It merely reassorts the genes so that individuals in each generation will have different gene arrangements and combinations, causing each person to be a unique creation. Because these gene arrangements or genotypes, discussed earlier, influence the characteristics, *recombination* is an important source of individual variability.

The Sex Chromosomes and Sex Determination

Sex determination is a complicated multistep process beginning at conception with the fertilization of the egg by the sperm. If an X chromosome is provided by the sperm, then the zygote will have an XX pair and will usually possess the genetic equipment to develop into a female. In the early weeks after conception, the embryo tissues begin to differentiate, and the region that will become the urinary tract and reproductive organs reaches a level of development with sex undifferentiated. There is a potential for becoming female should certain

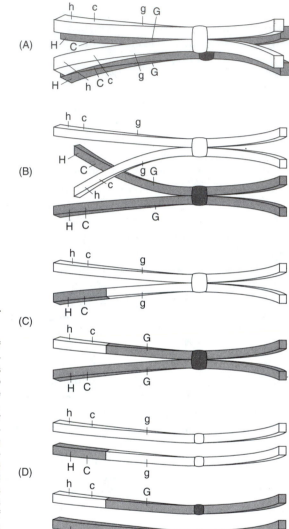

FIGURE 2-4
Crossover of X-Chromosome Fragments during Meiosis.

Occasionally, there is an exchange of fragments between homologous chromosomes (members of a pair). This exchange may take place due to breakage of chromatids during the prophase stage (shown in Figure 2-3). The parts are then rejoined to the other chromosome. The model of the X-chromosome illustrates the swapping of the section with the h allele (hemophilia) and c allele (colorblindness) with the fragment carrying H (normal allele) and C (normal visual). This event occurs during prophase, steps A and B. Step C shows a separation of the chromosomes—each is broken apart into its chromatids, step D. The final result is a realignment of genes.

conditions continue to prevail—that is, the embryo is a presumptive female. The ducts (Mullerian) that give rise to the ovaries and reproductive organs of the female will develop, while those ducts (Wolfian) that are precursors of male reproductive organs will regress. By the twelfth week the female sex will be established as the embryo enters the fetal stage of development.

If, however, the sperm carries a Y chromosome, then a complicated process of differentiation begins, initiating a series of steps leading to maleness of the embryo and hence of the fetus. The short region of the Y chromosome carries a gene essential for maleness—the testes determination factor (TDF). The products of this gene will stimulate the development of testes from the gonadal ridge by the sixth embryonic week. As this development proceeds, a potent form of testosterone is secreted that initiates a series of steps that leads to sex identification. One of the major changes initiated is the alteration of the neural pathways within the hypothalamus of the brain, the controlling center for endocrine function. This pathway regulates ovarian activity and controls menstrual cycling in the postpubertal female. However, the testosterone secretion of the male embryo changes this pathway in the male direction. The testosterone secretions also stimulate differentiation of the Wolfian ducts and formation of the male reproductive system consisting of the prostate gland, seminal vesicles, and vas deferens of the testis; they also organize the shaping and growth of the external genitalia. Another gene (the H-Y), carried on the long region of the Y, has been described as a possible controlling factor in sperm production. In addition, there are controls for cellular receptors of the male hormone, or for maintenance of androgen–estrogen ratios. Other hormones, under the control of genes carried on the Y chromosome, are being discovered even at this writing, and these add to the complexity of biochemical and physical sex identity. In summary, the early embryo stage follows a basic development plan that is female unless altered by the action of the products of certain Y-linked genes.

Chromosome determination of sex usually proceeds as expected and sex identity is established, but on rare occasions the opposite turns out to be the case. About once in 20,000 male births, there is an individual born with a pair of XX chromosomes. What has occurred is that during meiosis in the male parent a fragment of the Y carrying the gene for testes development (the TDF part) breaks and attaches itself to an X, which then is passed on in the sperm that by chance fertilizes the maternal parent's ovum. This means that even though the offspring has the XX pair, he still possesses the TDF critical for stimulating the products that cause the development of a male embryo. These rare individuals are, however, sterile since they lack the region of the Y chromosome necessary for sperm production. By contrast, XY females have occasionally been born, and here the explanation is similar in that the TDF was also involved, but the effect was opposite since it involved the lack of the TDF gene. During meiosis in the male parent, the TDF-bearing fragment of the Y was lost and a sperm was produced with this deficiency. Hence, an embryo bearing the X plus defect Y would develop, following the basic female body plan because it lacked the hormonal stimulation to determine the male sex.

There are numerous other variations in sex determination recorded, but these mostly involve differences in the number of the sex chromosomes. Such deviation from the sex chromosome pair usually yields an individual with abnormal developmental characteristics. Occasionally (about once in every 400 male births) an extra X chromosome is combined with the XY pair. The individual has a diploid number of 47 and is an XXY male with poorly developed sexual characteristics together with some female ones as well (*Klinefelter syndrome*). Males with an extra Y chromosome (47, XYY) have also been recorded. These are normal males, with the exception of their greater-than-average height. Early studies of this condition described a possible association with certain behavioral pathologies and pointed to a supposed high frequency of the XYY condition among mental patients and prison inmates. Subsequent studies, however, found that only a small number of individuals with this syndrome were institutionalized (about 4 percent), whereas the remaining 96 percent of XYY males had normal behavior patterns indistinguishable from those of the rest of the male population. The presence of an extra Y chromosome does not predispose a male to social pathology, but it has remained a karyotypic curiosity much misunderstood for a long time (Witkin et al., 1976). Another example is the birth of a female with only a single X chromosome (once in every 3,500 female births). She will have a series of anatomical defects known as *Turner syndrome* (45, XO) and the diploid number will be 45 instead of the normal 46. Such individuals have poorly expressed secondary sexual characteristics and tend to be shorter than normal.

The major significance of the X and Y chromosomes, in addition to sex determination, is the influence that the genes that are carried on these chromosomes have on the development of secondary sexual characteristics of form, final adult size, and growth rate and pattern during adolescence. Similar to the distinguishing influences seen in embryonic development, the sex chromosome differences continue to influence child growth. Females reach puberty and pass through their adolescent growth spurt an average of two years earlier than males, and during this growth period they acquire the secondary sexual characteristics that so distinguish male and female. Bodily proportions depart from the childhood form as the pelvic girdle grows more rapidly than the pectoral region (across the shoulders). But linear growth ceases sooner than in the male, resulting in a lower average height. Head and face growth also proceed more slowly, and females retain more of a childlike shape in these two regions. Males in most populations are significantly larger in body size and differ in bodily proportions. They differ also in body hair distribution and density from females, especially in facial hair. These differences, and more (detailed later in Chapter 5), are the result of certain genetic differences in the sex chromosomes, especially the Y-linked genes. Many of the male–female differences are the result of X and Y size contrasts.

The sizes of the twenty-two autosomes plus the sex chromosomes (the human karyotypes) are diagramed in Figure 2-5. Since the autosomes exist as pairs, each homologous chromosome being identical to its mate in size and shape, only a single member of each pair is shown—the haploid number. There is a comparable region on each member of the pair. For example, certain parts of each chromosome will take up a chemical stain, and these darkly stained areas of one chromosome will have a comparable location on the other one of the homologous pair. These stained regions are grouped on each chromosome into a *p* and a *q* region, the short and long arms above and below the cen-

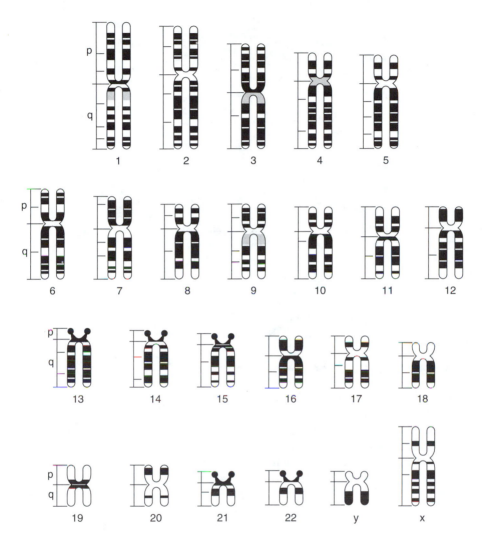

FIGURE 2-5   Human Chromosomes in Mitosis.

This illustration is drawn from a photomicrograph of human chromosomes in mitosis. The twenty-two autosome pairs are grouped according to size (karyotype) and the sex chromosomes are placed separately after pair twenty-two. The dark bands illustrate the locations stained by specific chemicals. The short and long arms of each chromosome are designated by *p* and *q* to assist in locating particular sites.

tromere where the chromatids are joined. The X chromosomes also pair up in a female, and homologous regions exist. A different situation exists in the male, however. There is little homology between the X and Y chromosomes.

The Y differs considerably in size and structure from the X. The Y is shorter, so that except for a very small region at the tip of the short arm (*p* region) there is no corresponding region on the X (see Figure 2-6). Any genes

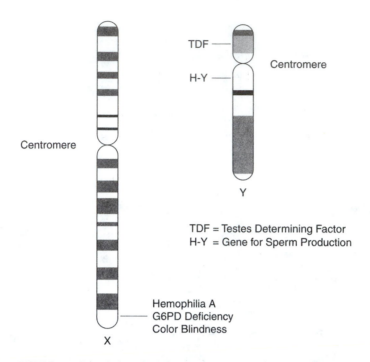

FIGURE 2-6 X and Y Chromosomes and Nonhomologous Region.

appearing on the nonhomologous region of the X chromosome will not be paired up in male cells, since the male is hemizygous (having only a single X chromosome). Therefore, a certain number of genes on the nonhomologous region of the X will express a gene product without any influence from a dominant allele that would be present in the female. This leads to the existence of certain recessively determined traits that occur more frequently in the male than in the female—for example, *hemophilia A* (the most common form of an inherited defect in blood clotting), and two genes for color sensitivity of the cones of the retina (the protan for the synthesis of a red-sensitive pigment and deutran for a green pigment). A recessive allele of either of these closely linked genes will result in defective vision for color in the red–green part of the spectrum that occurs in about 8 percent of males of western European ancestry and is commonly called *color blindness*. There is a third X-linked gene that in recessive form causes a deficiency of an important enzyme of carbohydrate metabolism, *G6PD*, whose function is detailed in Chapter 4. All three of these genes—hemophilia A, colorblindness, and G6PD—are positioned in nearby loci in a region at the lower end of the long arm of the X chromosome (Figure 2-6).

Little is known about Y-linked genes, although major advances have been made in mapping the Y chromosome in the last few years. The *p* region carries genetic loci for maleness, as described above, and some exchange during meiosis may be made of this psydohomologous region with the X. But few other traits have been traced to genetic loci on this short chromosome. A gene for male pattern baldness is one possibility, and a peculiar hairy growth over the outer edges of the ears, hairy pinna, are two traits that have been frequently mentioned. More recently, studies of regions of the Y chromosome (in some sexually dysfunctional males) with the aid of restriction enzymes (DNA probes—see below) have identified certain regions with particular influences on skeletal and dental growth, testes development, and spermatogenesis (see Vogel and Motulsky, 1986, and McKusick, 1994). These and other studies are beginning to define the role of the Y-linked genetic loci in the development of male secondary sexual characteristics.

THE GENE, DNA, AND THE "CODE OF LIFE"

Knowledge of the gene as a unit of inheritance underwent a slow but steady advance over the first half of this century after the rediscovery of Mendel's experiments. The earliest and perhaps the most important of these advances was an understanding of the intergenerational transmission of traits; parents do not pass on characteristics but transmit the "information base" needed for their development. The association of such information with the darkly staining material in a cell's nucleus was made early in the century, about the time the term "gene" was used to designate the hereditary unit of information. This was followed by a recognition of chromosome pairs, where the genes were thought to occupy a position or *locus* on each. The further advancements made in studies of cell structures and how they divide clearly demonstrated the basic mechanisms of particulate inheritance.

Understanding of the actual nature of gene structure and its varying functions, and of how genetic mutations occur, had to wait until a model was offered to define the structure of the nucleic acid components within the cell's nucleus. Though nucleic acid had been long suspected to be the hereditary material within the nucleus, the connection could not be made to the proteins that directed cellular processes and growth. These processes were thought to be dependent on the chromosome's involvement in the synthesis of products necessary for the cell's metabolism. The composition and structure of the nucleic acids seemed to be the key to understanding not only the nature of heredity but the functioning of the entire organism as well.

This led to a search for these products, and for many years investigators worked, with some success, to describe the structures of complex molecules, like proteins that were believed to control cellular metabolism or, in some cases, formed the basic components of body tissues. But the structure of the nucleic acids and their relationship to protein molecules escaped definition until mid-century. In 1953, James Watson and Francis Crick offered a model to explain the molecular structure of a compound, *deoxyribonucleic acid* (DNA), whose existence in the nucleus had been known for years. The model proved to be an accurate description of this complex structure, and their discovery had a momentous impact on biology and was just the type of breakthrough that the field needed to start a new phase of genetics research. The discovery was so important and basic to the understanding of the genetic code of life that Watson and Crick were awarded the Nobel Prize in 1962.[2]

DNA is a long, repetitive, chainlike structure made up of alternating phosphate and sugar (deoxyribose) molecules to which are attached one of four kinds of organic bases (thymine, adenine, cytosine, or guanine). The sugar-phosphate molecules form a basic backbone structure of DNA. The unit composed of sugar, phosphate, and base molecules is called a *nucleotide* (Figure 2-7a), which is joined with the next nucleotide, and this process is repeated over and over until a long chain has been formed. The bases of the nucleotides are attracted to other bases on a complementary DNA strand and the two are held together by a weak hydrogen bond. Each base only attracts one other type; thymine (T) is bonded to adenine (A) and cytosine (C) to guanine (G). The length of the two chains can be diagramed as a lad-

FIGURE 2-7A
Nucleotide Structure, the Basic Unit of the DNA Molecule.

A nucleotide is composed of a molecule of phosphate and a deoxyribose sugar to which is attached any one of four types of organic bases: adenine (A), thymine (T), cytosine (C), or guanine (G). This basic unit is attached to an adjacent nucleotide by bonding between phosphate and sugar molecules as shown. Three nucleotides, taken together, provide a particular *triplet code* because of the combination of the three organic bases they contain, and this code specifies a particular amino acid as discussed in the text.

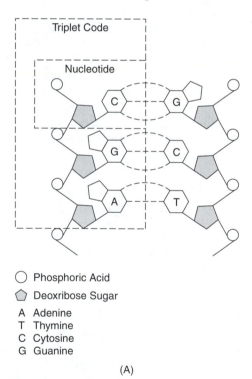

○ Phosphoric Acid
⬠ Deoxribose Sugar
A Adenine
T Thymine
C Cytosine
G Guanine

(A)

---

[2]Many researchers in several fields laid the groundwork for molecular genetics, and Watson relates a very interesting and personal account of the events leading to the discovery of the DNA structure. He also describes the fierce competition among scientists to be the first to identify the functioning of this key molecule (see *The Double Helix*, 1980).

derlike structure; the long parallel structures are formed by the sugar and phosphate backbones while the connecting rungs are the complementary base pairs (Figure 2-7b). The DNA strands are actually rotated about each other to form the double helix described by Watson and Crick.

The importance of the base-to-base attractions is well illustrated when a cell divides. The DNA strands pull apart and the unbonded bases attract new nucleotides and bond with complementary bases. These nucleotides attach over the length of the original strands, forming two new double helical molecules, as illustrated in Figure 2-7c. This DNA replication at cell division is described as semiconservative; one of the old strands is joined with a newly formed strand so each of the daughter cells will end up with its proper DNA complement. This process occurs repeatedly during cell divisions to produce new tissue and, provided that all replication is correct (no mutations), the daughter cells will be identical to parental cells.

The Gene: Structure and Function

Once the nature of the nucleic acids of the cell nucleus was described, the search was on for an explanation of how they related to cellular functions and division,

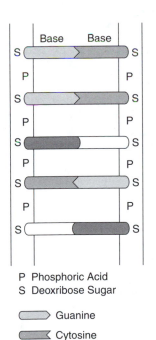

P Phosphoric Acid
S Deoxribose Sugar

Guanine
Cytosine
Thymine
Adenine

(B)

FIGURE 2-7B
Schematic Diagram Depicting the Ladderlike Arrangement of DNA.

The organic bases of opposite DNA strands are attracted and bound together by a weak hydrogen bond that causes DNA to be a double-stranded molecule. Because of their chemical structures, adenine will bind only with thymine and guanine with cytosine. These base-to-base bonds form the "rungs" of the "ladder" while the series of sugars and phosphates are long side pieces to which the rungs are attached.

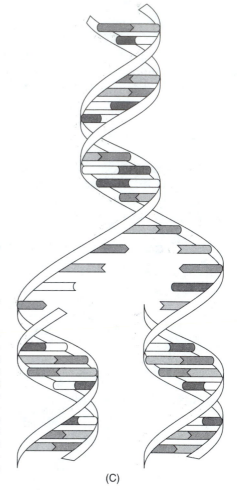

FIGURE 2-7C
Helical Shape of DNA Molecule and Semiconserv-
ative Replication.

DNA molecules are rotated so they form a double helical structure; the sides formed by the sugar and phosphates and weakly bound bases are connected as
shown in Figures 2-7a and b. When a cell divides the
DNA molecules must be duplicated in such a way that
the new cells will have the exact quanity and sequence
of nucleotides. This is achieved by a process of separation of part of the molecule at a time and bonding the
complementary nucleotides to the exposed unpaired
bases. When completed, this process has created two
daughter helixes, each composed of one of the original DNA strands bound to a newly synthesized one, a
process called semiconservative replication.

(C)

and what relation these acids had to the transmission of traits throughout generations of cells. The search was directed to protein molecules because of their
functions. They provide support (structural proteins) as in the example of collagen, an important protein of skin, bone, and many other tissues in the body;
regulate metabolic processes (enzymes), as in digestion, body temperature control, and production of skin pigment (tyrosinase); and influence gene expression through the action of thousands of enzymes in a cell or by hormones.

Proteins constitute a class of chemical compounds made up of chains of
smaller molecules (amino acids) linked together by peptide bonds.[3] The total

---

[3]The major organic molecules of living organisms are classified into four categories: carbohydrates (sugars and starches), lipids (fats), proteins, and nucleic acids.

of these linkages is described as a polypeptide chain. The proteins are composed of 20 kinds of amino acids arranged in a linear chain in some combination. The chain may be a few dozen amino acids long, as in human insulin, which has 51 arranged in 2 tightly bonded chains, or a protein may contain a hundred or more amino acids, as in globin of human hemoglobin, with 574 organized into 4 polypeptide chains, 2 alpha and 2 beta. The sequence or linear arrangement of the amino acids is critical and provides the protein molecule with a specific identity and hence its function. In Figure 2-8 the normal sequence is shown for the first 6 positions and for position 26 of the 146 in the beta chain of human hemoglobin. A substitution of amino acid, valine, for glutamic acid changes the identity from hemoglobin A to hemoglobin S (sickle cell type), and under certain conditions its function (oxygen transport) is radically altered. Other substitutions also change hemoglobin type as

FIGURE 2-8   Amino Acid Sequences of Three Types of Beta Globin.

These diagrams depict the amino acids at the first 6 and at the 26th position. Normal, type S, and type E hemoglobin have the same sequence of amino acids at all 146 positions of the beta globin chains with two very important and specific exceptions. Type S has a substitution of valine for glutamic acid at position 6 while type E is the same as the normal for that position but has a replacement of lycine for glutamic acid at position 26.

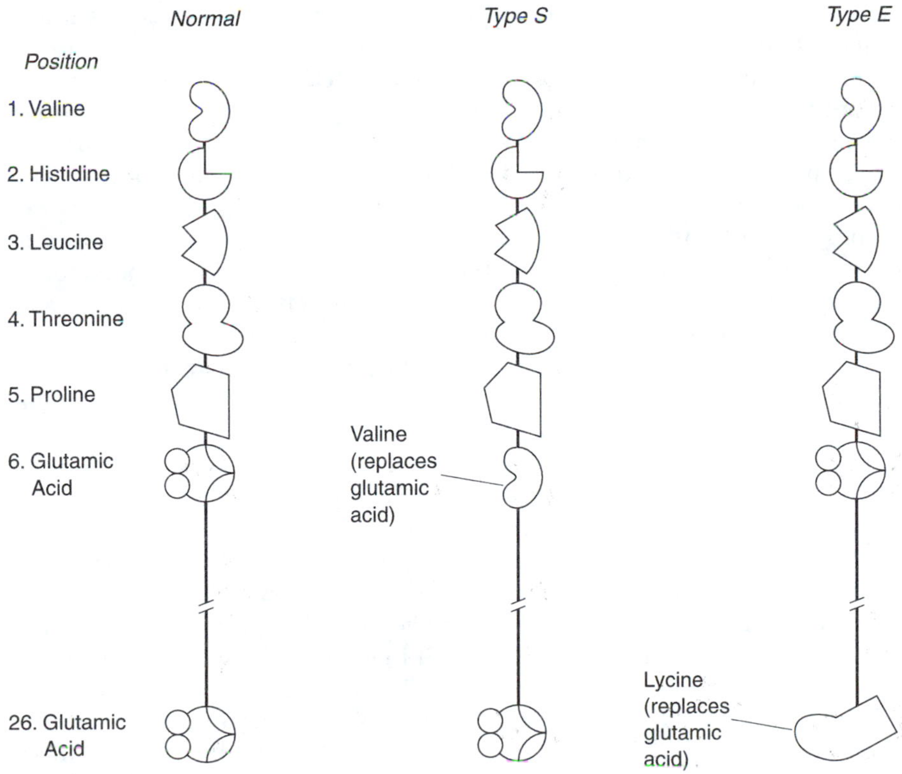

Normal   Type S   Type E

Position

1. Valine

2. Histidine

3. Leucine

4. Threonine

5. Proline

6. Glutamic Acid   Valine (replaces glutamic acid)

26. Glutamic Acid   Lycine (replaces glutamic acid)

shown. This importance of amino acid sequence raises the question of how cells and structures that synthesize proteins direct the correct organization of the polypeptide chains.

Because of a pattern of inheritance of different forms of proteins observed in family lineages over the years, protein synthesis was thought to be under genetic control. But the genetic material, though considered to be in the nucleus, was not identified until after mid-century. The major compounds within the nucleus, the nucleic acids, were at first ignored as the genetic code because their chemical composition, analyzed long before the Watson and Crick discovery of their structural arrangement, showed a presence of only four organic bases. Any hypothesis that these bases existed in a regular structural sequence made it difficult to understand how only four units could determine the linear arrangement of twenty types of amino acids into a string of dozens or more. Also, the proportions of the bases varied between DNA and RNA compounds. The major work after 1953 provided the answers and opened up the era of molecular genetics, which has enormously expanded the understanding of cellular function and its inherited basis.

The Genetic Code

Considering DNA as the genetic code, the problem of amino acid identification is solved when the nucleotides are "read" three at a time as a group instead of individually. Since each nucleotide is identical (phosphate and sugar) except for one of the four types of organic base attached, a group of three nucleotides gives the probability of 4^3 or 64 different coded combinations (three positions at which one of four kinds of organic bases may occur). This code then could account for more than twenty amino acids with a number of "codes" left over. After much research, different DNA triplets were shown to code for particular amino acids, and some amino acids could be coded for by any one of several triplets; the DNA code was said to be redundant (see Table 2-1). The problem that remained to be solved was how the DNA code in the nucleus could control synthesis in the cell's cytoplasm where the structures (ribosomes) and raw materials needed for the protein synthesis were located.

RNA.   This second nucleic acid compound (ribonucleic acid) proved to be the transporting agent or *messenger* that copied the code and relayed it to the sites of protein synthesis, the *ribosomes*. Figure 2-9 diagrams the basics of this process. It starts in the nucleus when an enzyme, *RNA polymerase,* causes the double strand of DNA to separate along a few triplets. The unbonded bases of one of the strands are temporarily bonded to complementary bases of RNA triplets (codons) that are formed into a chain as the enzyme moves along the DNA. Once a transcription has been made, the mRNA chain segment separates from the DNA. This process is repeated until a terminating triplet is reached (ATT, ATC, or ACT in Table 2-1). At this point a single-

TABLE 2-1 Genetic Code[a]

AMINO ACID	DNA (TRIPLET)	mRNA (CODON)
Alanine (ala)	CGA, CGG, CGT, CGC	GCU, GCC, GCA, GCG
Arginine (arg)[b]	GCA, GCG, GCT, GCC, TCT, TCC	CGU, CGC, CGA, CGG, AGA, AGG
Asparagine (asn)	TTA, TTG	AAU, AAC
Aspartic acid (asp)	CTA, CTG	GAU, GAC
Cysteine (cys)	ACA, ACG	UGU, UGC
Glutamic acid (glu)	CTT, CTC	GAA, GAG
Glutamine (gln)	GTT, GTC	CAA, CAG
Glycine (gly)	CCA, CCG, CCT, CCC	GGU, GGC, GGA, GGG
Histidine (his)[b]	GTA, GTG	CAU, CAC
Isoleucine (ile)[c]	TAA, TAG, TAT	AUU, AUC, AUA
Leucine (leu)[c]	AAC, GAA, GAG, GAT, GAC, AAT	UUG, CUU, CUC, CUA, CUG, UUA
Lysine (lys)[c]	TTT, TTC	AAA, AAG
Methionine (met)[c]	TAC	AUG
Phenylalanine (phe)[c]	AAA, AAG	UUU, UUC
Proline (pro)	GGA, GGG, GGT, GGC	CCU, CCC, CCA, CCG
Serine (ser)	AGA, AGG, AGT, AGC, TCA, TCG	UCU, UCC, UCA, UCG, AGU, AGC
Threonine (thr)[c]	TGA, TGG, TGT, TGC	ACU, ACC, ACA, ACG
Tryptophan (trp)[c]	ACC	UGG
Tyrosine (tyr)	ATA, ATG	UAU, UAC
Valine (val)[c]	CAA, CAG, CAT, CAC	GUU, GUC, GUA, GUG
Terminating triplets	ATT, ATC, ACT	UAA, UAG, UGA

[a]Symbols for bases in nucleic acids: A (adenine); C (cytosine); G (guanine); T (thymine); and U (uracil), used as a substitute for T.
[b]Essential in diet of young child.
[c]One of the eight amino acids that humans cannot synthesize and therefore must obtain from the diet.

stranded mRNA (messenger) has been produced, and the DNA strands are rejoined into the double helix as before.

The mRNA is only a primary messenger, however, because it includes a number of noncoding sequences of the gene, the *introns*. The primary mRNA undergoes a process of maturation that causes a looping of the strand over the intron area, which is then cut and discarded. The remaining ends are joined, linking together those segments of DNA that code for proteins, the *exons*. The finished mature product of mRNA then moves out to the ribosomes in the cytoplasm, the site of protein synthesis. This single chain of triplets (codons) provides an attraction for the bases of short strands of transfer RNA (tRNA) to attach temporarily. Each tRNA or anticodon (because its bases are complementary to mRNA) carries a particular amino acid. When the codon–anticodon bonds are established, the amino acids, carried by the tRNA, form peptide bonds, and the process is repeated until the stop signal is reached. The completed protein molecule is thus produced (Figure 2-10). The tRNA are free to pick up more amino acids and the process begins all over. The triplets (codons) of mRNA are listed with the corresponding DNA triplets and the

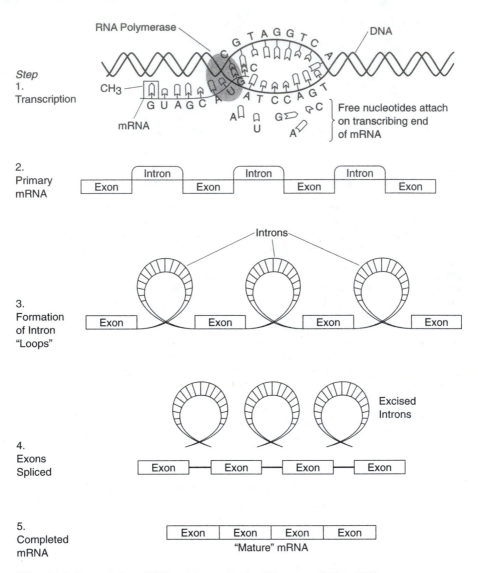

FIGURE 2-9 Transcription of DNA and the Synthesis of Messenger RNA (mRNA).

The five basic steps in the process of synthesizing mRNA to transcribe the DNA code are illustrated in this diagram. *Step One* begins by the separation of a segment of the double helix by the enzyme, RNA polymerase. The exposed bases of one of the DNA strands attract free nucleotides which become bound to one another, forming the single-stranded mRNA, which is a process similar to the formation of complementary daughter strands of DNA during replication. However, the major exception is that the mRNA soon separates, remains single-stranded, and uses the base uracil to bind with adenine instead of thymine. The enzymes move along the DNA and the process is repeated, and when a length of DNA has been "read" the strands rebind to one another.

Step Two is reached when the transcription is completed and the primary mRNA is separated. At this step the mRNA contains a copy of all of the DNA, both exons and introns.

Step Three is a maturing process that causes the introns, noncoding portion, to contract and form loops that result in shortening the mRNA, bringing the exons closer together.

Step Four excises the intron loops and splices the exons together.

Step Five produces the now shortened and completed strand of mature mRNA that contains the code to direct the production of polypeptide chains of amino acids.

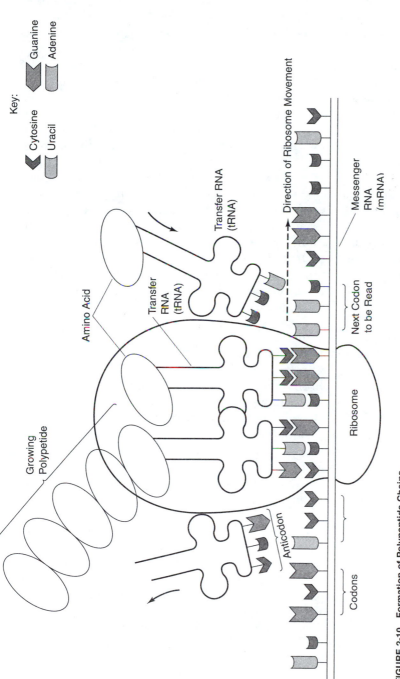

Key:

Cytosine
Guanine
Uracil
Adenine

Growing Polypeptide

Amino Acid

Transfer RNA (tRNA)

Transfer RNA (tRNA)

Direction of Ribosome Movement

Ribosome

Next Codon to be Read

Messenger RNA (mRNA)

Anticodon

Codons

FIGURE 2-10 Formation of Polypeptide Chains.

This drawing illustrates the roles played by messenger and transfer RNA in directing the orderly arrangements of amino acids to form polypeptide chains that make up proteins. The *ribosomes*, small granular bodies in the cell's cytoplasm, move along the mRNA and bring the anticodon of the tRNA into contact with the complementary codon of the mRNA. The amino acids carried by the tRNAs form peptide bonds linking together in a chain until the protein is produced. As the process proceeds, the tRNA is released and free to attach to another amino acid.

amino acids in Table 2-1. This code is universal; that is, the amino acids have the same codons throughout all living organisms, whether amoeba or human, and the universality of the code provides strong supporting evidence for the unity of life.

To summarize, a single-stranded nucleic acid (RNA) is transcribed from one strand of the DNA molecule, the sense or template strand. This mRNA is complementary to all those triplet regions between a start and stop triplet sequence and includes the coding (exon) and noncoding (intron) regions of a gene complex. The introns are excised from the primary mRNA and the exons are joined before it is released to the site of protein synthesis, the ribosomes. The mRNA begins to attract a tRNA that carries one amino acid specified by the codon–anticodon sequence. A series of these are attached along the strand and the adjacent amino acids react to form peptide bonds resulting in a long chain that is the protein. From the diagrams and descriptions it is apparent that the mRNA faithfully replicates from the DNA, a complementary chain of triplets that must be modified by removal of those noncoding portions, the introns, since the DNA carries many more triplet units than are used in the protein synthesis process. The discovery of this excess of nucleotide material leads to a reexamination of chromosome structure and the basic nature of the human genome.

CHROMOSOMES AT THE MOLECULAR LEVEL

Since the description of chromosomes, their structure, and their changes during cell division was made early in this century, knowledge has reached a point where the finer, molecular components can be defined. We now not only have a sharper focus of what is transpiring at the genetic level but we also have a fairly good idea of how all the genes fit together to form these large structures in the nucleus, the chromosomes.

The human genome contains enough DNA for over one million genes, but the real number of genes is closer to one hundred thousand or even less. This means that a large excess of DNA is replicated and transmitted between generations of cells but is not used in the coding of protein synthesis. This excess, or actually most of the DNA, has other than genetic functions, since DNA fragments may be regulatory, provide start or stop signals, or function simply as spacing devices as in the case of the introns. The scope of this excess may be appreciated by some comparisons. If stretched out to full length, the DNA equivalent in the total haploid genome of a gamete is a molecule one meter long that contains about one billion triplets. But all of the DNA must be contained in a cell nucleus with the dimensions of 10 μm by less than 1 μm. This placement of such a large mass in a restricted space is made possible by compaction due to "super coiling" of the helical structures.

The total DNA of the human genome is divided into chromosomes, and each is a long, continuous chain of DNA coiled and compacted; the longest is 82 μm and the shortest, the Y chromosome, is 2.15 μm. At the beginning stages of mitosis or meiosis (discussed above) a chromosome is composed of two chromatids held together by a centromere somewhere along its length. A visualization of this arrangement is provided by the drawing in Figure 2-11, which compares components of a chromosome at the structural, microstructural, and submicroscopic level. This knowledge of the fine structure of the chromosome, together with knowledge of the nucleotides and triplets of the gene, has contributed to a clearer understanding of genetic loci and has permitted the mapping of portions of the genome. In fact, a major project (the Human Genome Project or HUGO) is now under way to map or identify and label the position of each gene site.

FIGURE 2-11   DNA and Chromosome Structure.

This diagram illustrates, at several microstructural levels, the relationship of DNA strands to the chromosome. The *chromatids* are shown as densely compacted DNA linked together at a point near their centers, the *centromere*. The lower right chromatid shows a section of a fibril that is further magnified to illustrate the supercoiled DNA structures it contains. Further expansion of this segment reveals the particles of proteins and an individual DNA molecule. (Source: Modified and redrawn from Vogel and Motulsky, 1986.)

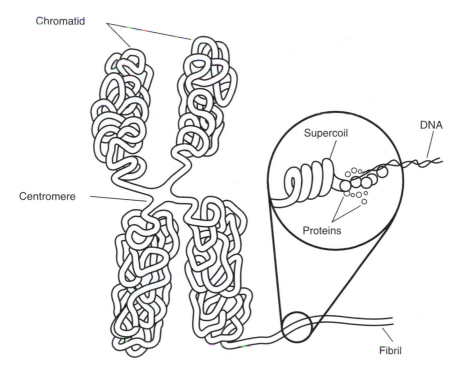

Regions along the DNA strand of a chromosome have certain noncoding functions or contain codes for particular gene products. The region or locus for certain genetic traits, identified earlier by linkage studies in family lineages described above, has been confirmed and is now clearly established by investigations of chromosome structure at the molecular level. This advance in our knowledge of inheritance has been made possible by the discovery of a class of bacterial enzymes that can cut the giant DNA molecule into shorter strands at specific base pair locations. These enzymes, *endonucleases*, have opened up a whole new frontier for genetic studies.

Endonucleases.   These restriction enzymes, so called because they cut the DNA molecule at specific points along the chain, have enabled investigators to separate much of the entire one-meter length of the human genome DNA into many shorter fragments. These fragments are of varying lengths (number of base pairs or Bp) and each has a specific triplet sequence at the point of cleavage; the triplet sequence plus one or two other nucleotides provide a point of attraction for one of these enzymes. Cleaving the entire human genome can produce about 500,000 fragments of from 100 to 10,000 Bp in length. These fragments can be separated by the *Southern blotting* method, a technique that separates the different fragments in an electric field and preserves them on a nitrocellulose filter (Southern, 1975). Basically, the technique takes advantage of the fact that fragments differ not only in size but in electric charge as well, a characteristic that will cause the fragments to move at different rates of speed through an agarose gel plate when an electric current is applied (electrophoresis). Once the fragments are separated, the fluid medium, a buffer solution, is blotted out by squeezing the gel between a weight, blotting paper, and the filter (Figure 2-12). This removes the fluid and leaves the fragments trapped and dispersed on the nitrocellulose filter as they were in the gel.

The hydrogen bonds of these DNA fragments are broken by treatment with an alkali solution separating the double strands. The now single-stranded fragments with specific base sequences can be examined individually by special chemical staining or by use of a radioactive probe. This probe is a short strand of DNA of known base sequence labeled with a radioactive isotope of phosphorus (^{32}P). The DNA probe combines with the complementary DNA strands and forms a double helical structure on the filter. A piece of photographic film is exposed to the radioactive labels over a period of several days. The result is a series of dark bands on the film that identifies the positions of those fragments that had combined with the probes. Because 500,000 fragments are an impossible number to deal with at one time, the chromosomes are first separated and then examined individually. The chromosome DNA may be cut by one or more restriction enzymes[4]

---

[4]There are hundreds of restriction enzymes (endonucleases) known at this time, with more being added to the list as the HUGO project proceeds.

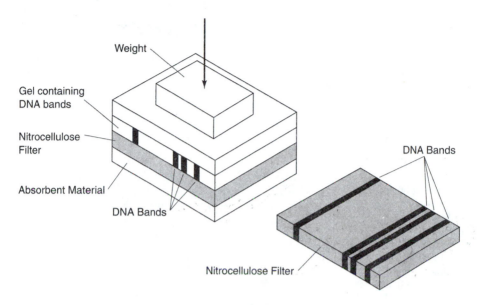

FIGURE 2-12   DNA Fragment Separation by the Southern Blotting Technique.

The weight in the drawing compresses the gel layer and squeezes the buffer fluid onto a nitrocellulose filter. The porous filter allows the fluid to pass through to the absorbent material while retaining the DNA fragments. These fragments are positioned as bands relative to one another as they were on the gel.

and the resulting fragments are then treated by the Southern blotting method.

DNA Probes.   A large and ever-growing "library" of probes has made it possible to pinpoint the location of a gene on a particular chromosome. These DNA probes are radioactively labeled single-stranded DNA, which attach to the complementary fragments forming a hybrid double helix on the filter as described above. This allows for identification of specific genes or gene clusters because of the way in which the DNA probes are produced, by a method called reverse transcription. Where mRNA is available for proteins of known amino acid sequence, as in the case of the hemoglobins, insulin, etc. (see Table 2-2), an enzyme, reverse transcriptase, assembles DNA nucleotides complementary to the mRNA chain. This process is, as the name signifies, the reverse of the transcription process that occurs in the cell nucleus to produce the mRNA. The difference is, of course, that the molecular geneticist assembles complementary DNA (cDNA) in the laboratory using mRNA material as a template. The cDNA, when treated, becomes a "probe" to hybridize with the DNA fragments produced upon cleavage of the chromosome DNA by restriction enzymes.

Briefly, a gene product of interest is identified (enzyme, structural protein, etc.), and the mRNA is obtained from a cell or assembled in a test tube,

TABLE 2-2   Examples of Genetic Diseases Detected by Gene Probes

Disease
Achondroplasia
Alpha1-antitrypsin deficiency
Diabetes mellitus (type 1)
Globin gene cluster (alpha)
Globin gene cluster (beta)
Growth hormone deficiency
Hemophilia A
Hemophilia B
HLA genes
Immunoglobulin genes
Lesch-Nyhan syndrome
Osteogenesis imperfecta (type II)
Phenylketonuria
Prealbumin (amyloidosis)
Sickle cell anemia
Thalassemias
Thrombosis III deficiency

Selected from various sources. For a complete listing, see Cooper and Schmidtke (1986).

which is possible when the amino acid sequence of the gene product is known. The mRNA provides a template for the synthesis of cDNA. The cDNA is used as a probe to locate the gene sequence on a chromosome fragment. A similar method, in situ hybridization, also uses a radioactive DNA strand, but adds the probe to chromosomes in their metaphase of division. The probe hybridizes with the intact chromosome DNA at a specific segment. These methods have permitted many highly imaginative genetic studies and, as investigation of human chromosomes expands at an accelerating rate, the number of useful probes and their applications increase rapidly. Some examples of the locations of genes for specific traits are given in Table 2-3. The location is listed by chromosome number, the area (*p* or *q* arms) and the site on the arm. For example, a collagen gene is located on the long arm (*q*) of chromosome 7 at the 22nd site. Development of these processes has taken place over years of intensive biochemical work, and many are highly sophisticated, so much so that no brief description can do them justice. For more details and elaboration of additional investigation to identify or "map" the human genome, the reader is directed to texts like Hartl (1988), Nichols, (1988), or Vogel and Motulsky (1986).

GENE CLUSTERS AND RESTRICTION FRAGMENT LENGTH POLYMORPHISMS (RFLP)

The various means of identifying gene location and the gene's finer structure have revealed some complications. The studies documented many more poly-

TABLE 2-3   **Sampling of Human Genes Identified by In Situ Hybridization**

GENE AND BASE PAIR (BP) LENGTH	LOCALIZATION CHROMOSOME AND REGION
Beta globin (4,400 BP)	11 p
Alpha globin (800 BP)	16 p
Insulin (900 BP)	11 p 15
LGH (550 BP)	17 q 22–24
Interferon	9 p 2.1-pter
IFN alpha + beta	12 q 24.1
Ig (6600 BP)	14 q 32
Ig Kappa (10500 BP)	2 p 12
Alpha-fetoprotein (380 BP)	4 q 11–22
Serum albumin (1600 BP)	4 q 11–22
Ig C lambda (203 BP) (gene family)	22 q 11
Myosin MHC (2200 BP)	17 p 1.2-pter
Collagen-gene	7 q 22

IFN   Interferon, gamma or immune type
Ig   Immunoglobins
LGH   Growth hormone (Lactogenic gene cluster)
Selected from Vogel and Motulsky, 1986.

morphisms of DNA than were expected, but, at the same time, there has been some clarification of the excessive amounts of DNA present in the human genome as noted above. Because of the intensive study of human hemoglobin over the last forty years, the genes, gene clusters, and RFLP of this protein may be used to illustrate some recent discoveries.

The genes that regulate synthesis of the alpha and beta globin genes have been located on two different chromosomes: the alpha globin gene of 800 base pair units on the 11th, and the beta gene, 4,400 base pairs, on the 16th. The identification of the beta globin gene offered some unexpected results. In the process of hybridization of beta globin DNA with complementary DNA (cDNA), some loops of unpaired nucleotides were produced on the beta globin strand that were visible under an electron microscope. These were segments of DNA not present as complementary regions on the cDNA. The explanation of the results was straightforward. Since the cDNA was a true copy of the mRNA made by reverse transcription, and since the mRNA represented the amino acid sequences of beta globin, then the unpaired DNA sequences were regions that were not transcribed into the completed mRMA. The unpaired regions were introns, as described above, and three are shown in the beta Hb gene diagramed in Figure 2-13a. The Hb gene actually is a cluster of three groups of nucleotide triplets (the black boxes) separated by noncoding units, the introns (white boxes). The gene is transcribed, and in step one all groups are represented. Then the introns are excised, the three exons are joined, and the mRNA is complete.

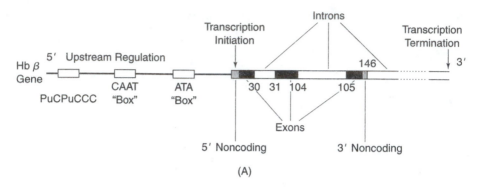

FIGURE 2-13a   **Diagram of the Beta Globin Gene of Human Hemoglobin.**

The *introns* (noncoding) and *exons* (coding) regions of the gene are shown as well as the transcription initi-
ation and termination "boxes." The numbers indicate the location of the codon for a corresponding amino
acid position of the beta globin.

These interesting findings opened up a new realm of investigation. First,
the search is on for the function, if any, of the introns. The second area of
interest is the evidence that a gene exists "in pieces" as a cluster of nucleotides
along a portion of the chromosome 11 DNA. There are, in addition to the Hb
gene, several other genes (embryonic globin, for example) in this cluster, and
a *"pseudogene,"* a DNA sequence similar to the functional gene[5] but not transcribed (Figure 2-13b). Additionally, the wide use of several restriction
enzymes revealed a great diversity in the size, and triplet sequences in the
noncoding regions near the beta globin gene.

RFLP. Because of the attention directed to the study of abnormal
hemoglobins, considerable information has been derived about the restriction fragment length polymorphism (*RFLP*). Table 2-4 lists some of the major
restriction enzymes used to cut the beta globin gene cluster at different
points. These sites, or points of cleavage in the DNA molecule, are illustrated
in Figure 2-13b. The considerable variation between individuals is due to single substitutions of nucleotides, or point mutations. Because much of the
DNA between gene clusters is noncoding, these substitutions causing
sequence variation have no known functional consequences—at least not at
this stage of our knowledge. Some of these variations in cleavage sites produce
fragments of different nucleotide sequences, and this series or cluster of
nucleotides is called a haplotype. They occur in greater frequency in one population compared to another and even among individuals. As shown in Table

---

[5]After consideration of units of nucleotides called exons, introns, and even pseudogenes,
it is necessary to redefine the term *gene*. It may be best defined as that region of the DNA that
contains the nucleotide sequence code for the production of a polypeptide chain through the
vehicle of an mRNA chain.

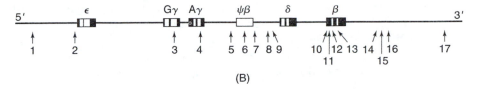

(B)

FIGURE 2-13b   Diagram of the Beta Globin Gene Cluster.

The coding parts of DNA are frequently linked to other DNA clusters that play no role in the production of the protein—in this case, globin. However, the thousands of base pairs of this cluster may be cut at specific sites by selected enzymes. The resulting fragments can be used to distinguish between populations and sometimes even individuals. The numbers in this diagram represent sites that are cut by the endonucleases corresponding to those listed in Table 2-4.

2-4, the RFLP produced by PVUII (number 5 in the diagram, Figure 2-13b) occurred only in the DNA sample obtained from the Greek population. The Hine II restriction site is recorded at high frequency in Greeks and Asians but is low in African Americans.

The nucleotide sequences (RFLP) vary in length and are repeated many times throughout the DNA. The larger ones called variable number of tandem repeats, or *VNTR*, are from seven or more nucleotides in length and have a high mutation rate of up to 7 percent. A shorter sequence, the short

TABLE 2-4   Frequency of DNA Polymorphic Sites in the Beta Globin Gene Cluster in Selected Ethnic Groups

POLYMORPHISMS	GREEKS	AMERICAN BLACKS	SOUTHEASTERN ASIANS
Taq I (1)[a]	1.00	0.88	1.00
Hine II (2)	0.46	0.10	0.72
Hind III (3)	0.52	0.41	0.27
Hind III (4)	0.30	0.16	0.04
Pvu II (5)	0.27		
Hinc II (6)	0.17	0.15	0.19
Hinc II (7)	0.48	0.76	0.27
Rsa I (8)	0.37	0.50	
Taq I (9)	0.68	0.53	
Hinf I (10)	0.97	0.70	0.98
Rsa I (11)			
HgiA (12)	0.80	0.96	0.44
Ava II (13)	0.80	0.96	0.44
Hpa I (14)	1.00	0.93	
Hind III (15)	0.72	0.63	
Bam HI (16)	0.70	0.90	
Rsa I (17)	0.37	0.10	

[a]Numbers in parentheses refer to the sites illustrated in Figure 2-13b, which are cut by the restriction enzymes.

Source: Modified from Vogel and Motulsky, 1986.

tandem repeat polymorphism, or *STRP*, has from two to five nucleotides and is more stable with a lower mutation rate (a tenth of a percent or lower). A third type is now identified, the SNP or single nucleotide polymorphism, that has a lower mutation rate still. All three of these forms of nucleotide sequences are interspaced among structural genes as seemingly useless satellites of DNA.

The continued application of different endonucleases has revealed more and more polymorphisms of satellite DNA (VNTR, STRP, and SNP). At this time, there are at least 20,000 DNA markers identified, and the number is growing (Kidd and Kidd, 1996). This work with RFLP sampled in populations from around the world has opened up a whole new frontier in the study of human genetic diversity, as explored in the following chapters. Since much of this polymorphism has no apparent functional significance, the RFLP serve well as population markers suggestive of a common history and of interpopulation relationships. The problems yet to be resolved are twofold; first, the selection of relevant markers, and two, the sampling of populations. These problems and their relevance to studies of human variation and evolution will be taken up in Chapter 4. Finally, the RFLPs are the result of changes in the base sequences or mutations, but these are mutations in the noncoding regions and probably do not influence survival. They may influence applications for certain forensic purposes, such as in paternity cases.

MITOCHONDRIAL DNA

In addition to the DNA in the nucleus, there is a quantity of DNA contained in small subcellular structures, the mitochondria, within the cell's cytoplasm. A typical cell contains about 100 of these mitochondria, whose main function is oxidation of carbohydrate, protein, and fat molecules to provide energy for cellular metabolism. These largely self-sufficient organelles, on average, replicate and divide with each division of the host cell and thereby continue a lineage of coded information contained within this special faction of DNA. This mitochondrial DNA (mtDNA), together with nuclear DNA (nDNA), codes for the production of polypeptide units that regulate the functioning of the oxidative processes of the mitochondria. In a sense, the coding and synthesis proceeds very much like that described above for the transcription, translation and protein synthesis from the nDNA. What sets the mitochondria apart is their number (there are about 100 per cell versus only a single nucleus), their variation in rates of growth and division, and the replication of mtDNA. What is most extraordinary and most useful is the small size of this mtDNA.

Mitochondrial DNA forms a circular single double-stranded helix only 16,569 base pair units long. Most of these 5,523 codons serve a coding function with no intervening sequences, unlike the nDNA coding units that are separated by noncoding units (introns). Each mitochondrion contains several of these circular DNAs and they are easily extracted and examined in the laboratory. A single messenger RNA transcript has been made of the entire mtDNA and cleaved by endonucleases into significant coding regions. As a result, the locations of all of the thirty-seven closely linked genes have been mapped and the nucleotides have been sequenced for each. The functioning of most genes is well established, and certain mutant forms have been related to several disorders of the neurological sensory and neuromuscular systems (see McKusick, 1994).

This cytoplasmic inheritance, as it was once known, offers many opportunities for studies of gene influence on cellular functions. An equally valuable purpose has been suggested for the study of human evolution. Because of mtDNA's high mutation rate (about ten times the mutation rate of nuclear DNA), mtDNA sequences may evolve rapidly. What is most significant is that, since the mitochondria are dispersed in the cytoplasm, it is inherited only through the maternal line; the ova contain hundreds of them while the few clinging to parts of the sperm do not enter the fertilized ova. It is this factor of unilineal inheritance and the high rate of genetic variation of the thousands of mitochondrial DNA that offer an opportunity to compare population relationships and origins by comparing estimates of times of divergence of ancestral groups. However, establishing phylogenetic, or family tree, relationships between contemporary populations by use of DNA polymorphisms (the RFLPs) depends on some broad assumptions about origins and time calibrations that have become a center of controversy over the use of "molecular clocks."

Comparisons of RFLP data taken from 147 people assumed to represent five population groups (African, Asian, Australian, Caucasian, and New Guinean) offered a reconstruction of human ancestry that started a controversy that has continued over the past decade (see Templeton, 1992). Briefly, researchers using RFLPs of mtDNA offered data that traced all geographic populations back to African origins. Their hypothesis was that modern *Homo sapiens* evolved in Africa approximately 200,000 years ago and expanded in numbers, migrating into other parts of the Old World. As these newly evolved populations moved into other geographic areas they replaced the archaic forms of genus Homo (*H. erectus*). Further, since the mtDNA is inherited through the female line, all living humans could trace their mitochondrial DNA back to a female (or females) living 200,000 years ago on the continent of Africa (Cann, 1987, 1988). This phylogenetic reconstruction gave rise to numerous imaginative and sometimes illogical interpretations; descriptions of an "African Eve" appeared in popular science and news magazines that explained that all of humankind could be traced to a single woman. The authors of the original theory of an "out of Africa" origin did little to slow this trend towards ever broader speculation and continued to expand descriptions of origins to include other populations like Native Americans, Australians, New Guineans, Pacific Islanders, et al. (Wilson and Cann, 1992). Wilson, Cann, and their co-workers argued that all of these geographical groups were of recent ancestry, an argument quite contrary to much of the archaeological record (Thorne and Wolpoff, 1992; Frayer et al., 1993). The stage was set for confrontation with paleontologists over theories of human origins when molecular biologists applied their many laboratory skills to anthropological questions.

There are several technical points to consider, however, when population RFLPs are compared. The first is that some regions of the mtDNA are less susceptible to change, while others fix mutations at higher rates (Jeffreys, 1989). This means that changes in base sequences occur at varying rates, contributing to high variability of mtDNA within a population. Second, the fact that all thirty-seven genes are closely linked limits the usefulness of the mitochondria for evolution studies (Spuhler, 1988). Third, and most important, is the difficulty in calibration of this molecular clock. Some calibrations assume a steady mutation rate (i.e., a constant change in base sequences) at 2 percent per million years, while others argue for a slower rate of less than 1 percent. These calibrations are obtained by comparisons of living human and ape mtDNA, mainly chimpanzee. The faster rate assumes that chimps and humans diverged from a common ancestor some five million years ago, a time estimated by an earlier molecular clock application of nuclear DNA data (see Templeton, 1985). The slower rate is obtained because paleontological evidence places the time of chimp and human divergence much earlier, approximately nine million years ago. This slower rate of mutational change pushes the "out of Africa" date back hundreds of thousands of years and is more compatible with the fossil record. Regardless of which date one chooses to accept, or how one may view the "Eve" theory, molecular genetics, with its new and efficient methods, has provided anthropology with an exciting way of measuring human variability. How this variability is to be interpreted and what the results mean have yet to be decided.

FORMAL HUMAN GENETICS

At this point, following a discussion of the finer structure of the gene, the reader might be tempted to conclude that genetic knowledge depended on the discovery of DNA and insight into the effects of mutations, or how changes in the genetic code began, with the availability of restriction enzymes, the endonucleases. No such conclusion is warranted, however, because the study of *formal genetics*, that is, the crossbreeding of experimental animals, insects, and bacteria to produce a particular series of traits in the offspring, laid the foundation for much of our knowledge of genetics before the DNA structure was defined. Human subjects have played an equally important role in the development of formal genetics. Even though *Homo sapiens* is a complicated organism with a long generation time and between 50,000 and 100,000 genes, a great deal has been learned about trait inheritance from studies of our own species.

Through analysis of traits over several generations, certain human characteristics have been related to simple gene combinations. Studies of human pedigrees and the identification of easily perceived phenotypes, even centuries ago, have added to our understanding of *dominant* and *recessive* inheritance. For example, Maupertius, a French astronomer and philosopher of the eighteenth century, began to satisfy a growing interest in biology by the study of a rare human condition called *polydactyly*, extra fingers or toes. He learned of a Berlin family with a number of individuals with extra digits. The father of the family had six fingers and toes like one of his parents; the other parent had the normal number. With the father's cooperation and interest, Maupertius traced the appearance of polydactyly through four generations of the family. Since the condition could appear in some of the children even if one of their parents were normal, he described the condition as a dominant trait. What was of special interest was that the polydactyly trait could be expressed differently. One of the two sons in the fourth generation had six toes on his left foot but the normal five on his right, while his right hand had six fingers and the left hand had only a poorly developed stump for the sixth digit.

Maupertius expanded his interest in family traits by studies of abnormalities of skin color. Reports of the occasional appearance of nonpigmented skin in children of dark-skinned parents in Africa and among Native Americans of Panama attracted Maupertius's attention. He also considered this abnormal trait a hereditary condition but somewhat different in its transmission between generations compared to polydactyly (Glass, 1955). Other scholars of the period and even of previous centuries made many observations on frequencies of rare characteristics occurring in some families. One such trait that attracted attention, even in biblical times, was the tendency for certain males to bleed profusely when cut. If a male infant showed this tendency, usually identified during the circumcision rite, then his brothers were excused from undergoing the rite. This inherited trait, appearing in the male line and now known as hemophilia, was later identified in the royal families of Europe. Genealogists have traced it back to Queen Victoria of England, who passed it on to several of her children and their descendants. One of the most famous of the recipients was the last Russian czar's son, Alexei.

Such keen observations of easily perceived traits distributed through family pedigrees prepared the way for the genetics studies to come. What is surprising was that it took so long (two centuries) for the potential to be fully realized. With the rediscovery of Mendel's work and the recognition of his two principles of particulate inheritance at the beginning of the twentieth century, the search was on for more evidence of human genes. Many new discoveries were made, but the rush to embrace particulate inheritance led down many blind alleys, especially in the realm of human behavior and developmental variability.

Dominant Inheritance

Some traits are inherited as dominants; that is, the presence of a single dominant gene will cause the traits to be expressed. *Achondroplasia*, a type of human dwarfism caused by arrested growth of the long bones due to a defect in cartilage development, is an example of a phenotype determined by a dominant allele. This dominant allele may appear in a family lineage with no previous history through a mutation that has been reported at a high rate in some northwestern European populations (see Table 2-5). A person who possesses the mutant allele for this condition will be significantly shorter than normal because of a failure of growth of the arms and legs; the body trunk is usually of normal size. Another well-known but unrelated affliction, the so-called *Hapsburg lip*, made famous by numerous individuals of this royal family of central Europe, is also determined by a dominant allele at another locus. Individuals with this condition have a protruding lower jaw and enlarged lower lip, and chances are that half of their children will show the same abnormality. The peculiar trait of a white streak or forelock in the hair is another example of the influence of the action of a dominant allele. These simple, easily perceived dominant traits fully express their characteristics in each generation, and a simple ratio or proportion exists: If one parent has the trait, there is a 50 percent chance that each child conceived will also possess it. However, if both parents have the trait, then the probability that their children will have it increases to 75 percent (Figure 2-14).

TABLE 2-5   Estimated Human Mutation Rates for Selected Traits

AUTOSOMAL DOMINANTS	MUTATION PER MILLION
Gametes	
Achondroplasia (dwarfism)	10–14
Retinoblastoma (eye tumor)	6–18
Huntington's disease (progressive degeneration of central nervous system)	1
Neurofibromatosis (tumors of nervous system)	13–25
Marfan's syndrome (disorder of connective tissue)	4–5
X-Linked Recessives	
Hemophilia A (bleeder's disease)	20–30
Duchenne's muscular dystrophy	30–100

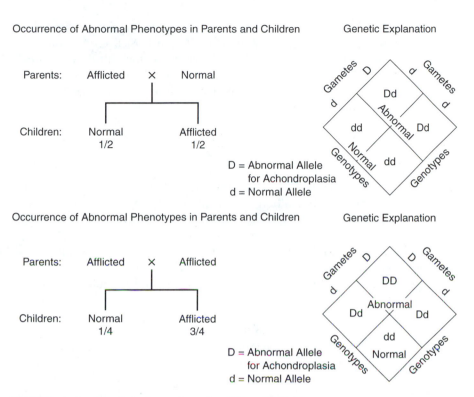

FIGURE 2-14　**Dominant Inheritance: Examples of Abnormal Traits.**

Recessive Inheritance

Unlike simple dominant alleles, the presence of recessive alleles cannot always be detected and sometimes causes characteristics to appear in children of unafflicted parents, often to their dismay. Rather than blame one's bloodlines or one's grandparents, or argue that devilish forces are at work, it is best to recognize that humans possess many sets of genes whose actions or potential actions are masked by the expression of the more dominant allelic form. Such genes, called *recessives*, can cause a characteristic to appear in an individual only when they combine as a pair (homozygous combination). A large number of human traits are determined in this way, from conditions of the skin to enzymes, or growth processes to blood types.

One example is a well-known condition that interrupts the synthesis of melanin pigment and causes the individual to be without color in the hair and skin; such an individual is known as an *albino*. This condition occurs in European populations only about once in 20,000 births, but once in 3,000 births in several Nigerian populations and once in 200 among the Cuna Indians of Panama. In a majority of these cases the parents are normal but each is a carrier of a recessive allele that affects the synthesis of an enzyme essential for the production of melanin; these genes may combine upon conception to produce an offspring who has the recessive pair. There are at least five other albinism types under the control of genes at other chromosome loci but they are much rarer than this albino type I. There is even a record of two albino parents producing a normal offspring; this led to the conclusion that the parents carried albino genes at different loci (see McKusick, 1994). The explanation for the varying frequencies in different populations will be discussed in Chapter 6.

Another example of recessive inheritance is provided by the ABO blood-group system. We all have an inherited blood type in this system, and within this century, the medical importance of blood type has been recognized. Accordingly, the mechanisms of inheritance have been well established. The allele that determines type O blood is recessive to both the A and the B alleles. Hence, it often happens that parents, neither of whom is type O, have an offspring with type O blood. There should be no question of paternity. The type O child simply demonstrates that the parents were carrying the type O allele, a recessive whose presence is masked by the action of either the A or the B allele (see Figure 2-15). If the genotype is AB, however, both alleles will influence the phenotype. This codominance of the A and B will give a blood type AB, as indicated in Figure 2-15. *Codominance*, where both alleles contribute to the phenotype, is found to be a condition at numerous genetic loci.

The ratio of recessive trait occurrence in each generation depends on the gene combinations of the parents and is somewhat more difficult to determine than the simple dominant ratio. If neither parent has the trait but both are carriers of the recessive gene, there is a 25 percent chance that a child they produce will have the trait. But if one parent is the carrier and the other parent has the trait, then there is a 50 percent chance that their child will have the combination (see Figure 2-16).

FIGURE 2-15   Inheritance of ABO Blood Types.

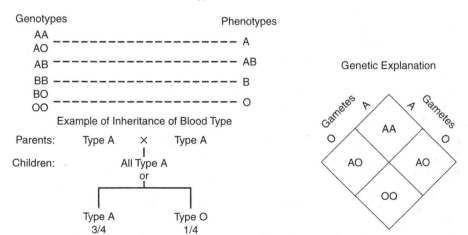

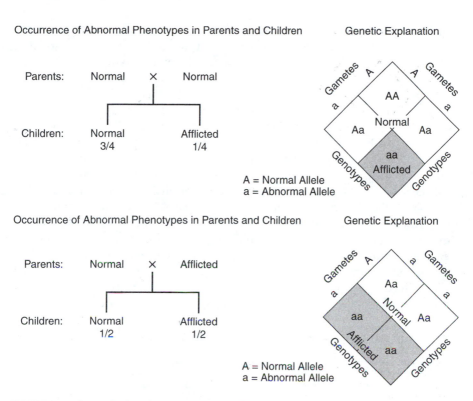

FIGURE 2-16   Recessive Inheritance: Examples of Abnormal Traits.

Gene Combinations and Interactions

The preceding examples shown in Figures 2-15 and 2-16 illustrate the relationship between genotype and phenotype; a certain allele or pair of alleles will determine a particular trait. Many human traits, however, are of complex inheritance, and several genes may determine the phenotype through their combined action. Such traits are called *polygenic* or multifactorial since the products of two or more genes at different loci interact to contribute to the development of a phenotype. Growth processes and body form are under the control of many genes exerting influence during critical stages of the life cycle, for example. Human skin color, another example, varies over a wide range throughout our species because the synthesis of the melanin pigment proceeds through a series of stages of biochemical processes under the control of several genes to produce the final product. The hue of the skin—that is, as the color appears to the eye—covers a broad and continuous range from very dark to light. The human eye is a poor measure of this range, so other means have had to be devised to evaluate "color." Measures made of the light-reflectance characteristics of untanned skin surfaces have been used instead. The skin reflectance properties of offspring of one dark-skinned and one fair-skinned parent measured between the ranges of their parents (Figure 2-17). This measure matches closely that suggested by the hypothesis that genes at three or four loci are responsible for the inheritance of skin color.

These measurements of skin reflectance are made on skin from an unexposed area of the body to avoid the tanning influence of the ultraviolet rays of the sun. If exposed, then skin pigment in most people will increase; even those with naturally dark skin will increase pigmentation. This illustrates environmental influence (sunlight) on a genetically complex phenotype (skin color), and the outcome of this interaction is a highly variable reflectance property. This property is measurable as a quantitative trait, or described as a multifactorial trait because of several genes and environmental interactions.

There are numerous other human multifactorial traits that demonstrate a range of environmental and genetic influence. Several *congenital* diseases (present at birth) and diseases of mature adults seemingly "run" in families; there is a history of appearing in one spouse's pedigree because some genetic or environmental factors influence the development of the fetus. Birth defects like neural tube anomalies (e.g., spina bifida), cleft palate, club foot, and heart defects are examples. The midlife diseases such as hypertension,

FIGURE 2-17   Skin-Color Distributions in Blacks and Whites. (From Bodmer, W. F., and L. L. Cavalli-Sforza, *Genetics, Evolution, and Man.* Copyright © 1976. San Francisco: W. H. Freeman and Company.)

Skin color is measured by the skin reflectance for light of 685 mμ wave length. For the F_2 generation, distributions shown are those expected under various hypotheses about the number of genes involved. Observations on F_2 and backcrosses tend to resemble those expected if the trait is determined by three of four genes.

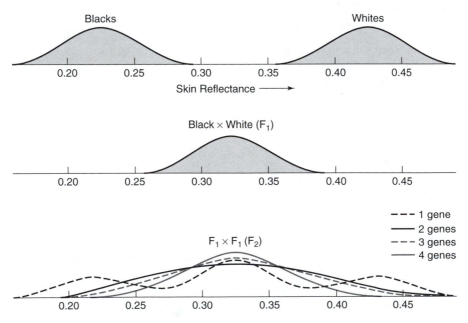

adult onset diabetes (type II), and coronary heart disease are other multifactorial conditions frequently studied in reference to combinations of familial and environmental influence. The blood pressure of close relatives of a hypertensive person is higher, on average, than for that age group in the general population. Likewise, the relatives of diabetics often show a lessened ability to regulate blood sugar levels and are at risk for developing the disease in later life if excess carbohydrates are consumed.

Further, complexity of the genetic system may cause a trait to vary in frequency or in expression. There are genes that are known to influence more than one trait, and these genes are said to be *pleiotropic*. Because the primary products of gene action are polypeptides (chains of amino acids, shown in Figure 2-10), they may be part of a biochemical pathway leading to the production of several other products. For example, a recessive allele that prevents the production of an enzyme needed in the metabolism of an essential amino acid, phenylalanine, can indirectly cause severe damage to the central nervous system through the accumulation of toxic levels of this amino acid. This condition, resulting from the inheritance of the pair of recessive genes controlling phenylalanine metabolism, is known as *phenylketonuria* (PKU). In addition, persons homozygous for this gene will have paler skin and a reduced thyroid activity because phenylalanine is not converted into a necessary ingredient for the synthesis of another amino acid, tyrosine. This amino acid is the precursor from which melanin, the skin pigment, is made. It also is the basic compound from which thyroxine (the active iodine compound of the thyroid gland) is formed.

Another contributor to phenotypic diversity is the fact that genes do not always cause a character to be expressed in the same way, and sometimes the phenotype does not appear at all, even though the genotype for it is known to be present. For example, the pedigree of a family that possessed a muscle defect of the small finger that causes the digit to be permanently bent showed a distribution of the autosomal dominant gene through four generations. One of the males in the third generation lacked this inherited defect, though he passed along the gene to both of his daughters in the fourth generation. This skipping of generations is an event that occurs when a gene is partly or incompletely penetrant. In some individuals autosomal dominant traits may be more severe than in other persons. This condition, known as *variable expressivity*, is illustrated by the presence of extra fingers or toes (*polydactyly*). As discussed above, a dominant allele causes the presence of extra fingers or toes, but the trait is not always expressed in the same way. Sometimes an extra digit will appear on both hands and feet, or sometimes only a hand or foot will have an extra digit. These and other traits recorded in family pedigrees illustrate some of the variety of expressions of complex traits. To understand them and their intergenerational transmission, it is necessary to consider the organization and clustering of human populations as they influence future generations.

BIOLOGICAL UNITS

The discussion of the mechanisms of inheritance and of the effects of genes on individuals now must be considered in the context of those groups or units within which individuals interact. These are the populations or species whose numbers and genetic composition will alter through time in response to environmental forces. Normally, a certain range of individual variability for many characteristics is encompassed, but the most favorable traits are present at the highest frequency, with some exceptions. Such frequencies are typically represented down through the generations. One of the major concerns, though, is how these traits may vary between generations. Equally important is the geographic distribution or spatial clustering of traits in population groups.

Species

The venerable idea of species is based on the observation of the striking discontinuity of life forms in nature. The study of this discontinuity among groups of living organisms developed into a discipline that recognized a species as something "different" and used these differences to classify plants and animals in the natural world. The earlier classifications, based on simple morphological traits, did not take into account the range of variability, and there was often misunderstanding, as illustrated by descriptions of polytypic species that emphasized an idealized form. This old typological approach has been replaced in biology by the recognition of the biological diversity in many species and the difficulty encountered when attempts are made to differentiate between groups of organisms solely on the basis of a few select morphological features.

The species concept has undergone a long history of development and change, especially in this century. As more has been learned about variation and its genetic basis, the definition of species has focused more on genetic variability, isolating mechanisms, and ecology. For example, many authors today stress reproductive isolation, natural habitat, and ecological niche in their attempts to define species. This follows Mayr's observations described in his extensive and important review of animal species (see Mayr, 1963). Mayr referred to *species* as the largest and most inclusive reproductive community and noted that a species is also an ecological unit. But even this perspective underwent further development, as illustrated by the definition that he offered years later: ". . . a species is a community of populations (reproductively isolated from others) that occupies a specific niche in nature" (Mayr, 1982:273).

Populations

The nature of species, especially of wide-ranging, complex organisms, encompasses a concept of gene pool today. The species' gene pool is composed of divisions or groups of interbreeding organisms called populations.

Within each of these populations are collections of individuals who bear a part or a small sample of the total species gene pool for the term of their life span. These individuals form what is described as a breeding population or *deme* and collectively represent a portion of the species. Within each population the gene combinations are reassorted each generation through the mechanisms involved in the reproduction process. The total number of combinations of all genes creates a *gene pool* whose composition will depend on the degree of interbreeding between populations; also, natural forces may alter the gene pool each generation. The distribution of characteristics among the individuals of a population may be described by a normal curve, as in the case of stature or skin color discussed above. This concept of gene pool contrasts with the idea of type or average, which emphasizes the central tendency (arithmetic mean). Typological comparisons between groupings of individuals or populations throughout the species rely on arithmetic means, stressing differences between one type and another, whereas in reality there is often a great deal of similarity between widely dispersed populations within our species. The populationist view considers the distribution of traits throughout the gene pool and attempts to show the similarity or dissimilarity between adjacent populations, which could be illustrated by the wide range of overlap of these normal curves of a population. Geographical distributions of many gene frequencies form a continuum over a wide area, and the gene frequencies of each population overlap those of its neighbors. The effect can be a smooth clinal distribution of gene frequencies.

FACTORS OF VARIATION AND EVOLUTION

Evolution has been described as "descent with modification," a definition that refers to a gradual change of populations of organisms throughout tens of thousands of generations, changes that accumulate and lead to the formation of new species. Such a definition is applicable to studies of paleontological species in comparisons with their modern living descendants who may be diverse in form, as in the examples of the variety of primate species living today. Many of these primate species can be traced through the fossil record to a few common ancestors tens of millions of years ago. This is an abbreviated way of describing an aspect of Darwin's theories of evolution. He emphasized that the world is not constant and that the diverse living forms were connected by descent to common ancestors. The similarities of certain characteristics among groups of species have been demonstrated through comparisons of morphology; hence, humans are grouped with the great apes of Africa rather than with baboons because there is greater anatomical similarity. The development of techniques that compare blood proteins and DNA have validated these earlier observations.

Since Darwin's theory was developed, the knowledge of genetics, and now the clearer understanding of the nature of the gene, has contributed to a new form of the definition of evolution. Geneticists and many anthropologists describe evolution as change in gene frequencies in a population from one generation to the next. This cannot be considered evolution unless these changes persist as a new pattern over time. The accumulation of these changes, often under the influence of natural selection, is described as *microevolution*. There is an abundance of examples in simpler organisms but it is more difficult to demonstrate microevolution among living humans, as we shall describe in the following chapters. Considering the new knowledge of genetics and the recognition of the significance of a species' environment, about mid-century *evolution* was understood as a change in the adaptation and in the diversity of populations of organisms. According to Mayr (1982, 1988), this emphasized the dual nature of evolution as a vertical phenomenon of adaptive change and a horizontal phenomenon of diversity among populations. The degree of change and its rate over time were subject to a variety of forces that affected population composition throughout the generations.

Stability or change within a biological unit (the breeding population or gene pool) depend on a great many factors. If these factors balance out so that a net change takes place and persists over generations, the result is evolution. If the elements that cause change are counteracted by those that tend to maintain stability, then there will be no net change in gene-pool composition. Such stability is, of course, an ideal situation. The actual condition of a population may be small gene-frequency variation among several generations, partly because each generation varies somewhat in number of individuals and in age distribution and sex ratio, more so in former times with high mortality rates than today with a longer life expectancy at birth. Treating population equilibrium or disequilibrium has always presented a problem because demographic as well as genetic factors must be considered. An important step was taken with the recognition of Mendelian genetics followed by the development of the foundation of population genetics.

Hardy-Weinberg Equilibrium

Early in this century, even after particulate inheritance was recognized, there still was considerable confusion over the relationship between dominant and recessive alleles. The question frequently raised was: If one allele was dominant to another, would not the dominant one eventually, after a period of time, come to be the most frequent allele in the population? The answer is no, of course not. In 1908, an English mathematician, G. H. Hardy, and a German physician, W. Weinberg, independently of each other, offered a mathematical formula $(p + q)^2$, which described in simple terms the proportion of a pair of alleles in a randomly mating population living under stable conditions. This formula explained why the dominant allele would not increase.

If the symbols of *A* and *a* are used to indicate the alleles, then the gametes (sperm and ova) will carry one or the other allele, and recombination through reproduction will occur at a constant frequency. The following combinations are expected:

SPERM

		A	a
OVA	A	AA	Aa
	a	Aa	aa

This simple table shows that one AA genotype is reproduced for every two Aa combinations and every one aa genotype—the *Mendelian ratio.* In the hypothetical situation in which the alleles A and a are present in equal numbers in a population, one-half of the gametes carry the A allele and one-half carry the a. Let p equal the frequency of A and q equal the frequency of a; then the allele frequencies of all combinations can be derived from the table:

	FREQUENCY OF *SPERM* CARRYING ALLELES A AND a	
	p (.5)	q (.5)
FREQUENCY OF *OVA* CARRYING ALLELES A AND a p (.5)	p² (.25)	pq (.25)
q (.5)	pq (.25)	q² (.25)

Adding up the frequencies of all combinations to derive a total for the population we get

$$p^2 + 2pq + q^2$$
$$(.25) + 2\,(.25) + (.25)$$
$$p^2 + 2\,pq + q^2 = 1,$$

and then $(p + q)^2 = 1$ because it is the binomial expression of the quadratic equation. Taking the square root of the equation we get

$$p + q = 1$$

which is a mathematical way of saying that, in a sexually reproducing population, the total number of alleles at any locus is equal to unity. Therefore, if we know the frequency of one, then the other can be determined (expressed as $p = 1 - q$, or $q = 1 - p$). This should be easy to comprehend if one recalls that only a single allele is present at a locus on a chromosome (though the other chromosome of the pair may carry another allelic form of the gene). In our example of two allelic forms, it is an either–or situation; the A or a is present. Given the random mating conditions, each type of sperm has equal opportunity to fertilize each type of egg, so the 1:2:1 Mendelian ratio of the genotypes AA, Aa, and aa will be maintained throughout the generations and there will be no change in gene frequency. The *Hardy-Weinberg Law* states that the frequencies of p and q will remain the same throughout any number of generations given a stable, random-breeding population isolated from other populations.

An example can be made of the number of individuals who are taste-sensitive to a chemical, *phenylthiocarbamide* (PTC), a substance that is bitter tasting to a majority of persons but tasteless to about 25 percent of Europeans tested. It was found some years ago that this tasting ability was inherited as a dominant allele (T). So a person either TT or Tt was a taster whereas the homozygous recessive tt was a nontaster. If a random sample of a population shows that there are 250 nontasters out of 1,000, then 25 percent of the population have the genotype tt. The gene frequency of the recessive allele (q) in this example can be calculated: $q^2 = .25$ and $q = \sqrt{.25}$, which is equal to .5, or one-half of the alleles for the PTC locus are the recessive form. The frequency of the dominant allele (T) would then be .5 or $(1 - q)$. Nevertheless, even though the alleles are of equal frequency in the population, three-quarters or 75 percent of the individuals have the taster phenotype. This is simply explained by reference to the ratio of the genotypes previously shown. One-half of the recessive alleles (t) are combined with the dominant alleles to form the heterozygote who is a taster (Tt). Throughout future generations, assuming random mating with respect to taste sensitivity, the gene frequencies of these alleles will remain the same and there will be the same number of individuals who are tasters (see Table 2-6).

The Hardy-Weinberg formula assumes, in addition to random mating, that certain conditions exist that contribute to population stability, and if these conditions are maintained, gene frequencies will remain invariable throughout any number of generations. Few natural populations fit this model situation exactly, but the basic formula established a reference against which change can be measured, and it provides a useful tool in studies of variation and evolution. The forces for change in a population's gene frequencies are *mutation, natural selection, genetic drift* (a sampling error), and *gene flow*.

Mutation

As noted earlier, the change in a genetic code results in an alteration in its action and introduces a new variety of allele. This adds different genotypes within a population. Mutation, then, is the ultimate source of all genetic vari-

TABLE 2-6 Frequencies of Offspring from All Types of Matings

GENOTYPES OF PARENTS	FREQUENCY OF MATINGS	FREQUENCY OF OFFSPRING			NUMBER OF INDIVIDUALS		
		TT	Tt	tt	TT	Tt	tt
TT x TT	p^4	p^4	—	—	625	0	0
TT x 2 Tt 2 Tt x TT	$4p^3q$	$2p^3q$	$2p^3q$	—	1,250	1,250	0
TT x tt tt x TT	$2p^2q^2$	0	$2p^2q^2$	—	0	1,250	0
2 Tt x 2 Tt	$4p^2q^2$	p^2q^2	$2p^2q^2$	p^2q^2	625	1.250	625
2 Tt x tt tt x 2 Tt	$4pq^3$	—	$2pq^3$	$2pq^3$	0	1,250	1,250
tt x tt	q^4	—	—	q^4	0	0	625
All Types	1	p^2	$2pq$	q^2	2,500	5,000	2,500

Adding up each column gives a total of $p^2 + 2pq + q^2$ = (all types of matings) and the numerical example adds up to a total of 10,000. This table shows, in a randomly mating population of this size with p of .5, that the numbers of individuals with the three genotypes will be distributed 1/4TT (2,500), 1/2Tt (5,000), and 1/4tt (2,500) each generation. Under conditions of stability, as described earlier, this distribution will remain unchanged throughout any number of generations.

ation in a population and may provide a species with an ability to respond to a variety of environmental conditions. Some mutations, however, cause such a radical metabolic disturbance that an organism cannot survive; many more are detrimental but are not lethal. Still other mutations may affect changes in the way organisms metabolize certain substances, resist parasites, or produce antibodies against infectious diseases. A question frequently raised in the past was whether or not all point mutations are "bad." All are seen now as an error in DNA coding with a greater or lesser effect on protein synthesis, depending on the amino acid substituted. If the substitution occurs in a polypeptide position that reduces or eliminates the protein's function to a level that places the individual's survival at risk, then it may be considered bad. In certain environments, however, the mutant allele, though depressing some metabolic processes, may convey a survival advantage to the carrier of the allele. The influence on survival of such an error, or change in code, will be taken up in the following chapters. Here, mutations, without evaluating effect (lethal mutations excepted) may be considered one of the sources of disturbance of genetic equilibrium between generations as measured by the Hardy-Weinberg Equilibrium.

In *Homo sapiens*, mutations apparently occur at a low rate, though this rate may be influenced by certain forces (for instance, ionizing radiation) from natural or human-caused sources. The results from exposure to radiation cannot be predicted—that is, which genes will mutate is not known. Some human mutation rates that occur due to unknown causes have been measured in family lineages and are listed in Table 2-5. As shown, the rates are very low, and population gene frequencies will be disturbed only slightly, but a mutant gene may convey an advantage and contribute to increased fitness in certain environments where selective forces favor the carrier of the mutant. This may cause the frequency of the mutant allele to increase rapidly in just a few generations.

Natural Selection

Though chance plays a role in the production of variation within a population of sexually reproducing organisms, the range of variability and composition of a breeding population is limited. All possible genotypes are not represented in each generation with equal frequency. There are factors that limit the extent of population diversity and determine the gene frequencies from generation to generation. A major factor that acts to limit and stabilize genetic diversity is called *natural selection.*

Some individuals, because of one or several combinations of genotypes, have characteristics that are adaptive in certain environments and enable them to survive at a higher rate, with an extended reproductive period. They reproduce at a higher rate than other individuals and, thus, contribute more offspring to the next generation. Such persons, by definition, are the fittest in the sense of *Darwinian fitness* (those who produce the most offspring). Even small inherited differences among individuals, over time, may lead to differences in the gene pool composition. Those genotypes that confer some reproductive advantage no matter how small will increase within a population throughout generations.

There are several mechanisms that determine reproductive success; the sum total of all those processes that determine survival and reproduction are lumped under the term *natural selection.* The word *natural* indicates that there are certain conditions that exist in the environment within which the organism lives that are relatively advantageous to some individuals. These natural conditions are in contrast to those created by the animal breeder who selects chickens or cattle and breeds only those animals that possess the economically desirable traits—rapid weight gain, for example. Selective breeding of farm animals, dogs, or race horses is a good example of the practice of artificial selection for desirable characteristics. Darwin, offering an explanation of how evolution occurred, noted that what humans have done in a limited way in an effort to domesticate plants and animals, nature has achieved on a grand scale through natural selection.

The effect of natural selection is the maintenance of certain desirable characteristics throughout the generations. Mutations, which occur spontaneously, may convey an advantage under certain environmental conditions, and the number of individuals possessing the mutant allele will increase each generation, perhaps slowly or rapidly, depending on the life span of the organisms and the intensity of selection. It has been difficult to demonstrate natural selection in human populations because of our long life span and because of the impossibility of exerting laboratory controls, but insects and certain mammals are another story and have provided some excellent examples.

There is a clear record of an increase in the number of insect species resistant, or even immune, to the effects of insecticides. Resistant strains of the common housefly began to appear throughout the world within two years after the insecticide DDT was introduced in an effort to control this and other insect pests. It appears that fly larvae of the resistant strains develop faster and survive better in a crowded environment than the DDT-susceptible strains. Studies of the DDT-resistant insect strains showed that the presence of a certain enzyme (dehydrocholorinase) aided in the metabolism of the insecticide. This enzyme was also present, but in lower quantities, among those flies most susceptible to DDT. It is not difficult, then, to reconstruct an evolutionary history for the flies that depicts a population heterogeneous for this trait (a mix of flies with high and low quantities of the enzyme). When their environment shifted drastically with the introduction of DDT, the resistant strain of flies survived longer and reproduced in greater numbers, until a majority in future generations were of the resistant type. The varieties were already present, probably due to past mutations, and if the rapid reproduction of flies is considered, then even a slight advantage of one genotype over another would cause major changes in the populations' response to their environment. More of a danger to humans has been the proliferation of resistant strains of malaria-carrying mosquitos.

Other examples of environmental change and natural selection are seen in the rise of bacteria strains resistant to certain antibiotics, a resistance that has made them more and more difficult to control. Each of these examples shows environmental changes caused by human intervention and is an excellent demonstration of the operation of natural selection on simpler organisms. Many populations of complex organisms also provide evidence for the action of natural selection, as in the case of the spread of rabbits in Australia and the attempts to control their population boom.

The European wild rabbit was introduced into Australia in 1859 when a colony of twenty-four were turned loose on an estate in Victoria in the southeastern part of Australia. By 1928 the fast-breeding rabbits, without any natural predators in their new homeland, had multiplied to an estimated 500 million, spread over much of Australia. The rabbits became a major pest, destroying grazing land and crops and causing millions of dollars' worth of damage each year. All attempts to control the rabbits with traps and poisons proved futile until 1950, when a virus (myxoma) lethal to rabbits was introduced into the population. From the first infection induced among rabbits in South Australia, the virus spread into most areas, killing 95 percent of the rabbits by 1953. After this drastic decline, however, the population recovered and began to increase due to the survival and reproduction of a few individuals whose genetic complement provided them with some degree of immunity. In addition, the virus itself underwent a transformation, and new strains appeared that were less lethal. Selection favored the disease-resistant rabbit, and there was a co-adaptation of the virus and host (rabbit). In order for a virus to survive long enough to multiply and to be transmitted to another host it must not be too lethal. If the rabbit dies before the virus can be transmitted to a new host (usually by mosquito), then the virus strain also dies. Selection, therefore, favored a less deadly virus and a rabbit with a degree of resistance to the infection. These results have been verified many times in laboratory tests and thus provide an illustration of the action of selection.

Reproductive success is the mark of fitness and ensures the survival of the species and the successful adaptation to environmental fluctuations. However, the mere success of a population may lead to a wide range of increases and decreases in population size. A case in point is the rapid-breeding field mouse (*Microtus awalis*). The female is fertile at 13 days and if bred will produce a litter (4 to 6) 20 days later. Fertilization can occur again immediately after the female gives birth, and a second litter can follow within 20 days. These mice have been bred in captivity and can produce 24 litters within 20 months. Such frequent reproduction increases the population to a point where it far exceeds the carrying capacity of the environment (usually measured in terms of available food), and widespread destruction of the resources occurs followed by a rapid population decline or "crash." Within months, the cycle can be repeated. Selection exerted by disease and the limitation of food resources tend to check population size, but in the case of rapid breeders, insects and even some mammals, the extremes in maximum and minimum population sizes can be enormous.

Slow-breeding animals have a different sort of problem. The elephant, the slowest of the mammals with a gestation period of 22 months, may, under favorable conditions, reproduce 6 offspring during its reproductive span. Even slight environmental variations can have profound effects. Drought and disease work a heavy toll and may have been responsible (probably aided by human predators—the Paleolithic hunters of the New World) for the extinction of the mammoths (prehistoric elephants) in the Western Hemisphere 8,000 years ago. In the case of the human species, with a shorter gestation period of 9 months, we, too, have a limited reproductive potential due to the lengthened dependency period of the young and the relatively short reproductive period of the female (compared with life span). Human reproductive potential is further restricted by numerous regulations imposed by society that forbid sexual intercourse between certain individuals. The net result is a reduction in the absolute numbers of offspring produced, which often is below the biological potential. In sum, natural selection refers to all those features of a population's environment that influence reproduction and survival contributing to a steady production of individuals over the generations who, as Darwin described, have a reproductive advantage.

In the case of human populations, natural selection is much more complicated, as will be explained in the following chapters. Throughout our history some populations have increased while others have declined. Diseases once a deadly menace have now declined to be replaced by others; in this decade, mortality from a previously unknown disease, acquired immune deficiency syndrome (AIDS), has risen dramatically. Until the last few centuries human existence had always been precarious. Frequently, high fertility was exceeded by an even higher mortality until human adaptation underwent a dramatic improvement. First, the Neolithic revolution, when plant and animal domestication began about 10,000 years ago, was a very successful adaptation with high fertility that contributed to major population increases. Then again during the Industrial Revolution of 200 years ago, Western Europe underwent a population "explosion"; fertility rates went up while death rates declined dramatically. A short time later, the rest of Europe and certain other parts of the world followed in this new pattern. Today, many national groups are undergoing a similar experience of population increase but at much higher rates. Those countries that had major growth throughout the period of the Industrial Revolution are now experiencing a lowering of birth rates together with a reduction of mortality rates that has brought the annual increase of population down to a lower level. There has been, throughout human history, disproportionate growth among human populations. No one regional group has predominated for very long, and there have been tendencies for fluctuations in population growth, as I will describe in Chapter 8.

Gene Flow

In addition to growth, there has been considerable population movement throughout human history, and much of this migration has occurred in the last few centuries. The migration and mixing of peoples increase genetic exchange, and populations that were isolated in past centuries have undergone a considerable change in gene frequencies. Interpopulation contact through migration, trade, or warfare has had a major influence on the genetic variability of many populations of *Homo sapiens*.

This *gene flow*, as it is often called, refers to exchanges between different population gene pools so that the next generation is a result of admixture of the parental population. This has been an important factor that has reduced the influences of isolation and reduces development of unique gene combinations within a breeding population. It has the potential for introducing new gene combinations, causing the population to be more heterogeneous. The relative influence of gene exchange between breeding populations depends, of course, on the size and length of time in contact. Invading armies, colonists, travelers, and traders have all had an effect on genetic distribution throughout our species. The distribution of gene frequencies today and in the recent past is quite different from what it was prior to the major colonial expansion of western Europe beginning in the fifteenth century, and it is continuing to undergo changes.

Genetic Drift

A critical factor influencing gene frequencies from generation to generation is the total number of individuals who make up the effective breeding population (males and females in their reproductive years). When this number is very small there is the possibility that not all gene combinations will be represented in the next generation. This may be described as a sampling error or genetic drift. The chance distribution of the genotypes of offspring from the mating of heterozygotes can serve to illustrate the influences of population size on sampling error. When there is a mating of heterozygotes (Aa × Aa), there is a probability of 25 percent that the offspring will be AA. If the couple produce five children in all, then the probability is less than .1 percent that they all will be genotype AA, while there is 1.5 percent chance that three children will have this genotype (see Table 2-7). Should either of these unlikely events occur and more AA genotypes be produced than either Aa or aa, the frequency of the recessive allele, a, would decrease through chance alone in a population with only a few matings in each generation. The larger the number of matings, the greater the probability that all genetic combinations will be reproduced, so the gene frequencies will remain stable from one generation to the next. By contrast, the fewer the matings each generation, the smaller the sample of the total gene pool. Under this condition there will be a greater chance that certain genes will not be passed on because of the small size of the sample.

There are a number of examples where genes have become fixed at high frequencies in human populations within just a few generations. Island populations throughout the Pacific and other regions, as well as religious colonists whose beliefs have resulted in self-imposed breeding isolation, doc-

TABLE 2-7   Distribution of Offspring of Two Heterozygous Parents (Aa × Aa)

GENOTYPE OF FIRST OFFSPRING	PROBABILITY OF FIRST OFFSPRING	GENOTYPE OF SECOND OFFSPRING	PROBABILITY OF SECOND OFFSPRING	TOTAL PROBABILITY
AA	1/4	AA	1/4	Both offspring AA, 1/16
AA	1/4	Aa	2/4	AA followed by Aa, 2/16
AA	1/4	aa	1/4	AA followed aa, 1/16
Aa	2/4	AA	1/4	Aa followed AA, 2/16
Aa	2/4	Aa	2/4	Both offspring Aa, 4/16
Aa	2/4	aa	1/4	Aa followed by aa, 2/16
aa	1/4	AA	1/4	aa followed by AA, 1/16
aa	1/4	Aa	2/4	aa followed by Aa, 2/16
aa	1/4	aa	1/4	Both offspring aa, 1/16

ument the influence of population size on gene frequencies. The smaller the size of the effective breeding population (ratio of males and females of reproductive age to total population), the greater the chance of gene frequency change between the generations.

The influence of the founders' gene combinations is another form of sampling error and is referred to as *founders' effect*, described by Mayr (1963). Because of the improbability of a small group of colonists representing all of the variety of the parent population, this initial error in sampling will have a major influence on future generations of descendants from the founding population. This restricted sampling, or "bottleneck" effect, may be repeated in future generations if, through natural catastrophe or disease, the population loses large numbers of its people over a short period. Consider the example of the small South Atlantic island of Tristan da Cunha, midway between South America and Africa. The 270 persons occupying the island in 1961 could trace their ancestry back to the original 15 colonists consisting of soldiers, shipwrecked sailors, and a few women who arrived in 1816.

The lonely, isolated island has no natural harbor to shelter ships from the rough seas and its environment is harsh, so, except for an occasional individual, there has been no immigration. Despite these restrictions the population had grown to 103 by 1855, when it suffered a setback with the departure of all but 33 persons. A second bottleneck occurred when a small boat, with 15 males aboard, capsized leaving no survivors. Following this disaster many of the widows and their offspring emigrated, reducing the island population from 106 to 54. The population recovered to reach 270 by 1961. The events that caused this small founding population to undergo an expansion, followed by severe reduction, and then expansion again have caused some rare genetic recessive traits and unique gene frequencies to exist among the modern-day descendants.

Even larger populations, descendants of a few founders, will often contain a high frequency of rare genetic defects. An example of such detrimental genes reaching high frequencies is the inherited defect *porphyria*. This metabolic disorder prevents chemical conversion of the porphyrin compound, the iron-bearing pigment of hemoglobin, and results in the excretion of excessive amounts in the urine. Persons with the South African type of *porphyria*, inherited as an autosomal dominant, are ultrasensitive to sunlight, which produces severe skin lesions. The accumulation of porphyrin in the blood leads to a number of symptoms of the digestive tract and to nervous system disorders, and persons with the affliction are sensitive, as well, to certain types of drugs like barbiturates. This metabolic defect is rare throughout the world, with most cases reported in the Afrikaans population. The gene responsible for this affliction has been traced through genealogies back to 1688 to a young girl from Rotterdam and her spouse, another immigrant from the Netherlands. The 8,000 carriers of this autosomal dominant allele today are descendants of this marriage. These findings are not surprising, considering that an estimated one million of three million Afrikaans are descendants of 40 original couples settling in the Cape area (see Dean, 1963).

Random Mating

The Hardy-Weinberg Equilibrium assumes that matings take place without regard to genotype; that is, they are random. Persons marry without considering the blood group genotypes; for example, persons do not select a mate of type A blood and reject one of type B. Therefore, calculations for many of the human gene frequencies will not be disturbed by a nonrandomness of breeding. However, random breeding in another sense does not usually apply in the choice of mates because a number of social as well as biological criteria are considered. In human populations all males and females do not have an equal chance of mating, and there are a number of barriers that reduce random mating. One is *positive* assortative mating, which describes a tendency for "like" to marry "like." Tall people tend to marry tall people and short people tend to marry short people. Also, there is a high positive correlation between the I.Q.s of husband and wife. Persons frequently marry those within their social circle and, until just a few generations ago, geographic distance played a major role in mate selection; marriages took place most often between individuals who lived near each other. Though the distances between prenuptial households is steadily increasing, marriage to "the boy or girl next door" was more fact than fiction until quite recently. Another factor that has effected random matings is society's rules that prohibit matings between close relatives, but these rules might be suspended when small community size limited mate choice, as described in Chapter 6.

Society's rules governing marriage have influenced a degree of outbreeding, or population *exogamy*, where mates are selected from outside of one's family or village, reducing homozygosity while increasing heterozygosity. Population *endogamy*, or inbreeding, causes the reverse—an increase in homozygosity. The consequences of the relative degree of inbreeding may be in evidence in health, growth, and genetics. Children of *consanguineous* matings (marriages of relatives of some degree) are smaller in size, have a higher frequency of congenital abnormalities, and exhibit greater mortality during the first six years of life (Morton, 1958, 1961; Schull and Neel, 1965). The degree of genetic relationship of the parents increases the chance of pairing deleterious recessives in the offspring because of a higher probability that the parents may be carriers of the same recessive alleles, due to their sharing of a close common ancestor. This increased homozygosity of recessives is shown by higher incidence of genetic diseases in certain populations. There is a greater frequency of consanguinity among parents of affected offspring than among the general population (see Table 2-8).

TABLE 2-8   Percentages of Affected Offspring of Cousin Marriages

TRAIT	% CONSANGUINITY[a]
Albinism	19–24
Alkaptonuria	30–42
PKU	5–15
Tay-Sachs	27–53
Xeroderma pigmentosum	20–36
Ichthyosis congenita	30–40
Congenital total blindnes	11–21

[a]This indicates the frequency of consanguinity of those parents who produced affected offspring. This should be weighed against the average for the general population, which is less than 1 percent.

Source: Data adapted from: Stern, 1973; Vogel and Motulsky, 1986.

GENES AND POPULATIONS: A SUMMARY

Mendel's experiments laid the foundation for modern genetics. The significance of these experiments was that they clearly demonstrated, for the first time, particulate inheritance, and the concept of inheritance by a blending of traits was at last put to rest. There are several points that should be emphasized. The first is that genes are transmitted in groups because they are a part of the chromosomes that exist as paired structures except when separated at meiosis to form the gamete. At this point in cell division, each chromosome goes its own way; there is an independent assortment that takes place, as Mendel showed with his experiments with dihybrid plants. Another way of describing this chromosome assortment is to consider that in humans, who have forty-six, one-half of the chromosomes are provided by each of the parents. However, this is not necessarily the same order in which they, in turn, will be passed to the next generation. As our gametes develop they will contain some mixture of chromosomes from each of our parents so it is highly improbable that any person will possess one-fourth of his or her genome from each grandparent. Recall Mendel's second law; the Law of Independent Assortment, which contributes to a large number of gamete types, over eight million.

A second point to consider is that a crossing of heterozygotes produces results that will usually differ somewhat by chance alone from the Mendelian ratio (1:2:1). This is to be anticipated, though, and simple statistical tests can show whether this deviation significantly differs from the expected or if it differs simply due to a chance variation. If the difference is statistically significant then one of the factors of the Hardy-Weinberg Equilibrium may be involved.

In considering a Mendelian population (breeding population), those sources of variation and the forces for stability will have to be identified and compared in order to understand any change in gene frequency throughout the generations. Sources of new genetic material (mutations) cause small, minor changes in gene frequency in contrast to migration, which can disturb equilibrium in a single generation. If the mutation is one that conveys an advantage, then natural selection can cause a rapid rise in the frequency of the new allele. Mutations, as discussed, play the role of supplying new genetic material and, considering the complexity in the copying of the genes at meiosis, it is surprising that mutation rates are so low. It is likely that many more mutations occur than have been measured, and that these mutations are responsible for the wide range of biochemical variability that we are beginning to recognize in the human species. Most of these deleterious mutations are, fortunately, masked by the normal allele except in those rare cases when they are combined in the homozygote. We now know of the many variations in DNA fragment lengths, recently described, that frequently occur from either crossovers or from base pair changes.

Population size is a critical consideration in any study of human variation because of the possibility of loss of alleles through chance alone. The *effective breeding population* consists of those in their reproductive years (generally considered to be between fifteen and forty-four) and is, on the average, roughly one-third of the total population. Add to this the restrictions imposed by society's rules dictating the matings allowed, and chance can be seen as a major factor in gene frequency change. Also, chance plays a role in reproduction (the variety of gametes is an example) but human behavior channels a good bit of genetic variability along a certain course, as we describe later.

This chapter has provided an overview of the biological basis of human inheritance and variability. These basic concepts are developed throughout the balance of this book, and appropriate examples are given. The examples offer evidence that *Homo sapiens* is subject to basic biological laws. Though human behavior may alter the direct effect of the forces acting on a species, our total gene combinations are still related to certain environmental variables that exert selective forces. The appreciation of the importance of these forces enables us to understand the development of biological diversity.

3

Human Biology I: Traits of Simple Inheritance

With the rise of molecular biology and analysis of DNA structure, more and more is learned about the many human phenotypes of simple inheritance determined by a dominant or recessive allele. Some of the better-known traits controlled by genes at a single locus (monogenic) include the various blood-group systems, hemoglobins, enzymes, and numerous serum proteins. This list of specific gene traits is continuously growing as improved techniques permit the identification of polymorphisms at more chromosome loci. The expression of these monogenic phenotypes is relatively little influenced by the environment, in contrast to the wide ranges of variation seen in polygenic traits (multiple gene loci). These monogenic traits are described as discontinuous; each trait is either present or absent, in contrast to the broad ranges of the polygenic traits discussed in later chapters. In the study of population genetics and of those factors that cause changes in gene frequencies, monogenic traits are most useful. Some of these simply inherited traits have also been used as markers to estimate the degree of genetic distance between populations and their probable ancestral relationships. Recently, the use of restriction enzymes to "cut" the DNA molecule at precise locations has added considerable knowledge of the restriction fragment length polymorphisms (RFLP) in many population groups and have added an important method of studies of human biological variation, as discussed in Chapter 4. Before discussion of the precise DNA markers, this chapter will take a more historical view and examine those traits of the blood and enzyme systems identified beginning in this century. A vast amount of data has accumulated on these traits, which are useful in comparing populations and their environments.

BLOOD COMPONENTS AND INHERITED TRAITS

Blood serves the vital functions of transporting oxygen and nutrients throughout the body and of removing the waste products of metabolism. Blood consists of specialized cells, *erythrocytes* (red blood cells), whose function is to transport oxygen to the tissues, and a yellowish fluid, the plasma. This fluid part of the blood contains a variety of substances vital to the metabolism. Major plasma constituents are *albumin,* a group of large protein molecules that combine with and transport a number of substances; blood-clotting agents—*fibrinogen,* several clotting factors, and small granular bodies called *globulin* fractions (see Figure 3-1). Another type of cell—the *leukocytes* (white blood cells), mainly granulocytes and lymphocytes—is also found in the blood. Normally there are few of these cells in circulation, but during infection their number rises dramatically as the body's defense against invading organisms.

In our discussion of inherited polymorphisms of the blood we are especially interested in the gamma globulin fraction that include immunoglobulins, antibodies that attack the foreign substances entering the body, usually bacteria or proteins. These *antibodies,* our main line of defense, are protein molecules that have the ability to attach to certain other chemical molecules on the surfaces of microorganisms. This attachment causes a group of these organisms to cling together (agglutinate). Many foreign substances such as

FIGURE 3-1 **Blood Components.** When a sample of blood is placed in a test tube and spun in a centrifuge the heavier components settle to the bottom with the lighter products and fluids at the top. The diagram lists these major components, the types of cells, and the products in the plasma.

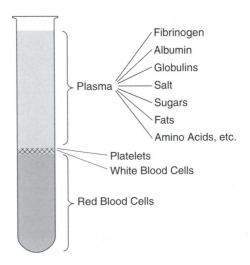

Plasma
- Fibrinogen
- Albumin
- Globulins
- Salt
- Sugars
- Fats
- Amino Acids, etc.

Platelets
White Blood Cells

Red Blood Cells

pollen, mold, virus, or bacteria may stimulate the synthesis of antibodies in the host's body; substances with this property are called *antigens*.

The antigen is often a complex molecule with multiple combining sites or locations where antibodies may connect, and may be viewed as a simple model shown in Figure 3-2. The antibody, however, is a simpler structure and has fewer combining sites. When the antibody connects with an antigen, there are still sites available to connect with other antibodies and antigens until all combining sites are full. The result is a linkage together of all the foreign antigens. This interaction ultimately makes it possible for the body's defense to destroy foreign substances or to render them harmless by preventing their multiplication. The efficiency of this system depends on the ability to produce antibodies of the right kind and in sufficient quantities.

The Blood Groups

There are antibodies in each person's system that are, of necessity, compatible with the individual's own circulatory system. But if blood from one person is mixed with blood from another, then a reaction may occur between the antigens and antibodies of the two individuals. Experiments that mixed red blood cells of

FIGURE 3-2   Diagram of Antibodies–Antigen Reactions.

These diagrams show the relationships between red blood-cell antigens (type A) and the two types of serum. No agglutination will occur when type-A cells are mixed with serum from a type-A person. The antibodies are anti-B type (β antibodies) and are not attracted by the combining sites of the type A (left diagram). When type-A cells are mixed with serum from a type-B person, the anti-A antibodies (α antibodies) combine with the cells and agglutination occurs, causing the cells to cling together in a group (right diagram).

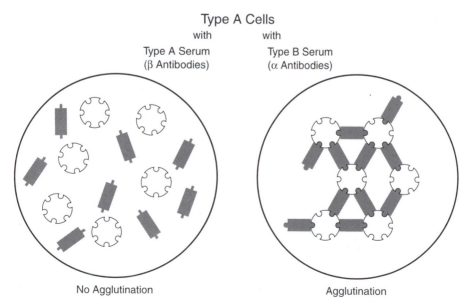

one species with samples of serum from another resulted in an attraction between the red blood cells causing them to cling together or agglutinate. This attraction suggested that there was some substance that attached to a sticky part of the red blood cell surfaces. Likewise, when samples were taken from different humans, the agglutination would occur frequently, but not always. These serological experiments over the last quarter of the nineteenth century indicated that there were some distinct differences in the surface components of the red blood cells and those within the blood serum. There was further demonstration of the variety of human blood components when blood transfusions were attempted on a large scale, for the first time, during the Franco-Prussian war (1870–71).

Prior to 1900, transfusions were used only as a last resort in an attempt to save the patient's life. Often the transfused blood would cause shock and even death because of agglutination of the incompatible antibodies and red cells, as we now know. At times, though, transfusions were successful, because some mixtures of blood were compatible. In 1900 Karl Landsteiner, an Austrian immunologist, began to systematically analyze the pattern of agglutination between the blood donor and recipients. Tests were made by mixing the blood serum from one person with red blood cells from another. Only certain combinations caused an agglutination of the red cells. If a reaction occurred between serum from person A and red cells from person B, Landsteiner found the reverse was also true; serum from B would agglutinate cells from A. Throughout thousands of tests Landsteiner found these results to be consistent, but there were some individuals whose cells could not be agglutinated by either anti-A or anti-B serum. Transfusions could now be made safely if the donor and recipient bloods were matched.

Since this original discovery, a number of other major blood groups have been identified by cross-reaction between red blood cells and serum from different individuals and also by reaction of blood cells to specially prepared antiserum. Such antiserum is prepared by injecting human cells into laboratory animals—rabbits, for instance—and extracting samples of antiserum made by the animal. This antihuman antiserum is then tested against a variety of human blood samples and the reactions tabulated. In testing of blood cells taken from numerous individuals, agglutination reactions are noted with some and not with others. Extracts of plant compounds have also been applied in this way. Table 3-1 lists several of the more clinically important blood groups, including those useful today in the study of human genetics.

The ABO Blood Group is the best known of a growing list of the red cell antigens because of its medical importance, and, since its discovery, millions of people throughout the world have had their blood types recorded. Analysis of these data and comparison of ABO types in families has shown that the type was passed on by Mendelian inheritance.[1] The antigens are under the

---

[1]The inheritance of blood types as Mendelian characters was demonstrated by Hirszfeld and von Dungern in 1910 but they identified only two alleles, A and B. Their work stimulated many others, and Bernstein in 1924 established that there were, in fact, three alleles that determined the ABO blood types (see Mourant, 1983).

TABLE 3-1 Major Blood Group Systems

SYSTEM	ANTIGENS	GENOTYPES	PHENOTYPES	DATE OF DISCOVERY
ABO	A_1, A_2, B	OO, AA, BB, AB	O, A_1, A_2, B, AB	1900
Lewis	Le^a, Le^b	Le^aLe^a, Le^bLe^b, LeLe	Le(a + b −), Le(a − b +), Le(a − b −)	1946
Rh	(see Table 3-6a)			
MNSs	M, N, S, s	MS/MS, MS/Ms, Ms/Ms, MS/NS, MS/Ns, Ms/NS, Ms/Ns, NS/NS, NS/Ns, Ns/Ns	M, N, MN, S, s, Ss	1927
P	P_1, P_2	P_1P_1, P_1P_2, P_2P_2 P_1p, P_2p, pp	P_1, P_2, p	1927
Lutheran	Lu^a, Lu^b	Lu^aLu^a, Lu^aLu^b, Lu^bLu^b	Lu (a + b −), Lu (a − b +)	1945
Kell	K (Kell) k (cellano)	KK, Kk, kk	K + k −, k + k +, K − k +, (K − k −)	1946
Duffy	Fy^a, Fy^b	Fy^aFy^a, Fy^aFy^b, Fy^bFy^b, FyFy	Fy (a + b −), Fy (a + b +), Fy (a − b +), Fy (a − b −)	1950
Kidd	Jk^a, Jk^b	Jk^aJk^a, Jk^aJk^b, Jk^bJk^b	Jk (a + b −), Jk (a + b +), Jk (a − b +), Jk (a − b −)	1951
Diego	Di^a	Di^aDi^a, Di^aDi, DiDi	Di (a +), Di (a −)	1955
Sutter	Js^a	Js^aJs^a, Js^aJs, JsJs	Js (a +), Js (a −)	
Auberger	Au^a	Au^aAu^a, Au^aAu, AuAu	Au (a +), Au (a −)	1961
Xg	Xg^a	Xg^aY, XgY, Xg^aXg^a, Xg^aXg, XgXg	Xg (a +), Xg (a −)	1962

Sources: Based on Buettner-Janusch, 1966; Giblettt, 1969; and Race and Sanger, 1975.

control of at least three alleles at a locus on chromosome 9; the alleles A and B are codominants whereas the type O allele is recessive. The genetics of the ABO system become more complex as additional alleles are detected. For example, there are actually two types of A, A_1 and A_2, that increase the number of alleles at the ABO locus to four.

Within the blood plasma of each person there are antibodies related to the "type" of red blood cell antigen. The antibody type as well as the antigen type are under genetic control, and the pattern of inheritance is listed here:

GENOTYPE	PHENOTYPE	ANTIBODIES
	(BLOOD TYPE)	
AA } AO }	A	anti-B
BB } BO }	B	anti-A
AB	AB	none
OO	O	anti-A, B

This diagram illustrates that the genotypes AA and AO determine the same blood type (the type of antigen carried by the red blood cell). Persons of this type will have anti-B antibodies in their plasma, so blood from a type-A person cannot be donated to a type-B person. These antibodies are "naturally" occurring—that is, they appear to have been determined by the ABO alleles. They are normally present in a person's serum and their production need not be stimulated by an antigen from external sources. The antibodies (A and B) in a type-O person are somewhat different; they are smaller in size and their reactions are weaker.

Soluble ABO Antigens and Modifying Genes

When the ABO group was first studied it was assumed that type O was simply the absence of antigens A and B and a type-O person's blood would not react to either antisera. Further study showed that certain antisera could be found that would react with type-O blood cells. The reaction indicated the probability of an antigen on type-O cells and was designated *type H*. The antigen is a molecular fragment on the surface of the blood cell that is common to both the A and B antigens, because type-A and type-O blood cells will also react with the anti-H serum. The reaction is weaker than that of the cells from a type-O person. However, the order of strength of reactions is $O > A_1 > B > A_2$. This H substance may be identifiable in the saliva and other bodily fluids just as the antigens of type A and B of most persons may be present in soluble form (around 75 percent in the British Isles and higher in other regions).

The presence of soluble ABH antigens in bodily fluids such as saliva, tears, semen, milk, gastric juice, and other watery secretions is determined by a dominant allele at another locus, and the person who is homozygous or heterozygous is described as a secretor. The inheritance of the ability to secrete the ABH antigens in soluble form is shown by the following genotypes:

GENOTYPE	PHENOTYPE
Se Se >————————————>	secretor
Se se >————————————>	secretor
se se >————————————>	nonsecretor

The existence of these water-soluble forms throughout the body tissues has made it possible to study the structure of the ABH antigens because they can be chemically analyzed. The antigen's molecular structure consists of a chain of simple sugar molecules linked to protein or lipid compound. The A and B antigens are alike except for a different sugar at the terminal end of a common chain forming the H antigen, as shown in Figure 3-3. Without one or the other of these sugar molecules (1 or 3), the molecular structure determines a type O (Race and Sanger, 1975). Since this structure was identified by analysis of the soluble antigens, the antigen on the red cell surface has been

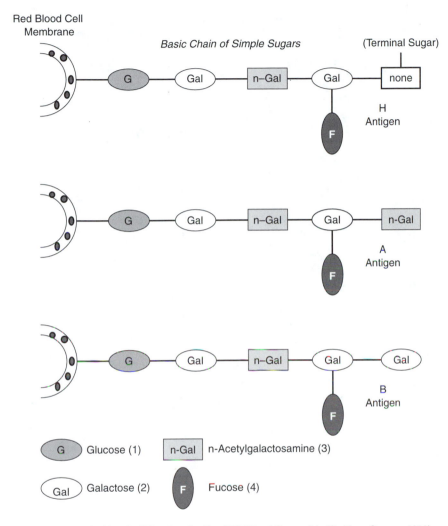

FIGURE 3-3   Basic Chemical Structure for the ABO Blood Group. (Modified from Ganong, 1993)

identified and confirms this basic structure (Hakomori, 1986). In Figure 3-4, the process of forming the completed structure is by synthesis of a precursor followed by the formation of a longer intermediate chain in which, if an H gene is present on chromosome 19, an H antigen is completed (shown as step 3). If the individual lacks an A or B transferase enzyme, no further synthesis takes place and the chain of sugars stops at step 3. However, if an A or B allele is present then an additional sugar is added as in step 4. The differences between the blood type antigens appear to be only simple base substitutions in a segment of the chromosome 9 DNA. These differences determine if the A or B transferase enzyme will be present to complete the change from step 3

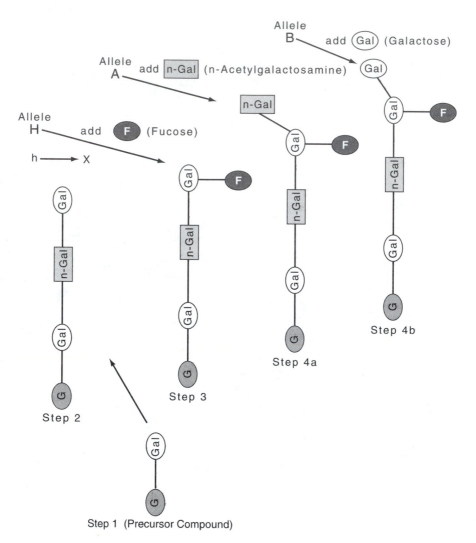

FIGURE 3-4   Synthesis of ABH Chemical Structure. (Data from: Hakomori, 1986; Mange and Mange, 1990)

to step 4. A critical point to consider is that the intermediate chain must be converted to the H antigen before the A or B antigens can be produced.

Bombay Blood Type

The complexity of the ABO system was underscored by the discovery of persons in India whose red blood cells did not agglutinate when mixed with anti-A, anti-B, or anti-H serum—added evidence that another genetic locus influenced the expression of the ABO blood types. These persons should have had an ABO type given the evidence from the studies of their family pedigrees, but they did not. Further surveys showed that this rare condition is seldom found in any population except among Mohorati speakers in and around Bombay, India, where the frequency is about one in 13,000, and on Reunion Island in the Indian Ocean (see Gerard et al., 1982). Such persons are said to have the *Bombay* blood type and lack ABH antigens on red blood cells or the soluble form in the serum. This condition, the Bombay blood group, is inherited as a simple recessive and may be understood as the lack of a substance that is essential as a precursor for the structure of the A or B antigen (see Figure 3-4). This process of intermediate (step 2) to H antigen is under the control of another locus on chromosome 19 where two alleles have been identified, a dominant and a recessive. Without a dominant allele (H) step 2 to 3 cannot be completed, and a person with such a genotype (hh) would not have either A or B antigen. The recessive (h) is rare and a homozygous genotype (Bombay type) is seldom found, but when it occurs, the person will not type as A or B and his or her blood plasma will contain anti-H antibodies.

The Significance of the ABO Blood Group

The importance of the ABO blood type for many forms of medical treatment is beyond dispute; it is essential to identify a person's type so a proper match can be made between donor and recipient. The question of what biological function this genetically controlled trait may have is another matter. Also, what, if any, is the significance of the pattern of geographical distribution among the world's people? These differences are unlikely to have arisen by chance alone, though genetic drift played some part earlier in human pre-history because of small founding populations. The key question is: Are different environments influencing survival? A complex of several disease organisms may be acting on different genotypes of blood components. Is there evidence for genetic adaptations? These are some of the questions that have been raised about this medically important trait.

The discovery of inherited differences in ABO antigens and antibodies intrigued many investigators and led them on in a search for a function. Did the fact that type B was more frequent in parts of Asia, while type A was more prevalent among northern Europeans, have any relationship to the environmental variables in each region? Other investigators followed the route that treated the blood groups as nonadaptive, that is, selectively neutral, and reasoned that differing frequencies of the types among populations were due to other factors that influence gene frequencies (Boyd, 1950). Despite this latter position, an enormous amount of work has gone into an effort to discover natural selection at the ABO locus. Since the initial discovery of the ABO system in 1900, many millions of persons around the world have been typed, and extensive research as been carried on in an attempt to discover correlations between blood type and the incidence of disease. The results have been inconclusive, but they have stimulated much speculation about the meaning of blood-group polymorphism in all of the red-cell antigens, plasma proteins, the HLA system, and the ABO blood groups in particular.

The average frequencies of the ABO alleles for the entire species may serve as a baseline against which individual populations or population complexes may be compared. Allele O (62.5 percent) is the most frequent and the B (16 percent) the least, with allele A (21.5 percent) slightly higher. Populations in many parts of the world deviate widely from these averages, but, with a few exceptions (Australian Aborigines and Native Americans in particular), alleles A and B are usually greater than zero and seldom rise above 50 percent. Figure 3-5 plots the A and B frequencies for 215 representative populations; most cluster within the ranges of 15–30 percent (type A) and 10–20 percent (type B) when gene frequency distribution is considered. Alice Brues (1954 and 1963) argued that such a distribution could most adequately be explained by balanced polymorphism at the ABO locus that was maintained by selection for the heterozygote, the AO genotype. Though the nature of the selection has yet to be fully understood, many workers now consider that the ABO alleles are adaptive and in some way influence survival.

Though the search for the meaning of ABO blood-group polymorphisms over this century has not been conclusive, a number of possible explanations have emerged. These explanations can be grouped into several categories of selection that influence allele frequencies over the period of human

FIGURE 3-5 Limits to the Range of Alleles A and B in the World's Populations. (From Brues, A. M., "Selection and polymorphism in the ABO blood groups." Copyright © 1954 by The Wistar Institute Press. Reprinted by permission of the publisher.)

Quantitative distribution of 215 representative human populations in respect to frequencies of the ABO blood-group genes.

PERCENT OF GENE A

PERCENT OF GENE B	0	5	10	15	20	25	30	35	40	45	50	55
0–5	6	7	1	2	4	3	3	2	1		1	
5–10	1	1	4	7	10	11	7	1	1	1		
10–15	1	2	8	13	15	16	8	1				
15–20		1	4	13	10	9	2					
20–25			2	9	6	2						
25–30			2	7	6	2	1					
30–35	1			2	2							
35–40												

evolution and population diversification. Selection in *Homo sapiens* functions to cause differential fertility, differential mortality, and infant mortality in particular. There have been studies that describe the effectiveness of selection in each of these categories; some genotypes had an advantage.

Differential Fertility

There was a difference in the rate of live births of type-O mothers that indicates some type of incompatibility; type-O women produced fewer children than expected when the fathers were either type A or B. In addition to reduced fertility in cases of incompatible matings, should the male parent be heterozygous AO or BO, then there was a significantly greater number of OO children produced by the type-O mother. The net result of matings incompatible for the ABO system is seen in Table 3-2.

The differential fertility acts in the following ways: First, there is a selection at the *prezygotic* stage (prior to fertilization of the ovum). In a type-O female there appears to be a greater chance of fertilization by the sperm carrying the type-O gene, so the genotypes differ significantly from the expected frequency shown by the Hardy-Weinberg equilibrium, as in the following:

Parents   AO (male) × OO (female)
Children   AO   OO (>50 percent)

With the parental AO and OO genotypes, there two possible genotypes of the offspring as indicated. The chance of either occurring is 50 percent (the Mendelian ration is 1:1), but, in fact, a statistically significant greater number

TABLE 3-2 ABO Blood Types and Fertility

	MATINGS WHERE THE ABO BLOOD TYPES OF MALE AND FEMALE ARE:			
	Compatible		*Incompatible*	
Total matings	812		617	
Pregnancies	2,639		1,928	
Abortions[a]	273	(0.10 per pregnancy)	295	(0.15 per pregnancy)
Living children[a]	2,108		1,341	
Couples childless[a]	80	(0.10)	112	(0.18)
Couples as yet infertile	66	(0.08)	72	(0.12)

[a]These differences between compatible and incompatible matings are statistically significant.
Sources: Based on Matsunaga and Itoh, 1958; and Matsunaga and Hiraizumi, 1962.

of OO offspring are produced. This apparent selection of the O-carrying sperm may be due to the antibodies in vaginal secretions, which react with sperm specific for type A. Sperm have been shown to possess specific antigen reactions, but the question still remains whether such specificity is due to the alleles carried by the sperm.

The second reason for reduction of fertility of incompatible matings is fetal loss due to antibodies A and B in the type-O mother. The naturally occurring A and B antibodies in the O mother do not readily cross the placenta, but some mothers make an anti-A and anti-B that can easily diffuse through the placenta membranes and enter the fetal bloodstream. Once there, they can disrupt development and may even cause fetal death. Overall, several studies show that women who carry fetuses with ABO blood types incompatible with their own have a greater risk of spontaneous abortion. The ease with which some antibodies from the maternal system can pass into the fetal bloodstream can be a danger similar to that known to exist for Rh hemolytic disease (see below).

In sum, fetal maternal incompatibility may contribute to a reduced fertility rate, increased abortion early in pregnancy, and hemolytic disease of the neonate (about once in a thousand pregnancies). These are strong selective forces favoring the increase in the frequency of the O allele over A or B and should lead to rapid fixation. In other words, all populations with such incompatible matings would eventually contain only type O (Figure 3-6). Such a condition exists in many Native American populations, but most of the world, as we have seen, has populations with a mixture of all three alleles. The question is: What factors cause the A and B alleles?

Disease Incidence and the ABO Blood Groups

The association between ABO blood types and certain diseases was considered early in the study of red-cell antigen systems. Namely, was there a significant correlation with a specific disease? Analysis of thousands of hospital records compared the blood types of patients with the disease for which they were treated. In this way a wide variety of diseases were listed, but the early results, because of statistical errors, were disappointing and discouraged further investigation for nearly twenty-five years. Later these errors were noted and the search for disease correlations was renewed.

A study of the frequency of stomach cancer in England revealed a difference between regions: The mortality rate was higher in the North than in the South. Aird and associates (1953) at first thought the difference might be due to some environmental factor, and there did prove to be a difference in water hardness; a higher calcium concentration was found in those areas with the lowest stomach cancer rate. The correlation was slight, but when the ABO blood types were compared there was a higher number of type-A persons with this type of cancer. These results encouraged a wide range of investigators to seek disease associations with this medically important blood group. Signifi-

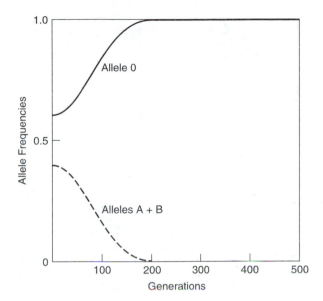

FIGURE 3-6   ABO Incompatibility Leads to Fixation of the O Allele.

Fetal–maternal incompatibility of ABO type contributes to reduced fertility in the type-O mother. The maternal antibodies select against a type-A or type-B fetus while favoring a type O. The result is that the allele O would become fixed in a population within about 200 generations if no counterselective forces are involved, that is, neither type-A nor type-B persons have an advantage in certain environments. Source: Etkin and Eaton, 1983.

cant associations were found with a number of tumors as well as with several other metabolic diseases (see Table 3-3). Interestingly, correlations continued to identify gastrointestinal type disorders, from duodenal ulcers to stomach and colon cancers and cancer of the pancreas. This turned attention to the soluble form of the ABO antigens and their function in the digestive tract.

Though the distribution of secretors and nonsecretors throughout the world's populations is not as well known as that of the ABO red cell types, their presence in tissues and fluids throughout the body may have a major significance in the response to foreign antigens. Some clues are provided by the relative gene frequencies at this locus. The record, to date, has established that most Native Americans are secretors and that the majority of nonsecretors are found in African populations south of the Sahara and in southern India. In the British Isles the alleles (Se, se) are approximately equal in frequency and there are about 25 percent nonsecretors (the se se genotype). The meaning of this distribution is not fully understood but there is a suggested relationship between the antigens and digestion. There may be some interactions between the macromolecules of food and bacteria in the digestive tract.

TABLE 3-3   Significant Associations between Blood Groups and Noninfectious Disease

DIAGNOSIS	NO. OF SERIES	NO. OF PATIENTS	CONTROLS	COMPARISON	
Neoplasias of the intestinal tract					
Cancer, stomach	101	55,434	1,852,288	A:O	1.22
Cancer of colon and rectum	17	7,435	183,286	A:O	1.11
Malignant tumors of salivary glands	2	285	12,968	A:O	1.64
Cancer, pancreas	13	817	108,408	A:O	1.24
Cancer, mouth and pharynx	2	757	41,098	A:O	1.25
Other neoplasias					
Cancer, cervix	19	11,927	197,577	A:O	1.13
Cancer, corpus uteri	14	2,598	160,602	A:O	1.15
Cancer, ovary	17	2,326	243,914	A:O	1.28
Cancer, breast	24	9,503	355,281	A:O	1.08
Multiple primary cancer	2	433	7,823	A:O	1.43
Nonmalignant tumors					
Nonmalignant salivary tumors	2	581	12,968	A:O	2.02
Other internal diseases					
Duodenal ulcers	44	26,039	407,518	O:A	1.35
				O:A+B+AB	1.33
Gastric ulcers	41	22,052	448,354	O:A	1.17
				O:A+B+AB	1.18
Duodenal and gastric ulcers	6	957	120,544	O:A	1.53
				O:A+B+AB	1.36
Bleeding ulcers (gastric and duodenal)	2	1,869	28,325	O:A	1.46
				O:A+B+AB	1.51
Rheumatic diseases	17	6,589	179,385	A:O	1.24
				A+B+AB:O	1.23
Pernicious anemia	13	2,077	119,989	A:O	1.25
Diabetes mellitus	20	15,778	612,819	A:O	1.07
				A+B+AB:O	1.07
Ischemic heart disease	12	2,763	218,727	A:O	1.18
				A+B+AB:O	1.17
Cholecystitis and choleli-thiasis	10	5,950	112,928	A:O	1.17
Eosinophilia	3	730	1,096	A:O	2.38
				A+B+AB:O	2.13
Thromboembolic disease	5	1,026	287,246	A:O	1.61
				A+B+AB:O	1.60

Sources: Examples selected from Mourant and Kopec, 1978; Vogel and Motulsky, 1986.

The presence of soluble antigens (ABH) in a majority of people, plus the fact that many food substances, once broken down into their molecular constituents, have specific reactions with the ABO substances, make it highly probable that there is a complex series of reactions between antigens and macromolecules within the gastrointestinal tract. Many of these reactions may enhance digestion or retard it, depending on the substances involved, or there may be chronic irritation of the fine mucous linings of the intestines. At any rate, it is more than a coincidence that a number of the diseases associated with the ABO system are localized within the digestive system. This area of research has not been fully explored, but immunological studies point out the likelihood of gut flora, similar to the blood group substances, stimulating the production of antibodies appropriate to the individual's RBC antigen. Hence, a type-A person will make anti-B antibodies in response to stimulus by substances in the gut flora and will tolerate antigens similar to type A (Roitt, 1988). Given the wide variety of foods that omnivorous *Homo sapiens* can and has subsisted on for thousands of years, the digestive system would be an area subject to natural selection.

In sum, the chronic diseases listed in Table 3-3 have been used to demonstrate the correctness of the original hypothesis that selection has been acting to influence polymorphisms of the ABO system. Note, however, that these diseases are of the type that usually afflict an individual later in adult life, near the end of the reproductive period. It is unlikely, then, that ulceration, diabetes, or cancer is going to influence a person's reproductive fitness. However, dietary–antigen relationships should be looked at carefully as an area of strong environmental influence.

Infectious diseases offer several interesting possibilities for explanation of the adaptability of blood groups. Certain blood types may cause an individual to be more or less susceptible to disease-causing organisms, and several relationships between blood type and diseases are listed in Table 3-4. Type O has been listed most frequently in disease associations that would account for a

TABLE 3-4 ABO Blood Groups and Infectious Diseases

DISEASE	REPORTED GREATER SUSCEPTIBILITY (TYPE)
Paratyphoid	O
Cholera	O
Plague	O
Scarlet fever	O and B
Escherichia coli (some strains)	B
Smallpox	A
Bronchial pneumonia	A
Rheumatic heart disease	A

Sources: Examples selected from Mourant and Kopec, 1978; Vogel and Motulsky, 1986.

balancing effect countering the fertility advantage of the Type O mother noted above. The second most frequent association is type A, with three important infectious diseases, in contrast to the seldom involved type B.

Some of the organisms that cause these diseases have been demonstrated to be similar, antigenically, to either the A, B, or H antigens; that is, they have chemical structures on the coatings of their outer shells that are very similar in form to the antigens on the surface of the red blood cells. The explanation follows that the more similarity between the chemical structures of disease organisms and ABH antigens, the less likely is the individual's defense system to make antibodies against the disease organism. Thus the smallpox virus has a chemical specificity similar to type-A antigen. A person with type-A blood would be more susceptible to smallpox than would an O or B type. The findings of Vogel and his associates (Vogel, 1975) described a mortality of 50 percent in type-A persons (approximately four times higher than in B or O persons) among populations in India, the region that suffered from the world's last smallpox epidemic. As a matter of fact, the frequency of A is much lower among populations of the Indian subcontinent than among Europeans, perhaps a reflection of India's long history of epidemics.

Another organism, the plague bacterium with its H antigen specificity, appears to be more lethal to type-O individuals. During the Middle Ages and later, plague epidemics were recurrent, with enormous loss of life. The first and most lethal pandemic of 1345 caused up to 50 percent mortality in the cities of western Europe. In wave after wave, this disease passed through the population, but with decreasing fury, until the last reported epidemic of 1645. If one considers the high rate of mortality even in the later periods, then the effectiveness of the disease as a selective agent can be appreciated. Any advantage of inherited resistance, no matter how slight, would be passed on to future generations. This seems to be the case for the blood groups. Those regions of the world where plague has the longest history are the very regions where type O is found at the lowest frequency today. Areas that had suffered through many outbreaks of the epidemic over the centuries have a proportionately higher A and B frequency today than regions where plague had never been reported.

Vogel (1975) points to central Asia, India, and Mesopotamia as major plague centers, areas where populations have the lowest frequency of O. The selection against a type-O person in populations with a long history of plague would, over the generations, decrease the frequency of this allele. If in the same populations there was selection also against type-A allele because of smallpox, then both the A and O alleles would be present in low frequencies. In such populations suffering from the double threat of smallpox and plague, type-B allele would occur at high frequencies, as it does in India, where B frequencies are among the highest in the world (Figure 3-7).

Another possible source of natural selection is the peculiar behavior of insects. Some species of insect vectors appear to prefer one particular host

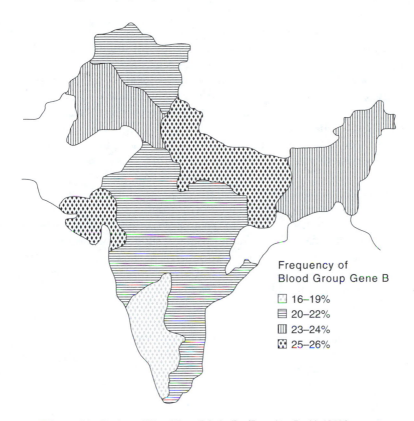

FIGURE 3-7 **Distribution of Blood Type B in India.** (Based on Buchi, 1968.)

Plague and smallpox have been major causes of death at all ages throughout India well into this century. These diseases were likely sources of natural selection at the ABO locus and are probable causes of the high frequency of type B.

over another. The temperature or color of the skin, or the chemical compounds excreted, may influence choice. Some studies have demonstrated that mosquitos have preferences in the blood they choose to feed on. How the insect choice is made or what chemical substance attracts them is not known, but type O was the most frequent preference. Volunteers were used to record the frequency of bites, and those persons with type O blood were bitten more often than those with type A or B. Should subsequent studies support these preliminary results, then malaria and other mosquito-borne diseases may be added to the list of disease selection at the ABO locus (Wood, 1974).

Population size is another factor that indirectly influences the course and intensity of natural selection. A glance at the chart of infectious diseases in Table 3-4 shows that many are of the type commonly found in larger populations who live in close contact within dense settlements and who are exposed to food and water pollution throughout their lives. One is tempted to speculate that only in relatively recent times has selection operated to pro-

duce the ranges of gene-frequency variation from the ABO blood types—
since the Neolithic, when *Homo sapiens* developed agriculture and adapted to
settled village life. Supporting evidence is provided by the fact that the more
isolated groups, especially those that have been involved with the development of dense, sedentary lifestyles only in the last few hundred generations,
are the ones with the highest type A and O frequencies—groups such as the
northwest Europeans. The Basques of northern Spain, Lapps, Australian Aborigines, and Polynesians are some examples of isolation and high A frequencies. Type B is consistently low except in a few Middle Eastern isolates (see
Table 3-5).

By contrast, the populations whose ancestors established the earliest
large, densely populated, agriculturally based communities are those with the
lowest A frequencies (Native American groups excepted). A majority of
India's populations, Thailand, and many Mideastern groups illustrate this
relationship. This speculation is based on the diverse data of the reactions
between the red-cell antigens of the ABO and several diseases. The problem
is a highly complex one; some selective forces may be acting in opposition to
each other, as in the case of smallpox and plague, but the net effect is to alter
a breeding population's gene combinations.

With all the information that we possess on the blood groups, explanations for their adaptive significance still escape us, and several recent author-
itative works on the human blood groups give little attention to natural selec-

TABLE 3-5 Blood Group Gene Frequencies in Isolates in and near Europe

	GENE PERCENTAGES					
ISOLATES	A	B	O	M	d	K
Icelanders	20	5	75	58	37	5
Irish (Republic)	17	7	76	57	43	4
Lapps	37	9	54	52	16	1
Basques	24	2	74	54	56	5
Béarnais	24	4	72	49	59	3
Corsicans	22	3	75	65	35	4
Sardinians	20	7	73	75	22	3
Walsers	21	5	73	51	41	8
Bergamasques	24	6	70	56	43	5
Valle Ladine	20	3	77	78	56	
Svani (Caucasia)	23	7	70	65	41	
Saudi Arabians	16	11	75	72	25	6
Towara Bedouin	16	9	74	52	31	13
Jebeliya Bedouin	12	26	62	66	54	18
Ait Haddidu Berbers	7	5	89	24	23	4

Source: Selected from A. E. Mourant, 1983.

tion. As Vogel (1968:366) stated, the blood-group antigens probably played an important role in *Homo sapiens* evolution and adaptation:

> In earlier centuries, infections have killed a high percentage of mankind before reproductive age. Hence, selective pressure was very strong, and genetic adaptation to infections must have strongly influenced our present gene pool.

Such influence is especially strong during infancy, that time of the life cycle when selection can be most influential in shaping the gene pool of future generations. High infant mortality, of 50 percent or more of live births, was once the norm and, even in this century, rates of between 10 to 25 percent have been reported. Often these deaths were due to various forms of gastrointestinal ailments, or infant diarrhea, which is especially severe in those populations that must use polluted water. This continues to be a problem in many underdeveloped countries today where life expectancy is short and infant and childhood mortality high (see Chapter 8).

Because diarrheal disease once was and continues to be a major cause of mortality today in many parts of the world, blood type probably has been a significant influence on survival. A high rate of infant infectious diarrhea caused by various strains of *E. coli* bacteria is frequently reported, and often the ABO antigens are implicated. The shifting of A or B type antigen specificity in *E. coli* strains during the epidemics in eastern Europe in the 1950s alternately caused more frequent episodes in type-B or in type-A infants. In both examples, the infectious diarrheal disease was more acute in both than in type-O infants (Vogel and Motulsky, 1986). Such a recent episode of selection due to infectious disease underscores the probable influences over the last few thousand years of human history as we became more sedentary with increasing population density.

Differences in reactions of the ABO antigens with several kinds of intestinal bacteria have been noted above, and, as a result, the severity of the diseases that the organisms cause may be expected to vary with blood type. There is no more critical period than when an infant is adjusting to the microbial groups common to his or her environmental setting. This period, and the period of stress on the young child's system during weaning, are times of extreme selective pressures. Add to this all of the parasites and amoebas found in many tropical regions, plus marginal diets and the lack of suitable "weaning" foods, and one can easily see that any difference in susceptibility to infection, even though slight, will lead to extensive differences in mortality rates.

The Rh Blood Group

The Rhesus system is second to the ABO in clinical importance and is the one most often involved in a blood disease of the newborn, *erythroblastosis fetalis* (hemolytic disease of the newborn). In this disease, the red cells of the developing fetus are destroyed by antibodies made in the mother's blood in a response to stimulus from certain antigens on the fetus's red cells—antigens that the mother does not possess. Though the disease was known for many years, no explanation was possible until 1940, when Landsteiner and Weiner showed that anti-Rhesus serum[2] agglutinated red cells of about 85 percent of white New York patients tested. The 15 percent of the individuals who did not react to the serum were identified as Rhesus (Rh) negative. The research continued and, about a year later, the investigators discovered that mothers who had given birth to infants suffering from a hemolytic disease (erythroblastosis) were Rh negative; their blood cells did not react to the anti-Rh factor but their infants did (see Figure 3-8).

Since the 1940s numerous studies of the Rh system have revealed a large number of Rh antigen types that are inherited through Mendelian mecha-

FIGURE 3-8   Reaction of an Rh Negative Mother to Her Rh Positive Fetus.

If the fetus of an Rh negative mother and Rh positive father is Rh positive there is the risk of the mother becoming sensitized by the fetal red blood cells. A few of these cells may enter the mother's bloodstream and, because they are Rh+, they will stimulate the production of antibodies. These antibodies can freely cross the placenta and destroy the fetal red blood cells.

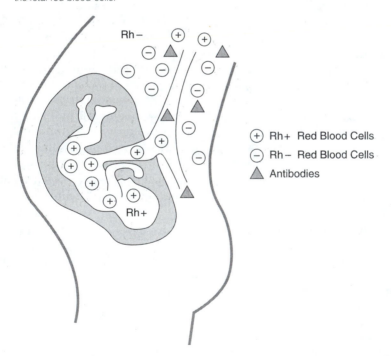

Rh−

Rh+

⊕ Rh+ Red Blood Cells
⊖ Rh− Red Blood Cells
▲ Antibodies

---

[2]Anti-Rhesus serum was made by injection of rhesus monkey cells into rabbits, who then made an antiserum specific for this species. Testing against human red cells showed that most would react with the anti-Rhesus serum.

nisms. Because of the number and complexity of the reactions to antisera tests, two different explanations have been offered to describe the kinds of reactions and modes of inheritance. The hypothesis by Fisher and Race postulates that the reactions or potentials for reactions are inherited as if they were determined by three closely linked loci, each with two alleles (each allele determines one antigenic response to an antiserum). They used the notations Cc, Dd, Ee to represent the pair of alleles at each locus; the lower case does not indicate recessivity or dominance, because each allele determines the presence of an antigen, though an antibody for d has not been discovered yet. Because the three loci are so closely linked that crossover rarely occurs, the loci are written together as a combination (haplotype) to represent the genotype. A typical genotype might appear as:

$$\frac{CDE}{cde}$$

which shows that all antigens in the systems are represented and would interact with the antiserum especially prepared for these tests. By contrast, Weiner, the codiscoverer of Rh, postulates that there is only a single locus with eight allelic genes, each responsible for determining an antigen that can combine with three or more kinds of antibodies. Both hypotheses are equally valid, though some immunologists prefer one over the other, and both notation systems are used to indicate blood type in the Rh system (Table 3-6a).

Each parent in this example (Table 3-6b) would test positive for C, but, because they are heterozygous for the alleles, the probability is that one out of four offspring would be negative for this antigen. The female, according to her genotype, is homozygous for gene d. She would not react to the anti-D serum test (this individual would be considered Rh negative). However, because her husband has both d and D, there is a 50 percent chance that a child produced by this mating would have the D allele and would be Rh positive. There is also a possibility, in this case, of the fetus's stimulating anti-D antibody production

TABLE 3-6a Genetic Notation and Rh Antigens

ALLELIC GENES (WEINER SYSTEM)	ANTIGENS (SPECIFIC ANTISERA REACTIONS)	THREE GENE LOCI (FISHER-RACE SYSTEM)
R^0	Rh_0, hr', hr''	cDe
r'	rh', hr''	Cde
r''	rh'', hr'	cdE
R^1	Rh_1', (Rh_0, rh', hr'')	CDe
R^2	Rh_2 (Rh_0, hr'', hr')	cDE
R^z	Rh_z (Rh_0, rh', rh'')	CDE
r^y	rh_y (rh', rh'')	CdE
r	rh (hr', hr'')	cde

TABLE 3-6b   Mode of Inheritance of Rh System (Fisher-Race Notation)

MALE GENOTYPE	FEMALE GENOTYPE
CDE	Cde
cde	cdE

Genotypes of offspring

gametes	Cde	cdE
CDE	CDE	CDE
	Cde	cdE
cde	cde	cde
	Cde	cdE

in the maternal system.[3] The anti-D antibodies from the mother's bloodstream easily cross through the placenta into the fetal circulation, where they agglutinate and then destroy the blood cells (see Figure 3-8). When such an event occurs, there is the risk of the fetus's developing the erythroblastosis disease. The risk increases with each pregnancy because the mother's system is sensitized by carrying previous Rh negative fetuses and the anti-Rh antibodies are at a high level. Naturally, if the genotype of the fetus is negative for D, there would be no danger. Though the majority of the incompatibility problem is caused by the D allele (about 90 percent), there are some cases due to the E and C alleles.

Over the decades since the discovery of the Rhesus system, treatments have been developed that reduce the risk of erythroblastosis. If the woman is identified as Rh negative and there is a possibility of an Rh positive fetus, then some way must be found to prevent her immune system from making antibodies against the antigen D (Rh+). This may be accomplished shortly after the first pregnancy (usually right after delivery) by injection of antiserum (anti-D). This antiserum will attack any fetal blood cells that may have crossed into the mother's bloodstream during labor. Since antibody production does not begin until after 72 hours from delivery, this prevents her immune system from becoming sensitized and thus reduces the risk for each succeeding pregnancy. As an additional protective measure, since fetal blood cells may rarely cross the placental boundary during pregnancy, some antiserum (anti-D) may be injected after the twenty-eighth week of gestation. Since such medical treatment has been available only since mid-century, the question is how allele (d)

[3]Except in unusual circumstances, blood cells do not cross the placenta to exchange between maternal and fetal circulation. At birth, however, when the placenta is separating from the uterine wall, a few fetal cells can enter the maternal circulation. If the mother's blood type is different from the fetus's then her system will make antibodies. The level will rise with each pregnancy and so will the risk of a fetus or newborn suffering from a hemolytic disease caused by maternal antibodies against the fetal red cells.

could be maintained at such a high frequency in parts of the world when it can cause such problems in pregnancy.

The answer to this riddle has been sought for decades, with no solid answer, nor is there any explanation of a selective value for the Rhesus negative. Clues may be found eventually in the frequencies of the alleles throughout the world's populations. The distribution of the Rh alleles shown in Figure 3-9 provides evidence that strongly supports the argument that selection may have acted on this locus also, though the only disease association thus far reported has been a higher than expected *type D allele* among patients suffering from rheumatic fever. The most frequent explanation offered for the Rh system is that hemolytic incompatibility serves to regulate the frequency of d(r). This allele, responsible for approximately 95 percent of the hemolytic disease in the newborn, approaches a frequency of zero in a population within a few generations when selection is most intense. Yet, despite the selection against offspring of Rh incompatibility matings, a high frequency of d(r) has been maintained in several populations throughout the generations. These high frequencies suggest that natural selection is operating to maintain a deleterious allele, probably through selection for the heterozygote as we have seen in other examples.

FIGURE 3-9 **Percentage Frequency of Blood-Type Allele r (RH negative).** (After Hulse, 1971.)

We do not know what the advantage may be to a heterozygote carrier of d(r) but, whatever it is, a balance has been maintained and the allele persists at high frequencies in several European and African populations.

Some Minor Blood Groups

In addition to the systems already considered there are a number of less well-known groups. These groups are discovered, often by accident, when a patient has an unexpected reaction to a blood transfusion or gives birth to an erythroblastic infant even though the mother was Rh+. Careful immunological studies eventually identify the particular antigen involved. Family and population tests with the new antisera often show a variety of responses among the people tested and a new antigen system is then established. Often these systems are under the control of a single pair of alleles and some of these new antigens have proven useful in population genetic studies because of an uneven distribution among our species. Such systems have relatively little clinical importance but are valuable as genetic markers.

The MN System. The *MN system* was first discovered in 1927 when Landsteiner and Levine were able to prepare two types of antiserum against human red cells that would identify three types of individuals.[4] The symbols M and N were used to describe the genotypes of this new system. Inheritance of MN type appeared to be of this kind:

MN	×	MN	Genotypes (parents)
MM	MN	NN	Genotypes (children)
M	MN	N	Phenotypes

These alleles are codominants and each determines a characteristic response to antiserum. The heterozygote (MN) individual would react with both antisera and this would distinguish this individual from the persons who react only with anti-M or anti-N. Unlike the ABO or the Rh systems, the MN system does not appear to have any medical importance—probably because no antibodies are known to occur in humans. Antibodies neither occur naturally (the genetically determined ones as in the case of the ABO blood group) nor are induced (as in the Rh system).

Another antigen, determined by a gene at a locus closely linked to the MN locus on the fourth chromosome, is referred to by the term S. There appear to be only two alleles at this locus, Ss, with S dominant, so there are

---

[4]Many of the blood-group systems have been discovered by mixing blood cells with antiserum made from plant extracts or with antihuman serum made by injecting human red cells into certain animals, usually rabbits. This results in antibodies against a variety of the proteins attached to the human red cell. This procedure provides a way of detecting a range of individual variation.

three genotypes: SS, Ss, ss. Both SS and Ss give a positive reaction to the anti-S test, whereas s does not react to the antiserum. The S and the MN loci are linked so closely that there are no known cases of crossover. This means, as in the Rh system, that the genes are transmitted as a unit, a haplotype: MS, NS, and so on.

The seemingly neutral selection of the MNS system results in an even distribution among most of the world's peoples. There are some notable exceptions, however. Native Americans have a high frequency of the haplotypes MS and Ms, in contrast to Australian Aborigines, who have extremely high frequencies of N, reaching from 65 percent to a high of 95 percent. Such highs of this allele have also been reported for certain populations of New Guinea, which is to be expected due to shared origins with Australian populations some 40–60,000 years ago when the island was linked to the continent. The total lack of the S allele among Australians while it is high among New Guineans is a puzzle, though.[5] Adding to the question are reports of an excess of MN genotypes (greater than expected by the Hardy-Weinberg equilibrium) reported in some populations. The significance of these population distributions of the MNS system, while interesting to the anthropologist, has yet to be determined, though they may be added as one more bit of evidence to compare ancestral relationship.

The Duffy Blood Group. There are three types of antiserum of this blood group, designated anti-Fy^a, anti-Fy^b, and anti-Fy^4. A majority of people from around the world have red blood cells that will react to either one or the other of the first two types, and many react to both. However, most people in central and west Africa, and many African Americans, are negative for both Fy^a and Fy^b but will react to the third type, Fy^4. Given these data together with numerous family studies, it appears that there are three alleles at this blood type locus on the first chromosome, codominants that determine the presence of a red blood cell antigen (see Table 3-7).

In persons of European descent the frequency of Fy^a reaches a high of 90 percent; the balance are Fy^b, and rarely some have been reported with Fy^4. Throughout central Africa, Fy^4 reaches 100 percent and a high frequency is seen in populations on both sides of the Red Sea and among Kurds of Iraq and Iran. Except for Africans and Europeans, the Duffy blood group has not been widely studied, and a summary of these allele frequencies are listed for several African populations in Table 3-8. Because antigens Fy^a and Fy^b are virtually lacking in most of these populations, these types have proven to be one of the most useful genetic markers for determining the degree of European admixture in

---

[5]The diversity of New Guinea in language (over 700 languages) and culture is nearly matched by genetic variation. For example, the Gerbich blood group exists only in a few New Guinean and nearby Melanesian populations. The extreme ruggedness of the environment, leading to near isolation of numerous breeding populations until late in this century, is the likely source, as will be discussed in Chapter 6.

TABLE 3-7   Duffy Blood Group

GENOTYPE	PHENOTYPE
Fy^aFy^a	Fy (a + b −)
Fy^aFy^b	Fy (a + b +)
Fy^aFy^o	Fy (a + b −)
Fy^bFy^b	Fy (a − b+)
Fy^bFy^a	Fy (a + b +)
Fy^bFy^o	Fy (a − b +)
Fy^oFy^o	Fy (a − b −)

African Americans. One of the interesting aspects of the Duffy system, however, is the probable role these antigens played in the survival of African slave populations when they were brought to the Western Hemisphere.

Africans and their descendants possess a degree of immunity to certain forms of malaria, a disease responsible for widespread illness and for mortalities reaching into the millions, even today. Most malarial infection in the Western Hemisphere is caused by the vivax parasite, one of the four species of malaria-causing protozoan but differing somewhat from the other three types,

TABLE 3-8   Frequency of Duffy Allele Fy^a in Various Populations

POPULATION	FREQUENCY OF Fy^a ALLELE (PERCENT)
Africa	
Upper Volta	0
Dahomey	0
Ghana	0
Nigeria	0
Kenya	
Kamba	0
Giryama	9.5
Bechuanaland	
Bushman (Central)	27.9
Bushman (Pooled sample)	31.2
South West Africa	
Bushman	15.7
Hottentot	27.9
Republic of South Africa	
Bantu	11.8
Congo	
Bantu	7.8
North America	
Black	21–26
White	43

Sources: Based on Hiernaux, 1966a; and Reed, 1969.

as discussed in the next chapter. Vivax malaria is widespread from tropical to temperate regions of the world, once extending as far north as the midwestern United States. It has been brought under control in North America by mosquito eradication in this century, but was once a major problem for early settlers and proved to be deadly to the Native American populations. The resistance of the African populations, in contrast to Europeans and Native Americans, is one of the explanations offered for their survival and expansion. This resistance is hypothetically due to the nature of malarial infection: Once the parasite is injected into the bloodstream by the bite of a female Anopheles mosquito, it must enter a blood cell to begin its life cycle phase in the human host. The red cell antigens of the Fy^a and Fy^b provide attachment points for the vivax parasite and facilitate entry. The Duffy Fy^4 does not, as demonstrated by laboratory experiments mixing parasites with red blood cells of differing Duffy type. Type Fy^4 were highly resistant, which explains the immunity of individuals of African descent from this form of malaria. These laboratory results, the epidemiology of vivax malaria, and the distribution of the Duffy types offer one of the important examples of the functioning of natural selection in humans (Livingstone, 1984, and Mourant, 1983).

The Diego Blood Group. Originally, this blood group was identified among certain Venezuelan Indians who had up to 30 percent positive response to the antibody (anti-Di^a). Its subsequent discovery among other Native American populations has caused it to be called an "American Indian" gene. It also occurs in some east Asian populations and among a few Papuan populations in New Guinea. Later a second allele, Di^b, was found to be the most frequent of the two in Asian populations. Diego types are absent in Europeans, Africans, and Eskimos. However, too few population surveys have been made to establish a more complete distribution. The Diego antigens apparently cause no known medical problem but, since the highest frequencies occur in tropical populations, suggestions have been made that there is some relationship to that type of environment. At this point, all that may be said is that the Diego system offers one of the few markers unique to Asian populations and to Native Americans. The Diego types join a growing array of genetic markers that may be used to distinguish between major population groupings.

Xg Blood Group. This blood group is primarily of interest because of its position on the X-chromosome. The Xg type has been frequently recorded because it provides an additional locus to assist in the "mapping" of this chromosome. A single antibody is known, anti-Xg^a, which identifies two types, Xg (a+) and Xg (a−). Family pedigrees suggest that the antigen is inherited as a codominant trait; Xg^aY males and Xg^aXg^a females react strongly to the antisera. The erythrocytes of Xg^aXg females have a weaker, more variable reaction. There has been no significant variation of frequency among those populations tested so far.

THE BLOOD GROUPS: AN OVERVIEW

Studies of the red-cell antigen systems provide a way of distinguishing among individuals on the basis of their reactions to several antisera. These responses, as we have discussed, are determined by complex molecules (antigens) on the surface of the blood cell that have a certain specific identity inherited as a Mendelian trait. For most blood groups, the ABO, Rh, and MN, for example, a majority of our species respond in predictable ways. For the rarer, lesser-known systems, reactions to the antisera tests have been recorded less frequently (as an example, the Diego system). There are many more systems (the "private" antigens) that describe rare cross-reactions with antisera in a single family lineage.

The complexity of the red blood cell antigens need not concern us, nor should the student become dismayed at the large variety of human blood types that have been identified. This variety merely demonstrates the range of genetic polymorphisms of our species and can be useful for many anthropological purposes in comparison of populations. The systems listed here also provide a vital tool for the study of human genetics, identifying paternity, and distinguishing a monozygous (single-egg or identical) twin from a dizygous (two-ova or fraternal) twin. Population studies also show that the red-cell antigens offer a means for analysis of population migration, admixture, and, perhaps, for study of the forces of natural selection, since many distributions may be more different than would be expected from chance.

A major question is why we possess this complex of inherited antigens: Just what are their functions? Further, is there any advantage of one type over another under certain environmental conditions? These are hard questions to consider here. Most of the evidence of natural selection has been indirect, as explained above for the ABO system. The Duffy does offer an example of the functioning of the antigen. This and other antigen systems are closely related to cell membrane functioning and probably influence the transport of various macromolecules, impeding some and facilitating others. At least that is what seems to be the case with the ABO that leads to a reaction of gut bacterial flora of specific types (see Roitt, 1988). As more is learned about the chemical composition of the red-cell antigens, comprehension of their functioning will grow. For the time being, the several blood "types" continue to be a useful example of human polymorphism.

WHITE BLOOD CELL (WBC) (LEUKOCYTE) ANTIGENS

Another major cellular component of the blood, the *leukocytes*, has become an increasingly important focus for the study of inherited antigens. The leukocytes or *white blood cells* (WBC) are a group of cells whose function is to protect the body against infectious organisms and, normally, they are present in small numbers; there are between 4,000 and 11,000 compared with about

5,000,000 red blood cells in a microliter of blood. The WBC number rises dramatically when the body is challenged by invading organisms. Unlike the red blood cells, the WBC are not confined to the blood vessels. The WBC can move freely through blood vessel walls and enter spaces throughout the body, circulating not only by way of the blood vessels but through the lymphatic system, a series of nodes and ducts containing plasma. This brings them into close contact with nearly all other tissues.

There are several types of WBC, but granulocytes and macrophages are the most numerous (about 50 percent of the total). These are large cells that play a key role against infection as they engulf virus, bacteria, and foreign proteins. Through a complex process in reaction to infection, the granulocytes release peptide particles (chains of amino acids) that stimulate the activity of other types of WBC, the lymphocytes (T and B cells) that are found mostly in the lymph nodes, thymus, and spleen. The effectiveness of these immune responses, including the activities of the other WBC, depends on the antigenicity of the invading organisms and the degree of similarity or dissimilarity to the host's tissues. In other words, the functioning of the WBC in their protective role depends on their antigen types and the antigen identity of the foreign substance, a recognition of "self" or "non-self."

A key process in the recognition and memory of foreign substances and subsequent immune response is the action of T and B lymphocytes. There are several varieties of T-lymphocytes; one is a cytotoxic form that destroys foreign cells, either transplanted, inhaled, or ingested. A second T-cell type serves as a memory to recognize a previous contact with certain foreign substances; consider as an example the lifetime immunity one retains once exposed to "childhood diseases" like measles. The third and fourth varieties are inducer or suppressor cells that regulate the antibody production of the B-lymphocytes. These inducer T cells do not make antibodies but communicate by chemical messenger to the B-lymphocytes to stimulate their antibody production. The B-cells also will divide rapidly and differentiate into antibody-producing plasma cells as a response to particular bacterial surface antigens. Through this complex of cellular interaction outlined in Table 3-9, the human immune system is able to respond to literally millions of "non-self" substances over the course of a lifetime (see Ganong, 1993). This scope of protective response is even more impressive when the underlying genetic mechanisms are considered.

After years of research on the immune system, skin grafts, and organ transplants, the WBC are recognized as having a highly variable antigen system, even more complex than that described for the red blood cell (RBC) antigens. There are many differences of the WBC in comparison with the RBC. The WBC are found not only in the blood serum within the blood vessels but also distributed throughout most tissues of the body in virtually every fluid surrounding the somatic cells. This wide distribution and their antibody functions explain, in part, the rejection of skin grafts and organ transplants.

TABLE 3-9   Immunity and Lymphocyte Cells

BONE MARROW LYMPHOCYTE PRECURSORS

give rise to:

T-Lymphocytes
    derived cells:
        1. cytotoxic (T_8) — — — — → cellular immunity
        2. memory
        3. inducer or helper (T_4)—act on B-cells
        4. suppressor(T_8)—act on B-cells

B-Lymphocytes
    derived cells:
        1. memory
        2. plasma types— — — → humoral immunity
            immunoglobulins Ig G, A, M, D, E

Attempts, over the years, to graft skin from one person to another failed because the recipient's system rejected the graft as material foreign to its own immune system. However, grafts between identical twins proved to be successful. This success of twin grafts suggested that the immune-rejection process was genetically determined. Further evidence was provided by studies of the blood serum from patients who had been given multiple transfusions; their serum contained a variety of agglutinins (antibodies). Tests of these antibodies against blood samples taken from the general population resulted in the agglutination of WBC in 60 percent of the cases (Dausset and Colombani, 1972) That is, some of the WBC "types" introduced into the patient through transfusion stimulated antibody production and some did not. However, the individual's WBC were not affected by the antibodies in his or her own serum. Following this evidence of individual differences in the ability to produce a variety of antibodies of specific identity, family and twin studies were conducted. The results obtained by cross-typing and matching blood cells of close relatives established the mode of inheritance of WBC antigens. These earlier studies were followed by many others over the next three decades and have identified a large complex system of WBC antigen types (human leucocyte antigens or HLA).

The Histocompatibility System (HLA)[6]

There are a series of glycoproteins, or antigens, on the surfaces of the WBC that function as a part of the antibody processing during the immune response outlined above. These antigen types of the WBC form are so diverse

---

[6]This system of WBC antigens exists in most vertebrates and is referred to by the general term *major histocompatibility complex* or MHC. In humans, the more specific term *human leucocyte antigen* or HLA is most often used.

that they constitute the most polymorphic system of inherited traits known, thus far, in humans. The antigens are, like the RBC antigens, molecules of sugars linked to a protein as part of the cell's surface membrane, and their presence is detected by a reaction with specific antibody form. In addition to their location on the WBC, these antigens are also found widely dispersed throughout tissues of the body and are attached to all other cells except RBC, sperm, and certain placental cells.

The antigen types are determined by several closely linked loci on chromosome 6 and designated HLA-A, HLA-B, HLA-C, HLA-D, and HLA-DR. Since there are from eight to forty alleles at each locus, the resulting multiplicity of allelic combinations of these loci make any simple designation impossible. Normally, a person's HLA system is expressed as a haplotype, the listing of the allele present at each of the loci. For example, in a study of 334 people in England, the haplotype HLA *A1-B8-DR3* was found among 10.4 percent, which was a world high for this particular haplotype while it was only half as frequent in most other Western Europeans. By contrast, the most frequent haplotype found among Japanese populations was HLA *A24-BW52-DR2*, which occurred in 7.8 percent of the sample. Table 3-10 summarizes a variety of HLA haplotypes distributed among several population groups (see Bodmer et al., 1987). With a clearer understanding of the antigenicity of the HLA system,

TABLE 3-10 Major HLA Haplotypes of Selected Populations

HLA HAPLOTYPES			POPULATIONS*												
			1	2	3	4	5	6	7	8	9	10	11	12	13
			percent of total sample												
A1	B8	DR3	10.4	5.1	5.1	7.1	8.9	9.1	12.1	5.3	—	1.5	3.7	3.6	2.2
A2	B35	DR4	0.1	—	0.4	0.1	—	—	—	—	1.9	—	14.8	3.6	—
A2	B35	DR5	—	0.4	0.7	0.4	—	—	—	5.3	0.6	—	—	—	—
A2	B35	DRW8	0.3	0.4	0.4	—	—	—	0.8	2.6	0.9	—	7.4	—	—
A2	B44	DR4	4.0	1.8	1.1	1.2	3.6	1.5	2.7	—	—	—	—	—	—
A24	B35	DR4	—	0.2	—	0.1	—	—	—	2.6	0.9	0.8	14.8	—	—
A24	B7	DR1	—	0.4	—	0.2	—	—	—	—	4.5	—	—	—	—
A24	BW52	DR2	—	—	—	—	—	—	—	—	7.8	—	—	—	—
A24	BW54	DR4	—	—	—	—	—	—	—	—	6.2	—	—	—	—
A26	B38	DR4	0.1	0.1	—	0.1	0.6	—	—	7.9	—	—	—	—	—
A28	BW58	DRW6	—	—	—	—	—	—	—	—	—	—	—	—	6.7
A3	B7	DR2	4.5	2.9	1.1	3.7	5.3	3.0	6.6	—	—	—	—	—	—
A30	B13	DR7	0.8	0.9	0.4	0.6	2.4	3.0	1.2	5.3	—	11.3	—	3.6	—
AW33	BW65	DR1	0.1	0.5	0.4	0.5	—	1.5	—	7.9	—	—	—	—	—

*Populations: 1. English, Celtic, Dutch, Scandinavian; 2. German, French, Italian, Spanish, Swiss; 3. Austrian, Yugoslavian, Czech, Hungarian; 4. American, Canadian; 5. Australian; 6. South African Caucasoids; 7. Other Caucasoids; 8. Jewish-Ashk; 9. Japanese; 10. Chinese (including Chinese subsets); 11. American Indians; 12. Mexican; 13. Black Africans.

Source: Modified and selected from Bodmer et al., 1987.

close tissue matches may be obtained by identifying the haplotypes of close relatives, a procedure that is a vital step in the preparation for organ transplants.

Because of the protective function of the WBC in the immune system,
disease–HLA type correlations have been sought. Over the past fifteen years
frequent associations have been reported between HLA types and specific
diseases. Eighty-nine percent of the patients with a chronic inflammation of
tendons and ligaments at specific skeletal joints (Ankylosing spondylitis) had
the B27 antigen. Celiac disease, a type of chronic inflammation of the
intestinal tract, is another association with the HLA system; 68 percent had
HLA type B8. Others, like rheumatoid arthritis, type I diabetes (juvenile),
and multiple sclerosis, also show a significantly higher frequency of certain
of the HLA types. Such associations between disease and the HLA system do
not prove cause, however, but do provide a reference point to study the chain
of genetic–environmental interactions that may result in a disease state.

In addition to its clinical significance and because of its diversity
throughout the species, the polymorphisms of the HLA system provide
another set of genetic markers of human variability. Several geneticists and
anthropologists have used such data to trace population migrations and to
reconstruct ancestral relationships on the basis of HLA haplotype similarity or
dissimilarity. The number of loci and the variety of alleles provide a means of
gaining a closer perspective on interpopulation relationships. Peopling of the
Pacific and relationships between Melanesian, Polynesian, and New Guinean
populations have been postulated on the basis of their similarities or differences in HLA types (see Serjeantson, 1984).

POLYMORPHISMS OF SERUM PROTEINS

In addition to the diversity of red and white blood cell antigens there are numerous proteins in blood plasma that have a variety of forms (polymorphisms) differing among peoples of the world. The synthesis of each protein is under
genetic control, and when mutations occur there are structural changes that may
alter the protein function. These differences in protein forms can be readily
identified, as electrophoresis separates many protein fractions into various
groups, as sketched in Figure 3-10. Each of the major groups—albumins, groups
specific (GC), globulins, and lipoproteins, transferrins, and haptoglobins—separate at a certain point along the starch gel strip because of their differing mobility in an electric field. The several globulin fractions show an enormous range of
variability, and the albumins, once thought to be a protein of little variation, now
are also known to be highly polymorphic (see Szathmary, 1993). Likewise, transferrins and haptoglobins are polymorphic, though in a more restricted range.
These polymorphisms are distributed among different regional populations in
some interesting ways. The meaning of this plasma protein polymorphism is not
always apparent, but some clues are provided by the following examples.

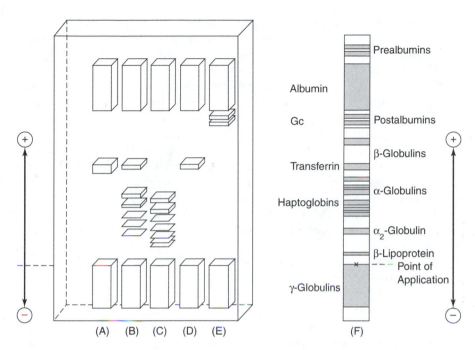

FIGURE 3-10   Relative Electrophoretic Mobilities of Protein Constituents of Human Serum. (a), (b), (c) Haptoglobins, phenotypes Hp 1-1; Hp 2-1, Hp 2-2, respectively; (d) transferrin, TfC; (e) group-specific component, -phenotype Gc 2-1; and (f) composite showing relative electrophoretic mobilities of important constituents of serum. (These diagrams show the relative positions of the various components after electrophoresis in alkaline starch gels; variations in conditions of electrophoresis lead to changes in resolution of some of the proteins.) (From Buettner-Janusch, J., *Physical Anthropology: A Perspective*, 1973. Copyright © 1973 by John Wiley & Sons, Inc. Reprinted by permission of the publisher.)

Immunoglobulins (Gamma Globulins)

These are a group of antibodies specific for certain foreign antigens introduced as mold, pollen grains, or the proteins of an infectious organism. Each person has the capacity to synthesize an enormous number of different antibodies, and this synthesis takes place within the B lymphocyte cells in circulation, as outlined above. Only a small part of our antibody production capacity is ever realized, however, since it depends upon the stimulation of the T and B lymphatic cells. Once stimulated, the B cells begin to divide, producing identical cells that secrete the antibody specific to the antigen. The result is a group of slow-moving globulins, whose variety is the result of a combination of an individual's genotype and environmental experience. This causes a difference from individual to individual while maintaining some shared types within each family or population. Pastoral people, like the Turkana living in Kenya, will share numerous immunoglobulin types as contrasted to those shared among native Australians. Likewise, Inuit (Eskimo) hunters in the Canadian Arctic will be in contrast to the pastoral Saami (Lapps) in Scandinavia.

The combinations of the HLA genes of these and other populations contribute to such differences, of course. But the genes determine the potential of response to certain environmental stimuli (in the form of foreign antigens) and the diversity of these stimuli further adds to population contrasts because of the nature of the formation of the gamma globulin types. These globulins consist of highly variable and complex protein molecules composed of four polypeptides, a pair of "heavy chains," each linked to a smaller or "light chain" (Figure 3-11). Most of the heavy chain is a constant region, a stable amino acid sequence, while the part that is linked to the light chain is highly variable. The amino acid arrangement of the light chain varies to conform to the identity of the antibody that attaches to this region. Comparisons of the constant heavy chain regions among the immunoglobulins reveal five classes whose functions vary as shown in Table 3-11.

The IgG group of immunoglobulins is the most plentiful and has been extensively studied. The constant part of the heavy chains shows a great deal of polymorphism and is described as the GM system, which has at least twenty specific antisera reactions. Though some of these reactions are inherited as simple codominant alleles and the amino acid sequence of each region of the chain is under control of a separate locus, it is not clear how many genetic loci are involved. The loci do appear to be closely linked on the fourteenth chromosome, each with several codominant alleles.

There is a variation in the frequency of occurrence of several of the *GM types* among the world's populations that have been tested. Table 3-12 illustrates this variation of the major GM groups. The haplotypes are the clusters of specific GM types that occur together in an individual. They apparently are transmitted genetically as a unit, and distinct differences are found between

FIGURE 3-11   Diagramatic Representation of Antibody Structure.

The antibody is a complex of light and heavy chains of polypeptides linked together by two sulfur atoms (S-S). They consist of a basic constant chain linked to a variable region that has a structure specific for a particular antigen. This recognition site binds and inactivates the antigen as illustrated.

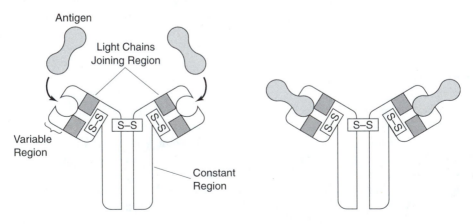

TABLE 3-11   Types of Immunoglobulins

TYPE	PLASMA CONCENTRATION (μ/ml)	FUNCTIONS
IgG	12,100	Inactivates bacteria and virus
IgA	2600	Neutralizes toxins
IgM	930	Inactivates bacteria and virus
IgD	23	Unknown
IgE	0.5	Activates allergic responses

several populations. This distribution of the antibody system's polymorphisms suggests varying levels of ability to react to certain classes of disease-causing organisms. Combinations found in some populations but not in others suggest that natural selection has been operating, but direct correlations between GM types and a particular disease have not been made.

Haptoglobins

The haptoglobins are another group of serum proteins that are of particular interest. They are part of the alpha$_2$ globulins and have the capacity to combine with the oxygen-carrying pigment, hemoglobin, when it is released into the plasma upon the destruction of old red blood cells at the end of its life span of about ninety days. This attachment to the haptoglobin prevents the loss of

TABLE 3-12   Common GM Haplotypes in Various Populations Tested for Eleven Factors

	A	B	C	D	E	F	G	H	I	J	K	HAPLOTYPES
European (Caucasoids)	+	+	+									A (1, 17, 21) B (1, 2, 17, 21)
Mongoloids	+	+					+	+				C (3, 5, 13, 14) D (1, 5, 13, 14, 17)
Ainu	+	+					+		+			E (1, 5, 14, 17)
New Guinea	+	+		+				+				F (1, 5, 6, 17)
Australian	+	+										G (1, 5, 6, 14, 17) H (1, 13, 17)
African (Negroids)				+	+	+	+					I (1, 3, 5, 13, 14) J (2, 7, 21)
Bushmen	+			+			+				+	K (1, 5, 17)

hemoglobin through excretion by the kidneys. The haptoglobin–hemoglobin complex is carried through the circulatory system to the liver, where it is broken into the iron-bearing heme group and globin portions. The heme is converted to bilirubin and then to bile in the gallbladder, while the atoms of iron are recycled in the production of new red blood cells in the red bone marrow. The globin chains provide a resource of amino acids for protein synthesis. A most important aspect of the haptoglobins is this preservation and transport of the free hemoglobins.

Three types of haptoglobin have been identified, each apparently under genetic control through the action of a pair of nondominant alleles at a locus on chromosome 16. The genotypes and phenotypes would appear as:

GENOTYPES	PHENOTYPES
Hp^1Hp^1	Haptoglobin 1-1
Hp^1Hp^2	Haptoglobin 1-2
Hp^2Hp^2	Haptoglobin 2-2

The population distribution of haptoglobins varies widely, as shown in Table 3-13. The highest frequency of Hp^1 appears in tropical populations who, typically, have high parasite loads that increase the rate of red blood cell destruction, thereby suffering from low red cell counts. Because Hp^1 has a greater affinity for hemoglobin and hence a higher binding capacity, possession of this haptoglobin type would be an advantage in populations where hemolytic anemia is very high and quantities of free hemoglobin must be conserved.

Transferrins

Another serum protein variant is a beta-globulin (transferrins) that binds atoms of iron and transports them to the tissues as needed, especially to the bone marrow where hemoglobin is formed. Also, transferrins assist in the absorption of iron through tissue membranes, especially dietary iron through the gut wall. The necessity of the protein for iron transport is best documented by examples of persons with a rare recessive allele that results in a total lack of transferrin in their plasma. Such persons suffer from severe iron deficiency anemia despite an excess of the mineral due to the failure of absorption and transport (McKusick, 1994).

Transferrins exist in at least seventeen forms as identified by electrophoresis methods, and each seems to be under genetic control of an autosomal nondominant allele. The several variants fit into one of the three groups; the majority are in group TfC and a slower group (TfD), whereas only a few types occur in group TfB. These polymorphisms are distributed unevenly throughout the species and several populations have only a single type (Table 3-14). TfC is the most common, but TfB is not widely distributed. The significance of this polymorphism of the iron-binding protein is not known, but there may be some relationship to a variation in iron-binding

TABLE 3-13   Geographic Distribution of Hp[1] Gene

POPULATION	NUMBER TESTED	HP[1] FREQUENCY
Europe		
Norway	1,000	0.36
France	406	0.40
England	218	0.41
Italy (South)	752	0.32
Poland	151	0.36
Africa (North)		
Nigeria: Yoruba[a]	99	0.87
Senegal	398	0.63
Africa (East)		
Uganda[a]	165	0.63
Africa (Central)		
Congo: Metropolitan	151	0.77
Tutsi	86	0.52
Pygmies[a]	125	0.40
Africa (South)		
Zulu	113	0.53
Hottentot	59	0.51
Bushmen	113	0.29
Asia		
China: Hong Kong	122	0.29
Japan	822	0.28
Thailand	682	0.24
South India: Tamils	291	0.09
Todas	89	0.35
Pakistan	392	0.21
North America		
Alaska: Eskimos	418	0.30
Arizona: Navajo	263	0.45
New Mexico: Apache	98	0.59
Mexico: Lacandon	89	0.92
Central America		
Panama: Cuna	174	0.38
South America		
Ecuador: Quechua	192	0.78
Bolivia: Aymara	71	0.70
Brazil: Xavante	78	0.46
Pacific Islands		
Australian Aborigines		
North Queensland	493	0.17
New Guinea	82	0.66
Philippines	293	0.38
Samoa	80	0.59
Tonga	200	0.60

[a]Hp[0] phenotype greater than 10 percent

capacity. Such a difference would make certain forms more efficient in populations suffering from a high rate of red cell loss, as was suggested for haptoglobins. An increase in combining capacity would be advantageous to populations in which a large percentage of the people were subject to chronic anemia. Any advantage, no matter how slight, in the absorption and transport of this vital element would contribute to survival.

INBORN ERRORS OF METABOLISM

Some of the most useful of the genetic markers in the study of human populations are various types of inherited biochemical defects. Many of these defects are due to a lack of enzymes that regulate important steps in our intermediate metabolism. Because of these deficiencies, proteins are not synthe-

TABLE 3-14   Frequencies of Three Transferrin Groups

POPULATION	NUMBER TESTED	FREQUENCY		
		TfC	*TfB's* (Fast)	*TfD's* (Slow)
Asia				
India				
Tamil	291	1.000		
Toda	89	1.000		
Ceylon				
Singhalese	159	0.988	0.006 B_2C	0.006 CD_1
Tamil	140	1.000		
Veddah	64	0.890		0.094 CD_1 0.016 D_1
Japan	822	0.984	0.001 BC	0.015 CD
Africa				
Nigeria				
Habe	120	0.850		0.150 CD_1
Fulani	111	0.937		0.063 CD_1
Fulani	68	0.838		0.147 CD_1 0.015 D_1
Ibo	70	0.871		0.129 CD_1
Congo				
Nonmetropolitan	446	0.933		0.067 CD_1
Pygmy	121	0.934		0.066 CD_1
South Africa				
Hottentot	59	0.932		0.068 CD_1
Zulu	116	0.974		0.026 CD_1
Bushmen	113	0.876		0.115 CD_1 0.009 D_1

Source: After Buettner-Janusch, 1966. Copyright © 1966 by John Wiley & Sons, Inc. Reprinted by permission of the publisher.

sized, carbohydrates are not converted to energy, lipids (fats) are not properly utilized, or other essential substances are not transported or stored. Examples of all of these problems have been identified in the human genome, many of which are due to a recessive allele. Fortunately, most of these inherited conditions are extremely rare, with only a few cases identified in the medical literature. A catalog of Mendelian traits in humans has been prepared that lists these genetic defects together with all known traits of the human genome, and is updated periodically (see Morbid Anatomy of the Human Genome, in McKusick, 1994).

The few examples described below illustrate how a slight change in a single step in a biochemical pathway can have major, sometimes fatal consequences. Since Garrod's classic paper in 1902 describing an inherited biochemical defect, *alkaptonuria,* there has been a continuous search for other such disorders, and many inherited enzyme defects have been reported. A majority of these traits result in a pathology of the metabolism that may be more or less lethal. Some manifest themselves as a lack of a single enzyme that results in an interruption of a biochemical pathway and are easily identified, such as phenylketonuria (PKU). Other types of inherited defects may cause the individual to be more susceptible to certain environmental conditions. An example is provided by the degenerate lung disease (emphysema) that occurs more frequently in susceptible individuals (persons inheriting ineffective forms of alpha antitrypsin, the inhibitor of the digestive enzyme, trypsin) when they are exposed to air pollution. A partial list of the more common recessive diseases in *Homo sapiens* is provided in Table 3-15. These examples all suggest the extent of the possibilities of error in a complex metabolic system like our own. All population groups have their share of inherited diseases, though there is considerable variation because of a past history of natural selection, genetic drift, isolation, or gene flow.

Phenylketonuria

Phenylketonuria (PKU) is a disease caused by the inheritance of an autosomal recessive gene on chromosome 12 that prevents synthesis of the enzyme phenylalanine hydroxylase (PAH). Individuals homozygous for this allele are unable to metabolize an essential amino acid, phenylalanine, which occurs in most dietary proteins. In homozygous normals and heterozygous carriers, the excess phenylalanine not used for protein synthesis is oxidized into tyrosine. The homozygote recessives lacking PAH enzyme have a block in their metabolic pathway (see Figure 3-12) and the phenylalanine amino acid is metabolized more slowly through an alternate pathway. This slower conversion process results in accumulations of phenylalanine in the blood of up to fifty times the normal levels. The excess levels of phenylalanine are toxic to the developing central nervous system in most infants and young children. If the substance persists in the bloodstream over time, brain dam-

TABLE 3-15   Incidence of Common Recessive Diseases

DISEASE	INCIDENCE PER MILLION BIRTHS
Severe mental defects (excluding aminoacidurias)[a]	800
Deafness (severe)[a]	500
Cystic fibrosis	400
Blindness[a]	200
Adrenogenital syndromes[a]	100
Albinism	100
Phenylketonuria (PKU)	100
Treatable aminoacidurias (excluding PKU)[a,b]	50
Untreatable aminoacidurias (excluding PKU)[a,b]	50
Mucopolysaccharidoses (all forms)[c]	50
Tay-Sachs disease	10
Galactosemia	5
Total	2,365

[a]These diseases exist in multiple forms.
[b]Aminoacidurias are diseases, like PKU, that are caused by accumulation of an amino acid because of an enzyme block owing to an inborn error of metabolism. Some thirteen diseases are included under these two headings.
[c]Mucopolysaccharidoses are diseases, like Hurler's syndrome, that are caused by a defect in the metabolism of certain types of complex sugars (the mucopolysaccharides), whose accumulation in various tissues causes a variety of gross developmental abnormalities.
Source: From Jones, A., and W. F. Bodmer, *Our Future Inheritance: Choice or Chance*, 1974. Copyright © 1974 by Oxford University Press. Reprinted by permission of the publisher.

age will result. Untreated, the PKU individual will suffer severe mental retardation and that person's mental capacity, as measured by IQ tests, will be significantly lower than normal; from 20 to 80 is a victim's usual IQ range (Figure 3-13). Note also the lower range of head size and differences in reflectance properties of the hair; the PKU infant tends to lighter hair color due to lower amounts of melanin. All represent the pleiotropic effects of the PAH allele. It is important, therefore, to identify those infants at risk as early as possible.

The Guthrie test for PKU in newborns was begun in the 1960s in Europe, North America, and Asia, and since then millions of infants have been examined. Europeans and Americans of European descent had the highest frequencies, from one in 6,000 to about one in 20,000 births. It is extremely rare among Japanese, African Americans, and Ashkenazic Jews. Even among Europeans the gene frequency for the PKU recessive is highly variable; eastern Ireland has about one PKU infant per 7,000 births (a calculated gene frequency of 0.014) in contrast to one in 18,000 births in London (a gene frequency of 0.007). Scandinavian populations have even lower frequencies (.0038) while in several eastern European populations the PKU trait is nearly as high as in eastern Ireland. These tests have proven to be very useful in the identification of those infants at risk, and if the PKU condition is

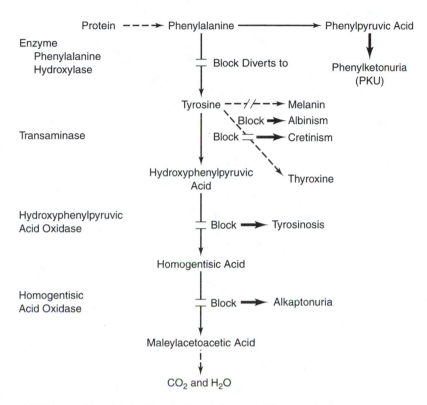

FIGURE 3-12   Metabolic Pathway for Phenylalanine and Tyrosine. The first step in the metabolic breakdown of the essential amino acid phenylalanine is mediated by a liver-produced enzyme, phenylalanine hydroxylase. This enzyme is responsible for the substitution of an OH group for an H atom in phenylalanine, converting it to the amino acid tyrosine. Tyrosine, in turn, through a series of intermediate steps is converted into melanin, the skin pigment, and other substances. It is also broken down further along the pathway illustrated, in which the existence of intermediary steps is indicated by dotted arrows. If phenylalanine hydroxylase is absent, phenylalanine is in part converted into phenylpyruvic acid, which accumulates, together with phenylalanine, in the bloodstream. These substances are toxic to the central nervous system and lead to phenylketonuria. Other genetic metabolic defects in the tyrosine pathway towards oxidation are also known. As indicated in the diagram, absence of enzymes operating between tyrosine and melanin is the cause of albinism. Two other blocks illustrated produce tyrosinosis, a rare defect that causes hydroxyphenylpyruvic acid to accumulate in the urine, but requires no treatment, and alkaptonuria, which makes urine turn black on exposure to air, causes pigmentation to appear in the cartilage, and produces symptoms of arthritis. Another block in a different pathway, somewhat more complex, produces thyroid deficiency leading to goiterous cretinism. (From Lerner, M. I., and W. J. Libby, *Heredity, Evolution and Society*, 2nd ed., 1976. W. H. Freeman and Company. Copyright © 1976.)

identified at birth, treatment begins immediately. By careful management of the dietary levels of the amino acid phenylalanine, the infant can grow and develop normally.

Since the wide-scale measure of blood levels of phenylalanine was instituted, individuals have been identified with abnormally high levels of phenylal-

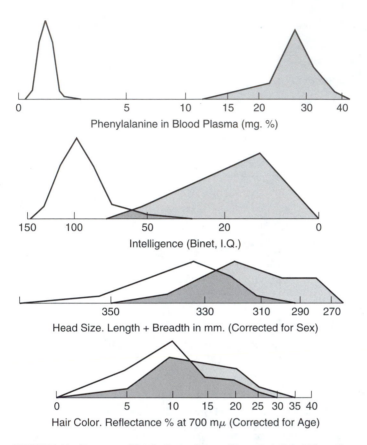

FIGURE 3-13   **Frequency Distributions of Some Characteristics of Phenylke-tonuria in Phenylketonuric Patients (Shaded) and in Control Populations.** Hair color and head size show pronounced overlap, and intelligence shows some over-lap. The level of phenylalanine in the blood, however, is higher in all phenylke-tonurics than in controls. If intelligence were the only phenotype used in the analy-sis, the genotype would be said to be nonpenetrant in a small proportion of cases. When plasma level of phenylalanine is the phenotype, the genotype is found to be fully penetrant. (From McKusick, Victor A., *Human Genetics*, 2nd ed., 1969. Copy-right © 1969 by Prentice-Hall, Inc. Redrawn from Penrose, *Ann. Eugenics*, 16 [1951], 134.)

anine but without the symptoms of the PKU disease. These persons developed normally and appeared to tolerate the abnormal levels by some unknown mechanism. The metabolism of the amino acid turned out to be more com-plex than first thought, and several pathways have been defined, each with some degree of partial deficiency in metabolism. Different types of PKU have also been defined in different family kindreds (see Mange and Mange, 1990). This increase of diversity in the genetics of an amino acid metabolism is to be expected as research expanded through analysis of the DNA region at the PAH locus. The fact is that individuals vary in their effectiveness in converting an essential amino acid, and pathological conditions exist at high levels in some populations due to one or another of the autosomal recessives at the PAH locus.

Consider the biochemical pathway in Figure 3-12 and note the range of steps beginning with the conversion of *phenylalanine.* There is a succession of conversions, each leading to a variety of products and are affected by the efficiency of the first conversion. Defects at this stage actually affect the subsequent series of biochemical steps. At certain of these steps other enzyme defects occur that are inherited as recessives. One of these is *alkaptonuria,* which causes alkaptones to be excreted in the urine. These cause an affected person's urine to turn black when exposed to the air, as described by Garrod (1902). No severe effects result from this condition. However, darkly pigmented granules appear in the affected person's cartilage, and occasionally symptoms of arthritis result. This defect is rare—approximately one case in a million—and is only noted here as another example of inherited metabolic defects. What is of special interest, though, is the reduced quantity of the amino acid tyrosine in persons of impaired phenyalanine metabolism. Because tyrosine is a precursor for the processes that lead to the production of melanin, these persons tend to have fairer skin, light-colored hair, and blue eyes. The effects on the production of thyroxine, a hormone of the thyroid gland, are not recorded, but there may be differences between those persons of normal and subnormal levels of tyrosine due to the lack of synthesis. Since some tyrosine is obtained through food proteins, persons with reduced synthesis of this amino acid still are able to produce the pigment, unlike those persons with total or near total impairment of melanin production.

Albinism

Many of the inborn errors of human metabolism require sophisticated biochemical methods to identify, but a few traits result in obvious, easily recognized phenotypes. The most striking and highly visible of these phenotypes is *albinism*—total or near total lack of melanin, the pigment of skin, hair, and the iris of the eyes. Albinism has been recognized for many centuries, even back to biblical times (Noah was reputed to have been an albino). The albino phenotype varies in frequency from one in 20,000 births among Europeans to one in 1,100 among the Ibos, a large ethnic group of West Africa. In several small, isolated, inbred populations the frequency is reported to be as high as one in 146 live births; the Cuna, a Carib Indian group occupying islands off the Caribbean coast of Panama, and the Hopi of Arizona are populations with such exceptionally high frequency of albinos.

There are several autosomal recessive alleles at loci on chromosomes 9, 11 and 15 that affect the synthesis of melanin. Two major types of albinism have been defined: a type I, where the afflicted person lacks tyrosinase, the enzyme needed to convert tyrosine to a precursor compound for melanin production; and a type II, where the afflicted person tests positive for tyrosine enzyme but is still unable to synthesize melanin. This type II, tyrosinase positive form, accounts for the majority of albinism, occurring once in 35,700 births, and it is the type seen most frequently in Africans and Native Americans. In contrast, type I occurs once in 67,800 births and is the type most frequently responsible for albinism among Europeans (Witkop et al., 1989). Numerous inherited defects in melanin synthesis have been identified and this raises doubts about any single model of explanation; fourteen types of albinism have been defined and at least sixty alleles at the tyrosine locus are known. The complexity of the pigment system is underscored when albino parents give birth to normally pigmented children. This phenomenon of *complementation* (the additive effect of gene products from different loci) was offered to explain how a male and female, apparently with the same defect, produce phenotypically normal individuals. Though both parents lacked pigmentation, mother and children tested positive for tyrosinase. The father tested negative for this enzyme, as expected for an albino (type I). The explanation is that the parents were albinos because of different metabolic reasons and there were at least two different genetic loci involved in the production of melanin. This is illustrated in the following way:

$$\text{Parents} \quad \frac{\text{aaBB}}{\text{(albino)}} \times \frac{\text{AAbb}}{\text{(albino)}}$$

$$\text{Children} \quad \frac{\text{aABb}}{\text{(normal)}}$$

Some Variations in Sugar Metabolism

The major source of energy for the metabolic processes of the body is a simple sugar, glucose derived from several kinds of complex carbohydrates of the diet. These complexes of starches or sugars must first be broken down into simpler structures in the small intestine so they can be absorbed into the bloodstream. This hydrolysis or cleavage into smaller molecular structures is mediated by enzymes for that particular carbohydrate compound. For example, *amylase* is the enzyme that brings about the hydrolysis of starches, *sucrase* the enzyme for sucrose (cane sugar), and *lactase* the enzyme that causes hydrolysis of milk sugar, lactose. There are many more enzymes that play essential roles in the digestion, energy conversion, or storage of carbohydrates that are ingested by the human diet. A reduction or an absence of certain of these enzymes is known to be inherited as autosomal recessives.

Deficiency of the Lactase Enzyme.   As in the case of most mammals, the newborn human's source of food for the first few months or even years is the milk secreted by the mother's mammary glands. In addition to protein and fat, the secretion contains an important carbohydrate, lactose, the principle source of energy for the growing infant. This milk sugar is a large, complex molecular structure that cannot be absorbed directly into the bloodstream. It must first be split into its simpler components, glucose and galactose, which are then absorbed through the cells lining the upper intestinal tract. The enzyme *lactase* catalyzes this breakdown of the lactose sugar, and this enzyme is secreted in large quantities by the cells lining the walls of the upper intestinal track throughout infancy and childhood, diminishing in adolescence. Following the weaning period as individuals change their diet to solid food, the lactase enzyme reduces to 10 percent or less of the level present in the infant. This level and activity of the enzyme may be maintained into adult life in some individuals, depending, perhaps, on the continued use of fresh milk from dairy herds. A majority of people do not maintain lactase into adult life and hence lose their ability to digest fresh milk.

Most adults and adolescents rarely consume fresh milk; even many pastoral peoples with a ready supply of this rich food source ferment the milk into some form before consumption and seldom use it fresh. In its fermented form, bacteria do the job of the lactase and split the milk sugar into digestible products. Most humans are classified as lactose malabsorbers (LMA) because they lack an allele for lactase, probably a dominant. This group includes virtually all Asians and Africans as well as many Europeans (see Table 3-16). There are populations, however, where a large percentage of adults maintain an ability to digest lactose and are classified as absorbers (LA). Such individ-

TABLE 3-16   Frequency of Lactase Deficiency

GROUP	NO. OF SUBJECTS	PERCENT DEFICIENT
American Negro	97	74 (approximately)
Batutsi (Rwanda)	12	17
Bahina (Angola)	11	9
Australian Aborigines		
Papunya (all less than 15 years old)	25	90
Maningrida (age range 6 to 48 months; mean 22 months)	19	80
Greenland Eskimos	32	72
American Indian (Chami, Colombia)	24	100
American Indian	3	67
Chinese	20	85
Formosa	7	
United States	3	
Phillippines	10	
Baganda (Africa)	17	94
Bantu (Africa)	35	89
Thai (Thailand)	140	97
Thai (Thailand)	75	100

Source: Based on McCracken, 1971.

uals are found mainly in northern Europe and among a few pastoral tribes in East Africa. All have had a long history of direct consumption of fresh milk from their cattle, goats, or reindeer. This experience over the centuries, plus the genetic factor, has contributed to a population with a high rate of lactose digestion. Careful analysis of family pedigrees in Finland, for example, showed that those adults who were unable to digest lactose had inherited the lactase deficiency as an autosomal recessive; adults who were absorbers were either homozygous dominants or heterozygotes, while the malabsorbers were homozygous recessives (see Sahi, 1978; Flatz et al., 1982).

Avoidance of fresh milk is the major indicator of malabsorption (LMA) because of the gastrointestinal distress caused by undigested lactose, which is converted to lactic acid, carbon dioxide, and hydrogen in the colon. The continued use of fresh milk into adulthood is considered an indication of effective digestion. Anecdotal description of milk use among many of the cattle herders of East Africa is considered evidence of a high frequency of the lactase allele. For example, among the Orma, a cattle-herding people of Kenya, fresh milk is frequently consumed, especially during the dry seasons. All adults and children partake without the distressful symptoms of the malabsorption syndrome, except for the story of one twelve-year-old male of mixed parentage; his mother was Bantu, an agricultural group living nearby (Ensminger, 1990). A more precise way of determining lactose tolerance is by measures of hydrogen (H^2) in a "breath test"; an individual's malabsorption of lactose results in higher levels of H^2 in expired air. Applications of this test to Sudanese populations revealed much the same relationships between a dairying economy and lactose absorption as seen among the Kenyan populations. Sudanese from tribes of pastoral nomads had a higher percent of lactose tolerant individuals (62 percent) than did the agriculturists (36 percent) on the Sudan–Egyptian border (Bayoumi et al., 1981).

Similar observations have been offered for Europeans where the observed differences in use of milk by adults have been confirmed by laboratory tests for lactase phenotypes (see Flatz et al., 1982). Milk-using experience and lactose tolerance correlations vary somewhat, however. Among the Saami (Lapps), groups with 300 years of experience in fresh milk consumption, the range of LMA in adults varies from 25 percent to as high as 60 percent. Rural populations of southern Finland, with 3,000 years of milk consumption, have as few as 17 percent LMA individuals (Sahi, 1978). In sum, milk-using experience has contributed to a high frequency of the gene for adult lactase persistence in some peoples of the world. Those able to digest lactose have an advantage in their ability to use a rich source of carbohydrate, but they may also be endowed in another way. Since lactose sugar facilitates the absorption of calcium through the gut membranes, those consuming and digesting milk on a regular basis may be at an advantage in the far northern temperate zone. In the higher latitudes, the short hours and weak sunlight reduce the synthesis of vitamin D, a vitamin necessary for calcium absorption and the growth and maintenance of skeletal tissue. Hypothetically, then, in areas where people are deprived of adequate vitamins, anyone who can compensate by increased calcium intake may be at a selective advantage. Such a hypothesis overlooks, however, the experiences of lactose absorbers in Africa, where sunlight and vitamin D sufficiency is not a problem. The hypothesis is worthy of consideration within a broader context of skin pigmentation, diet, and evolution as discussed in Chapter 5.

Galactosemia. There are a number of other genetic abnormalities of carbohydrate metabolism, though, fortunately, most are rare. One of the better-known defects is *galactosemia,* which is the inability to convert galactose to glucose. This metabolic defect is inherited as an autosomal recessive trait. Persons homozygous for the allele lack the enzyme (galactose-1-phosphate uridyltransferase) necessary to convert galactose, one of the sugars produced when a molecule of lactose—milk sugar—is split during digestion. Heterozygotes have quantities of the enzyme that are intermediate between normals and the afflicted person.

Within a few days or weeks of birth, the afflicted infant begins to show signs of distress and an impairment in its ability to digest milk. If allowed to go untreated, the accumulation of galactose in the blood leads to several serious conditions: stunted growth, enlarged liver, mental retardation, and cataracts. Fortunately, galactosemia is rare (from 1 in 65,000 births in Europe to 1 in 118,000 reported in Massachusetts) but the several known cases may be due to a recessive at different loci. The galactosemia cases do provide, however, another example of inherited defects in metabolism that result from the lack of a single enzyme (Vogel and Motulsky, 1986).

Some Other Metabolic Defects

In addition to inherited disorders of carbohydrate metabolism, there are a number of examples of enzyme deficiencies that affect metabolism of the organic bases of the DNA or partially block synthesis of the lipid (fat) coverings of nerve fibers. Most are quite rare, occurring only in a few inbred lineages, while some are present at distressingly high frequencies. McKusick (1994) lists several thousand for which the mode of inheritance is known. A few disorders are described below as examples of those genetic defects that are of anthropological interest.

Errors in Purine Metabolism. Whenever there is an excess of purines like the organic bases of the DNA and RNA nucleotides, adenine and guanine, for example, the compounds are converted through several steps to an ultimate end product, uric acid. A normal person excretes a soluble form of the excess uric acid through the urine. There are several metabolic abnormalities that cause uric acid to accumulate in the tissue in crystalline form, causing much pain. *Gout* is a common term for this disease, which actually occurs in a number of forms and more often in males than in females. Some individuals have a tendency to develop this disease because of an inherited enzyme defect, which appears to be an X-linked recessive. Overeating, especially a diet high in proteins, increases the uric acid produced and can bring on the symptoms of joint pain and swelling.

Another form of purine acid metabolism deficiency is accompanied by an elevated uric acid excretion and a peculiar form of self-destructive behavior. The afflicted child, always male, chews off his lips and if not restrained will bite off the ends of the fingers. This *Lesch-Nyhan* syndrome has attracted much attention since its description in the 1960s, and biochemists have identified an enzyme deficiency in the pathway of conversion of the purine nucleotides. The deficiency is inherited as an X-linked recessive and though the female carrier can be identified she does not show any of the disease symptoms.

Errors in Pyrimidine Metabolism. The end products of pyrimidine (organic bases like cytosine, thymine, and uracil) metabolism are highly soluble, unlike the products of purine metabolism. Thus, an overproduction of pyrimidines does not cause any pathological symptoms to appear, but there are certain enzyme deficiencies in pyrimidine metabolism that are inherited and that result in certain detectable compounds. One such compound is beta-aminoisobutyric acid or *BAIB*. This substance is formed by the breakdown of pyrimidines and is further reduced to carbon dioxide and ammonia by the action of a transaminase enzyme. High rates of excretion have been measured in some people who are homozygous for this recessive allele. Their metabolism is otherwise normal except for the excretion rate of BAIB. In addition, persons undergoing radiation treatment for cancer excrete large amounts because of the high rate of destruction of DNA in the cancer cells.

There appears to be no pathology associated with high excretion of BAIB. Persons who are low excretors (less than 40 mg/day) appear to be no more or less fit than high excretors (300 mg/day). With the exception of a correlation with radiation treatment for cancer just noted, there appears to be no disease correlation for BAIB excretion. However, there is a significant geographic distribution of populations that are high excretors (see Table 3-17). Large numbers of excretors are seen among Asians; in contrast, Europeans and Americans of European descent tend to be low in number (only 10 percent are high excretors). Among African Americans, excretors are more frequent but they still number far below the percentage of high excretors in Asian populations. Though the meaning of this metabolic variation is not clear and fitness does not appear to be influenced, the phenotype provides another interesting marker for the study of human polymorphisms.

Tay-Sachs Disease. There are numerous rare disorders of the metabolism of lipids (fats) and associated complexes formed with sugar molecules.

TABLE 13-17   Distribution of BAIB Excretors

POPULATION	NUMBER TESTED	FREQUENCY OF HIGH EXCRETORS
North America		
European descent		
Michigan	71	0.03
Texas	255	0.10
New York	218	0.10
New York	148	0.11
African descent		
Michigan	25	0.20
New York	38	0.15
Indians		
Apache	110	0.59
Apache	113	0.42
Eskimo	120	0.23
Chinese	33	0.45
Japanese	41	0.41
Central America		
African descent (Black Caribs)	285	0.32
Asia		
India	16	0
Thailand	13	0.46
Marshall Islands		
Rongelap	188	0.86
Utirik	18	0.83

Source: After Buettner-Janusch, 1966. Copyright © 1966 by John Wiley & Sons, Inc. Reprinted by permission of the publisher.

Such disorders are inherited as recessives that occur at very low frequencies so the chance of a homozygote recessive is very remote, somewhere in the range of once in a million conceptions. In certain populations, however, a recessively inherited disease may occur at high frequencies even though the homozygous recessive is a lethal combination. There are several diseases of this type, but one of the best known is *Tay-Sachs*, a neurodegenerative disorder that causes death before two years of age. Despite its mortality, it occurs among the Ashkenazic Jewish populations of eastern Europe and the United States once in every 2,500 births. This frequency contrasts to 1 in 500,000 non-Ashkenazi births (Ludman et al., 1986). Given these relative frequencies, one in twenty-five persons in the Jewish population are carriers but show no signs of the disease.

Tay-Sachs disease is caused by the accumulation of a lipid-sugar molecule, ganglioside, an important constituent of cell membranes. Synthesis of this molecule occurs by a regular and continuous process as sugar molecules are linked to a type of long-chained lipid molecule. Excesses that are produced beyond the normal cell membrane requirements are degraded by removal of sugar molecules from the lipid portion of the chain, thus maintaining a balance of gangliosides in cell cytoplasm. This is an especially important process in the fast-growing and dividing cells of newborns and infants. In Tay-Sachs individuals this regulation process is interrupted and excess gangliosides accumulate in neuronal cells, causing the brain to become swollen and distended. Brain functions are severely impaired and the infant fails to develop normal neurological responses; muscular control degenerates, followed by paralysis, and loss of hearing and sight occurs by the end of the first year.

Excess gangliosides are degraded by two enzymes called hexoaminidase A and B. Because of inheritance of recessive alleles, Tay-Sachs victims lack hexoaminidase A (Hex A) and, hence, are unable to normally metabolize ganglioside molecules. The recessive allele has been localized to the short arm (region p) of chromosome 15, and the mutation is a single base substitution (G to C) in intron 12 of the DNA sequence. Other mutation forms have also been identified, most resulting in loss of the ability to synthesize the enzyme. In another population with a high frequency of Tay-Sachs, French Canadians of Quebec, a different mutation has been identified (Myerowitz and Hogikyan, 1987). The phenotype of both groups, however, is the same; they lack the enzymes necessary to process the ganglioside molecules. Measurements of the Hex A enzyme levels can identify newborns or fetuses who are at risk. Parents of such infants would be carriers of the defective allele (heterozygotes) who, though they show no symptoms of the disease, have less than normal levels of the enzyme. The measurement of the Hex A enzyme level can identify the carriers and can assist in genetic counseling for prospective parents whose families have a history of Tay-Sachs disease.

The persistence of the high frequencies of this detrimental gene has perplexed scientists for years, and thus far only two explanations have been offered. The first relates to the effect of population size and isolation. The Ashkenazi Jewish populations today probably descended from between 1,000 and 5,000 people who migrated from the Middle East about 1,000 years ago. This small founder size, followed by generations of near isolation and inbreeding, would be in the range for genetic drift to be effective. However, since there are at least two abnormal Hex A alleles now known, genetic drift seems less likely as the cause of Tay-Sachs frequencies. A selection favoring the heterozygote is an alternate explanation (Chakravarti and Chakraborty, 1978). Arguments have been advanced that the crowded ghetto environments fostered the persistence of typhoid and tuberculosis diseases at high levels. Continued exposure acted as selective forces that favored certain genotypes; infections were less acute and mortality was lower. In this case, the argument continues, carriers of the Hex A deficient allele suffered lower mortality rates, survived longer and had higher fertility rates that compensated for the loss of Tay-Sachs infants. Thus far, family studies over several generations in Poland support this hypothesis; families with a history of Tay-Sachs produced more living children in the tuberculosis-typhoid environment. The exact mechanisms involved in this hypothetical relationship of Hex A levels and infectious disease have not been demonstrated but it is founded on similar hypotheses of balanced polymorphism in the persistence of other lethal recessives in certain disease environments—for example, the high frequency of the cystic fibrosis gene in certain populations.

Cystic Fibrosis. The most common lethal genetic disease in European and European-derived populations is cystic fibrosis (CF), inherited as an autosomal recessive. The disease is a disorder of the exocrine glands, those glands that excrete their products into tubules (pancreatic enzymes or parotid salivary glands, for example) in contrast to endocrine glands (pituitary, thyroid, or adrenal are three examples) that release their hormone products directly into the blood. The CF patient suffers from respiratory and digestive problems due to secretions of thick, viscous substances that block tubules and do irreversible damage to several organs, the lungs and pancreas in particular. By blockage of the pancreatic ducts, the enzymes are prevented from reaching the digestive tract, and accumulation of the thick mucus in the smaller air passages of the lungs impairs respiration. This deadly combination of respiratory and digestive problems causes cystic fibrosis to be one of the leading causes of childhood mortality. Before 1950 few survived past infancy, and even today with treatment available, life expectancy is still only twenty-four years. The disease prevalence is from 1 in 500 to 1 in 3,800 births in those of European ancestry. It is extremely low among Africans (1 in 17,000) and rare in Asians (1 in 90,000 births of Asians in Hawaii). The high overall rate among ancestral Europeans in the United States gives a carrier frequency of one in twenty (Weiss, 1993).

The location of the CF gene and identification of its product represents one of a growing number of success stories in genetic research. For years the search was handicapped by incomplete understanding of the physiology of the disease; a high rate of excretion of sodium and chloride in the sweat (about five times normal) was recognized but the connection with some gene product was not established. The locus was isolated to chromosome 7 by 1985, but it was several years before the gene structure was described. The DNA sequences of 500,000 base pairs were finally established as the code determining a large, complex protein called the cystic fibrosis transmembrane conductance regulator (CFTR). This complex unit encompasses a number of cell membrane functions, mainly ion transport (see Ganong, 1993). Thus far, twenty-four different mutations have been identified with CF disease. The high frequencies of several of these mutations in certain populations raises the question of the maintenance of a lethal recessive just as in the case of Tay-Sachs. If the homozygous recessives die before the age of reproduction (as was the case prior to the 1960s), and if those that survive now have such low fertility rates, then what accounts for the one in twenty carrier frequency among many European populations?

The CF allele is correlated with the distribution of tuberculosis, which is believed to have appeared in epidemic proportions in England during the sixteenth century. It then spread to the Continent with the expansion of the Industrial Revolution, which contributed to concentrations of growing European populations in urban centers. Eventually, by the late nineteenth century, this "white plague" or "consumption" became a major cause of death on both sides of the Atlantic. Any individual who had a resistance to this disease, no matter how slight, would enjoy a longer life and a higher reproductive rate. A convincing case is made for carriers of the CF allele in this kind of environment (see Meindl, 1987). The heterozygote (carrier of the mutant allele) had an increased capacity to secrete highly viscous fluids containing large amounts of mucopolysaccharides in the lungs and could more rapidly repair cellular tissue damage caused by invading tubercular bacteria. In sum, the carrier's abnormal levels of these activities, while not as severe as in the homozygous recessive, conveyed an advantage in certain disease environments. This is an interesting hypothesis that offers to explain the high rates of CF in tubercular exposed populations, but it does not consider the CF rates among the Ashkenazim. It is comparable to the hypothesis for Tay-Sachs persistence in eastern European Jewish populations not considering other ethnic groups exposed to the same disease environments. These disease-genetic associations should be analyzed among a broader range of peoples but, unfortunately, there is no published data on CF or Tay-Sachs outside of those populations mentioned.

POLYMORPHISMS OF ANTHROPOLOGICAL INTEREST

Taste Sensitivity

There is a wide range of taste sensitivities in humans. Some of us detect certain chemical compounds more easily than others. Hence, detection of levels of saltiness, bitterness, or sweetness in foods and beverages differs among us all (Williams, 1956). There is good evidence that some of this sensitivity is inherited, as has been thoroughly demonstrated by at least one substance. Perhaps no other polymorphism is so easily detected by a simple test as is taste sensitivity to a substance called phenylthiocarbamide or *PTC*. In high concentrations this substance tastes bitter to some people but not to others. Since the accidental discovery of this condition over fifty years ago, millions of people have been tested and the frequency of tasters and nontasters has been calculated.

This ability to detect the substance PTC is determined by a dominant allele (T): Persons who are TT or Tt can detect a bitter taste. In almost all populations tested there are tasters and nontasters, but as more careful tests have shown, there are various degrees of sensitivity. The homozygote dominant individual (TT) is more sensitive than the heterozygote (Tt) or the homozygote recessive (tt) and can detect the bitterness in more dilute solutions. The frequency of the nontaster in a sample of ethnic groups is shown in Table 3-18. We can see a range of variation of nontasters from a low of less than 2 percent in aboriginals of Taiwan (Formosan natives) to a high of over 40 percent in residents of the city of Bombay, India. As described in Chapter 2, given the percent of homozygous recessives, frequencies for both dominant and recessive alleles can be calculated. These calculations give frequency ranges of .134 to .652 for the recessive (t) and .865 to .342 for the dominant (T), comparing Taiwan to Bombay. Most European and European derived populations have frequencies within the middle of these ranges.

The significance of this taste polymorphism is not certain, though it may be widespread among primates. Studies of chimpanzees and rhesus monkeys revealed taste sensitivity variation over a broad range (Eaton and Gavan, 1965). The question of the significance of this polymorphism becomes more difficult when we recognize that the substance, PTC, used for these tests as well as for testing of humans is a synthetic compound not found in nature. However, the whole chemical compound does not cause the bitter sensation: it is a small cluster of atoms, a carbon, nitrogen, and sulfur tightly bound and acting as a single unit (a radical, in chemical terminology) that causes the bitter taste. This radical of carbon-nitrogen-sulfur (CNS), or thiocyanate, is widely distributed in nature in many common, widely used food plants. Several plants of the Cruciferae family (cabbage, turnips, mustard greens, and so on), as well as cassava (manioc), a tropical root that is a dietary mainstay for millions, contain this thiocyanate group. There is some evidence that avoidance of the bitter-tasting foods containing CNS may be an advantage enjoyed by the taster.

Nontasters are more susceptible to thyroid deficiency, and a higher frequency of nodular goiter is found among them than in people who are tasters. This is due to a depression of iodine uptake by the gland because CNS is a component of a class of chemical compounds, thioglucosides, that can block iodine absorption under certain conditions. Reduced thyroid function results from lowered iodine levels that, in turn, affect lowered metabolism, particularly in child growth or in lowered fertility in adults (Jackson, 1993). One hypothesis explaining taster polymorphism is that persons able to reject CNS-bearing plants would reduce the degree of thyroid interference in contrast to nontasters. This could be a major advantage among those populations in iodine-poor areas of the world. Food avoidance, special food preparation, as in the case of cassava from which most CNS is extracted, or use of high iodine content salt, all contribute as adaptive mechanisms to maintain normal metabolic levels.

Cerumen (Ear Wax)

The waxy substance that accumulates in our ears has two forms that are under the control of a pair of alleles. The wet, sticky form of wax is determined by a dominant whereas the dry, flaky form is determined by a recessive. In addition

TABLE 3-18   Frequency of Nontasters

POPULATION	NUMBER TESTED	PERCENT NONTASTERS
Formosan (Natives)	1,756	1.8
Cree and Beaver Indians (N. Alberta)	489	2.0
Ramah Navahoes	264	2.0
Chinese (in Malaya)	50	2.0
Africans, mostly West African	74	2.7
Bantu, Kenya	208	3.8
Aborigines (Senoi), Malaya	50	4
Lappish (Finland)	140	6.42
Japanese (Brazil)	295	7.11
Japanese (Japan)	656	8.23
Chinese (in London)	66	10.6
Negro (white admixture; Brazil)	534	12.83
Chilean	216	13.43
Jewish (north Africa)	340	15.00
Malays	50	15.6
Malayan	237	16.04
Northeastern Hindu (Riang)	401	16.21
"Cabocio" Brazil	258	16.28
Negritos, Malaya	50	18
Jewish (Ashkenazim; Europe)	440	20.68
Jewish (non-Ashkenazim; Balkan)	101	21.78
Northeastern Brazilians	296	23.31
Belgian	425	23.76
Portuguese	454	24.0
Spaniards, northeastern	306	24.8
White (Italian admixture; Brazil)	74	24.32
Basques, Spain	98	25.0
Eskimos, N. Alaska	68	25.8
Arab (Sudan)	1,963	25.40
Tamils in Malaya	50	27.2
Finns	202	29.2
U.S. white	3,643	29.8
Hindu	256	29.30
Norwegians	266	30.5
White (Rio de Janeiro, Brazil)	164	30.49
Danes	314	31.8
Swedish	200	32.00
English (London)	541	32.90
Indian (Guajiro, Venezuela)	100	40.00
Eskimos, Labrador	130	41
Bombay Indians	200	42.5

Sources: Based on Allison and Blumberg, 1959; and Saldanha and Nacrur, 1963.

to the stickiness or dryness, the waxes differ in their lipid (fat) content and in the quantity of antibodies that they contain.

The ear wax types vary throughout the world's populations. A majority of Asians (80 to 90 percent) have the dry type, in contrast to Europeans and Africans, who usually have the wet ear wax. Among Asians and populations of Asian descent, though, there is a cline of variation that correlates with temperature. Dry ear wax is frequent in northern Asian populations while the wet type is found more often among tropical populations in both Asia and the Americas. For example, 93 percent of Mayan Indians in the Yucatan of southern Mexico have the wet type of ear wax. Because of this clinal distribution and because of lipid and antibody differences, there is a possibility that wet ear wax may serve some protective function in hot, humid climates. However, there is no conclusive evidence. The distribution of cerumen alleles provides another example of the growing list of polymorphisms that require further study before their adaptive significance can be understood (Petrakis et al., 1967).

TRAITS OF SIMPLE INHERITANCE: SOME CONCLUSIONS

The advances in human biology have been rapid and remarkable over the past fifteen years. Not only have many new genetic markers been reported, but chromosome locations have been noted as well. Additional population data have also been obtained, and frequency distributions are more readily available for many simply inherited traits. Blood components and enzyme systems for numerous non-European populations are being published more frequently. In addition, one of the greatest single achievements has been the study of the finer structure of genes and those numerous strands of noncoding units that separate the functional segments. The use of DNA fragments has aided in describing human diversity, and these DNA pieces of varying lengths have been added to a growing list of polymorphisms. The study of human biological diversity has moved from an examination of the end product of gene action, the phenotype, to the recording of the actual genetic code itself. However, these developments have not been an unmixed blessing; they have revealed an enormous range of variability right down to the level of an individual's identification by nuclear DNA polymorphisms. The comparisons of populations now must take into account this new information, and anthropological explanations of population structures and gene flow become ever more important.

4

Human Biology II: Hemoglobin Variants and DNA Markers

Polymorphisms of certain traits such as blood groups, enzymes, and proteins differ markedly in frequency among populations, as described in Chapter 3. The several factors that contribute to gene frequency change offer a way of explaining these trait differences. Influence of such factors as population size, migration, or gene flow can often be well documented by reference to historical events, linguistic similarities, or archaeological evidence. It has been and still is difficult, however, to demonstrate natural selection in humans, and there is little direct evidence of superior fitness of heterozygotes for one or another polymorphism. The hypothesis of phenotype fitness in certain environments, such as the relative immunity of heterozygote carriers to a particular disease, is difficult to test in humans. The postulated fitness of heterozygous carriers of lethal genes described in the last chapter offers some explanation for the persistence of high frequencies, but there have been few direct links made between survival of some genotypes and disease. Much of our data comes from epidemiology and demography, comparisons of differential survival or fertility rates of normal homozygotes and carriers of a lethal gene. However, more complete evidence for disease selection is offered by human hemoglobin variants in malarial environments. This chapter describes these hemoglobin variants, their distribution, and probable disease relationships, and considers the use of DNA markers for population comparisons.

HEMOGLOBINS: NORMAL AND ABNORMAL

The red blood cells contain a variety of proteins, most of which is hemoglobin, approximately 85 to 90 percent. Hemoglobin is a large, complex molecule composed of four long chains of amino acids (polypeptide chains). Each polypeptide encompasses a heme group, a large molecule (porphyrin ring) containing an atom of iron that can carry a molecule of oxygen (O_2) and, incidentally, gives blood its red color when oxygenated. These iron atoms, within the center of the heme groups, combine with two atoms of oxygen in the lungs and then transport the O_2 throughout the circulatory system, releasing it as needed by the surrounding tissues. This uptake, transport, and then release of oxygen is a complex process dependent on several characteristics of the enzymes within the RBC, the structure of the heme groups, and the oxidative state of the atoms of iron they contain.[1] One of the most significant of the factors influencing red blood cell function is the structure of the globins, that is, the amino acid composition of the alpha and beta chains.

The structure of hemoglobin is the most thoroughly studied of any protein and its large size enables ready comparisons of electrophoretic mobility, a technique applied by Linus Pauling for comparative studies of proteins (Figure 4-1). Since the 1940s when Linus Pauling showed the molecular differences of hemoglobin of persons with sickle cell disease (Pauling et al., 1949), samples of this blood protein have been examined for millions of people from around the world. Hundreds of hemoglobin variants have been detected. Most are rare variants, occurring only in a few families, and some are polymorphic, reaching frequencies of greater than 1 percent (see Livingstone, 1985). Many of these variants differ by only a single amino acid in the entire polypeptide sequence of 141 of the alpha chain or the 146 of the beta chain. A sample of these changes in amino acid sequences is listed in Table 4-1. Note the substitution of *histidine* (His) by *tyrosine* (tyr) at position 58 in a variant of the alpha chain called Hb M Boston, named for the city where it was first discovered, or consider the Honolulu G variant at position 30. Position 6 of the beta chain shows two variants; if *valine* (Val) is substituted for *glutamic acid* (Glu) then Hb S is produced, but if *lysine* (Lys) is the substituted amino acid than Hb C is produced. Most substitutions appear to have little or no effect on hemoglobin function and hence red blood cells and health are normal. But changes of amino acids at certain critical positions, Val or Lys at position 6 and Lys at position 26 of the beta chain, for example, may reduce or radically alter hemoglobin shape and interrupt the normal RBC function of oxygen transport. The Hb S variant can result in a high rate of blood cell loss fol-

---

[1]Oxidation of iron from its Fe^{++}(ferrous) state to Fe^{+++}(ferric) may occur when blood is exposed to a variety of chemical compounds. The poison cyanide and the gas carbon monoxide are two of the better-known agents that convert iron. Such hemoglobin with the ferric iron is called methemoglobin and is unable to take up oxygen.

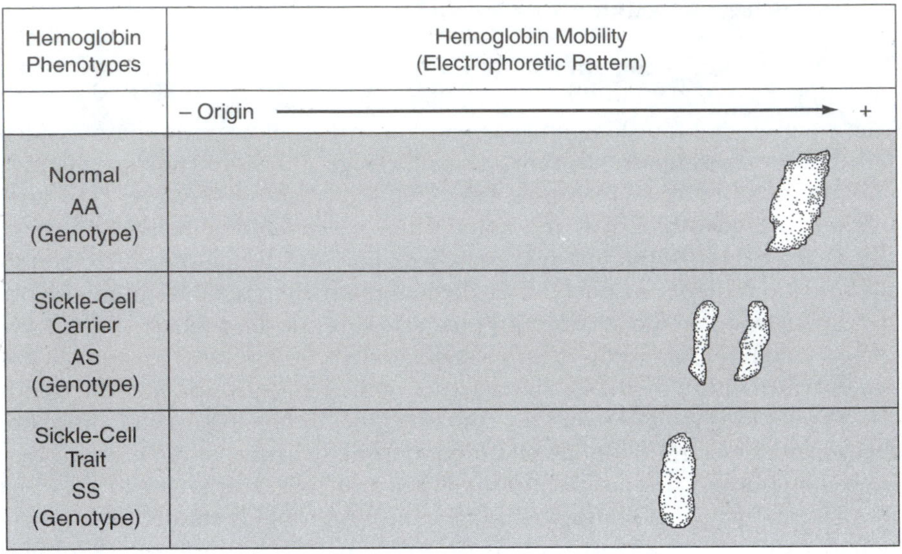

Hemoglobin Phenotypes	Hemoglobin Mobility (Electrophoretic Pattern)		
	− Origin ⟶ +		
Normal AA (Genotype)			
Sickle-Cell Carrier AS (Genotype)			
Sickle-Cell Trait SS (Genotype)			

FIGURE 4-1   **Separation of Hemoglobins by Electrophoresis.**

lowed by severe anemia (sickle cell anemia) contributing to a host of circulatory problems and early death.

These sequences of amino acids in hemoglobin are under genetic control, as noted earlier in Chapter 2. The variants then are transmitted between generations according to Mendelian laws. If the symbol of normal hemoglobin is Hb^A and Hb^S signifies the abnormal sickling type, then the mode of inheritance can be written:

Parent's genotypes: $Hb^AHb^S \times Hb^AHb^S$
Their children's genotypes will be: Hb^AHb^A or Hb^AHb^S or Hb^SHb^S

The expected ratio of these will be 1:2:1, the Mendelian ratio of offspring produced from the mating of heterozygous parents. The individuals with the Hb^AHb^A hemoglobin will produce beta globin strands with a particular sequence of amino acids and, since this is the most frequent type, it is considered the normal form. However, the Hb^S allele codes for a single amino acid substitution as noted above. The alleles Hb^A and Hb^S are codominant, that is, a heterozygote person's blood-forming tissues will produce normal and abnormal hemoglobin. Their red blood cells will then contain mixtures of molecules of both types, but a larger proportion will be of the normal hemoglobin A. The homozygote recessive person (Hb^SHb^S, or simply SS) can produce only hemoglobin molecules with the valine substitution in the beta chain.

If all hemoglobin has this simple change in amino acid sequence, the cell may undergo a deformation in shape when oxygen is taken up by the sur-

TABLE 4-1 Major Alternation in Amino Acid Sequences

ALPHA CHAIN

POSITION	1	2	16	30	57	58	69	141
	Val	Leu	Lys+	Glu-	Gly	His+	AspN	Arg
Hb variant								
Hb1			Asp-					
Hb G Honolulu				GluN				
Hb Norfolk					Asp-			
Hb M Boston						Tyr		
Hb G Philadelphia							Lsy+	

BETA CHAIN

POSITION	1	2	3	6	7	26	63	67	125	150
	Val	His+	Leu	Glu	Glu	Glu	His+	Val	Glu	His+
Hb variant										
Hb S				Val						
Hb C				Lys+						
Hb G San Jose					Gly					
Hb E						Lys+				
Hb M Saskatoon							Tyr			
Hb Zurich							Agr+			
Hb M Milwaukee-1								Glu-		
Hb D Punjab									Gin	

Source: Reprinted by permission from Watson, James D., *Molecular Biology of the Gene*, 4th ed. Menlo Park, Calif.: The Benjamin/Cummings Publishing Company, Inc., 1987, figure 8–8, p. 193.

rounding tissues. As oxygen is released by the hemoglobin molecules, the polypeptide chains begin to alter their spatial orientation and will change to a series of helical-shaped fibers. The more oxygen removed, the more the hemoglobin molecules will alter until enough of these long fiber bundles have formed that they, in turn, stretch and deform the blood cell. As this process proceeds, the shape of the deformed cell becomes crescent or sickle-like in appearance instead of its normal round shape; hence the term "sickle cell" (Figure 4-2).

Persons with the SS hemoglobin may develop what is called sickle-cell disease (SCD). They may survive for long periods without clinical symptoms of the disease and few of their cells will undergo the sickling process, depending on the rate of oxygen consumption. When, however, there is a greater demand for oxygen, which would occur during vigorous exercise, surrounding tissues take up more oxygen from the RBCs as they pass through the peripheral blood vessels. This causes more of the molecules to become deoxygenated; shape change follows, which brings on a sickling crisis. The distorted cells lose flexibility and clog smaller blood vessels, especially in the peripheral circulatory system. To remove this blockage, the body's immune system responds by attacking and causing the cells to *lyse* (break apart). Hemoglobin is released from the red blood cells as they rupture and, because of a reduction in cell number and increased free hemoglobin, anemia and a whole host of associated afflictions will result (Figure 4-3). The SS homozygote may be at greater or lesser risk, depending on age, disease, work habits, diet, and geography. A manual laborer is at greater risk of sickling than a person who has a sedentary occupation, for example. Exercise in the thinner atmosphere in the mountains, or flying in

FIGURE 4-2 Normal and Sickled Human Red Blood Cells. (Photo Researchers, Inc.)

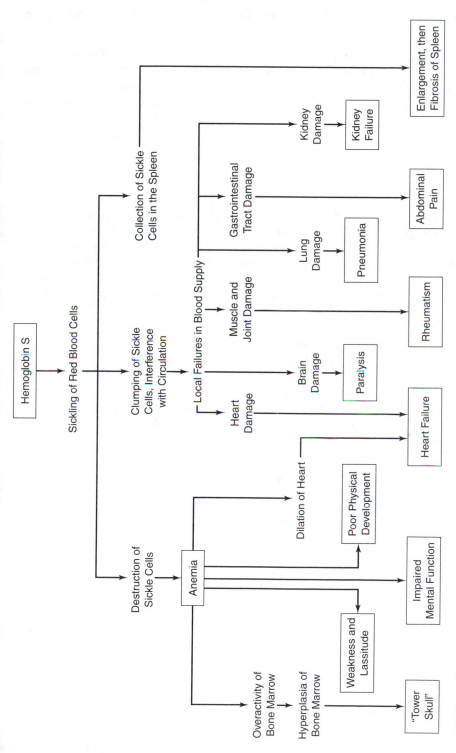

FIGURE 4-3 Physiological Effects and Clinical Symptoms of Sickle Cell Disease. (From Buettner-Janusch, J., *Physical Anthropology: A Perspective*, 1973. Copyright © 1973 by John Wiley & Sons, Inc. Reprinted by permission of the publisher.)

planes with unpressurized cabins, could bring on a crisis. The SS genotype is a near-lethal combination because all hemoglobin is of the S type, and sickling crises can be frequent with a high mortality rate. Few live to adulthood; average life expectancy is about forty years in the United States but much lower in Africa. Though there are reports of some adult homozygotes leading normal productive lives in Ghana, West Africa, the odds are heavily against the survival of individuals with SCD (Konotey-Ahulu, 1982).

By contrast, heterozygote carriers of the sickle cell trait (SCT) enjoy a high degree of protection because a majority of their hemoglobin is normal and the Hb^A molecules combined with the Hb^s prevents the abnormal hemoglobin (Hb^s) from forming fibers distorting blood cells. The heterozygote's red blood cells function normally under most circumstances, and only very rarely do these cells, with a mixture of hemoglobin types, sickle (Edelstein, 1986). However, there has been considerable confusion over the relative health risks faced by heterozygous persons (AS) compared with homozygous normals (AA). This has been especially true in the United States, where about 10 percent of African Americans are carriers. A carrier (SCT) has been thought to be at greater risk when exercising heavily or when working at altitude, and flying in planes was thought to be beyond their physiological capability. Throughout the 1970s the Navy tested recruits and nearly all officers coming on active duty for the presence of the sickle cell trait. Army personnel were also screened but only those applying for airborne duties were examined. Major commercial airlines also joined this confusion by grounding or even firing personnel with the SCT (Bowman, 1977). Such misunderstanding had been grounds for rejection of African Americans with SCT from the Air Force, and was the cause of at least one forced resignation from the Air Force Academy in Colorado Springs (see Duster, 1990). By 1981, the ban on cadets with SCT was ended but several major corporations have continued to test prospective employees (see Kevles, 1995).

Since these reactions twenty years ago to a trait common in African Americans as well as in several other ethnic groups, the issue or non-issue of physical disability of heterozygotes has diminished in public attention. But the confusion still can occur, as in the groundless fears over blood transfusions, misunderstanding of genetic counseling, and confusion of SCT with SCD. What it means to be a carrier is not the risk of disease or of early death but the probability of producing a child with the sickle cell disease (SCD). If both parents are carrying the S allele then there is a 25 percent chance of producing a child with genotype SS (recall the Mendelian ratios). Then, if the number of carriers is considered, the chance of producing a sickle cell child can be calculated for an entire population group. African Americans may be used as an example.

Given that the frequency of the Hb^s gene averages about 5 percent in the entire African-American population of about 33 million and, of this number, 10 percent are carriers (heterozygotes; AS genotypes), there is a probability of

1 in 100 that the mating of heterozygotes will occur (or 0.10 × 0.10). This assumes that matings are random in regard to the hemogobin locus. The probability of producing an SS child from such matings can be calculated from the Hardy-Weinberg equilibrium:

African Americans

$$0.10 \text{ (AS)} \times 0.10 \text{ (AS)} = 0.01 \text{ (or 1 out of 100 probability}$$
$$\text{of heterozygotes mating)}$$

The expectation of SS newborns from these matings is then calculated by:

$$0.010 \times 0.25 \text{ (homozygote probability)} = 0.0025.$$

This is about 1 in every 400 births in the entire African-American popu- lation, given that the average of SCT individuals is about 10 percent. Actually, the frequency of newborns with SS genotype varies by region; it is higher in parts of the southeastern United States, where there are about 15 percent het- erozygotes (SCT), and lower in northern cities like New York, with the gene at only about 3 percent.

The prevalence of the sickle cell gene is much higher in Africa, about 10 percent or higher in some regions, which increases the probability of het- erozygote matings. If the frequency of heterozygotes is considered to be 20 percent, then the following probability can be calculated:

Africans

$$0.20 \text{ (AS)} \times 0.20 \text{ (AS)} = 0.04 \text{ (probability of heterozygote mating)}$$
$$0.04 \times 0.25 \text{ (probability of SS newborn)} = 0.01 \text{(or 1 in 100 births)}$$

The chance of these with SCD living to the age of reproduction is less; their fitness relative to the other genotypes ranges from zero to about 10 percent. These differences of genotype fitness have raised many questions, and the answers have offered an excellent model of natural selection operating on the human species. Despite the Hb^s (or S) allele being near lethal, it still exists at high frequency (from 10 to 20 percent) in numerous populations, especially in Central Africa. With few if any homozygotes living to adult- hood and reproducing, there is a high loss of S alleles each generation. The allele frequency should decline over time, but such is not the case. This question of the maintenance of the S allele despite selection against it was addressed in the 1950s by Allison and others (Allison, 1954). They consid- ered and then discarded the possibility that mutations (Hb^A to Hb^s) replaced the lost alleles, since a rate 100,000 times higher than any known human mutations would have had to be maintained (see Livingstone, 1958 for a review). With replacement by mutation ruled out, differences in fitness of the genotypes was considered in those African populations with the highest S frequencies. Fifteen percent of the homozygous normals (AA) and 90 percent of the homozygous abnormals (SS) die between birth and the age of reproduction relative to the heterozygotes (AS). This may be presented as genotype fitness:

$$AA = 0.85; AS = 1.0; SS = 0.10.$$

DISTRIBUTION OF HEMOGLOBIN S

These relative fitness values favor the carrier and maintain a balance of the two alleles (A and S); in other words, some environmental factor or factors selectively favored the heterozygotes. They lived longer and reproduced at a higher rate, compensating for the lost S alleles, which maintained a balanced polymorphism in the population. Malaria, because of its high mortality and concordant geographical distribution with certain abnormal hemoglobins, was considered as a likely selective force. Just as Haldane had suggested in the case of thalassemia (another hemoglobin variant), the AS heterozygote was probably more resistant to the mosquito-borne disease malaria. This possibility of the relative resistance of the genotypes stimulated data collection on malarial epidemiology and evidence for the distribution of abnormal hemoglobins (Figure 4-4).

The highest frequencies of Hb^S occur in central Africa, northeast India, and Arabia. High levels are also found around the Mediterranean, especially in Greece. Turkey, and Arabia, may also be included in this list, shown in Table 4-2. Such a distribution in some countries bordering the Mediterranean results in cases of SCD reported among Europeans, much to the surprise of some physicians.[2] Explanations for this distribution outside of Africa are often related to the history of the area, which experienced an ebb and flow of diverse peoples, resulting in the establishment of colonies and the importation of slaves from sub-Saharan Africa, beginning probably as early as 2,000 years ago in the Mediterranean. Much of the distribution of the Hb^S alleles probably occurred during the years of Islamic rule from about A.D. 825 to 1060. These events of conquest plus widespread trade continued to disperse the S allele

---

[2]The question was raised in a recent issue of the *Journal of the American Medical Association* by a writer who wanted to know if there were any documented cases of SCT or SCD occurring in persons of European extraction. Powars (1994) replied in a short review of Mediterranean population movements that, yes, it was possible to be blond and blue-eyed (look non-African) and still have the trait. The brief summary, however, did not mention Arabia or India and so left the impression that Hb^S was strictly an African gene. The response also confused perception and appearances with genetics.

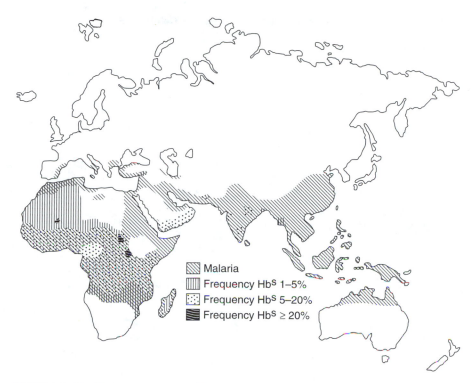

FIGURE 4-4 **Distribution of Malaria and Sickle Cell Anemia.** (Redrawn from Buettner-Janusch, 1966.)

over the course of hundreds of years. The more recent importation of African slaves into the Americas, however, was condensed into a period of less than four centuries, bringing people from specific African areas to the New World. The history of the slave trade offers a special case of distinctive environmental variables acting within a limited time frame, as will be considered below.

In India, trade and some colonization from Africa are also known to have occurred, events that offer a possibility of introduction of the Hb^s allele. It is difficult to explain the presence of such a high frequency in several parts of India, however, solely on the basis of the importation of slaves or the establishment of colonies (Figure 4-5). There is a possibility that an allele such as Hb^s, which is advantageous under certain conditions, appeared in several populations throughout human history by random mutations. The allele then would become fixed at high frequencies. Such occurrence of spontaneous mutations would rule out the need to associate a gene with a particular ethnic group. Though the question is far from settled, there are supporters for both sides of the argument: for gene distribution by migration or by independent mutation. One group of scholars explain that a few mutations in a central area could have resulted in a gene, such as Hb^s, advantageous in certain environments. From that area, supposedly in eastern Nigeria, the

TABLE 4-2   Some Examples of Populations with Sickle Cell Trait (SCT)

NATION OR REGION	SCT %
Africa	
Senegal	5–12
Guinea	8.5–20
Liberia	.07–28
Nigeria	18–32
Zaire	4–36
Angola	4–35
Kenya	0–25
Mediterranean	
Sicily	2.0
Greece (Orchomenos)	23.0
Turkey (Mersin)	13.0
Saudi Arabia	5–12.0
India	
Madras	14–17.0
Nilgiri district	8–31.0
Baster district	16–38.0
Americas*	
United States	3.2–15.1
Panama	5–14.0
Brazil	3–8.6

*Populations sampled had African ancestors.
Sources: Erhardt, 1973; Livingstone, 1985; Schroeder and Munger, 1990.

gene spread by population migration and interpopulation contact, increasing in frequency because of its selective advantage. This spread has been classically associated with the expansion of populations of Bantu speakers, early agriculturists who successfully exploited tropical rain forests because of their possession of iron tools and an efficient food crop, the yam. Such a reconstruction, however, would make it difficult to explain how the gene arrived in more remote areas noncontiguous with the main African homeland and outside of the ancient trade route networks—areas such as northeastern India, for example.

Significant clues to understanding the occurrence of the SCT are not found simply in histories of population movements, but also in the nature of the environments in several areas where SCT is frequent. Because of the concordant distributions of malaria and Hb^s, we have an important example of genetic adaptation of *Homo sapiens*. Populations with long histories of contact with the disease malaria usually exhibit the highest frequency of SCT (and also other hemoglobin abnormalities). The apparent relationships between these abnormalities and malaria are explained on the basis of a hypothesis that states: An individual who is a heterozygote (a carrier of the abnormal gene) enjoys a relative degree of immunity to infection by the malarial parasite in comparison with a person with the normal genotype.

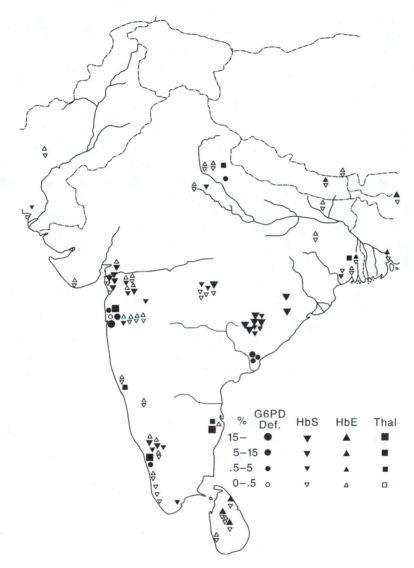

FIGURE 4-5   Hemoglobin S and Other Red-Cell Defects in India. (Reprinted from Livingstone, F. B., *Abnormal Hemoglobins in Human Populations*, 1967. (Chicago: Aldine Publishing
Company, 1967; copyright © 1967 by Frank B. Livingstone. Reprinted by permission of the
author and Aldine Publishing Company.)

MALARIA AND NATURAL SELECTION

The dreaded mosquito-borne disease malaria is endemic in many areas of the
world, mainly tropical areas, where people are continuously infected throughout the year. In subtropical regions infection is more cyclical, following the
rainfall patterns and increases in mosquitos. Malaria was once more wide-

spread, occurring in much of the Eastern United States and even in parts of Europe well into this century. Continuous efforts to eradicate the malaria-transmitting mosquito have eliminated the disease as a major problem in these areas. In many developing countries in the tropics, however, the disease remains the number one cause of sickness and death, with an incidence of between three to five million cases resulting in approximately two million deaths annually (Starke, 1996). If deaths owing to complications arising from malarial infection are added, then the death rate is actually greater. In areas of the world where the death rate from all causes is extremely high, recent control of malaria has reduced this rate by one-third to one-half. This illustrates the rather stringent control that malaria has exerted on population size; it has probably been a major selective force acting on humanity for many centuries. The negative effects of malaria, however, are seen in many other ways besides death rates. The endemic malarial conditions that exist among tropical populations mean that individuals carry a quantity of parasites in their bloodstream from time of birth, and, in many areas, are reinfected year round. This, together with the burden of other parasites common to the tropics and limited nutrition, lowers general health, reduces energy levels, and increases susceptibility to other diseases. All of these factors affect life expectancy, but malaria appears to be the major contributor.

The disease we call malaria is caused by several species of the genus *Plasmodium*. Humans are hosts to four species of *Plasmodium*, each of which causes a different type of malaria: *vivax*, the most common form and with a wide geographical distribution; *ovale*, the rarest form native to West Africa; *malariae*, a broadly but unevenly distributed parasite causing a mild form of the disease; and the fourth and most deadly type of malaria, *falciparum*. The species requires a warm climate to flourish, and its distribution is largely limited to the tropics (Harrison, 1978). These single-celled parasites have a complex life cycle, part of which is spent in the body of a mammalian host, where it enters the red blood cell and, using the cell's energy supply, divides, eventually destroying the host cell. The released parasites accumulate in the larger blood vessels, especially those in the liver and spleen.

The disease is transmitted to humans by the bite of a female *Anopheles* mosquito infected with the parasites, or an uninfected mosquito may suck up the parasites when biting an infected human. Either way, the mosquito is an important link in the distribution of the disease and can deposit malarial organisms in uninfected persons. Since mosquitos are carriers or vectors for malarial transmission, the distribution and spread of the disease depends on the habits and life cycle of the *Anopheles* species. Of the 100 species known to function as a vector of the *Plasmodium* parasites, there are only about twenty important ones because the parasites develop better in some species of mosquitos than in others. Each world region provides an environment that seems to favor certain species; for example, the species *A. gambiae* is the major vector for distribution of *falciparum* malaria in Africa and Arabia; *P. falciparum* accounts for 80 to 90 percent of the malarial infections found among the populations in these regions. Throughout India, Southeast Asia, and New Guinea, other species are important vectors of *vivax* and *falciparum* malarial parasites.

The part humans play in this host–vector disease organism scheme is important and complicated because of the specific habitat needs of the major species of mosquito. These needs are often provided for through human disruption of a natural environment, a disruption that creates expanded breeding places for the insect. The changes are particularly evident in the example of slash-and-burn techniques of the tropical rain forest horticulturists who radically alter the flora and drive away many mammals that might have been hosts to the mosquitoes. This style of agriculture involves the cutting and then burning of trees, and this removal of the tropical rain forest cover exposes the thin tropical soils to rapid erosion in high-rainfall areas. Stagnant pools of water collect and provide mosquito breeding places; further, humans locate their dwellings in groups where numerous families live in close contact. All of these conditions provide an ideal situation for the transmission of malarial parasites on a continuous basis, causing up to 100 percent of the population to be infected. For example, the *A. gambiae* mosquito, the efficient vector for the most lethal malaria, *falciparum*, is best adapted to those conditions that exist around human habitations in tropical rain forests with village clearings, stagnant pools of water, and open sunlit garden plots. In contrast, it does not breed well in thickly forested areas with few open areas; other mosquito species predominate but are less effective vectors (Livingstone, 1958).

Primitive agricultural activities and adoption of sedentary village life not only caused many environmental changes but contributed to a significant increase in human population, accompanied by a decline in the number of wild mammals in the vicinity of the settlements. In the past, the *Anopheles*, or their ancestral forms, may have preyed on other mammalian hosts, just as many mosquito species still do. Through the development of human sedentary life since the Neolithic, several mosquito species have come to depend on humans as their major host. Also, sedentary human populations provide many more hosts than did wandering bands of nomads. This has allowed our species to increase with the expansion of agriculture, which offered somewhat conflicting conditions for life in prehistory and early historic times. As humans gained skills in plant domestication, a surplus of food was produced that supported larger populations, but food production and the settlement patterns in turn altered the environment, favoring an increase of malaria. This disease caused a high mortality, but the losses of human life were more than balanced by gains made with the adoption of agriculture.

Under these conditions of early agricultural life, any degree of immunity that some people may have had because of their genotypes would contribute to their longevity and an increase reproduction rate. Since malarial parasites depend on red blood cells for nutrients during part of the parasite's life cycle, red blood cell metabolism under disease conditions has been under study for years (Edelstein, 1986). The results show that red blood cells containing some types of abnormal hemoglobin are less able to support malarial parasite growth. Also, these red blood cells are more fragile, with a shorter life span, and have a lower energy level. These factors reduce the multiplication of parasites and result in fewer number of cells in circulation. The most clear-cut relationship between malaria and all of the red-cell variants appears in the case of Hb^S; in endemic malarial areas, persons with SCT have lower parasite counts than do normals.

In areas where *falciparum* is endemic, there are several examples of natural selection favoring the survival of individuals with SCT. They are less likely to die from *falciparum* malaria than persons with all normal hemoglobin. There is a significantly greater number of heterozygotes in the forty-five-plus age group, which indicates a longer life span compared with homozygous normals. In addition, fewer die in infancy and more reach adolescence. Also, fertility is higher among female carriers. They have a higher live birth rate and lower parasite counts than do women with all normal hemoglobin. Though untested, fertility is likely to be higher among heterozygous males due to fewer episodes of high fever associated with malarial attacks, since spermatogenesis is impaired by prolonged elevated body temperature. Table 4-3 lists a summary of the evidence for differential fitness of the AS heterozygote in malarial environments. The combined data gained from laboratory tests and demography make a strong argument, but more convincing are the distributions of the S allele and malaria (see Figure 4-4). The hypothesis that the concordant distributions of gene and disease are the result of natural selection is reinforced by the evidence of several other inherited hemoglobin defects.

TABLE 4-3   Malaria as a Selective Force

	HETEROZYGOUS **AS**	HOMOZYGOUS **AA**
Fertility		
Female	Higher	Lower
Male	Higher sperm count	Impaired spermatogenesis(?)
Demographic		
Child	More children (age 1–4 yrs) Highest frequency among juveniles	Fewer adolescents
Adult	Greater number with SCT	
Morbidity		
Parasite count	Lower	Higher
Cerebral malaria	Less frequent	A major cause of adult mortality
Epidemiology		
frequency of Hb^S	Highest in areas of endemic malaria	No correlation

SOME OTHER ABNORMAL HEMOGLOBINS

Several inherited abnormal hemoglobin types exist at polymorphic frequencies and have wide distributions. Most of these types, in the homozygote state, do not cause disease as serious as SCD, though some may result in anemia under certain conditions. Because of their concordant distribution with malaria of the *falciparum* and *vivax* types, there is probably a higher survival rate of the carrier of one of these hemoglobin types, just as was the case for the sickle cell carrier.

Type E Hemoglobin. This major hemoglobin is also the result of a point mutation in the beta globin gene (amino acid lysine for glutamic acid; refer to Table 4-1). Hb^E, the third most frequent hemoglobin type (after Hb^A and Hb^S), has a more limited distribution that begins approximately where Hb^S distribution ends. It occurs in very high frequencies (>15 percent) among populations extending from India, through Southeast Asia, to New Guinea. The homozygote (EE) does not suffer as severely from acute anemia as does the (SS) nor is there cell distortion, but there appears to be a difference in fitness between the genotypes that favors the heterozygotes. The distribution in New Guinea demonstrates this well; the hemoglobin E is most frequent among populations living in the coastal plain, where vast, swampy low-lying areas support malaria. Away from these areas into the highlands of greater population density, malaria disappears as a health problem (until recent times) and frequencies of Hb^E diminish to zero.

Other hemoglobin abnormalities with polymorphic frequencies are found in a more restricted range of populations; examples are Hb C in a limited area of West Africa and Hb O$_{Arab}$ in the southern part of Arabia. Hemoglobin D$_{Punjab}$ is another, located in the region of India it is named for. No hemoglobin abnormalities are known to exist among native peoples of the New World. Those abnormal hemoglobins that are found in the Americas today occur in persons who are descendants of African slaves or in a restricted sample of Europeans who had migrated from malarial areas where certain hemoglobin abnormalities were present in high frequencies (as noted above).

The Thalassemias. The abnormal hemoglobins listed above are due to a single nucleotide substitution in the beta globin gene resulting in an amino acid substitution; beta globin is still produced but with a different amino acid sequence. In the case of the *thalassemias,* synthesis of either the beta or alpha globin chains is reduced, the amino acid chain shortened, or blocked altogether. This large group of abnormal hemoglobins result from point mutations that cause a shift or a deletion in entire DNA sequences of either the exons (the part that carries the code) or introns (the noncoding, intervening sequence) of the alpha or beta globin genes. Instead of single amino acid substitutions in the globin chain, DNA transcription is interrupted or shifted so

the codons of mRNA are not produced in a correct sequence or are even eliminated (see below). In some types, the globin chains may have a normal
sequence but are produced in reduced amounts, or a chain may be shortened, and, in some cases, the alpha or globin chain is totally absent. These
numerous variants of globin chain syntheses can result in severely handicapped hemoglobin function and frequent loss of the red blood cells. The
individual with such an affliction may have a life-threatening anemia, depending on the type of the inherited abnormality. These defects of globin chain
production, or thalassemias, are among the most commonly inherited disorders in *Homo sapiens* and may account for an estimated 100,000 child deaths
per year.

The first disorder to consider is *Thalassemia major* (formerly called Coo-
ley's anemia after its discoverer, a Detroit pediatrician), originally described as
a form of inherited anemia found among populations of several countries
bordering the Mediterranean Sea. This condition is inherited as an autosomal
dominant in part of the beta globin gene cluster on chromosome 11. This
mutant allele (beta thalassemia) decreases or halts the synthesis of the
beta-Hb chain. A reduced amount results in an imbalance of the quantity of
alpha and beta chains in the completed hemoglobin. Red blood cells with this
imbalance are unstable and are lost through hemolysis at a rapid rate in the
homozygous person. A total lack of beta globin chains, as in the case of the
beta°39, the most common type in Sardinia and other Mediterranean areas,
causes the cells to be even more unstable.[3] Homozygotes for this allele will suffer a severe form of anemia, called thalassemia major, and few will survive adolescence. The heterozygotes (thalassemia minor) may have a milder form and
usually live free of symptoms, since the reduction of beta-Hb production in
the heterozygote is somewhat compensated for by a continued synthesis of the
fetal hemoglobin form well into adult life. Such compensation enables them
to have a normal life expectancy.

Comparisons of beta thalassemia are made difficult by the fact that
thirty-seven genes around the DNA of the globin gene affect rates of synthesis. Various mutations of these genes have been found distributed unevenly
around the Mediterranean; one predominates in the western region while
another is more common in countries along the eastern shores (see Table 4-4).
Each affects a thalassemic condition resulting in anemia but with varying
degrees of severity. In fact, each ethnic group appears to have its own mutation in some of the genes that regulate hemoglobin production. Thalassemia
of the beta°39 type accounts for 95 percent of thalassemias in Sardinia but
only 65 percent in Spain. In Greece and other countries of the Eastern
Mediterranean, intron 1, a beta⁺ type, is in the majority. Despite severe selection against the homozygote of some types, beta thalassemias are widespread

---

[3]There are now at least thirty-seven different mutations that affect the beta globin chain
synthesis, and some cause a more critical disruption of globin synthesis than others.

TABLE 4-4   Beta Thalassemias of Selected Ethnic Groups

ETHNIC GROUP	BETA THAL MUTATIONS	TYPE	FREQUENCY
African American	TATA box (29)	β+	39%
	Poly A site	β+	26%
Mediterranean	Intron(110)	β+	38%
	β 39 term.	βo	29%
Indian	Intron 1(5)	β+	36%
	Deletion (61)	βo	36%
Chinese	Frame shift (71/72)	βo	49%
	Intron 2 (654)	βo	38%

Source: Data selected from Vogel and Motulsky, 1986.

throughout much of the Old World. In certain regions of Italy, for example, 35 percent of the people are carriers of alleles for some form.

Similar high frequencies of beta thalassemia alleles are seen in many African populations, especially in North Africa and in certain pastoral tribes in Sudan. Beta thalassemia is also frequent in Thailand, Southeast Asia, and parts of China (Chan et al., 1987). The severity of the disease varies from lethal to mild depending on the site of the mutation. These approximately thirty-seven sites also vary among populations. Considering only those mutations that result in a complete absence of beta globin production, $beta^o39$ and 6 are the principle mutations in the Mediterranean, $beta^o17$ and 41 in south China, and $beta^o15$ and 8 in India. As investigations of the thalassemias broaden, additional mutation sites are being discovered in specific ethnic groups that range at this time from Europe and Africa, through the Mideast to India and Thailand, with South China and Taiwan included on the far eastern edge of this distribution (refer to hemoglobin section in McKusick, 1994). From these eastern outlyers with beta thalassemia genes to New Guinea, a new group of hemoglobin variants (alpha chain mutations) become the predominant form as they began to appear in high frequencies.

Alpha Thalassemia. Deficiences of alpha chain production are highly variable, resulting in a greater variety of clinical expressions than reported for beta thalassemia. This is due to a more complicated mode of inheritance; there are two loci on chromosome 16 that carry the structural genes. Mutations at one or both of these loci, usually gene deletion types, cause clinical thalassemias that vary from mild to severe to lethal. Homozygotes for mutant genes at two loci are unable to produce any alpha globin, while in contrast, a carrier of a single affected gene has less than a normal amount, but the hemoglobin remains functional (see Table 4-5). Between these two extremes are carriers of a mutant at two loci, or homozygous at one loci and a carrier at another. Such individuals will produce varying

TABLE 4-5   Alpha Thalassemias of Selected Ethnic Groups

ETHNIC GROUP	ALPHA THAL MUTATIONS	TYPE
	CHAIN TERMINATION	
African American	UAA to GAA	Seal rock
Mediterranean	UAA to AAA	Hb Icaria
Indian	UAA to UCA	Hb Koya Dora
Southeast Asian	UAA to CAA	Hb constant spring
	OTHER TYPES	
Arabian	RNA cleavage(α2 gene)	α2 gene
	Frameshift codon 14	α1 gene
Sardinian	AUG to ACG	α2 gene

Source: Data selected from Vogel and Motulsky, 1986.

amounts of alpha globin, and since the hemoglobin varies in stability, suffer different rates of hemolysis.

The alpha thalassemias are one of the more common inherited disorders, but the deletion mutation combinations vary among the ethnic groups just as noted above for the beta thalassemias. Deletions at one alpha gene are common worldwide with the highest frequency (33 percent) in East Africa and the Mediterranean. In contrast, deletions at both alpha loci are the most frequent types in Southeast Asia. Mutations of the nondeletion type that interfere with mRNA also show wide ethnic variation. Different ones are reported for populations in Greece, Sardinia, India, China, Southeast Asia, and Melanesia.

Some thalassemia types appear in high frequencies despite the homozygous disadvantage. This is explained by the hypothesis that selection favors the heterozygote in malarial environments, as in the case of sickle cell anemia. The majority of the alpha thalassemias are milder, especially those expressed in Southeast Asian and Melanesian populations, but the frequencies still follow the distribution of malaria. A case in point is New Guinea, where a study was made in populations of the coastal areas to test the malarial hypothesis. Frequencies of alpha gene deletion type mutations ranged from 22 percent to 68 percent in coastal areas. In the central highlands, an area of greatest population density, the deletions drop to between 2 and 5 percent. Malaria is endemic in New Guinea, where both *falciparum* and *vivax* types are present in particularly virulent strains resistant to antimalarial drugs. Its incidence is highest in the marshy coastal areas and drops appreciably with altitude; the highland areas are believed to have been malaria-free before European contact. The distribution of the thalassemia mutations likewise falls with increasing altitude and diminished risk of malarial infection. Hill (1986) showed a high correlation between the mutations and malaria, and he also recorded a clinal variation from New Guinea through the Solomon Islands to New Caledonia as malaria and alpha thalassemia decline. He argued that selection favors the heterozygote of even this mild form of thalassemia when malaria is present. Thalassemia mutants are low or absent in the Fiji Islands, which are free of malaria. This distribution of hemoglobin mutants is similar to the relationship in the Mediterranean areas and also relates to a malarial parasite's survival and growth in red blood cells with defective hemoglobin.

The Enzyme G6PD (glucose 6 phosphate dehydrogenase)

While considering hemoglobin variants and their influence on survival, an enzyme, G6PD, should be noted because of its many inherited forms. The enzyme is present in all cells of the body, where it catalyzes a variety of functions, but one of the most essential of these functions is performed in the red blood cells. The enzyme initiates a step in a biochemical pathway, a chain of conversions that enables the red blood cell to reduce harmful oxidative products of cell metabolism (hydrogen peroxide, for example), and thus protect the cell membrane. These processes and the stages of chemical conversion are too complex to consider here (see Ganong, 1993 for specific details). It is sufficient to say that G6PD is a vital substance for red blood cell function, and the cell's life span is directly related to the quantity of the enzyme present. This is especially true when red blood cells are under oxidative stress from either chemical or parasitic sources. Nevertheless, enzyme function varies over a wide range because of different G6PD polymorphisms.

The G6PD enzyme is under control of a gene on the X chromosome as described in the discussion of sex linkage in Chapter 2. There are a number of alleles of this gene, and some code for the production of an enzyme form that operates less efficiently. Many altered forms of the G6PD enzyme have a lower level of activity and are described as deficient (G6PDD or Gd–). Under most circumstances this does not prove to be a health problem for the individual. Even mild infections will increase the level of oxidative products in the cells and will depend on a more active series of reducing agents to render these waste products harmless. Under such conditions, the level of G6PD activity is important, even critical, in cases of serious infection or parasitation. In Gd– persons, when confronted with such oxidative stress, blood cells increase in fragility and frequently lyse. This results in hemolytic anemia of varying levels of severity depending on the acuteness of the disease. Certain toxins in drugs or in plants can have the same effect, and can cause a transient form of anemia—that is, the production of new red blood cells will bring cell concentration back up to normal when the oxidative substance is removed. Recognition of the effect of these toxins eventually led to the discovery of the inherited defect in the red blood cell enzyme system.

The drug sensitivity of the RBC of some people has been recognized since the 1920s, when synthetic antimalarial drugs were first introduced as substitutes for quinine, the natural product used for centuries in the treatment of "fevers." Among the drug's earliest applications was in the British army, whose widespread occupation of many tropical areas placed tens of thousands of personnel at risk of malarial infection. Adverse responses to the drugs were soon reported among many of the Asian troops. Later, in World War II and during the Korean War, sensitivity was again noted among people of non-European origins. About 10 percent of African-American soldiers suffered from anemia following administration of drugs such as primaquine. This repeated the experience of the British army earlier; some ethnic groups suffered from a debilitating level of anemia when given certain drugs to prevent malaria. Though the genetic connection had not yet been made, doctors recognized that some deficiency condition existed in the RBC of these patients that caused cell destruction on exposure to these drugs. The anemia diminished when the source of the irritant was removed, and cell count gradually returned to normal.

The exact nature of the cell deficiency was determined in the late 1950s through laboratory tests devised to identify the susceptible individuals. It was found that these individuals had lower G6PD activity in their RBC than those persons whose cells did not hemolyze (burst apart) under the test procedures (Beutler et al., 1955). Once these test procedures were refined and proved effective in identifying afflicted individuals, many thousands of blood samples were examined. Deficiencies were found to occur more frequently in males than in females, suggesting that G6PD synthesis is under the control of an X-linked locus, which is now mapped to the same region as the colorblindness and hemophilia loci. Males with normal G6PD have Gd A or B, the most common types, whereas the deficient males have either Gd A– or Gd B–. Females who are G6PD deficient would be homozygotes for the defect Gd A– or Gd B– alleles. Heterozygote females tend to have a mixture of normal and abnormal RBC because only one of their X chromosomes is active in each of the cells of the blood-forming tissues.

Since these original studies, 325 other variants of G6PD have been reported. Fortunately, most of these are quite rare and only a few of the variants appear to be malarial drug sensitive. The major variants exist in numerous populations from New Guinea to India, Italy to Africa, and throughout the Middle East (Table 4-6). The highest frequency of Gd– is found in countries around the Mediterranean, particularly among Egyptians and populations on the island of Sardinia. The variant Gd(A–) is frequent—about 20 percent among Africans. The more severe variant form, Gd(B–), is found in frequencies of 15 to 20 percent in Greece, Sardinia, and the Middle East. China and Thailand also show high frequencies of variants with low activity levels (Beutler, 1983).

A surprising relationship exists between several of these Gd– variants and a widely used food plant, the fava bean (*Vicia faba*). It has long been known that some people had a hemolytic response following consumption of these beans or even exposure to its pollen. Such sensitivity is referred to as favism. Very much as in the drug-induced reaction, there is a recovery from the

TABLE 4-6   Classes of Some Common G6PD Variants

CLASS	POPULATION	ENZYME ACTIVITY
Gd B	Majority	Normal level
Gd A+	African	Near normal
Gd A–[b]	African	10–60% of normal
Gd B–[a,b]	Mediterranean	0–5% of normal
Gd Canton[a,b]	Chinese	4–25% of normal
Gd Anant[b]	Thailand	Near normal
Gd Mahidol[b]	Thailand	5–16% of normal
Gd Mahidol[b]	Thailand	5–16% of normal
Gd Hektoen	Thailand	Above normal

[a]Sensitive to fava bean.
[b]Sensitive to certain oxidizing drugs.
Sources: Data selected from McKusick, 1986; Vogel and Motulsky, 1986.

anemia when exposure ceases. Yet these fava beans have been a dietary staple of many populations of the Mediterranean region for centuries, and it is in these same populations that have the highest frequency of the Gd(B–) allele, coding for the most deficient enzyme form. Also, southern China, the largest producer of fava beans in the world, has populations with high frequencies of the more severe form of G6PD deficiencies.

The explanation for this relationship between such a potentially harmful plant and an inherited defect relates to the malarial environments in which these people live, as considered above for the abnormal hemoglobins. The plant toxins (divicine and isouramil) place an oxidative stress on the red blood cells, so in Gd– persons many more of their RBC are prone to lyse, if not already destroyed, as in the case of older cells. The rate of destruction is a function of the quantity of the plant toxins ingested. The RBCs maintain a very narrow or precarious balance, and any additional oxidative stress can increase hemolysis rates; cell life span is shorter and more immature cells enter circulation. The intake of malarial parasites tips this balance and hemolysis increases, thereby reducing parasite multiplication. The blood cells are sustaining activity within a narrow level. Assisting in this balancing act the blood cells must endure is probably a taste sensitivity to the fava bean that limits consumption, thereby reducing the hemolysis rate until challenged by parasites. Though not identified yet, this taste sensitivity is hypothetically an adaptation that assists in resistance to malaria. Possibly there are other common food toxins as well that work as low-level hemolytic agents, but the fava bean is the only one studied for this property (Greene, 1993).

Finally, these red blood cell variants, the abnormal hemoglobins, G6PD deficiency, and thalassemia, are not confined to a single geographical area nor are they unique to a particular "racial" group. The genes for these variants are widespread among many populations and closely follow the pattern of malaria distribution. No simple explanation of population migration and admixture has been able to account completely for these distributions. Major migrations of the world's peoples have undoubtedly been involved in the dispersal of these mutant genes, as in the case of African Americans, but selection in a malarial environment remains the most important factor. Several studies of the concordant distribution of the genes and disease support this conclusion, and one of particular interest is on the isolated island of Sardinia.

DISTRIBUTION OF RED-CELL VARIANTS IN SARDINIAN POPULATIONS

The island of Sardinia lies 126 miles (200 km) off the Italian coast. Its mountainous terrain isolates many of the towns and villages that are home to 1.5 million people (1993). They trace their ancestry to several European and Muslim invaders. Until modern times, the islanders have been relatively isolated from the mainland, following periods of colonization from Spain, France, Italy, and North Africa. Though these ancestral groups left limited genetic traces, according to Cavalli Sforza (1994), gene flow tends to be directed and limited by the geography and history of the island, so gene frequencies of certain markers today vary significantly from area to area. The populations of coastal communities differ in many ways, linguistically, historically, and genetically, from villages above the coastal plain. One of the most notable of these differences are the genetic markers that relate to a malarial environment. Until 1944, when a major mosquito control effort was begun, parts of Sardinia were among the worst malarial areas in the Mediterranean, and the area provides some extensive epidemiological data.

Studies of Sardinia offer substantial evidence to support the hypothesis of relationships between thalassemia, G6PD deficiency (Gd^{B-}), and malaria. Most significantly, a clear inverse correlation was found between altitude and frequency of thalassemia and G6PD deficiency (Figure 4-6). At higher elevations, as one moves away from the coastal plain, the rate of malarial infection decreases because the environment is less favorable to the mosquito vector. Changes in gene frequencies are also seen; there are fewer carriers of the genes for Gd^{B-} and thalassemia among the populations of villages in the mountains and foothills (note the major drop in G6PD deficiency above 400 meters). Thalassemia also declines, but at a lower rate. The declines with altitude offer a successful test of the malarial hypothesis—the carriers for these defects are favored. Where the risk of malaria is less, the frequency of the gene defects decline.

Some Sardinian villages, however, do not fit the correlations. In other words, the selective force (malaria) is present, but there are few people who are carriers of the genetic traits (G6PD and thalassemia) that would provide them with a degree of immunity; an explanation must be sought elsewhere. The villages of Carloforte and Usini, both in a malarious area, were settled in

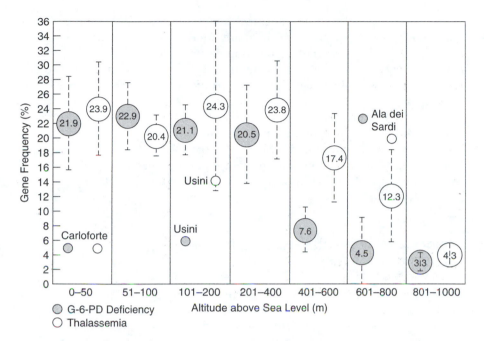

FIGURE 4-6 Incidence of G6PD Deficiency and the Thalassemia Trait in Relation to Altitude above Sea-Level. (From Siniscalco, M., et al., "Population genetics of hemoglobin variants, thalassemia and glucose-6-phosphate dehydrogenase deficiency, with particular reference to the malaria hypothesis." Copyright © 1966 by World Health Organization. Reprinted by permission of the publisher.)

The figures in each of the large circles are the averages of the gene frequencies found in the villages that fall within the ending altitude groupings (0–50 meters, 51–100 meters, etc.).

the last 200 years by immigrants from other regions, Spain (Usini) and Genoa (Carloforte). These founders did not possess the Gd^B or thalassemia genes. This reconstruction is further reinforced by the genealogical evidence; the few individuals with these traits can trace their ancestry to an earlier Sardinian origin (Siniscalco et al., 1966).

If the malarial hypothesis is accepted, then the genes for such abnormalities as Hb^S, Hb^E, thalassemia, and G6PD deficiency are an advantage for populations living in the area where malaria is endemic. The survival value of being a carrier living under malarious conditions outweighs the disadvantage. The selection for the heterozygote establishes a balanced polymorphism that maintains the abnormal gene at high frequencies. These relationships probably have existed for as long as humans have practiced agriculture in the tropics—about 3,000 to 4,000 years. The situation in the subtropics is more complex, and the insect vectors are different, as are the types of malarial disease that they transmit. The association between agriculture, settled village life, and malaria is probably the same, however. Skeletal remains from Greek Neolithic sites show extensive signs of bone modification associated with chronic anemia, and some investigators believe these conditions to be due to thalassemia, which is still found in many Mediterranean populations today (Angel, 1966). Because these same populations are those suffering from a high incidence of malaria, it is assumed that the early agriculturists brought about environmental changes in the subtropics that contributed to a rise in the disease. The links between human action, disease, and natural selection continue to this very day, as will be explored in later chapters. The numerous polymorphisms of the globins genes remains the best illustration of these links, as is further illustrated when a major selective force is reduced or removed entirely. Such a condition of rapid and radical change was created when hundreds of thousands of people were transported as slaves from their African homelands.

AFRICAN AMERICANS AND EVIDENCE OF GENE FREQUENCY CHANGES

The discovery and occupation of the Americas by Spaniards and Portuguese starting in the fifteenth century opened up a black page in human history. Not only were death and destruction wrought on native peoples of the New World, but about ten million Africans were enslaved and transported to North and South America. From about A.D. 1502 until the 1860s, slave ships landed their human cargos in ports stretching from Virginia in the north through the Caribbean to Brazil in the south. The sugar plantations of the Caribbean, with a high mortality and a need for a large labor force, absorbed most of the slaves. About 51 percent of the total of the slave imports over the three and half centuries were divided between the Caribbean colonies of Spain, Britain, and France. The largest number of slaves, 38 percent, were imported into the Portuguese colony of Brazil. The United States imported only 6 percent, and a majority were landed between 1720 and 1820.

Conditions were harshest, and mortality was highest, on the sugar plantations, requiring a continuous replacement of new slaves. It was many years before natural increase (an excess of births over deaths) began to stabilize populations in these areas. In contrast, the working conditions and less severe disease environments in the North American colonies (later the United States) fostered a rate of natural increase that gradually reduced the proportion of African-born slaves. Even during the peak of slave imports (1780 to 1800), those of African birth accounted for only 20 percent of the slave total (Fogel and Engerman, 1984). This uneven distribution of founders, and the varying rates of survival in the different colonies, contributed to the genetic diversity we find among African-American descendants today.

Most notable are the differing frequencies of the sickle cell trait. As noted above, African Americans in the United States have, on average, less than one-half to one-fourth of the Hb^s found among West African populations today (5–10 percent versus 20 percent). Assuming that the West Africans had this same frequency centuries ago when the slave trade began, then the reduction among their American-born descendants is highly significant. This reduction, occurring over the three and half centuries of their occupation in the New World, is rapid and may be accounted for either by admixture with Euro-Americans or by an elimination of the selective advantage of the carrier of the sickle cell trait. First, considering admixture that is estimated at about 20 percent, it should be noted that there is a considerable variation recorded among African-American communities; admixture is higher in large urban areas of the North and West while much lower among populations in the southeastern United States, especially along the Atlantic coast (Pollitzer, 1994). Admixture could account for some reduction in Hb^S since it is those very populations with fewer genes of European origin that retain the highest frequencies of African-derived genes. That is, hemoglobin C and S are more frequent in Charleston, South Carolina then in Pittsburgh, Pennsylvania.

This brings up the second possibility for explaining the decrease in hemoglobin S—the selection favoring the carrier. Malaria is probably not indigenous to the New World. But it has spread rapidly, mainly in South and Central America, since its introduction at the time of colonization. The major types, *vivax* and *falciparum*, have adapted to native mosquito species and still prove to be a major problem in many tropical areas. Also, malaria was once a major disease in the southeastern United States as well, but since the late nineteenth century, when mosquito eradication programs became widely applied, it has disappeared except for an occasional outbreak of "traveler" or "airport malaria." However, during earlier centuries the disease was a major health problem, rising to epidemic levels at times in some southern areas. Nowhere in North America, however, was malaria mortality comparable to the West African experience. In addition, the malaria was probably of the *vivax* type since this is the most frequent outside of the tropics (Harrison, 1978). There is a possibility that some *falciparum* appeared in the extreme southern fringes of the country, as suggested by health department reports. The coastal regions of South Carolina, for example, probably experienced this type (Pollitzer et al., 1966).

Consideration of malarial types is an important consideration because of the difference in mortality of each, *vivax* being least deadly. Most important, though, Africans appear to have an immunity to *vivax* because of their Duffy blood group type, discussed in the last chapter. Such a resistance would mean that, in areas where *vivax* was the predominant type, malarial infection could not act as a selective force favoring the carrier of the sickle cell trait if that person also had the Duffy blood group type Fy°. With mixed parasite types (*vivax* and *falciparum*) and with some gene flow into the African-American population, plus differences in climates and environments, malaria as a selective force diminished over the generations since arriving in North America. Declines in the Hb^S frequencies would be slow in the earlier generations, but the rate of decline would accelerate rapidly into the early twentieth century as mosquito control programs became effective and there were fewer outbreaks of malaria. The area where malaria persisted the longest, South Carolina, is home to African Americans with the highest Hb^s frequency today—the residents of the offshore Gullah Islands (Pollitzer, 1958). They are also one of the few groups in America with significant amounts of Hb^c, the allele otherwise restricted to a region around northern Ghana and Volta in West Africa. Questions of the distribution of sickle cell hemoglobin, both here and in the Old World, have become even more important with the rise of the newer genetic technology.

DNA MARKERS OF HUMAN VARIATION

With the use of endonucleases (restriction enzymes to cleave DNA at particular sites), as described in Chapter 2, an enormous amount of knowledge has been gained about the nucleotides of the noncoding sequences. This rapid advance in biotechnology has provided us with an ever-growing record of diversity at the DNA level, measured by the strings of base sequences cut into various lengths. These restriction fragment lengths vary from person to person, identifying a uniqueness of our individual genome, the so-called DNA fingerprints. Some, however, occur more commonly and are present at polymorphic frequencies which, in turn, differ among populations. Many RFLPs have proven useful as a type of genetic marker, particularly those in the noncoding DNA sequences in the region of major structural genes. Identifying and locating a major gene with its surrounding RFLPs may provide a means of population comparisons to record its distributions and relationships among populations. Most useful have been the genes for hemoglobin, especially the globin gene on chromosome 11 that shows seventeen sites of cleavage in the globin gene cluster. The degree of RFLP variation among several ethnic groups illustrates one of the earlier applications of restriction enzymes as discussed in Chapter 2 (refer to Table 2-4). Because of its broad distribution, the cleavage sites around the sickle cell gene have received the most attention.

Following the report by Kan and Dozy (1978) that there were at least two different RFLPs in the globin gene sequence of persons carrying the sickle cell trait, the search was intensified to discover other restriction sites that might be common to this gene sequence. Samples were taken from a broad spectrum of peoples, from Africa, Arabia, and India to the United States. Numerous RFLPs linked to the Hb^s were discovered but certain combinations appeared more frequently than others. Several of these cleavage sites (usually eight) were considered together in what is called haplotypes because of their close linkage (recall the blood group haplotypes). Many of the RFLP haplotypes occur only rarely but there are four major ones frequently found in populations with a high frequency of the sickle cell gene. These are named after the ethnic group in which the haplotype was discovered and where it is the predominant type: the African types of *Senegal, Benin,* and *Bantu,* and the *Asian* or Arab-Indian type, which is the predominant one found from eastern Arabia to India. A fourth African type, *Camaroon,* has been recently described. Table 4-7 lists these haplotypes for eight restriction sites indicated by a plus or minus if the fragment is cut at that point.

With this record of different haplotypes associated with the sickle cell gene a number of new questions emerge that relate to population movements, the spread of the gene, natural selection, and the possibility of independent mutation in the different populations. Considering the question of population movements first, we may look at the origins of Hb[s] and its frequency among modern-day African Americans. Reviews of their African origins (Curtin, 1969) show that regions within a 2,000 mile range from north to south supplied differing proportions of slaves for the North American market (Figure 4-7). The majority (70 percent) came from an area defined by the borders of modern-day Ghana and Nigeria, the area where the *Benin* type predominates. The balance came from the Senegal region to the northwest and the Bantu area in the south. The result is that most African Americans with SCT have the *Benin* type (Antonarakis et al., 1984). In addition, since Senegal was the major supplier to South Carolina for a time, the Senegal haplotype is found more frequently there than among African Americans today in Virginia (Labie et al., 1986). By contrast, the Bantu or Central African haplotype is the predominant type among sickle cell carriers in Brazil, reflecting the region of African origins of modern-day descendants because of the trade routes established by the Portuguese between their colonies in Africa (Angola) and Brazil (Zago et al., 1992). Differences are also seen in the Caribbean as a reflection of its population history, and comparisons of three national groups of African descendants show these contrasting frequencies of sickle cell haplotypes in Table 4-8.

TABLE 4-7 Restriction Site Haplotypes for the Beta Hemoglobin S Gene

HAPLOTYPES[a]	RESTRICTION SITES[b]	
Senegal	− + − + +	+ + +
Benin	− − − − +	+ − +
Bantu	− + − − −	+ + +
Arab-Indian	+ + − + +	+ + −

[a]Haplotypes found in populations in three African regions, Arabia, and India.
[b]Combinations of DNA sites cut by restriction enzymes above and below the beta hemoglobin gene S. The + indicates a fragment cut at this site and − no reaction to the enzyme.

Sources: Data selected from Livingstone, 1989, and Williams, 1985.

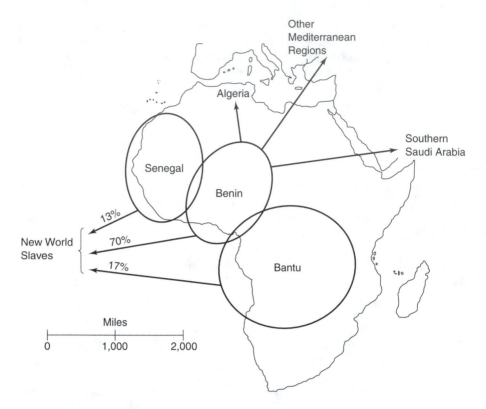

FIGURE 4-7   Origin and migration of African groups carrying three different Hb^s chromosomes (area of origin indicated by ellipses). Each chromosome, or haplotype, is defined by a distinctive pattern of RFLPs in the 60-kb length of DNA surrounding the β-globin locus. A separate mutation of Hb^A → Hb^s occurred in each background haplotype sometime in the past and is detectable today by restriction enzyme analysis. (From Mange and Mange, 1990, Sinauer Assoc. Reprinted by permission.)

A second major question relates to the origin of such haplotype diversity; there are over twenty for the restriction sites along the sixty-eight kilo-bases of the beta globin gene cluster. Most Hb^s haplotypes are rare, present in less than polymorphic frequencies in a few populations, but the wide distribution of the four major types, three African and one Asian, raises the possibility of differing population histories and perhaps contrasts in the expression of the sickle cell

TABLE 4-8   Haplotypes of the Sickle Cell Trait among People of African Descent (in percent of those with SCT)

HAPLOTYPE	JAMAICA	UNITED STATES	BRAZIL
Senegal	10	15	1
Benin	72	62	26
Bantu (CAR)	17	18	73

trait. The existence of these RFLPs in the beta-Hb cluster have been explained by independent mutations. That is, the Hb^s allele arose by mutation in each of four regions at different times (Hill and Wainscoat, 1986). There was the same substitution in the globin gene DNA sequence (valine for glutamic acid at position 6), but different replacements occurred in the non-coding flanking sequences. The hemoglobin of carriers of the sickle cell gene enjoys a degree of resistance to the malarial parasite, as explained above, regardless of haplotype. The homozygotes differ, however, in the severity of sickle cell disease (SCD). The time when a sickling crisis occurs and the clinical course of the disease varies between the haplotypes. The Asia (*Arab-Indian*) type is a milder form, with fewer sickling crises and a longer life span, probably due to a retention of fetal hemoglobin gene activity. The persistence of fetal hemoglobin into adulthood moderates the influence of Hb^s molecules. Red-blood-cell–carrying fetal hemoglobin reduces the rate formation of the stiff fibrous bundles when oxygen is taken up by the tissues from the globin S strands, thereby preventing distortion of the cell. The *Senegal* S haplotype also has a milder form of SCD, particularly in comparison to the *Benin* type; *Senegal* S homozygotes retain a higher percentage of fetal hemoglobin, as do the Asia types, and they also have a lower sickle cell count. These differences in the expression of SCD, along with the retention of a resistance to malaria, tend to support an argument for independent mutation in each of the four major areas.

The question of sickle cell origin is by no means settled. Another perspective is that, because the beta globin gene cluster region is subject to high rates of recombination and given that the Hb^s gene is under intense selection favoring the heterozygote, the beta globin underwent only a single mutation somewhere in the Mideast. It then spread rapidly with the advance of agriculture. Through population movement into new areas and diffusion between adjacent populations, Hb^s became established at high frequencies following the increase in malaria as a major disease. The various haplotypes we record today may be the result of recombinations from the original haplotype, probably the Asian (Arab-Indian) type (Livingstone, 1989). This explanation of the rapid spread of an advantageous gene in malarious environments offers a plausible counterargument to the multiple mutation hypothesis, and only additional studies may offer a test of the hypothesis. But the evidence we have to date does illustrate the importance of recording RFLP haplotypes around major genes and opens the way for new applications of genetic data. In addition to the genetic code of the structural genes we now have markers that can broadly describe population movements and their modern origins.

Gene Geography

Technology has been advancing rapidly since the earliest applications of restriction enzymes to the studies of human DNA sequences. The formation of the Human Genome Project (HGP) in 1990 with the goal of identifying each gene location on its chromosome and then sequencing the entire three billion nucleotide base pairs of the human genome is an example. The mapping of many important genetic loci has been accomplished—4,000 as of 1995. The sequences of 36 million base pairs have been recorded, only a small fraction of the total, but the rate of sequencing is accelerating as labs around the world improve their methods (Guyer and Collins, 1995; Venter et al., 1996). The biomedical benefits derived from such an ambitious undertaking are many, not the least of them a clearer understanding of gene function. The HGP, as originally conceived, will result in "model genomes," a composite of DNA sequences gained from samples of a few individuals, mainly European. The project, however, does not include a study of sequence variation at the population level that reveals differences in the frequency of occurrence of certain DNA polymorphisms. At this point in time, 150 years after Mendel's discovery, we should not have to be reminded that there is a broad range of genetic variation throughout the species and across generations. We are not variants of some "standard" or core type of *Homo sapiens* genome (Kidd et al., 1993; and Weiss, 1993). Recall the range of genetic markers described in the last chapter and the hemoglobin polymorphisms discussed above.

Considering that much of this genetic diversity may be underrepresented or even lost if sampling is limited to persons of European descent, it is essential to broaden the genome record to include representative samples of non-Europeans.[4] Further, anthropological studies over this century have identified many small, relatively isolated indigenous populations that have maintained unique languages and cultural traditions. Groups scattered about the vast Amazon basin of South America are examples, and people living in the more remote parts of New Guinea provide others. In more accessible areas there are many small populations that have managed to retain an ethnic identity despite sustained contact with influence and pressure from larger national communities. Tribal groups in Africa and hunter-horticultural groups in Southeast Asia are other examples of indigenous people that come to mind. But this only notes the "exotic" populations that are rapidly being absorbed; the millions of people divided into ethnic groups within Asia are also an important source of information on population diversity. Such groups must be considered as breeding populations if any human genome study encompasses questions of genetic variability distribution.

To meet this requirement, a group of anthropological geneticists have come together to plan a program to collect and disseminate knowledge of DNA diversity. This program, *The Human Genome Diversity Project*, has as its goal to collect blood samples for genetic analysis from a wide range of indigenous peoples. The focus is on geographically isolated people of distinct culture and

---

[4]I use "non-European" here to contrast the data sources of the ongoing genome research since it is difficult to select an unambiguous name or label to identify populations. Ethnic group, indigenous, aboriginal, exotic peoples, or a geographic label are terms that have been used by different authors, but these have been inconsistently applied. I avoid racial classifications for the reasons discussed in the first chapter.

language who, it is expected, will yield more information about diversity than large genetically admixed urban communities. Europeans, Euro-Americans, and African Americans are well represented in samples and are under study in numerous laboratories, but most indigenous peoples are fast disappearing as distinct populations. The goal is to add them to the DNA record to broaden the sample for the human species, a kind of "gene geography."

Since as early as 1984, several laboratories have been collecting blood samples from numerous indigenous groups of Africa, South America, and New Guinea. Blood cells, usually lymphoblasts, are grown in specially prepared cultures and multiplied many times, forming perpetual cell lines to serve as a resource for present and future DNA analysis. This DNA resource provides a data bank of genetic markers of significantly different population clusters around the world (Cavalli-Sforza et al., 1986). New blood samples are being added each year in addition to the expansion of the number of DNA markers that are recorded, increasing our knowledge of human polymorphism. With systematic analysis of RFLPs (restriction length polymorphisms) of these DNA samples, as described in Chapter 2, for example, it is now possible to discuss global patterns of DNA marker variation. Differences in short fragment sequences, deletions, or even single nucleotide changes in the intron regions offer an excellent data resource for population comparisons. As new genes are mapped to their chromosome loci, the surrounding noncoding base sequences are recorded, revealing that many are present at polymorphic frequencies.

A study of three Native American populations typed by thirty RFLPs of nuclear DNA is an example. Compared with a mixed sample of Europeans, the Native Americans showed a range of differences and less average heterozygosity (Kidd et al., 1991). The record of 100 DNA polymorphisms gained from five populations on four continents demonstrates even more emphatically the need for spreading the human genome study more widely across diverse populations. Bowcock and associates started with 47 markers and then expanded the number to 100 four years later (Bowcock et al., 1987, 1991). A majority of the markers (86) were bi-allelic and 14 were multi-allelic. These RFLPs were taken from clusters about the loci of well-studied genes that code for a variety of proteins from hormones and haploglobins to enzymes and receptors. Table 4-9 offers a selection of ten DNA markers as examples. The gene abbreviation and product is listed as is the gene's locus; e.g., TH, the gene coding for an enzyme, tyrosine hydroxylase, is located on position 15.5 of the short arm (p) of chromosome 11. The restriction enzyme, Taq 1, cuts the DNA flanking this gene into three fragments, 4.3, 2.3, and 2.0 kilobases long (see Alleles column). The next five columns list the frequencies with which these restriction fragments occur in each of the five population samples. The 4.3 fragment was found in 11 percent of the Pygmies of the Central African Republic, 45 percent in Melanesia, and 5 percent in the Chinese sample, for example. Considering the RFLPs at all ten loci, some alleles (fragments) occur at nearly 100 percent or are absent altogether.

What this means is that mutations, probably deletion types, arose in certain base sequences within the noncoding flanking sequences of a gene.

TABLE 4-9 Frequency of Ten Selected DNA Markers

GENE	LOCUS[1]	ENZYME[2]	ALLELES[3]	CAR PY[4]	ZAIRE PY[5]	MELANES[6]	CHINESE[7]	EURO[8]
APOB (apolipoprotein)	2p24	EcoRI	14	0.18	0.07	0.00	0.32	0.20
			12, 2.1	0.82	0.93	1.00	0.68	0.80
sample sizes				38	59	23	44	40
SST (somatostatin)	3q28	EcoRI	12	0.60	0.76	0.41	0.84	0.91
			6	0.40	0.24	0.59	0.16	0.09
sample sizes				35	51	22	51	360
ADH2 (alcohol dehydrogenase)	4q21	RsaI	1.25, 1.5	1.00	1.00	0.70	0.18	0.67
			0.58, 1.5	0.00	0.00	0.30	0.82	0.33
sample sizes				17	22	23	67	36
GHR (growth hormone receptor)	5	BstN1	1.4, 2.1	0.15	0.35	0.03	0.06	0.00
			0.6	0.85	0.65	0.97	0.94	1.00
sample sizes				88	91	32	62	66
TH (tyrosine hydroxylase)	11p15.5	Taq1	4.3	0.11	0.07	0.45	0.05	0.16
			2.0, 2.3	0.89	0.93	0.55	0.95	0.84
sample sizes				37	57	22	60	92
APOA1 (apolipoprotein A-1)	11q23	XmnI	8.3	0.40	0.43	0.52	0.59	0.82
			8.1	0.17	0.03	0.10	0.08	0.00
			6.6	0.42	0.54	0.38	0.33	0.18
sample sizes				40	35	21	83	78
IGF1 (insulin-like growth factor 1)	12q23	HindIII	6.3	0.00	0.00	0.07	0.18	0.20
			5.8	1.00	1.00	0.93	0.82	0.80
sample sizes				43	49	27	17	174
RB1 (retinoblastoma)	13q14.2	BAMIII	4.4	0.96	0.79	0.50	0.37	0.23
			2.3, 2.1	0.04	0.21	0.50	0.63	0.77
sample sizes				53	57	32	106	48
HP (haptoglobin)	16q22	BamHI	9.2	0.62	0.55	0.56	0.64	0.57
			7.5	0.38	0.45	0.44	0.36	0.43
sample sizes				47	55	32	88	58
GH (growth hormone)	17q22	BgIII	13.0	0.04	0.09	0.31	0.54	0.32
		10.5	0.96	0.91	0.69	0.46	0.68	
sample sizes				47	81	32	87	111

1. Chromosome and locus.
2. Restriction enzyme.
3. Kilobases of fragments cut by enzyme.
4. Biaka pygmies of Central African Republic.
5. Mbuti pygmies of Zaire.
6. Nasioi Melanesians from Bougainville, Solomon Islands.
7. Chinese residents of San Francisco born in mainland China.
8. Europeans or Euro-Americans (northern or central European origins).

Source: Data selected from Bowcock et al., 1991.

When a restriction enzyme (the Taq 1 of our example) is applied to a sample of DNA, three different bp lengths are cut, since the 2.0 and 2.3 bp alleles are so close their frequencies are counted together as a single allele. This allele is the most frequent type found in four of the five populations, ranging from 0.84 to 0.95. In the Melanesian sample the alleles are nearly equal, 0.45 and 0.55. The other RFLPs also show differences among the five populations. The explanation for allele diversity may relate to a long history of population isolation and variable mutation rates; selection probably can be ruled out since these flanking sequences of DNA probably do not influence the gene expression. Comparisons of RFLPs, then, offer an important series of markers for use in the comparison of population relationships. Comparisons of all 100 markers by distance formula enable the construction of a tree of descent leading back to a hypothesized common lineage (Felsenstein, 1973). As expected, Melanesians are further removed from the European branch than Chinese, and the Pygmy sample is at a greater distance still (Figure 4-8).

FIGURE 4-8   Tree Diagram Estimating Genetic Distances between Five Population Groups. (Data from Bowcock, et al., 1991)

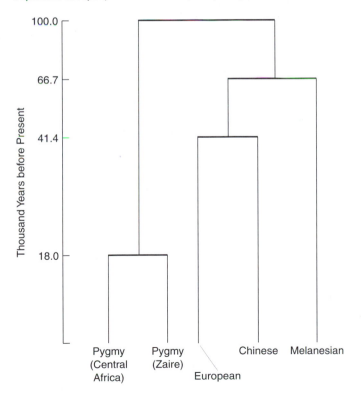

Still another set of nuclear DNA markers is provided by the variable number of tandem repeats (VNTR) in the noncoding flanking sequences. They may vary at polymorphic frequencies and, if considered together with adjacent markers within the gene cluster, are useful for postulating population origin and dispersal. The gene (CD4) that encodes for a glycoprotein on the surface of the T lymphocyte offers such an example. Located on the short arm (*p*) of the twelfth chromosome, the CD4 has two regions of polymorphism of interest (Figure 4-9). The first is a series of short tandem repeats of

FIGURE 4-9   Two Polymorphic Markers in the Noncoding Region of the CD4, Chromosome 12.

This schematic diagram represents a segment of chromosome 12 that carries the exons (1, 2, and 3) of the CD4 gene. Also shown is the noncoding region that contains a region of short tandem repeats of the TTTTC base series and the Alu series, a string of 285 bp. (Data from Tishkoff, et al., 1996)

Polymorphism 1
The TTTTC is a base sequence that is repeated from four to fifteen times. Adding the products of flanking sequences and those from amplification by PCR (polymerase chain reaction), the total base pairs will vary from 80 bp for a *four repeat allele* to 135 bp for a *fifteen repeat allele*. These short tandem repeat polymorphisms (STRP) vary widely among populations tested.
Part A shows a STRP of 110 bp in contrast to a STRP of 90 in Part B.

Polymorphism 2
The Alu, a string of from 250–300 bp repeated up to 500,000 times throughout the human genome, has a deletion type mutation at the CD4 locus on chromosome 12. This results in deletion of 256 bp from the more typical 285 bp represented by Alu(+) in Part A and Alu(-) in Part B representing the deletion.

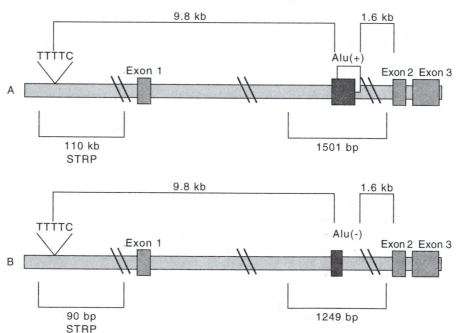

the bases *TTTTC* located before exon 1. This string of bases is repeated from 4 to 15 times, which, with flanking sequences, results in 80 bp for a tandem repeat of 4. For 15 repeats, there are 135 bp and there are 10 other base pair lengths recorded between these two extremes. Counting the number of base pairs as alleles, there are as many as 12 found among 13 African populations; fewer alleles are found in the Native American, Asian, and European samples (a total of 32 non-African populations). These data are used in conjunction with a second polymorphism, the Alu deletion in the flanking sequence before exon 2 of the CD4 gene.

The Alu cluster (named for the Alu 1 enzyme) is a fragment of 250–310 bps in length repeated throughout the human genome about 500,000 times widely dispersed among all of the 46 chromosomes. In the case of the flanking sequence of the CD4 gene, there has been a mutation that deleted 256 bp (Alu–) of the 285 bp (Alu+). Because this 256 bp deletion has not been found in the great apes, the Alu+ is considered the ancestral type and the mutation is likely to have occurred after the divergence of the human ancestral lineage from the chimps some four to six million years ago, plus or minus a million years (Wolpoff, 1996). Such a time frame for the divergence of human ancestors from the great apes has also been used to estimate a time of modern *Homo sapiens* migrating out of Africa as described in Chapter 1, and it is applied here with the use of the two polymorphisms of the CD4 gene cluster.

Both markers (haplotypes of the STRPs and the Alu–) were typed in unrelated individuals of 42 geographically dispersed populations, and the frequency with which the different STRPs occurred with the Alu+ or Alu– were recorded (Tishkoff et al., 1996). The deletion Alu– rarely occurs in Asians, Pacific Islanders, or Native Americans, less than 2 percent, and when it occurred there was the 90 bp STRP. The Alu– is frequent among Europeans (25–30 percent) and Africans (7–28 percent) and appeared most often with the 85 bp STRP. Considering all haplotypes, Africans have a greater variation in contrast to all others. Because of this haplotype variation at the CD4 locus, the explanation of recent origins of non-Africans is proposed as the most acceptable by Tishkoff and associates. They offer an estimate of 120,000 years before present for the earliest modern humans in Africa and about 90,000 years as the earliest outside of Africa (Middle East). These estimated dates coincide with those derived by mtDNA analysis and relate well to a presumed appearance of modern human fossilized skeletons. However, such a reconstruction of human ancestry is not universally accepted, as noted earlier, and depends on many assumptions discussed below. Ancestral origins and times of migration aside, the use of sequences of noncoding DNA as RFLPs, STRP, deletions, or combinations as haplotypes provides some useful markers of population relationships. Even the uniqueness of certain of the VNTRs has proven useful in the identification of individuals.

DNA Fingerprints

The use of various radioactively labeled DNA probes (short segments of single-stranded DNA) has provided an even finer focus of our view of DNA polymorphisms.[5] These probes will bind with the other DNA wherever there are complementary base sequences in the noncoding regions or minisatellites around the structural genes. Each chromosome has many repeats of these minisatellites, and mutations, unequal crossovers during DNA replication, contribute to polymorphisms as we have described above. Because of the thousands of repeats, the Alu for example, and the variations in base pair spacing, it is highly improbable (once in tens of millions) that any two people will have the same sequences. This means that when a sample of DNA is chemically extracted from cells, treated, and subjected to electrophoresis, the smaller fragments move more rapidly than the larger ones and after a time lapse all fragments will be separated according to size.[6] These fragment groups are fixed in place on a paper (membrane), ready for analysis, and each individual's DNA will produce a unique pattern.

A final step is to render the strands radioactive. Radioactive DNA probes are washed over this paper and the probes will attach to every fragment where there is a complementary base sequence. This hybridization of probe and satellite DNA results in differing radioactively labeled fragment lengths. These are then detected by exposing film over several hours to the radioactive labels. This results in a series of dark bands on the film very much like the bar codes seen on almost all items on sale in markets today. The band positions of the hybrid DNA fragments on the film have the same relationships as the fragments on the electrophoresis gel plant. Figure 4-10 diagrams this process, with person A showing only a single DNA fragment repeat between the enzyme cuts in contrast to persons B, C, and D. The DNA fragment of A will migrate furthest in a given time.

These regions, repeat sequences or "minisatellites" in the noncoding regions (introns), are hypervariable and will result in unique "bar codes." Jeffreys, a British geneticist studying restriction enzymes and DNA probes, recognized the potential applications for human identification (Jeffreys et al., 1985). Jeffreys and his colleagues isolated a fragment of DNA near the myoglobin gene containing a 33 base sequence, which was repeated more than 20 times within the fragment. The repetitiveness of this minisatellite attracted their attention and, after cloning, a probe specific for the region was produced. Applying the probe by methods described in Chapter 2 to other DNA sequences, they found that the minisatellite was repeated fre-

---

[5]Nucleotides with a phosphorus 32 (a radioactive isotope) are added to short segments of complimentary DNA (ᶜDNA).

[6]The process is multistaged: (1) DNA is chemically extracted and cut at various sites by a selected enzyme; (2) These short segments are separated into single-stranded units; (3) the DNA single strands are subjected to electrophoresis.

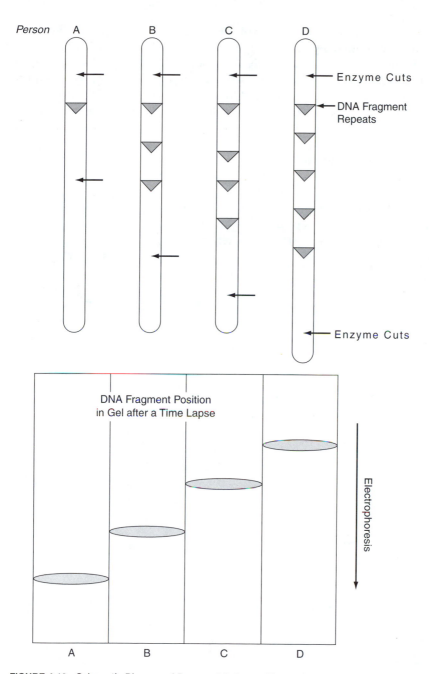

FIGURE 4-10 **Schematic Diagram of Fragment Polymorphism.**

quently throughout the entire genome. Comparison of samples taken from several people showed a pattern of hypervariable regions specific to the individual (Figure 4-11). That is, the alignment of the pattern of dark bands on the film, the regions of hybridization with the radioactive probe, differed for every person tested except in the case of monozygotic (identical) twins (Gill et al., 1985). There was nearly 100 percent heterozygosity in small populations, and a study of four generations of an inbred lineage demonstrated that the bands followed the laws of Mendelian inheritance, but new bands frequently appeared in children because of crossover during replication (Vogel and Motulsky, 1986). This work opened up an entirely new avenue of human identification we now call "DNA fingerprinting."

The DNA identification method has been applied many times since it was first used by Jeffreys to settle an issue of maternity in Britain in 1985. A young Ghanaian boy, living with his father in that country, wanted to migrate

FIGURE 4-11   DNA Fingerprints: A Schematic Illustration.

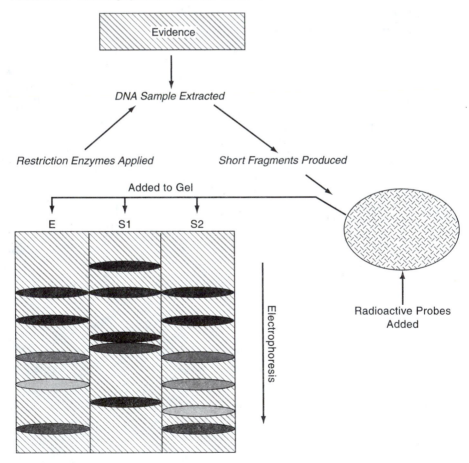

to Britain to live with his mother. His plans were blocked by immigration officials, who claimed that the woman claimed as his mother was, in fact, his aunt. Imposing new restrictive immigration policies that allowed admittance of only the biological children of parents in legal residence, the officials refused to grant a visa. Jeffreys was asked to help settle the issue of the mother or aunt relationship. DNA samples were taken from the undisputed offspring of the woman who were living with her in Britain, and these were compared to the boy in Ghana. The closeness of the hypervariable regions studied demonstrated that all of the children had the same biological parents. The woman was, in fact, the mother, as she had claimed, and the visa was granted so the boy from Ghana could be reunited with his mother in London.

This case gained considerable publicity and drew the attention of the police in Leicester County, England, who had tried in vain to solve a series of brutal rapes and murders of young girls. The police had samples of the murderer's semen from the girls' clothing and thought that it might provide evidence to help convict a confessed suspect. When blood and semen were compared in what was the first application of DNA fingerprinting to forensics, Jeffreys showed that the suspect could not be the killer, but that the same man had killed both girls. Still without a solution but with a growing confidence in this new technology, the police proposed to collect blood samples from every male within the districts surrounding the locations where the bodies had been discovered. This makes for a very unusual crime story, related in all its police and forensic details by Joseph Wambaugh in his novel *The Blooding*. The blood tests could only be voluntary, since, under British law, testing could not be compulsory. Most males cooperated; eventually over 5,000 were eliminated as suspects, and in the process DNA fingerprinting acquired the image of an infallible tool of science. It was this image of scientific infallibility that eventually gave the murderer away; his fear of the test was so strong that he paid a friend to assume his identity and take the test for him. When this was revealed months later, the police had their suspect and an eventual conviction. Since then, DNA has been more and more widely applied to convict the guilty or exonerate the innocent—but not without some mistakes and errors along the way, as labs struggled to improve techniques and develop standards for comparison.

The matching of the VNTRs between an evidence sample and a suspect's is not as simple and straightforward as implied. Misalignment of the gels or ignoring of certain bands has led to equivocal results; sometimes mismatches are made, or two individual samples are said to be from the same person when they are not. The famous case of an abandoned stillborn baby illustrates one type of error. A female insurance executive in Maryland left her car to be towed to a garage for repairs. The mechanic claimed to have found the body of a dead infant in the back seat, and examination of tissue samples showed, according to lab reports, that the car's owner was the mother. Despite obstetrical evidence that the woman had not given birth, the lab's DNA match pointed to the infant–mother relationship. The origin of the dead infant was not resolved, but the obstetrical examination proved that the DNA match was wrong. Months later, the woman gave birth to an infant, and sonographic records showed that she had conceived about two weeks before the infant's body had been found.

What the problem was with the laboratory's procedure has never been revealed, but enough other errors have been made by other facilities to raise questions about test standards. The Orange County, California sheriff's department sent 50 samples of blood and semen from 20 individuals to three reputable laboratories engaged in DNA testing. One lab wrongly identified 1 of 50, and another 1 of 44, while the third lab could only correctly identify 37 of the samples. Even the FBI had some difficulty in standardizing methods in the newly established DNA lab in the late 1980s. Tests were carried out on 225 agents, but on retesting, 37 samples could not be matched with the originals. Such results have raised questions about the fallibility of the DNA test methods and have caused a move toward setting standards for labs engaged in forensics work. The main issue remains one of near blind faith that the public has in the complex science of human genetics, as discussed by Hubbard and Wald (1993).

Comparisons of VNTRs between samples can rule out identity—the possibility that they came from the same person—because of a broad difference in banding patterns in the gel. However, establishing that a single individual's VNTRs are present in both samples is a matter of probability—the chance that two individuals could have the same banding pattern. Frequently, this probability is stated in terms of one in ten or a hundred million—very long odds that have had impressive impacts in criminal cases. Such probabilities depend on the data base from which sample VNTR banding patterns are taken. The frequencies of the occurrence of DNA fragments, produced by restriction enzymes, are measured in several population samples. Usually four or five enzymes are used, and averaging the results provides a reference base to calculate probabilities. The problem is which populations to select and how they should be grouped in a society of such diverse origins as ours. The establishment of data bases—Caucasoid, African American, Asian, and Hispanic—are assumed to provide representative samples, adequate for forensic comparisons. If a suspect is identified as Hispanic then the DNA sample refers to the Hispanic data base, Caucasoid to Caucasoid, etc. The assumption is that the data base is derived from a homogeneous, randomly mating population and that randomly selected samples are representative of the whole.

This practice has been vigorously challenged (see Lewontin and Hartl, 1991). Lewontin and Hartl argued that the race/ethnic data bases have been derived from heterogeneous groups, e.g., African Americans, Hispanics, and European. They used frequencies of several blood groups in Europeans as examples that stressed differences between Italians and Poles. Because of the mixed origins of Euro-Americans, they contended that the VNTRs' frequency estimates are liable to serious errors. Even more serious errors would be found in the other ethnic data bases. Their objections to probability calculations were answered by Chakraborty and Kidd (1991), who argued that the samples were sufficiently homogeneous and mating was sufficiently random to provide the essential reference data bases. Though the exchange between the authors continues, they are not that far apart in agreement on the value of DNA analysis for forensics; it is a valuable method of identification. The disagreement is founded largely on how to calculate the probability of a random match and the choice of ethnic data bases (Lewontin and Hartl, 1992).

GENETIC MARKERS AT THE DNA LEVEL: SOME CONCLUSIONS

The development of technology to identify the finer structure of DNA has led to a multitude of population studies. Distinguishing between populations on the basis of various markers within the noncoding regions has added a new dimension to recording human diversity. Before conclusions are reached about origins and ancestral relationships, caution is warranted, however. The high mutation rates of VNTRs, about 7 percent, and the frequency of crossover and recombination, contribute to an uncertainty and can lead to wrong conclusions. The lower mutation rates of STRPs (0.12 percent) cause them to be more useful in cross-population comparisons; that is, these markers of shorter DNA repeats are applicable to a longer time depth, while the VNTRs are limited to a more recent time frame. The 15–20,000-year separation of Native Americans from eastern Siberian origins may be measured by STRPs in contrast to the few generations of Euro-Americans and their European ancestors. The increased use of single nucleotide polymorphisms (SNPs) for population comparisons have added a new dimension in the study of identity by descent. These three types of nuclear DNA markers, together with an increasing variety of restriction enzymes, provide anthropology with a rapidly expanding store of data. There are 20,000 markers recorded for Europeans, the most thoroughly studied of any regional group. As more laboratories become involved, the store of data is growing for other ethnic groups as well.

Different laboratories are studying different sets of markers, resulting in little population overlap. If such a situation continues to exist, there will be a vast store of knowledge about human nuclear DNA variants, but scant basis for population comparisons. It is comparable to a hypothetical example: If, over the last fifty years, one lab had recorded only the ABO blood group in Great Britain while another lab recorded the Rhesus types in eastern Europe, the result would be knowledge of the ABO in one area and Rh types in another, and there would be no data for comparison. A more relevant example is the paucity of data on the haplotypes of the HLA system among people of African descent in contrast to the wealth of information that exists for

Europeans. Such an information gap has impeded the search for suitable transplant donors among different ethnic groups.

Because of this problem of investigative diversity, there has been an appeal for marker standardization (Kidd and Kidd, 1996). Though there is no reason for preference of one marker over another, except for ease of typing and utility for population studies, they offer a recommendation. They suggest three markers (PLAT, HOXB, and DRD2) that have already proven useful in population studies, in addition to the CD4 described above. These markers, together with those for the alpha and beta globin chains, provide an excellent start in standardization. The authors conclude their appeal with a warning that "Our history as a species is written in our DNA sequence and in the distribution of variation in that sequence within and among human populations. However, we need a concerted, coordinated effort to study enough of that message that we truly understand it and are not led astray by fragments read out of context" (Kidd and Kidd, 1996:12).

That such an appeal is necessary after more than a decade and a half is, I believe, a testimony to the rapid application of a new, complex technology and the confusion that has been generated. It is a prime example of technology outrunning interpretive frameworks. We simply have acquired so much data on human biological diversity that we cannot place it within a frame of historical reference—the record of species origin and dispersal gained from the fossil and archeological record. At least, not yet. We are trying to survey the human landscape at the submicroscopic level, nearly an atom at a time. Imagine doing a survey of a forest for marketable timber content by counting leaves instead of whole trees. In the process, the intervening sequences (the noncoding regions where the markers are identified) are assumed to be neutral in that they do not contribute to the expression of the gene sequences. There may be some doubts about this neutrality; consider the variation in clinical problems of the sickle cell hemoglobin haplotypes.

The DNA-based studies, to date, document the depth of similarities among peoples of the entire planet. These studies emphasize the shallowness of our perceived differences based on simple visual appraisals of skin, hair, size and shape. The record of DNA markers does not tell us how we gained certain of these complex traits—how we acquire a certain size and appearance, a skin color, or rates of growth. Simply, the environmental influences on expressions of DNA codes are little known, with few exceptions. We explore these influences on human diversity in the next chapter.

5

Traits of Complex Inheritance

In the preceding chapters I have described some traits of simple inheritance, phenotypes of blood types, enzymes, and hemoglobins that are determined by single genes. Also, markers of RFLPs were added to the list of genetic polymorphisms. Though such polymorphisms are now known to vary widely among population groupings, they have seldom been used as identity labels for ethnic groups or races. Rather, the classic race labels continue to be used to identify a group of individuals from which blood or tissue samples are collected for genetic study. Differences in gene frequencies are then compared on the basis of such race/ethnic group labels. The inherent inconsistencies of such a method are many. Besides the application of a discredited classification system, the major problem is that the use of easily perceived traits ignores the broad and continuous variability of the traits that is strongly influenced by environmental factors. Traits such as skin color, face form, body size, and head shape have all been applied to the classification of "races," but similarities do not necessarily denote common ancestry or membership in a particular "racial stock." Similarities of traits among different populations mean much more.

These traits are the result of a complex of environmental forces interacting with the products of several genes over the course of one's lifetime, especially during growth. Such traits are described as multifactorial or polygenic and under environmental influence produce continuously varying phenotypes, as is well illustrated by the diversity of human body form and size. Factors of climate or diet influence development and growth. Though a person may inherit groups of genes that could promote the development of a large size leading to a tall adult, poor nutrition or disease occurring at critical growth stages would limit size below one's maximum potential. Also, there is individual variation in size and form even among sibs because of unique individual responses to similar conditions. These and other phenotypes of complex inheritance vary over a continuous broad range within a population, and there is a great deal of overlap between ethnic groups. The same applies to that favorite label, skin color. A number of enzymes and hormones affect the synthesis of melanin (skin pigment); that, in turn, is affected by energy in the ultraviolet portion of the solar radiation spectrum. There are numerous widely dispersed populations in Africa, India, and Australia with darkly pigmented skin. While they differ in frequencies of many of the gene markers, skin pigmentation is one of the few common phenotypes that they share. This chapter will describe the range of variation of such complex traits and will explore the origins and meanings of such variability.

HUMAN FORM AND ITS VARIABILITY

The different sizes, shapes, and colors of the world's peoples are often described as representative of certain distinct groups, each possessing special typical features. Seldom do we appreciate that the range of human diversity extends in gradual degrees throughout the species. The human form varies over a wide range of sizes and shapes, and there is considerable difference among human populations living today. From pygmoid peoples to tall, slender Nilotics of East Africa, and from Eskimos to southern Europeans, we find that the ratio between stature and body weight differs in ways that may reflect environmental conditions of climate, diet, and disease as well as that of genetic influence.

Body Size

The height of normal adults in our species ranges from around four feet to well over six feet. These limits are exceeded occasionally but seem to represent a norm for modern stature. This variation in human stature is distributed among the world's peoples in some very interesting ways. Though there appears to be a tendency toward taller people farther from the equator (as in northwestern Europe) and shorter people nearer the equator, numerous exceptions exist. There are many examples of tall people living close to very short or even pygmoid groups. For instance, the Mbuti Pygmies of the Ituri Forest in the Congo live just a few hundred miles from a group, the Watusi, considered to be among the tallest people in the world. Another contrast in body size is seen among Native Americans of the Southwest; Hopi of northern Arizona average four to five inches shorter than the Papago who live about 200 miles to the south. Every racial or ethnic group seems to have its tall and short people, and stature covers such a broad range that general statements are precluded. Figure 5-1 offers diagrams depicting mean statures for several populations of our species. Though the Pygmy is at the low end of the range, several other populations have comparably short stature.

In all populations there is a range of sizes—people who are taller or shorter than average—just as there are differences of sizes among siblings. These differences reflect an influence of the genetic component as described later in this chapter under variations in growth. One of the most clearly defined differences in size attributable to genetic influence is seen when comparisons are made between adult males and females. Males tend to be larger than females in any population, and though there often are taller females and shorter males, average male size exceeds female body size by 5 to 10 percent (see Figure 5-2). This difference between the sexes is referred to as sexual dimorphism and refers to the many other contrasts in body size and proportions as well as to stature.

Body Form

A relatively simple way of determining body proportion is to compare a person's standing height with his or her sitting height. The *cormic index*[1] or ratio between the two measurements indicates proportion of stature owing to the legs or the trunk. In populations with relatively short torsos and long legs, such as the Australian Aboriginals and many Africans, the cormic index is less than 50 (a ratio of 50 would indicate the legs and trunk plus head were approximately the same length). The tall stature of Nilotic groups in East Africa north of Lake Victoria (Dinka, Shilluk, Nuer) is due more to their very long legs than to trunk length, whereas most descriptions of the Pygmies note their elongated trunks and short legs and long arms. Many Chinese populations, as well as groups of Native Americans, have cormic indices as high as 54 percent, which indicates rather long trunks and short legs (Figure 5-3). Likewise, the ratio of arm to leg length (intermembral index) indicates another bodily proportion and shows some population differences. Though many populations show a tendency toward a particular body form, characteristics of shape are not reliable as a single racial criterion. A case in point is provided by the results of an extensive anthropometric survey of Australian Aborigines. Abbie (1975) reported extremes in adult stature of 146 to 190.6 cm for males and 137.6 to 174.3 cm for females; the cormic index ranged from 40.8 to 53.4 cm for males and 41.3 to 54.3 cm for females. Some had very long legs while

---

[1]Proportions of body length are easily measured by dividing sitting height by standing height. This gives an index that describes the contribution of the head and trunk length to total body height, which is in the area of 50 percent.

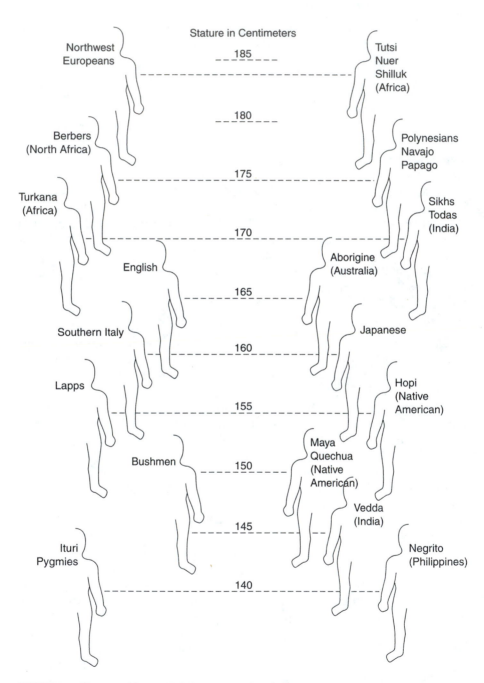

FIGURE 5-1 Diagram of Stature Variation between Populations.

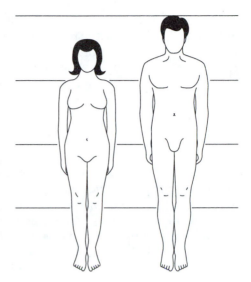

FIGURE 5-2 Sexual Dimorphism: Differences in Size, Shape, and Proportion of Male and Female Body Form.

This drawing depicts the average 5–10 percent difference between male and female. Some populations show a greater or lesser dimorphism. Shape and proportions also vary due to secondary sexual characteristics and differences in the relative widths of the pectoral and pelvic girdles.

FIGURE 5-3   Drawings of Three Distinct Body Forms: Nilotic, Eskimo, and Pygmy.

Three distinct body forms are represented in this drawing. The Nilotic form illustrates a tall, slender shape found among many of the pastoralists of East Africa (Watusi, Masai, and Nuer). The Eskimo shape is in stark contrast, with shorter stature and heavier body. By comparison, the Pygmy is not only the shortest and lightest human but has a relatively long torso with short legs.

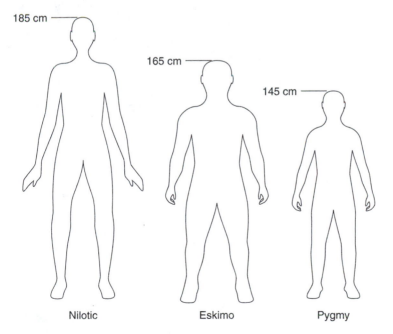

185 cm

165 cm

145 cm

Nilotic   Eskimo   Pygmy

others had very short ones. Another example is the short legs and long torsos of Japanese populations, a characteristic of Asian populations. This high average cormic index is changing as children have accelerated in their growth rates since the 1950s, as described later in this chapter in the section on human growth patterns and environmental influences.

Body Weight

As with size and shape, weight also varies over a wide range, but it does not correlate closely with stature: Some tall people are light in weight compared with heavier shorter people. Adult weight ranges from about 70 pounds to more than 200 pounds depending on diet and, perhaps, on genetic factors as well. There seems to be little ethnic variation in body weight or in response to a surplus dietary intake, though many groups of Native Americans, Pacific Islanders, and Australian Aborigines become extremely obese when they change to the refined high-carbohydrate, high-fat diets typical of American diets today. Usually, the excess weight is stored as layers of fat just below the skin, distributed over the body but more concentrated over the abdomen. There are some striking examples of differences, however, in the distribution of excessive subcutaneous fat, as in the case of steatopygia of Hottentot and San or !Kung women of South Africa, who, when well fed, develop especially large buttocks (Figure 5-4). In this condition, the buttocks are expanded by an enlargement of fat cells that are supported by bands of fibrous tissue. This may be an adaptation to high environmental temperatures, because the concentration of fat more in one region would lessen interference with the body's ability to dissipate metabolic heat through the skin's surface. The fat layer, if

FIGURE 5-4 Steatopygia of a !Kung female.

Steatopygia is one of the characteristics for which the Bushmen of South Africa are famous. It is an enormous increase in the size of the buttocks by an accumulation of fatty tissue. The shape is maintained and the weight is supported by an addition of fibrous tissue. The condition is most accentuated in females.

evenly distributed over most of the body, acts as insulation and would reduce the dissipation of body heat through radiation, a decided disadvantage in the hot climate of the homelands of these people.

Though dietary quantity and quality affect bodily proportions and weight, there is a close correlation with mean annual temperature. Generally speaking, in colder climates people are much heavier for their height than people in warmer regions, and the ratio between height and weight of the individual may be even more significant than limb ratios or trunk limb proportions. Table 5-1 lists some representative populations selected for variation in size and for the extreme temperature of their habitats. All "racial groups" contain some populations that have high stature–weight ratios (indicating a tall, thin person) as well as groups with low ratios (short and heavy). Among groups in the warmer regions, particularly the wet tropics, there is a tendency

TABLE 5-1 Body Size and Stature–Weight Ratio

POPULATION (MALES)	STATURE (CENTIMETERS)	WEIGHT (KILOGRAMS)	RATIO
Kazakh (Turkestan)	163.1	69.7	2.34
Finland	171.0	70.0	2.44
Iceland	173.6	68.1	2.55
Eskimo	161.2	62.9	2.56
England	166.3	64.5	2.58
Sicily	169.1	65.0	2.60
Venezuela	164.2	62.4	2.61
Ecuador	157.7	57.5	2.73
North China	168.0	61.0	2.75
Scotland	170.4	61.8	2.76
Yambasa (Africa)	169.0	62.0	2.78
Berbers	169.8	59.5	2.85
Korea	161.1	55.5	2.90
Mahratta (India)	163.8	55.7	2.94
Central China	163.0	54.7	2.98
Thailand	161.0	53.2	3.03
Japan	160.9	53.0	3.04
Sudanese	159.8	51.9	3.08
Annamites	158.7	51.3	3.09
Batutsi (Africa)	176.0	57.0	3.09
Kikuyu	164.5	51.9	3.17
Hong Kong	166.2	52.2	3.18
Vietnam	157.6	49.1	3.21
Burma	161.5	49.9	3.24
India	163.0	48.2	3.38
Efe	143.8	39.8	3.61
Pygmies	142.2	39.9	3.56
Bushmen	155.8	40.4	3.86

Sources: Based on data from Dobzhansky, 1962; and Frisch and Revelle, 1969.

to have a slender build, whereas in contrast, populations in the temperate or arctic regions are heavier for their stature.

A further example of the relationship between climate and body size is illustrated in Figure 5-5, which plots a body mass index (BMI) of several populations listed in Table 5-2 against mean annual temperatures of their environments. These examples of body form and size variability under differing environments demonstrate the great plasticity of human development. The responses to conditions of climate, diet, and disease are characteristic of many mammals and, in humans, the responses cross all ethnic and racial boundaries. These effects on size and shape have been described by general laws, called the Bergmann and Allen rules, which relate body surface area to heat dissipation or to conservation.

Bergmann and Allen Rules

Over a century ago a German physiologist, Carl Bergmann, observed that populations of many wide-ranging species of mammals varied in body size relative to mean annual temperature. Those populations inhabiting the colder regions of the species' range tended to be larger and heavier than those inhabiting the warmer areas. This was a matter of energy conservation, since differences in size-to-weight ratios vary the amounts of body heat lost in, for example, the Arctic winter. The opposite was noted in the tropics, where high environmental temperatures make efficiency in dissipation of body heat an important adaptive characteristic; average body size was smaller. Some thirty years later, an American zoologist, John Allen, also observed that mammalian

FIGURE 5-5   Body Mass Index versus Mean Annual Temperature.

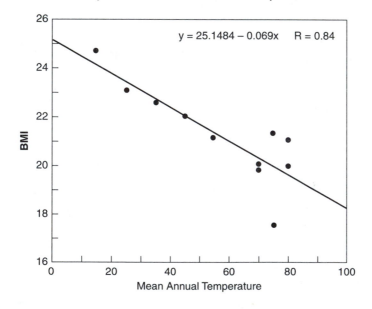

The chart shows: $y = 25.1484 - 0.069x$ $R = 0.84$

TABLE 5-2   Body Mass Index and Mean Annual Temperature

POPULATION	WEIGHT (KG)	HEIGHT (M)	HT^2	BMI	TEMP
Turkana	55.0	1.77	3.133	17.555	70–80
San	50.8	1.60	2.560	19.844	70–80
CAR Pygmies	41.5	1.44	2.074	20.010	80
Australia	60.0	1.73	2.993	20.047	70–80
CAR Farmer	54.6	1.61	2.592	21.065	80
Japan	61.0	1.70	2.890	21.107	50–60
Yanomama	50.0	1.53	2.341	21.358	70–80
Quechua	58.5	1.63	2.657	22.017	40–50
U.S. (EA)	69.1	1.76	3.098	22.305	—
Saami	66.1	1.71	2.924	22.606	30–40
Evenki	59.8	1.61	2.592	23.071	20–30
U.S. (AA)	72.2	1.76	3.098	23.305	—
Xavante	69.8	1.70	2.890	24.152	70–80
Inuit	66.7	1.64	2.690	24.796	10–20
Samoa	81.2	1.72	2.958	27.451	70–80

BMI: body mass index (Wt/Ht^2)
CAR: Central African Republic; EA: Euro-American; AA: African American
Source: Data selected from Eveleth and Tanner, 1976 and 1990.

body proportions were correlated with climate. He proposed a rule that the protruding parts of the body (tails, limbs, ears, face) tend to be shorter at the colder end of a species range. Conversely, these body parts were longer in the warmer regions. Taken together, these rules offer an explanation of the role that form plays in the maintenance of body temperature under varying climatic conditions.

These rules are based on sound observations of mammalian physiology and on the recognition of simple geometry. First, mammals must maintain body temperature within a narrow range, and second, metabolic heat production is proportionate to body weight—i.e., the heavier the individual the greater the amount of heat produced at rest or during muscle exertion. This generation of metabolic heat maintains the animal's body temperature, and if an excess is produced then it must be dissipated to prevent raising the animal's temperature, as easily happens on a hot day. On colder days, more heat is lost to the colder air surrounding the body so the metabolism increases, generating more metabolic heat. By small adjustments of metabolic processes, the animal is able to maintain a normal body temperature while at rest. However, this ability depends on the ambient temperature of the air surrounding its body. If the ambient temperature is too far below the animal's normal body temperature, then increasing metabolic rate alone cannot compensate. If the temperature is too far above body temperature then there is a difficulty in dissipating excess heat generated during exercise. Each mammalian species has evolved mechanisms to cope with these thermoregulation problems. Hibernating animals, for example, tolerate a significant lowering of their normal temperature during their hibernation. Another of the major adaptations has been changing body proportions to suit the environment.

Since most metabolic heat lost is through radiation (the flow or heat transfer by electromagnetic waves), the body's surface area-to-weight ratio is most significant. This relationship is summarized by Fourier's law of heat flow: heat lost per minute is directly proportional to (a) the body surface and (b) the difference between body core temperature and the environment (ambient temperature). Additionally, heat loss is inversely proportional to the thickness of the "shell." Simply, the greater the surface area, the greater the heat flow for a given body weight. The shell thickness refers to structures, principally skin and fat, that act as insulation and reduce the heat flow. Also involved as a major factor is the volume of subcutaneous blood flow. Below the skin is a rich network of blood vessels that constrict or dilate, alternately increasing or reducing the flow of blood near the surface. This aids in thermoregulation, since the flow regulation can increase or decrease the quantity of heat brought close to the surface.

A consideration of simple geometric shapes offers an illustration of the relationships between body surface and weight. In the case of a cylinder, the lateral surface area changes linearly while volume changes as the square. This means that volume increases at a higher rate than does area. Compare the formula: Area = $2\pi rh$; $V = \pi r^2 h$. The result is that an increase in the radius of the figure from 1 to 2 reduces surface area-to-volume ratio, the critical ratio in thermoregulation, from 2:1 to 1:1 while doubling the length maintains the same ratio (Figure 5-6). In the case of a mammalian body, the longer, narrower-shaped figure will have more surface area to dissipate metabolic heat generated in proportion to weight. A simple exercise can further illustrate this relationship. The cube in Part B has a measure of two units on a side and a surface-to-volume ratio of three, while doubling the length of the sides to form a rectangle doubles the volume but the surface-to-volume ratio is reduced only to 2.5. Though mammalian bodies are not geometric shapes like

FIGURE 5-6   (a) and (b) Changes in Surface Area to Volume.

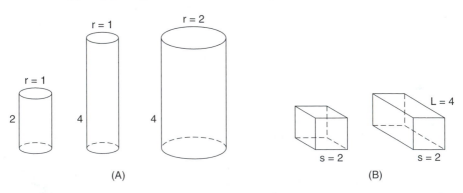

cubes, cylinders, or spheres, they generally do attain shapes with advantageous surface-to-volume ratios.

The question is whether geographic variation in human body shapes conforms to the Bergmann-Allen rules. Do not clothing, shelter, and dietary variations enable humans to grow and achieve a body form independent of climatic influences? The distribution of stature–weight ratios offers evidence that climate does, in fact, influence body form—people heavier for their height are found more frequently in colder areas, which relates to a need to conserve body heat and avoid the risk of hypothermia (see Table 5-1). Taking body mass index (BMI), or weight divided by height squared, shows a close negative correlation with temperature (see Table 5-2 and Figure 5-5). There are numerous exceptions to these correlations. The peoples of the Pacific are one of the first examples that come to mind. Samoans, though occupants of the tropics, have one of the highest BMIs of any population; also Fijians, Hawaiians, and Maori are large people with high BMI ratings. The explanation for these residents of warm climates who have stature-to-weight ratios and BMIs in the ranges of those found among arctic and subarctic natives may be found in their history of ocean voyaging.

Between 3,000 and 4,000 years ago humans began to extend their voyages further and further into the vast Pacific, probably from bases in the western Pacific scattered about the Solomon Islands. The voyages were made in open sailing canoes and extended over several weeks. During this time, the sailors were exposed to the cold, wet conditions found at sea even in the tropics. The wind-chill factor plus inability to shelter one's body from the sea spray caused body heat loss that could be life-threatening. The rate of loss of body heat depended on body proportions. Houghton (1996) graphically describes these conditions encountered by these early seafarers and argues that the largest, heaviest individuals had the best chance of surviving the trip. He noted that some of the largest and most muscular people are found in Oceania, and, far from being an exception to Bergmann's rule, their bodily proportions conform to the expected. The conditions that their ancestors were exposed to during the crossing of open ocean selected for those individuals who could grow large and accumulate body fat rapidly. Certainly, experiences of many modern-day sailors document the conditions at sea, and physiological experiments record the variation in rates of heat loss that closely correlate with body proportion and composition. A thinner individual with a higher surface-to-mass ratio will lose heat faster, undergoing a drop in body temperature three times as fast as a larger, heavier person.

Away from the marine environment, thinner people with high surface area are generally found in the tropics, as noted above. The selection under hot, humid conditions is for those individuals whose body forms enhance the rate of heat loss and so are best able to work under extremely hot conditions. Sweating, which can account for up to 27 percent of metabolic heat dissipation, works well as a thermoregulatory mechanism in dry climates but is less efficient under conditions of high humidity. Most body weights and heights of tropical peoples conform well with the Bergmann and Allen rules, and their bodily proportions aid in preventing elevation of body temperature to a dangerous level resulting in heat exhaustion. A major exception are pygmoid peoples of Africa, with their long torsos and shorter legs that give them a lower surface-to-weight ratio than expected for tropical people.

Pygmies. These African populations are exceptional for their small size and are, in many ways, in stark contrast to neighboring groups. The general relationships between body size, diet, climate, and growth seen in many of the world's peoples do not seem to apply to these dwarfed peoples. They are short in stature (under 144–145 cm), well below the mean for most other populations, but they have a long torso with short appendages. Most of their cranial and facial dimensions are near "normal," within 95 percent of the means for other African populations of the region. Pygmy faces are broad and marked by exceptional nasal breadth, well above the African average (Cavalli-Sforza, 1986). Such collections of characteristics are more typical of some pygmy groups than of others, as in the case of those in the Western and Central areas of the Pygmy range. According to Hiernaux, people called pygmies are those below 150 cm, while others up to 160 cm are properly called pygmoid. He notes that applying this label based on body length is difficult and can be misleading since many agricultural populations are shorter than some groups called pygmoids (Hiernaux, 1977:189).

Today, approximately 150,000 Pygmies live in small groups scattered throughout the tropical rain forests of central Africa, from near the Zaire–Uganda border in East Africa to the Central African Republic and Cameroon in the west. These groups are believed to be descendants of prehistoric hunters who have been progressively reduced and thinly scattered over the area as early agriculturalists began to occupy portions of the tropical rain forest approximately 2,000 years ago. The Pygmies have been pushed farther and farther into the more remote, agriculturally less desirable regions until, today, the largest numbers of Pygmies in Africa are concentrated in central Africa around the Congo basin and along the tributaries of the Congo River. In these areas the Pygmies have established a close trading relationship with the agricultural groups, trading labor or the proceeds of the hunt for cultivated foods. Many are becoming highly acculturated, integrated into the farming villages and seldom follow their former nomadic ways. The best known are the Efe, Batwa, and Bakanga who live in the regions east of Kisangani (Stanleyville) in Zaire. A few groups, such as the Babinza, however, live in the western region of central Africa; these western groups are far less numerous and more widely dispersed. It is interesting to note that the shortest people in the world, the Mbuti of the Ituri rain forests in Zaire, live within two to three hundred miles of the world's tallest and thinnest people, the Tutsi of Ruwanda, referred to as "elongated Africans" (Hiernaux, 1977).

Pygmoid populations called Negritos, sometimes referred to as Oceanic Pygmies, are dispersed throughout many of the more remote areas of South Asia, the Philippines, and New Guinea. They are found in the jungles of the Malayan Peninsula and on the island of Sumatra; these are the Semang and the Senoi (Sakai), who are only slightly taller than the average African Pygmy, with a mean stature of 152 cm (five feet). Off the west coast of the Malayan Peninsula are the Andaman Islands, inhabited by three distinct groups of Negritos: the Minicopies, the Onge, and the Garawa. They all are similar in features and a bit shorter than the Semang, 149 cm (four feet, ten inches). The Onge are quite fat, and the women develop large fleshy buttocks, similar to the steatopygia on the San and Hottentot females. On the Philippine Islands of Mindanao, Palawan, and the northern part of Luzon are a few remnants of pygmoid populations. Among the best known are the Aetas, whose mean stature has been given as 147 cm (four feet, nine inches). Other Negrito groups are found in the remotest parts of the mountains of western New Guinea; the Tapiro tribe, with a mean stature of 144 cm (four feet, seven inches), is an example.

The general characteristics of the Negritos, besides small stature, are very dark skin color, woolly hair, scant body and facial hairs, broad nose, and slight to moderately developed brow ridges. All groups do not share equally in these features, and there is a considerable variation between certain populations. In the case of skin color, some Negritos, as in the Philippine populations, have lighter brown or even yellowish skin, whereas the Andaman Islanders have very dark brown to black skin. Facial features also differ considerably, from smooth, rounded foreheads to heavy brows (usually in New Guinea groups) that match well the facial features of many Australian Aborigines.

A major problem that has puzzled students of human variation has been the origins of these dwarfed peoples, which centers on the question of the relationship between the two divisions, the African Pygmies and the Southeast Asian Negritos. How are they related? Do they, as once supposed, share close common ancestry, or are they members of a unique pygmoid race? Casual visual comparisons suggest that they are descendants of the same ancestors because of their comparable size, skin color, and hair form. In the past, Pygmies and Negritos had been classified as a single race, and certain anthropologists even suggested elaborate migration routes to get the ancestors of Southeast Asian Negritos from an African homeland to their present distribution. Other studies of pygmoid peoples have pointed out, however, that the African Pygmy and Negrito are two independent types with only their short stature and certain other features in common (Boyd, 1963). Each pygmoid population studied shared several traits of blood type and protein composition with their normal-sized neighbors. In fact, dwarfed peoples, in general, may be no more than local inbred populations (Abbie, 1967). The question of the cause of the pygmoid condition is still unresolved.

Some clues may be provided by the extensive studies of genetic and physiological characteristics of the African Pygmies. During six expeditions over a ten-year period teams of experts collected a broad spectrum of biological and anthropometric data from western Pygmy groups (Cavalli-Sforza, 1986). A great deal was learned about their physiology and genetic markers, but the most relevant to understanding their small size were the studies of growth hormone secretion. Though Pygmy size suggests a deficiency in human growth hormone, the tests revealed that they secreted an amount within the normal range. Further tests showed that they were unresponsive to the effects of growth hormone, however. This lack of response is due to a low level of a protein called insulin-like growth factor (IGF), a short polypeptide chain that is essential for cartilage and bone growth. There are two forms thus far identified, an IGF_1 and an IGF_2. Type 2 is present at normal levels, but type 1 is abnormally low in the Pygmies tested and appears to be genetically determined (Merimee and Rimoin, 1986). Such studies of growth hormone responses have yet to be performed on other dwarfed peoples and the specific gene or genes are still not identified, but it is likely that there are several factors that modify tissue response to growth stimulation.

In addition to their short size, the Pygmies have a totally different body form from their neighbors, a form that reduces the efficiency of heat radiation even though they are seemingly well adapted to hot, humid conditions. Because of the near 100 percent humidity of their environment, heat loss due to sweating is not useful in dissipation of body heat and is not a possible compensation for radiation. Pygmies may compensate through a reduction of internal heat production through a reduction of basal metabolism or of muscle mass, which can be accomplished with weight reduction. A 25 percent weight decrease lowers metabolic heat production by 18 percent, but if the weight reduced is in muscle mass, metabolic heat is lowered as much as 23 percent. This is a possible explanation offered for Pygmy heat tolerance. Cavalli-Sforza (1986) describes the relative lower muscle mass of Pygmies as represented by their thin calves, upper legs and arms. Comparisons of these dimensions with those of other Africans place Pygmies in the lower end of the range. This hypothesis of muscle mass and heat tolerance has yet to be fully tested, but muscle/metabolic activity is probably an explanation for survival under conditions that challenge the major mechanisms for maintaining a thermal balance as an individual goes about a routine of work.

HEAD SIZE AND SHAPE

The shape and size of the head have been under intense study by many generations of anthropologists, and numerous descriptive measurements have been devised. The human head has been of special interest because it houses that most important and mysterious part of our anatomy, the brain, and because of the wealth of well-preserved skulls from prehistoric times. Representative skulls from these extinct ancient populations often show a collection of characteristics that apparently sets them apart and has been used to suggest relationships between past and present populations. These characteristics were also presumed to be indicative of certain behavioral attributes; hence the profound interest.

Among the many skull features examined, the one most frequently used in the past for establishing racial groups has been the shape of the head, defined by the cephalic index, as noted in Chapter 1. This index, the ratio of the breadth to the length of the skull, provides an approximation of shape without regard to size. The skull of our species varies from long and narrow to short and broad—a variation of cephalic index from 70 (breadth = 70 percent of length) to about 90. Certain populations tend toward one or the other end of the range, as indicated in Table 5-3, which lists Australian Aborigines as having the narrowest heads, whereas at the other end of the range, Norwegian Lapps have the broadest head shapes.

Despite its frequent use in the past, the index has to be discounted as a racial criterion because of its broad range and because there are similar indices found for such disparate groups as Quechua of the Andes and central Europeans, Norwegians and Otomis (Native Americans), and Africans and Australian Aborigines. If several cranial and facial dimensions, describing face

TABLE 5-3   Cephalic Indexes

GROUP	MEAN INDEX
Australians (Arnhem Land)	71.8
Central Bantu	74.1
South Africa (Bushmen, Hottentots)	75.1
Vedda	75.6
Ituri Pygmies	76.5
New Guinea and Melanesia	77.7
Eskimo	78.0
Madagascar and Indian Ocean	78.7
Sioux (central United States)	79.6
Iran, Armenia, Assyria	80.2
Japanese	80.8
Norwegians	81.0
Eastern Chinese	81.7
Germans	82.5
Negritos (Philippines)	82.7
Hawaiians	84.0
Norwegian Lapps	85.0

The index is obtained by taking the ratio of maximum skull breadth divided by maximum skull length times 100.

Sources: Data from Biasutti, 1959; and Harrison, Weiner, Tanner, and Barnicot, 1977.

and head shape, are taken in combination and examined by modern statistical techniques, however, then distinctions are found among many populations. Degrees of relationships—that is, relative distances from a common ancestor—have been estimated in this way. The average cranial-facial morphology of northern Europeans differs significantly from that of southeastern Europeans, for example. The cranial remains of ancient peoples who overran central Europe throughout recorded history have also been differentiated by this method (Schwidetzsky and Rosing, 1982). The peopling of the Pacific and the Americas presents a challenge to prehistorians, but their studies are now being aided by extensive comparisons of cranial-facial shape of prehistoric populations (Brace and Hunt, 1990; Pietrusewsky, 1990).

Such studies are possible if care is taken in selecting dimensions of various features, because there is a strong component of inheritance regulating growth and the final form of the structure just as there is in stature. The component of inheritance in head shape was demonstrated by Osborne and De George (1959), who compared monozygotic and dizygotic twins and showed a closer similarity between the monozygotic (identical twins) than between nonidentical or dizygotic twin pairs. The mode of inheritance is not known, however, because head shape is not a simple character depending on a single gene; rather, it is determined by a multiple gene complex subject to strong environmental influences. The overall rate of growth and body size also influences shape because there is a positive correlation between stature and skull length; taller individuals have longer heads. Because of these factors, plus the pattern of distribution of cranial shape, cephalic index remains an element of interest in the study of bodily proportions. However, it should be considered as a part of the overall growth and development pattern influenced by environmental factors. Recall the changes in growth and head form among American-born children of European immigrants reported by Boas, as discussed in the first chapter. These and later studies proved that head form could significantly change in a single generation as living conditions improved.

Climatic conditions could also exert influences. For example, Beals and co-workers (1984) made a comparative study of 20,000 skulls from populations around the world and found a close correlation between environmental temperature and head shape. Populations in colder climates had, on the average, rounder heads than peoples in the tropics, a characteristic that is likely to be of adaptive significance. The relationship of surface area and mass of parts of the mammalian body form influence the radiation of metabolic heat and affect temperature regulation. The closer a structure approaches a spherical shape the lower will be the surface-to-volume ratio. The reverse is true as elongation occurs—a greater surface area to volume is formed, which results in more surface to dissipate heat generated within a given volume. Since up to 80 percent of our body heat may be lost through our heads on cold days, one can appreciate the significance of shape. For, as discussed above, the relation between surface area and volume is a critical factor in heat radiation.

Cranial Capacity and Brain Size

Perhaps more speculation and nonsense has been written about the size of the human brain and its relationship to intelligence than about any other aspect of our anatomical variability. This is probably because the size of the cranial vault differs so much among peoples today and has increased throughout the fossil record of human evolution (Table 5-4). The estimated volume of the cranial vault or cranial capacity increased from a low of 450 cubic centimeters (cc) in one of the earliest hominids, the Australopithecines, to the highest in archaic and modern *Homo sapiens.* The modern range for brain volume, estimated from cranial capacity, was achieved relatively early in human evolution, approximately 100,000 years ago, among the Neanderthals of Europe. In fact, the estimated mean size of the Neanderthal fossils' cranial capacity (1,450 cc) is actually higher than the mean for modern humans (1,345 cc).

The increase of brain size during the last two or three million years of evolution was an extremely important event for paleontological studies, and comparisons of cranial capacities of the different fossils can be useful to some extent. When comparisons are made between fossils over broad time spans, some conclusions may be made about intelligence if advances in technologies are also considered. The brain, represented by estimates of gross size, can then be said to have evolved, say between the earliest hominids (Australopithecines) and *Homo erectus* some two million years later, but note that brain size reached its modern range about 100,000 years ago (Neandertals). Since then there has not been an increase in means of brain size. What is especially notable is the wide range in variation among contemporary populations, and the lower end of the range extends well below the volumes estimated for certain early hominids—*Homo erectus,* for example (see Table 5-4).

Should we conclude that some of our fossil ancestors were more intelligent because of a larger average cranial capacity? Of course not! There is no evidence that individuals with small cranial capacities, and hence small brains, are any less intelligent than persons with larger cranial vaults housing larger brains. The differences among modern populations' brain sizes do not have any relevance to mental ability. As von Bonin (1963), a foremost neu-

TABLE 5-4   Range of Cranial Capacity in Some Fossils and Modern Humans, Including Two Pongids

	RANGE OF CRANIAL CAPACITIES
Chimpanzee	275–500 cm³
Gorilla	340–752
Australopithecine	450–700 (approximately)
Homo erectus (Pithecanthropus, Sinanthropus)	850–1,250
Neanderthal	1,100–1,700
Homo sapiens	1,000–2,200

Sources: Based on Montagu, 1960; Schultz, 1926; and Tobias, 1971.

roanatomist, once stated, the correlation between brain size and mental capacity is insignificant in modern *Homo sapiens*. In other words, differences of few hundred cubic centimeters of brain volume do not matter. The wide-ranging differences among the members of the same population show no correlation to behavior differences or to intellectual attainment. There are abundant examples of extreme differences in brain size in all populations that have no bearing on ability or achievement. Many famous statesmen and literary figures in recent history had cranial capacities at either end of the range—from Anatole France and Turgenev (1,100 cc) to Oliver Cromwell and Lord Byron (2,200 cc), while the great poet Walt Whitman had to get along with only 1,282 cc of brain space (Tobias, 1970). Females average 10 percent smaller cranial capacities than males—a difference that is related to the smaller average female body size. Also, brain size is closely correlated with body size; most studies, especially the earlier ones that are often used for comparison, seldom considered the overall size of the individual. Taller individuals have larger brains, as documented by numerous studies; brain weight is positively correlated with height (Pakkenberg and Voigt, 1964). Simply, larger people have larger brains. In addition, brain volume or weight is difficult to measure, either by estimation from cranial capacity of the dry skull, from the head of the living individual, or from the brain at autopsy when age and cause of death are important influences. The methods used to remove and separate the brain from the spinal cord, as well as the skill of the investigator, will influence the results.

Nevertheless, there are authors, even today, who insist on recording and emphasizing so-called racial difference in cranial capacity as if it were a meaningful indicator. See, for example, Burnham (1985), who argued that brain size is a significant indicator of intelligence, or Rushton (1992), who has revived the old argument of inherited inequality (see Chapter 7). Because of this persistent use of estimated brain size, a series of select populations is shown in Figure 5-7 to illustrate size ranges. Before the reader draws any conclusions, it should be pointed out that variation of more than ±100 cc about the mean is evident within most European populations; there are people with small heads and some with large heads, and differences of 400 cc or more are not unusual. In sum, individuals with larger or smaller cranial capacities are normally functioning and intellectually competent individuals, and neither individuals nor groups can be sorted by such a highly variable measurement as cranial capacity. Similarities or differences become understandable when growth processes and body size are considered.

FACE FORM

The human face is highly variable in its shape and size, and distinctly individual forms occur. We can easily recognize our friends by their facial appearance, and we automatically and even subconsciously group people according

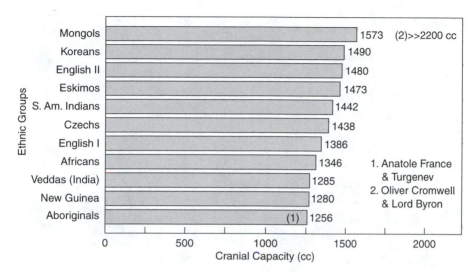

FIGURE 5-7   **Mean Cranial Capacity.** (Data from Montagu, 1960, and others.)

to their expressions or the dimensions and proportions of the face. One worker went so far as to divide faces into ten different categories or types, from elliptical to oval, including such classifications as rectangular and pentagonal. Even with many gradations among these categories, it was still impossible to apply them to all members of a population. Any scheme devised to describe facial characteristics of certain populations is just a rough approximation that will include only a portion of the individuals in the group. The form of the mouth, prominence of the chin or nose, and the position of the eyes are visual clues that enable recognition. We all group people into broad categories and we see these groupings as related to the major racial divisions of our species; the terms Eskimo, Aborigine, or Chinese project a mental image of what a person in that category looks like before we ever see the individual. Figure 5-8 offers an example of the human diversity of face form.

Little is known about the causes of such diversity or about the genetic influences. The soft tissues of the face are arranged in any number of ways and change with age; family resemblances are strong and population affinities are usually clear. Also, there appears to be a geographical distribution of face form that suggests some adaptation to climate; the flat, broad face of northern Asian peoples has been described as an adaptation to cold ever since the earliest days of anthropology, while at the same time the large, probably bulbous nose and the expanded maxillary sinuses of the European Neandertal were also considered cold adapted. There are few physiological studies to support such an explanation, however. A clearer understanding of facial structures is provided by studies of the facial skeleton.

Human face shape is complex and is the result of several large and small bones organized about three basic structures; the eyes, the nose, and the

FIGURE 5-8   Faces of *Homo sapiens*. This composite photograph illustrates the range of variability of our species. (Source: Courtesy of United Nations.)

mouth. The development and placement of these structures must be coordinated to provide sufficient space and symmetry to enable the functions of sight, respiration, and alimentation, each with special requirements of shape, size, and position in the overall facial arrangement. The spacing of the orbits of the eyes, for example, influences the visual field and affects appearance to a large extent, while the size of the nasal aperture allows for inhalation through the upper respiratory tract and is related to the bony structures of the roof of the mouth and the midface. The mouth, in turn, has a size and shape closely related to the size and spacing of the teeth in the dental arcade.

The shape of the human face has changed a great deal from the heavy prognathic structure possessed by our fossil ancestors to the reduced structure in modern *Homo sapiens*, which is rather small in proportion to our large head. This change has come about over a long period of time through evolutionary processes, as our ancestors relied less on their jaws and teeth for procuring and manipulating food, which, in turn, reduced the natural selection for large facial bones. The structures of the face, whose major function is to support the chewing apparatus, therefore diminished in size. These structures are primarily the brow ridges (the ridge of bone over the eyes), the cheekbones (or zygomatic arches), and of course the upper and lower arches of bone that support the teeth. With a reduction in these elements, the human face began to take on a new look, and the proportions were drastically altered. All of the world's populations did not undergo exactly the same pattern of change, however, nor were their faces altered at the same rate. Many of the facial features have maintained large sizes in some populations, such as the Eskimo and Australian Aborigines who have continued heavy dental use well into this century.

One rather distinctive facial characteristic clearly involved in the evolutionary process is prognathism, the forward protrusion of dental arches. A comparison of modern humans with recent or ancient and fossil Neanderthals illustrates the reduction in the lower face of modern humans (Figure 5-9). Many modern populations today have prognathic profiles, yet this does not indicate a close affinity with fossil ancestors; rather, it is the result of the presence of large teeth in broad dental arches. Because the major purpose of the bony structures in this part of the face is the support of the dentition, the bone arches of the maxilla and mandible are correspondingly large.

Teeth have proved to be significant in the study of human variability because of their importance as evidence in evolution and adaptation to environmental conditions. Teeth served *Homo sapiens* well as cutting, grinding, and shearing implements in past times, as the heavily worn dental remains of prehistoric and earlier historic humans demonstrate (Brace, 1962; Molnar, 1971). In fact, human survival up until recent times depended a great deal on a sturdy dentition and a heavy, well-formed skeleton, as illustrated by the robust dental arches in Figure 5-10. With the rise of technological efficiency to process the raw materials necessary to sustain life, however, there was less

FIGURE 5-9 Alveolar Prognathism. These sketches diagram the facial distinctions of several phases of human evolution. In contrast to the modern profiles, the lower face—mainly the anterior tooth row and chin— was much more robust and the teeth protruded further forward. The cheekbones (zygomatic arches) and brow ridges were also larger in earlier human ancestors.

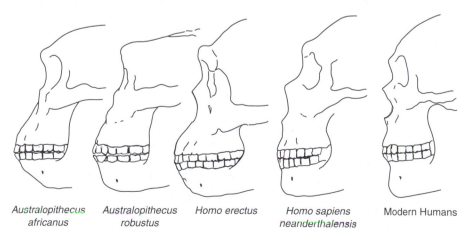

| *Australopithecus africanus* | *Australopithecus robustus* | *Homo erectus* | *Homo sapiens neanderthalensis* | Modern Humans |

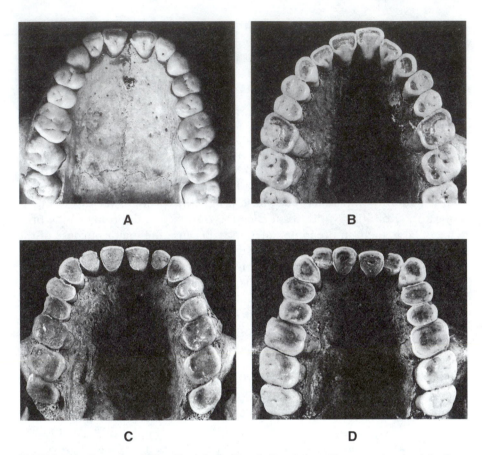

FIGURE 5-10 Examples of Worn Teeth in Prehistoric Populations. The upper dental arch is shown at several stages of wear. The unworn teeth of a sixteen-year-old (A) are compared to three adults who have suffered various degrees of tooth loss because of a tough abrasive diet requiring heavy chewing. A younger adult, about twenty-five (B), shows less wear than C, a thirty-five-year-old, and D, a forty-five-year-old (Source: Iva M. Molnar).

reliance on the dental arches as implements, so in modern times our teeth often are looked on as annoying items of our anatomy that frequently require dental treatment.

Teeth have characteristics of shape and size that increase the dentition's utility as a chewing implement—extra molar cusps and reinforced enamel ridges are examples. Throughout evolution these characteristics varied from population to population so that, today, the many ethnic groups show considerable diversity in these dental features because of the differences in selective forces for sturdy teeth that have been operating on each group. Tooth size, especially the diameter of the molar crown, shows great variation. From the large crowns of the Australopithecine molars (approximately 15 mm diameter in the cheek-to-tongue direction) to the small sizes of many European populations (11.5 mm diameter of the first molar) the dentition of humans and their ancestors has steadily reduced in size over time. This reduction has not been equal nor has it been constant in all of the world's peoples; today some people, such as the Australian Aborigines, still possess large teeth, well within the range of those found in European fossils of the mid-Pleistocene.

Shovel-shaped incisors are another dental feature that occurs more frequently in certain populations than in others. This term describes an incisor tooth that has thickened margins on the lingual surface (tongue side of the tooth). These raised surfaces provide structural reinforcement that prevents or reduces the possibility of breakage. In many Asian peoples—Chinese, for instance—most individuals have these types of incisors, and children suffer far less from breakage of the upper central incisors in childhood accidents than do European children.

Several other features of the dentition also show a great deal of variability and, in some cases, have been grouped according to race. More often, though, there is only a variability in the frequency of the occurrence of the particular trait, and all the major groups of humanity possess it to some degree. The molar cusps are an example, because their number and arrangement on the molar crown have often been used to identify racial affinity. Some groups frequently do tend to have one or another pattern; for example, there are very seldom fewer than five cusps on the lower first molar of the Australian Aborigines, whereas the first molars of many Europeans tend to be reduced in size with only four cusps. Many individual Aborigines differ from this "typical" pattern, however, and often have a sixth cusp. So it is with other "racial" characteristics of the teeth; though members of a group may have a higher frequency of one or more dental traits, they are seldom unique possessors, and other segments of humanity may have the same traits (as in the case of shovel-shaped incisors, Table 5-5). To sum up, the range of variability of the dentition of modern *Homo sapiens* is so great that several characteristic features must be considered together before racial or population affinity is described.

Morphology and Size

Tooth morphology and size are under close genetic control and have been shown to be very stable through time, a feature that allows comparisons of skeletal as well as living populations. These traits must be considered as a group or cluster, as Turner (1990) has done successfully to establish common ancestry and to trace origins. He recorded the frequency of twelve different dental traits, including shovel-shaped incisors, as they occurred among Asians, Native Americans, and Pacific peoples. The trait frequencies were analyzed by multivariant statistics, and clusters were derived that arranged representative

TABLE 5-5   Shovel-shaped Incisors

POPULATION	PERCENT MALE	PERCENT FEMALE
Chinese	66–89	82–94
Japanese	78	
Mongolian	62–91	91
Eskimo	84	84
Pima Indians	96	99
Pueblo Indians	86–89	86–89
Aleut	96	
American Black	12	11
American White	9	8

Sources: Based on Carbonell, 1963; and Comas, 1960.

samples into "trees" or dendrograms that located population samples according to degree of similarity. The results provided strong evidence for northern Asia as the original homeland of Native Americans while establishing a distinctive difference among Asian and Pacific populations. The advantage of Turner's method compared to other techniques is that skeletal remains thousands of years old could be used to determine the presence of the traits in different world regions.

Nose Form

The nose dominates the midfacial region and contributes a great deal to a person's distinctive identity. Form and size vary over a wide range; there are people with short, broad or long, narrow noses and all combinations in between. The linear measures are easily made on either the living or the dry skull, and many thousands of measurements have been recorded. Nasal index (width/length × 100), an approximation of shape like cephalic index, is also easily derived and has received a great deal of attention because nose shape has a pattern of geographical distribution and was once thought to be a distinctively racial trait. In some ethnic groups a certain shape does appear more frequently. An index of 104 describes a nose that is slightly wider at the nostrils than it is long; it is found among the Pygmies of the Ituri Forest area in Central Africa and Aborigines in central Australia. Narrower noses, represented by low indices (85 and below), are found among numerous groups throughout the world, in many Native Americans, North Africans, Europeans, and Eskimos. A narrow or a broad nose form is not confined to any particular race. For example, the long, narrow noses found among the peoples occupying the highlands of east Africa are in contrast to the wide noses of the tropical dwellers in the Congo Basin.

Because the nose performs the vital functions in the upper respiratory tract of filtering, warming, and moistening the inspired air, its size and shape variation among populations has been frequently studied. The nose is lined with mucosal membranes covering a dense bed of fatty tissues through which a rich supply of blood flows. These membranes can secrete large amounts of water, up to 1 liter per day, which serves to moisten the inspired air. The moistening function serves to help maintain the inspired air at the relative humidity of 100 percent required by the lungs. Other structures of the respiratory track contribute moisture, but the lining of the nose serves most effectively in this function. This means that the amount of total surface area of the internal nose and adjacent structures become more important in drier areas. Natives of arid regions of the world have a longer, narrower nose form—a geometric shape that provides the greatest surface area per unit size (Wolpoff, 1968). Among desert and mountain peoples the narrow nose is predominant, and it predominates even in the colder and drier climate of the Eskimos. A narrow nasal aperture provides an efficient mechanism for warming as well as moistening the inspired air. It is a simple matter of geometry that a high, narrow nasal opening can warm and moisten air more efficiently than a short, broad one, and in climates where the moisture content of the air is very low, selective forces act on this particular nose form, whether the dryness is due to intense heat or intense cold. Table 5-6 shows examples of average nasal indices among populations living in a variety of climates.

Because face form is a result of a complex of the growth processes of several facial bones, any single feature is the result of interacting forces. This is especially true of nose form, whose width is related to the size and proportion of the upper dental arch. As the palate gets wider, the nasal aperture becomes broader, and the Australian Aborigines are a good example. Though most live in some of the driest areas of the world, their noses are extremely broad as noted earlier. This dimension is related to the large anterior teeth and to chewing processes exerted on the dental arches during childhood, which stimulates the palatal growth. Also, prognathism tends to be associated with a short, broad nose, and a significant correlation has been found between the length of the skull base and nasal width.

TABLE 5-6   Mean Nasal Indexes of Select Populations

POPULATION	MEAN NASAL INDEX
South African Bushmen	103.9
Mbuti Pygmies	103.8
Aborigines (Australia)	99.6
Northern Bantu	95.5
Central Bantu	93.8
Vedda (India)	85.5
American Indian (Plains)	72.0
Eskimo	68.5
European	66.0
Iran	63.7

These factors of climatic influence and structural interrelationships suggest that human face form is extremely complex and that numerous variables are involved in growth and development to a certain adult form. Conclusions should not be drawn too quickly about relationships between any two populations solely on the basis of a similarity in structure, because face form, like other bodily dimensions, develops according to local factors of natural selection acting on the genes that regulate growth. It is not necessary to postulate migrations and intermixtures to explain similarities between populations, as was once done for the Nilotic face form found in groups like the Nuer, Watusi, and other East African pastoralists. At one time their long, narrow noses were believed to be one of the features resulting from admixture between African and western Asian populations. Subsequent genetic studies have not borne this theory out. No doubt, during a period of thousands of years, contact with western Asian populations may have occurred and some interbreeding may have resulted, but people with the Nilotic face are the result of local selective forces acting on the population; it is not merely a matter of interbreeding between races.

FACTORS OF GROWTH AND DEVELOPMENT

The shape and size an adult acquires are results of a complex of processes that occur during infancy and childhood. Over a span of our first dozen or so years of life we pass through several stages that affect the size and function of our bodies. The growth and development of the body's organs and structures are under control of a complex of genes that interact with the environment to produce the various dimensions and proportions discussed above. Nutrition, climate, and disease all act to regulate how we grow and at what rates. We resemble our parents, of course, but with improvements in environments seen in succeeding generations in this century, we often exceed our parents in rates and attainments of growth. The genetic influence is there but hard to define, and racial/ethnic variations in body form and size diminish as more diverse groups come to occupy similar growth environments. Responses are much the same in most groups for which there is comparative data. In effect, we are the products of our growth experiences. From the !Kung of southern Africa to Australians and Arctic Inuits (Eskimos), all children respond to favorable conditions in the same ways. Maturity is reached earlier, final adult height is greater, and body shapes are more similar. Children the world over are achieving their genetic growth potential. There are still short and tall people, fat and thin, and proportionate differences, but not as broadly expressed as in prior generations. Though conditions favoring growth are better understood, the genetic influences have not been established.

What has been clearly established is that there are several markers or "way-stations" that may be used to measure the relative quality of human growth. All humans pass through these well-defined periods during which growth may accelerate or slow down in response to environmental stressors, reflecting a major means of human adaptation. The age or time of certain periods—the onset of puberty, for example—varies from group to group. The passage through these stages is relatively similar, however; all humans spend approximately one-third of their lives preparing for the remaining two-thirds. These growth periods are listed in Table 5-7. Note that male and female timing is nearly the same except for an earlier onset of puberty in the female.

Comparisons with other mammals show that the time spent at each of these growth periods varies widely among species (Table 5-8). Humans are the most long-lived and, though their gestation period is not significantly different from that of the great apes, a greater amount of time is spent in childhood and adolescence. This lengthened development period is a major characteristic of our species, and the increased time allows for a longer learning period, which is an important correlate to our increased brain size and development. Throughout human evolution the lengthened learning period has been turned to advantage in the development of culture.

The average birth weight of Euro-Americans is 3.3 kg, while African Americans average 5 percent less; to achieve this size during the 270 days of gestation, the original weight of the fertilized ovum must be increased several billion times. From conception to birth the single cell is transformed into a complex organism consisting of billions of cells divided into numerous specialized tissues. Growth and development must occur at varying rates so that each unit will have its correct functional proportion by birth. The embryo grows at a linear rate of 1.5 mm/day during the second month, which is an enormously rapid growth rate; for example, if this rate were continued after birth, a thirty-foot-tall adult would be produced. From about the eighth week, growth slows until the sixth and seventh months, when fetal growth begins to accelerate. After this peak during the fetal stage, infant and child growth

TABLE 5-7   Classification of Growth Periods

PERIOD	MALE	FEMALE
I. Infancy (neonate)	Birth–1 year (First 4 weeks)	Birth–1 year (First 4 weeks)
II. *Childhood*	*1–16 years*	*1–16 years*
early	1–6 years	1–6 years
mid	6–9 or 10 years	6–9 or 10 years
late	9 or 10–16 years	9 or 10–16 years
III. Puberty (in late childhood)	13–14 years	12–13 years
IV. Adolescence	14–18 or 20 years	13–18 or 20 years
V. Adult	20 years +	20 years +

Source: After Krogman, 1972. Copyright © The University of Michigan Press. Reprinted by permission of the publisher.

TABLE 5-8   Developmental Periods of Select Mammal Species

SPECIES	GESTATION (IN DAYS)	AGE AT PUBERTY	LONGEVITY (IN YEARS)
Rat	22	6–9 (weeks)	4–5
Rabbit	31	6–9 (months)	10–15
Dog	63	6–8 (months)	15–20
Cat	63	12–15 (months)	20–30
Pig	112	7–8 (months)	12–20
Elephant	660	9–14 (years)	60–70
PRIMATES			
Bush-baby	120–146	1½–2 years	14
Lemur	120–140	1½–2 years	27
Rhesus	150–180	2–4 years	29
Baboon	180–190	2½–3½ years	29
Gibbon	210	8–10 years	31
Orangutan	220–270	8–13 years	30
Chimpanzee	216–260	8–9 years	41
Gorilla	250–290	6–8 years	33
Human	260–280	13–15 years	a

[a]Though average longevity ranges from 45 years to 75 years in different societies, there have been frequent reports of persons living beyond the century mark.

slows, but it begins to accelerate again in late childhood to another peak in adolescence (the "growth spurt").

Different body regions grow at varying rates at different stages, as in the example of the head, which accounts for a major proportion of growth during the fetal and infancy stages. This emphasis on cerebral development, one of the hallmarks of our species, is illustrated by the body-weight and brain-weight changes from the second month of gestation through the child's seventh year (Table 5-9). The brain weight accounts for 93 percent of the total weight, until the last four months of fetal development, when other parts of the body begin to enlarge rapidly; then the brain is only approximately 10 percent of total weight at birth. The human brain is at the maximum size that fetal metabolism can maintain because of the brain's higher energy requirement; the adult brain consumes about 20 percent of the body's total. From birth until the seventh year the brain grows much more rapidly than other tissues (except for the lymphoid tissues). By age seven a person has about 95 percent of his or her adult brain weight and brain development is nearly completed.

By comparison, after the first year of life, other tissues become slower in their growth until adolescence, when body size increases rapidly and the reproductive organs mature. The weights of several organs at various growth stages show a linear increase from birth to adulthood (Table 5-10). By the time puberty (adolescence) is reached, the brain is very close to its adult

TABLE 5-9   Age Changes in Brain Size*

AGE	BODY WEIGHT	BRAIN WEIGHT	% OF BODY SIZE	VOLUME OF BRAIN	CRANIAL CAPACITY	PERCENTAGE
Newborn	3,100	380.0	12.3	330	350	94.3
3 months	—	—	—	500	600	83.3
6 months	—	—	—	575	775	74.2
9 months	—	—	—	675	925	73.0
1 year	9,000	944.7	10.5	750	1,000	75.0
2 years	11,000	1,025.0	9.4	900	1,100	81.8
3 years	12,500	1,108.1	8.9	960	1,225	78.4
4 years	14,000	1,330.1	10	1,000	1,300	76.9
6 years	17.800	1,359.1	7.6	1,060	1,350	78.5
9 years	25,200	1,408.3	5.6	1,100	1,400	78.6
12 years	37,100	1,428.0	3.8	1,150	1,450	79.3
18 years	59,500	1,444.5	2.4	1,200	1,500	80.8

*Weights in grams. Volumes in cubic centimeters.

Sources: Based on Tobias, 1971; and Young, 1971.

weight. The thymus gland, a lymphoid organ in the lower neck that functions as part of the immunological system, decreases in size by contrast. Body size and proportions of head, trunk, and legs also change.

Growth Rates

The several growth processes that occur at varying rates are under the influence of factors noted previously. The interplay of these factors may lead to retarded or advanced growth. At each point in time we are expected to be at a particular point in our life cycle, but many of us deviate from this established norm. We may be taller or shorter than our classmates, reach puberty

TABLE 5-10   Average Weights (in Grams) of Organs at Different Ages

	NEWBORN	% OF ADULT WEIGHT	1 YEAR	6 YEARS	PUBERTY	ADULT
Brain	350	26%	910	1,200	1,300	1,350
Heart	24	8	45	95	150	300
Thymus	12	80	20	24	30	0–15
Kidneys (both)	25	8	70	120	170	300
Liver	150	9	300	550	1,500	1,600
Lungs (both)	60	5	130	260	410	1,200
Pancreas	3	3	9	—	40	90
Spleen	10	6	30	55	95	155
Stomach	8	5	30	—	80	135

Source: Reproduced with permission from Lowrey, G. H., *Growth and Development of Children*, 7th ed. Copyright © 1978 by Year Book Medical Publishers, Inc., Chicago.

earlier or later, or our skeletal system may develop at other than expected rates. In other words, our developmental age often will not coincide with our chronological age. One good measure of growth and development is the degree of skeletal development or "skeletal age" as compared to chronological age.

Skeletal Maturation. Most bone development begins during the embryonic period when the bones' characteristic shapes are formed in cartilage; the exceptions are cranial bones and the clavicle, which are developed from membranous tissues. During the latter part of the embryo state, mineralization of the cartilage starts from ossification centers and progressively increases until major portions of the bones have calcified. Bones continue to grow by this process of cartilage formation and then mineralize with calcium phosphate throughout childhood and adolescence, infusing the cartilage with this hard substance. Throughout childhood the secondary centers of ossification become established and contribute to growth. The ends of the bones, or epiphyses, remain separated from the diaphysis by a cartilage plate until late in adolescence when they fuse with the diaphysis. It is through this process of cartilage formation, followed by mineralization, that growth occurs. The active formation at the epiphyses near the ends of the long bones contributes to an increase in length. Each bone of the skeleton has a characteristic growth rate, and skeletal age or maturation is based on the degree of ossification of these centers and on their ultimate fusion with the main shaft (Figure 5-11).

In young children many bones of the skeleton remain unfused, and some bones (in the wrists, for example) have not yet begun to form. Radiographs of the hands of a child from the fourth to the seventh year show the development of the wrist bones (carpals), which begin to develop at different times during early childhood. Their relative sizes and degree of calcification show quite clearly (Figure 5-12). The fingers (phalanges) and the adjacent metacarpals (wrist bones), which grow in a pattern similar to the long bones of the arms and legs, show up clearly in this radiograph. The details of the diaphyses and associated epiphyses are shown at various stages. Thousands of individuals in many populations have had their hands radiographed during several years of growth, and standards of skeletal age have been established relative to chronological age. In this way, individuals with retarded growth may be identified early and, if owing to dietary or hormonal deficiencies, corrective measures can be taken.

There are many examples of deviation in skeletal development and epiphyseal fusion rates that are due more to general health and nutritional status than to ethnic differences. The timing of skeletal growth is much the same in all children given equivalent environmental quality, though Asian children are slightly more advanced. Where major contrasts exist due to socioeconomic standards, disparities between groups appear. Developmental age, as

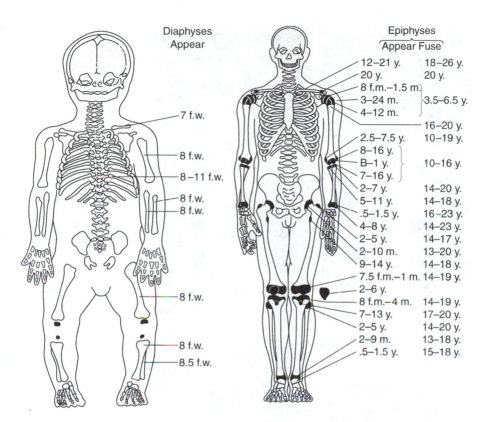

FIGURE 5-11 First appearance of the shafts (diaphyses) and joint ends (epiphyses) of the appendicular skeleton (f.w.: fetal weeks; f.m.: fetal months; m.: months; y.: years). (From Robertson, G. G., "Developmental Anatomy," in *Morris' Human Anatomy*, 12th ed., ed. B. J. Anson. New York: McGraw-Hill Book Company, 1966. Reproduced by permission.)

measured by skeletal maturity, may lag from several months to as much as a year behind chronological age.[2] This variation cuts across all ethnic boundaries and is class related as discussed below. In addition, there is a clear sexual dimorphism; females are between one to two years earlier in their skeletal development.

Skull. At birth, the bones of the cranium are separated by unossified membranes, which allow great flexibility and permit the passage of the infant's head (averaging 35 cm in circumference) through the birth canal. Starting from birth, there is considerable activity at the ossification centers, and the cranial bones increase in size until they meet and eventually fuse,

---

[2]Radiographic atlases of children have been in use for several decades as standards against which development may be measured. The two best known are the Greulich-Pyle, produced from a study of Cleveland, Ohio schoolchildren, and the Tanner Whitehouse, compiled from children in Britain (see Eveleth and Tanner, 1990).

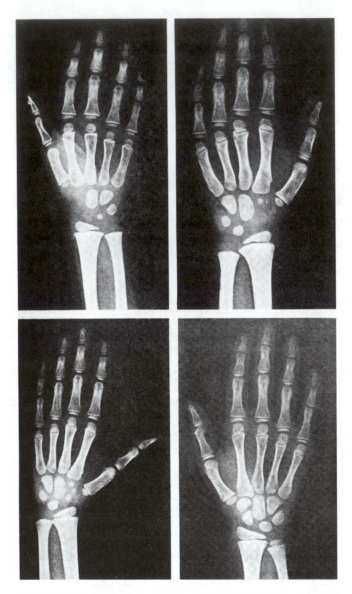

FIGURE 5-12   The development of the carpal bones (wrist bones) and the appearance of the epiphyses of the metacarpals and phalanges at ages four (top left), five (top right), six (bottom left), and seven (bottom right). (Reproduced with permission from Lowrey, G. H., *Growth and Development of Children*, 7th ed. Copyright © 1978 by Year Book Medical Publishers, Inc., Chicago.)

later in adult life. Certain cranial bones, however, fuse soon after birth. For example, the halves of the mandible fuse at the mandibular symphysis (the chin region) during the first year, and also the left and right halves of the frontal bone of the skull fuse along a suture through the middle of the forehead. Other cranial bones remain separated for many years and are joined at an irregular unmineralized junction (the sutures). These sutures gradually calcify with age, and the adjoining bones eventually become fused together. The older the individual, the less distinct will be the cranial sutures. This process of cranial bone mineralization covers a broad time range because each suture fuses at a different rate (Figure 5-13).

Dental maturation. At birth, the deciduous teeth are nearly complete, and some are ready to erupt within the first few months. Below their roots, buried deep within the jaws, are the developing permanent teeth, which gradually replace the deciduous teeth as the individual grows (Figure 5-14). This process of dental development is long and complicated; starting at about the sixth week in the embryo and continuing until the sixteenth year, there are some teeth in various stages of development while other teeth are fully formed.

FIGURE 5-13 Suture Closure of the Skull. The superior figures indicate the age at which the portion of the suture begins to obliterate; the inferior figures, the age at which obliteration is completed. The * indicates that the suture never completely closes. The figures on the upper teeth give the usual ages in years of the eruption of each permanent tooth. Owing to the great variability involved, these figures must be used with caution. (From Montagu, M. F. Ashley, *An Introduction to Physical Anthropology*, 3rd ed., 1960. Courtesy of Charles C. Thomas, Publisher, Springfield, Ill.)

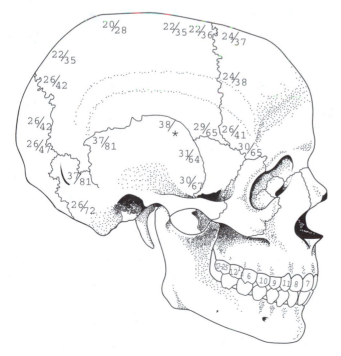

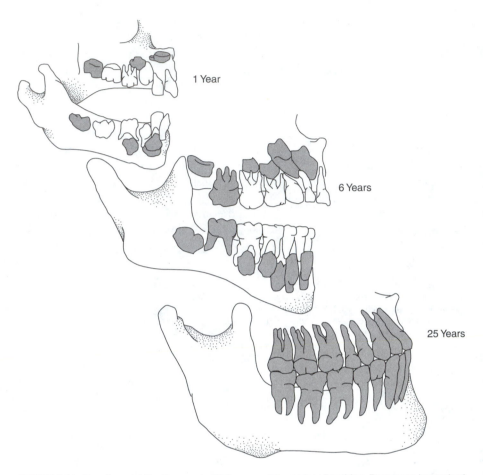

FIGURE 5-14   Eruption and Replacement of Primary and Secondary Dentition. Permanent (secondary) teeth are shaded. (From Harrison, R., and W. Montagna, *Man*, 2nd ed., 1973. Reprinted by permission of Prentice-Hall, Inc., Englewood Cliffs, N.J.)

The first teeth (deciduous incisors) erupt during the sixth to ninth month, while the crowns of the permanent first molars, incisors, and canines are just beginning to form. This process of development and eruption continues until the twenty-first year (an average among Euro-Americans), when the third molar (wisdom tooth) erupts, if the person is fortunate. Often, the third molar is impacted within the bone and must be removed surgically. The timing of dental development is listed in Table 5-11. Note that the crowns are completed and eruption occurs before the roots are fully formed.

Tooth-calcification sequences are fairly regular and provide a good indicator of age analogous to the skeletal ossification centers. Eruption times, however, are quite variable and are subject to several factors. There are strong environmental influences caused by diet and disease. Earlier eruption

TABLE 5-11   Chronology of Human Tooth Development

TOOTH	ONSET OF CALCIFICATION	CROWN (COMPLETED)	ERUPTION	ROOT (COMPLETED)
Deciduous				
Central incisor	4–4.5 months (in utero)	1.5–2.5 months	6–8 months	1.5 years
Lateral incisor	4.5	2.5–3	8–10	1.5–2
Cuspid	5	9	10–20	3.5
First molar	5	5.5–6	12–16	2.5
Second molar	6	10–11	20–24	3
Permanent				
First molars	Birth	2.5–3 years	6 years	9–10 years
Central incisors	3–4 months	4–5	7	9–10
Lateral incisors	10–12	4–5	8	10–11
Canines (cuspid)	4–5	6–7	11	12–15
First premolars (bicuspid)	1.5–2 years	5–6	10	12–13
Second premolars (bicuspid)	2–2.5	6–7	11	12–14
Second molars	2.5–3	7–8	12	14–16
Third molars	7–10	12–16	[a]	18–23

[a]The eruption time of the third molars is highly variable, with a range of 16–22 years.
Sources: Modified from Logan and Kronfield, 1933; and Schour and Massler, 1944.

appears to be the rule among higher socioeconomic groups. Sex differences also exist; tooth eruption is, on the average, a few months earlier in females. No definite genetic pattern has been established, though there have been several reports of ethnic differences in tooth eruption. Tooth eruption among Europeans and Euro-Americans is later than among Native Americans, Asians, and African Americans. Australian Aborigines appear to have the earliest tooth eruptions, especially the third molars, which have been known to erupt as early as thirteen years.

Sexual Maturation

Toward the end of childhood (eight to nine years in females and ten to eleven in males), a series of morphological and metabolic transformations begin that continue over a period of several years, transforming a child into a young adult. The body gradually begins to increase its growth rate with the approach of puberty. Changes occur in hair patterns and bodily proportions, and the sex organs begin to mature and increase in size. Approximately two years after entering this stage the individual begins the adolescent growth spurt (a time of rapid gain in size). The voice deepens (in males), breast development begins to be apparent (in females), and other secondary sexual characteristics appear—changes in fat distribution and development of hips (in females), for example, and increase in shoulder size in males. Pubic and axillary hair begins to appear in both sexes, and males start to show signs of facial hair.

There are wide individual variations in the time of puberty and the onset of the growth spurt, depending on sex, diet, general health, and genetic factors. In males, the growth spurt may occur anywhere between twelve and sixteen years, approximately two years later than in females (ten to fourteen years). After a year, growth decreases but continues slowly into the teens or early twenties. If measurements are taken throughout a person's growth years (longitudinal study), then a rapid gain can be easily seen, as shown in Figure 5-15, which plots average height increment gains for early- and late-maturing groups. Some individuals may gain 10 cm or more in height in a single year. Similar changes occur in weight, fat distribution, and bodily proportions. These changes, however, are more gradual and continue over longer periods.

FIGURE 5-15   Amount of Increase in Height per Year of Early-Maturing and Late-Maturing Girls and Boys. Although late-maturing girls show the peak rate of growth almost two years later than early-maturing boys, they still reach this stage nearly two and a half years before late-maturing boys reach the same peak velocity of growth. The curves of growth for height and weight are related to the maturation of the skeleton. This, in turn, is related to maturation in general (including the hormonal changes associated with sexual maturation). (From Tanner, J. M., *Growth at Adolescence*, 1962. Copyright © 1962 by Blackwell Scientific Publications, Ltd. Reprinted by permission of the publisher.)

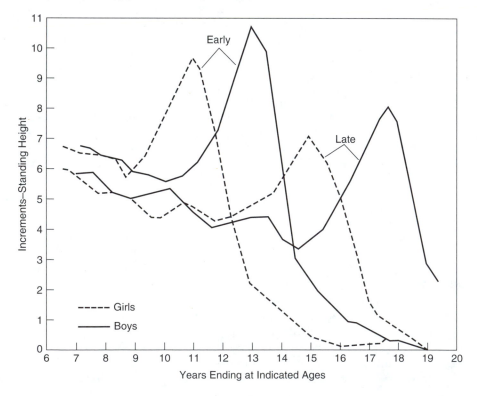

There is no clear-cut indicator of sexual maturity in the male; the increases in the sizes of the sex organs and their hormonal secretions are gradual and continue over a long period. In the female, menarche, the onset of the first menses, which occurs within a year of the growth spurt, is an excellent marker dividing prepuberty and postpuberty phases, however. There has been a trend over the past century toward a decrease in age at menarche, especially among children in the developed countries. For example, where records have been kept for one and a half centuries an average of seventeen years was registered in 1840 (Table 5-12). Today the average age at menarche is between twelve and fourteen, with 95 percent occurring between 11 and 15 years of age in the United States. No further decrease in age has been recorded, and there are several indications that the trend toward earlier menarche has ceased.

Neither racial/ethnic group nor climate appear to be a factor in the timing of female maturity, though both have been examined extensively during the past few decades (Eveleth and Tanner, 1976). More likely menarche is related to those same environmental factors that contribute to accelerated growth and changes in body composition. During and immediately after the adolescent growth spurt, female body composition changes radically. The rapid weight gain during this time is greatest for body fat—a 120 percent increase as compared with the lean body component (muscle and bone) increase of 49 percent. This significantly shifts the lean-body-mass-to-fat ratio

TABLE 5-12   Age at Menarche

POPULATIONS	AVERAGE AGE (YEARS)
European	
Various populations	12.5–13.5
Nineteenth century	15–17
New Zealand	
Maori	12.7
European	13.0
United States	
Afro-Americans	12.5
Euro-Americans	11–15
Chinese	
Hong Kong	12.5–13.3
Africa	
Nigeria	14.1
Uganda	13.4
Watusi	16.5
Hutu	17.0
New Guinea	
Bundi	18.0

Source: Eveleth and Tanner, 1976 and 1990; Frisch, 1988.

from 5:1 in the prepuberty years to a 3:1 ratio at menarche, indicating a significant rise of stored energy (male lean body ratios are around 5 or 6 to 1, by contrast). Rose Frisch (1988) has argued convincingly that it is this change in composition that provides the energy requirements of the female reproductive physiology. A minimal amount of 17 percent body fat is needed to initiate menses; in a girl of 165 cm (65 inches) tall, a total body weight of 49 kg (97 lb) is needed, or 38 kg (83.8 lb) for a person 155 cm (61 inches). The earlier attainment of these sizes and of the changes in body composition, as in the case of children in well-off socioeconomic groups with optimum nutrition, contributes to earlier age at menarche. Frisch notes that delays in menarche are experienced by many adolescent female athletes and ballet dancers, whose vigorous workouts reduce their fat/lean body ratio below the critical level.

In populations where children are relatively malnourished with insufficient food to meet the energy demands of growth, weight gain is significantly lower than in well-nourished populations. The girls grow more slowly, enter their growth spurts later, and slowly accumulate a store of body fat—all factors contributing to a later menarche. Contrasts by socioeconomic class have been reported in all countries. In Europe, urban girls enjoying better economic conditions reached menarche one year sooner than their rural cohorts; Indians of higher social class in Punjab reached menarche one and half years earlier than girls from poorer families. The same contrasts are seen between economically well-off urban Nigerians and rural poor; the well-off had a menarchial age close to the European average. The latest ages have been reported for New Guinea. Children of the Bundi tribe in the highlands of New Guinea, for example, had the slowest growth recorded in the world today, and girls reach menarche at about eighteen years, while the tribes living on the coastal plains grow faster and reach menarche at fifteen despite the location of their homeland in a malarial area. Additional evidence of nutritional influence is provided by European populations who lived through the hardships of two world wars. Many populations subsisted for long periods at or near starvation levels. The average age at menarche during these times increased by two years to age sixteen, a point not too far from late-eighteenth-century levels.

Males do not show as dramatic a change on reaching puberty, but they also suffer from diet and disease factors that interrupt growth. A major marker of these stressors, often described, is a later and less pronounced growth spurt (Figure 5-16a). Poor adolescent boys in London through the late eighteenth to early nineteenth century were described as so short that today only two of the eighty-one ethnic groups for which height data is available are smaller. These boys working in factories or wandering the streets averaged 6 to 11 cm shorter than boys of the middle class, and, as can be seen in Figure 5-16a, b, fell well below the British standard of 1965. Factory girls likewise fell below standards but not as much as the males (Figure 5-16b).

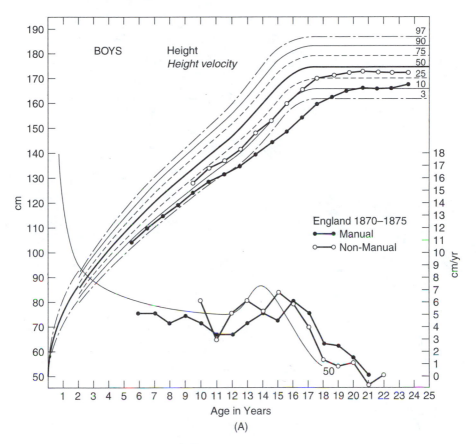

FIGURE 5-16 (A) Heights of boys of the manual worker class and of the nonmanual, mostly professional, class, in about 1870 in England. Values from Roberts (1874–76). Means are used for the manual group up to and including 15.0; modes thereafter. Means are used for the nonmanual group throughout.

This sorry state of child health was, perhaps, one of the low points in modern British social history. Alarms were raised about deterioration of the "lower classes" and there were fears that there would not be lads strong enough to carry rifles for the army or man the ships of war. Among the responses were the founding of various charitable organizations and the passage of laws relieving some of the worst aspects of child labor. The Marine Society was founded to provide shelter and training for homeless vagabond boys, and the Factories Regulation Act was passed to try to lessen the harshness of the conditions of child labor; among other things, it prohibited hiring of children under the age of nine and required rest and a meal period of one and one half hours each day. Not much, considering the typical twelve-hour workday, but an improvement and a recognition of the need for social change. Out of the Marine Society came further improvements, reflected in the heights of male adolescents shown in the graphs in Figure 5-17. Between

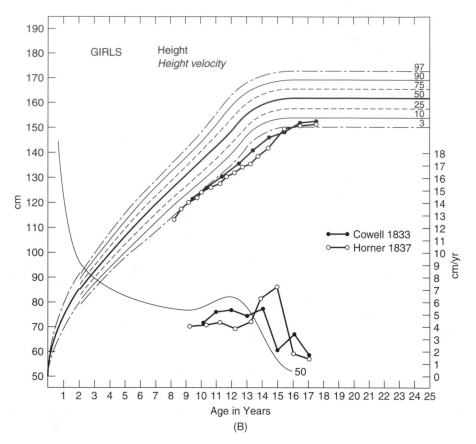

FIGURE 5-16 (B) Mean heights of girls working in factories in the Manchester–Leeds area in 1833 and 1837. Means for 1833 have been adjusted by subtraction of 0.5 cm for footwear. Source: From J. M. Tanner 1981. *A History of the Study of Human Growth.* Reprinted with the permission of Cambridge University Press.

1770 and 1810 no changes are seen, but thereafter, considerable improvements in growth are reflected in the larger sizes between fourteen and sixteen years of age (Tanner, 1981). The accumulation of these and other data from many studies of the health and welfare of children document some striking contrasts between generations and point to some significant trends. During the past century children have been reaching maturity earlier, as described above, and are larger at all ages than previous generations.

Longitudinal Growth Trends

Growth data from several European countries and North America show an average gain of 1 cm in adult height per decade during the last century. To a large extent, this is part of a trend toward earlier maturation; individuals obtain their adult height at an earlier age. Males in the United States today

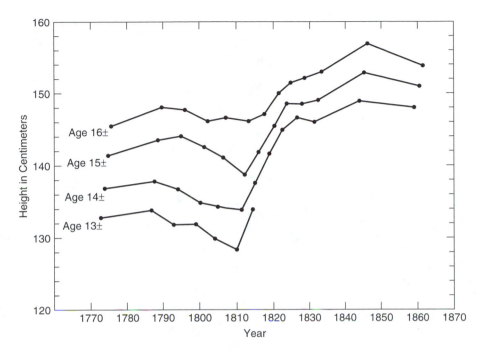

FIGURE 5-17 Heights of Marine Society recruits aged 13±, 14±, 15± and 16± from 1769 to 1860. Each point represents a 5–15 year cohort. Source: From J. M. Tanner. 1981. *A History of the Study of Human Growth*. Cambridge, MA: Cambridge University Press.

reach their adult height at around eighteen years, whereas their great-grand-fathers did not attain their full adult height until age twenty-six. Improved living standards in many societies have enabled children in many populations to grow to their maximum genetic potential; this increase in size during the past several generations is called *secular trend* (Figure 5-18). The graphs compare average heights of four groups from age four to twenty-three and show a 15-cm increase in adult height since 1833. The group of boys measured in 1833 were factory hands whose growth was retarded in late childhood and adolescence. Their height at age fourteen was a full 20 cm less than the standard of 1965, but slow growth over a prolonged period made up for some of this deficit. This catch-up period suggests that depressing environmental effects are more influential on growth rate than on final size.

Environmental Influences and Ethnic Differences

Boys and girls in the developed countries are heavier and taller than their parents. This secular increase in size has caused the height and weight tables of a generation ago to be far outdated. Reasons for this secular trend are often related to a general improvement in nutrition and health care with a reduction of infectious diseases (especially the "childhood diseases"), and to more

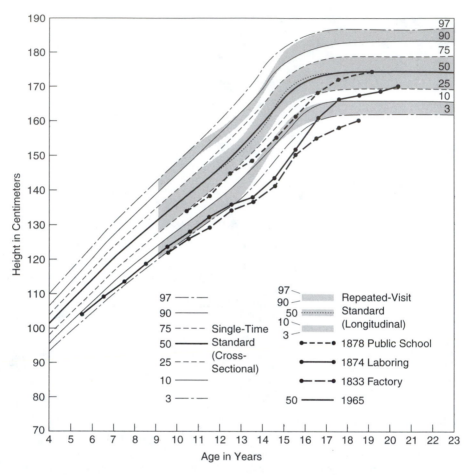

FIGURE 5-18 Secular Trend in Height. Secular trend in height is shown by surveys of the height of English boys in the years 1833, 1874, and 1965. Data are reproduced on a standard growth chart. "Single-time standard (cross sectional)" refers to the average result from cross-sectional surveys. "Repeated-visit standard (longitudinal)" refers to the average result from longitudinal surveys. The numbers 97, 90, 75, and so on indicate percent of the male population shorter than a given height. (From Tanner, J. M., "Growing Up," September 1973. Copyright © 1973 by Scientific American, Inc. All rights reserved.)

adequate housing. To this list of factors should be added the reduction or elimination of child labor. Most of these changes have occurred in this century. Differences still remain among socioeconomic groups in many countries, but the extremes are less than last century. Further, secular changes cut across all of the so-called racial/ethnic boundaries.

This phenomenon of increased growth and earlier maturity occurs in all groups whose socioeconomic circumstances allow children to be raised at optimum levels of nutrition and health. African Americans, a much studied group, show increases of body size over the past few generations despite their higher morbidity and mortality rates; however, this rate of increase is significantly less than that of Euro-Americans. They now attain an adult height by age eighteen that places them among the tallest in the world (see Tables 5-1, 5-2). Broader ethnic group comparisons show that Euro-Americans, Europeans, and Africans who are raised under similar economically well-off circumstances show few differences. The growth of Africans and Europeans is very similar, but Chinese are shorter at all ages and complete their growth earlier. What is most interesting is the case of the Japanese, who have increased approximately 10 cm between 1932 and 1982, despite a 2-cm decline during the war years of 1939–1945. This secular trend will probably soon cease and will bring the Japanese within 5 cm of British averages. Of special note is that sitting height has changed little. The stature increase has been by increased growth of the legs, which will bring bodily proportions nearer to those of Europeans (Eveleth and Tanner, 1990).

By contrast, groups of similar genetic composition raised under differing environmental circumstances differ in average body size at all ages. Children whose parents are members of the professional or managerial classes mature earlier and are 2 cm taller than children whose father's occupation is unskilled labor. At adolescence, the difference between children of these classes increases to 5 cm. Comparisons of seven-year-old children, grouped according to socioeconomic class based on the father's occupation and number of children in the family, are shown in Figure 5-19.

FIGURE 5-19 Differences in Height of Seven-Year-Old Children According to Occupation of Father ("Social Class") and Number of Siblings in Family. Sexes pooled. (Adapted from Goldstein, H., *Human Biology*, vol. 43, no. 1. Copyright © 1971 Wayne State University Press. Reprinted by permission.)

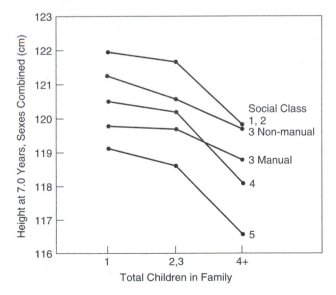

Further evidence of these characteristic growth responses to varying environments have been documented by many records of immigrant populations and their children, as in a study of stature increase among second-generation Italian-Americans in the Boston area (Damon, 1965). Groups were divided into decades from twenty to fifty-nine years of age; stature increased from the oldest to the youngest age groups. The greater stature of the youngest age group suggests that as economic standards and hence living conditions improve, populations' average stature and weight increase.

The many studies of human growth demonstrate that the effects of environment are quite similar for several ethnic groups. The tempo of ossification especially appears to be determined entirely by environment. Growth and attainment of adult height provides evidence of social conditions, and, in fact, economic historians have used stature as a proxy for the economic conditions of society during various periods of recent history. Appreciation of the influences environment has on growth will make it easier to understand human variability of form and size. We are, after all, the result of our growth experiences. There appear to be few ethnic distinctions and little evidence to point out genetic polymorphisms influencing body form and size, except for the insulin-like growth factor found in the Pygmies. Body form, shape, and size all are poor markers to distinguish between peoples, but is the color of our skin any better as a tool for classification?

THE STRUCTURE AND FUNCTION OF SKIN

Up to this point I have been describing morphological traits that can be measured or weighed even though they are the result of a complex of gene environment interactions. Now I must consider some traits not so easily defined and whose significance has often been misunderstood. We humans are visually oriented, so it is not surprising that we tend to view our world in terms of colors. This is especially true when categorizing ourselves. We still, all too frequently, cling to the antiquated classifications of black and white or brown and yellow as if nature has "color-coded" our species for ease of identification. So ingrained is this color concept in our thinking that we become surprised on discovery that no such divisions exist and that colors are the result of biochemistry and optic phenomena. To understand these phenomena we have to consider first the skin and its functioning under various environmental stresses.

The human body is clothed in a protective covering of renewable, elastic skin that wears off and is continuously replenished throughout our lifetime. Its functions are varied: from protection of underlying muscle tissue, glands, and blood vessels to carrying a large lymphatic system that plays a major role in immunological response to invading microbes and insects. Skin also functions in thermal regulation (maintenance of body temperature within its normal range) through surface radiation aided by the rich network of blood vessels just below the surface. These subcutaneous vessels can quickly expand, increasing the blood flow to aid metabolic heat loss, an important function during heavy work in hot climates. Constriction of these same vessels conserves body heat under cold conditions, maintaining skin temperatures lower than that of the core body. Assisting in thermal regulation through the skin are sweat glands distributed in varying densities over the body. These glands are capable of excreting large amounts of water that evaporate, cooling the body; heat of evaporation requires 600 calories per gram of water. In addition to this heat loss, the sweat glands excrete metabolic waste products, minerals, and some vitamins. So sweating can have both a positive effect (cooling) and a negative effect (water, mineral, and vitamin loss). Another function, and an extremely important one in the northern latitudes, is the synthesis of vitamin D (the vitamin essential for mineral metabolism). A final function is protection against the harmful effects of the ultraviolet rays of the sun, a function that involves both skin color and structure.

Skin consists of several structures organized in two major layers, the *dermis* and *epidermis*. The innermost or dermal layer consists of thick collagenous fibers and contains the blood vessels, nerves, hair follicles, and gland cells (sweat, sebaceous, and apocrine). This layer is covered by a thinner protective sheath of epidermis, a tissue with very active keratinocytes (basal cells). These basal cells or keratinocytes divide frequently and migrate upward. They gradually lose their vitality until they form flattened cells consisting mostly of keratin, a dense inert protein, the major constituent of nails, hair, and outer skin. This outermost skin layer of keratin is that part that wears away or flakes off.

An important component of skin structure, and the major contributor to its color, are specialized cells called *melanocytes* located in the lowest level of the epidermis. These cells have long, fingerlike projections, or *dendrites*, that are spread out from the cell body and come into close contact with the newly divided basal cells. The major function of these melanocytes is the synthesis of a substance called *melanin*, a pigment widely dispersed among vertebrate species. As the pigment granules are formed, they are concentrated into packets, or *melanosomes*, that are dispersed into the dendrites. From there, the melanosomes are injected into the basal cells (Figure 5-20). These cells then carry these granules as they migrate outward from the lowest layer of the epidermis, distributing the melanin throughout the upper layers of the epidermis. The skin color of all of us depends on how much of this pigment is distributed in our skin, which, in turn, depends on the rate of synthesis.

What is especially significant to our investigation of human variability is the considerable range of difference in melanin within and between populations. The number of melanocytes is approximately the same in all people (even albinos have a normal number), but the degree of melanin density varies widely. Color differences must be due, then, to a difference in the activity of melanocytes. In dark-skinned peoples, the cells function at a high level, synthe-

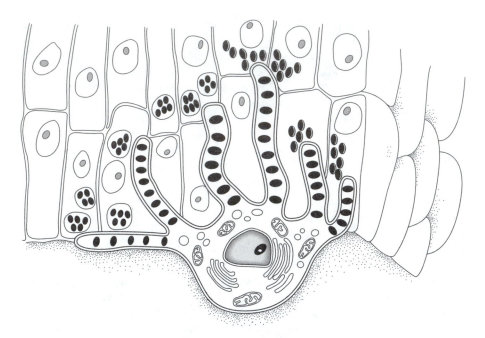

FIGURE 5-20 Epidermal melanin unit, showing the structural and functional relationship between melanocyte and surrounding cluster of keratinocytes to which it transfers melanosomes. (From A. H. Robins, *Biological Perspectives on Human Pigmentation*. Copyright © 1991 Cambridge University Press, with permission of the publisher.)

sizing large quantities of melanin, whereas in the fair-skinned northern Europeans, the cells make very little melanin. This activity is influenced by several genes, as suggested by comparisons of parents and their children. Offspring of a fair and a dark parent will produce melanin at an intermediate level (Figure 5-21). This figure only shows the averages of reflection characteristics at several wavelengths of light in each group. The ranges among family members is not indicated, but these comparisons do suggest the significance of genetic factors. What these genes are and how many are involved is a matter of dispute; from four to six genes have been proposed. Though supported by the reflectance data, this number seems to be too small. Consider that there are fourteen different types of albinism known under control of different genetic loci. One group of ten albino types lacks the tyrosinase enzyme, and the other four are tyrosinase positive but still are unable to make melanin (McKusick, 1994).

There are multiple mechanisms involved in synthesizing pigment. The amino acid tyrosine is the starting point for all of these processes and we all, even albinos, have large amounts concentrated in our melanocytes. The key to conversion of tyrosine is the enzyme tyrosinase, but the amounts of melanin produced is not related to the quantity of this enzyme. Even fair-skinned northern Europeans have sufficient quantities that could make them very dark. But there are inhibitors of tyrosinase that function more in some people than in

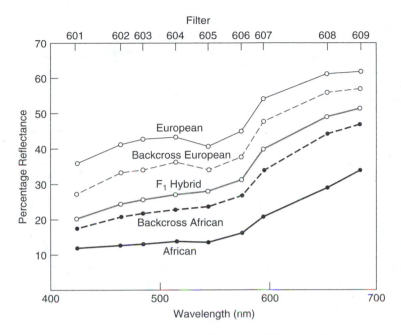

FIGURE 5-21 **Mean Reflectance Curves of European, African, and Various Hybrid Groups.** (Source: G. A. Harrison, et al. 1988. *Human Biology.* Oxford: Oxford University Press.)

others, and these inhibitors are likely regulated by several genes that vary from group to group. Australians and pygmoid peoples of Southeast Asia are dark because of processes different from those of sub-Saharan Africans, and Asians are different still in their melanization processes. What these processes are and how many genes are involved have yet to be discovered. The range of variation can be appreciated if the processes of melanin synthesis are considered.

The conversion of tyrosine to melanin pigments can be summarized by the steps listed in Figure 5-22. First, note that the bulk of the amino acid is provided by hydroxylation of phenylalanine and only about 5 percent from the diet. Tyrosine serves as a major component in hundreds of proteins, while another pathway leads to the formation of hormones of the thyroid gland, thyroxine. Tyrosine also is the starting ingredient for important hormones, the neurotransmitters: dopamine, noradrenaline, and adrenaline. The DOPA compound in pathway A (see left side of figure) is converted to a dopaquinone, which is then converted to either a brown-black melanin (eumelanin) or, if the amino acid cystine is added, a phaeomelanin (red-yellow) is formed. These processes occur in the melanocytes, and the several stages of chemical conversion are catalyzed by tyrosinase. The chemical derivatives at each step have been identified as well as certain of the enzymes, but those that regulate the processes and inhibit the enzyme effect are unknown. Another important pathway, pathway B as shown in the figure, also

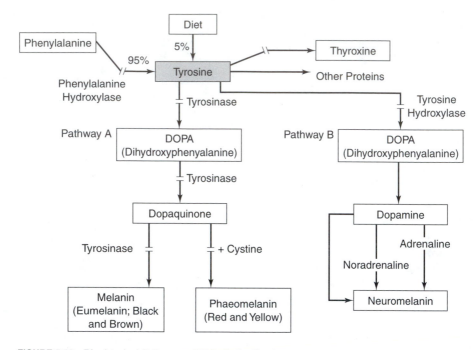

FIGURE 5-22   Biochemical Pathways of Melanin Synthesis.

begins with the conversion of tyrosine to DOPA, but there is a different enzyme, tyrosine hydroxylase, which is not present in melanocytes but is found in those tissues that produce the several neurotransmitters. This pathway is of interest because of its end product, neuromelanin, a pigment that appears in parts of the brain. Neuromelanin is formed in cells in the brain stem by autoxidation of some of the neurotransmitters, and it has been mistakenly related to skin melanization and used to construct a speculative Afrocentric theory of human evolution (de Montellano, 1993). The two melanins are not related except for starting with tyrosine; they are the products of different biochemical pathways (Ganong, 1993). We all have neuromelanin regardless of how much skin melanin we may produce; even albinos who are tyrosinase negative synthesize neuromelanin.

This brief overview underscores the complexity of the melanization process, and this complexity is extended further when external factors are considered. Certain hormones, some diseases, and perhaps mineral deficiencies (copper or zinc, for example) influence melanocytes, but the greatest stimulus is provided by the energy of ultraviolet radiation (UVR). Increased melanin production following UV exposure explains the ability of most lighter-skinned people to tan during the summer months with more hours of sunlight. There is a wide range of individual tanning ability, however, from little among northern Europeans to a rapid buildup of melanin among peoples native to the Mediterranean area. Even among people who are normally dark-skinned, their melanin density increases on prolonged exposure to the sun. Sex and age also influence melanin density and sensitivity to the effects of UV rays. Newborns of dark-skinned parents are lighter in color, sometimes even pink, and as they grow older their skin darkens until it reaches, by adolescence, an intermediate range between their parents. In addition, females of any population average less melanin than males. These factors of age and sex may have relevance to health and protection from disease or even survival.

The ability of humans to endure periods of direct exposure to solar radiation for prolonged periods varies and depends largely on the concentration of melanin, which functions as a filter blocking the ultraviolet portion of sunlight from penetrating through the epidermis to the dermal layer where blood vessels, nerves, and gland cells are located. Some studies have shown that heavily pigmented skin filtered out about 95 percent of the ultraviolet, whereas fair skin blocked only about 50 percent (Quevedo et al., 1985). Ultraviolet radiation can also be blocked by keratin, which is quite dense in thicker corneum layers, and this could play an important protective role. Albinos in West Africa develop thick, callused pads on the backs of their necks, for example (Harrison, 1975). It has even been suggested that "Mongoloids" have thicker skins, reducing the wrinkling effects of old age as well as protecting from UVR. The dense, near-inert keratin no doubt aids in filtering UVR, but melanin is more effective. In the dark skin of Africans, even the corneum is packed with melanin granules, which adds to its protection.

SKIN COLOR, GEOGRAPHY, AND NATURAL SELECTION

Before the major migrations brought on by colonization, the darkest-skinned people inhabited a region roughly defined by the Tropics of Cancer (Northern Hemisphere) and Capricorn (Southern Hemisphere), as noted in Chapter 1. This tropical zone has the longest, most intense daily solar radiation, with little seasonal variation. The distribution of dark-skinned peoples coincident with solar radiation intensity has caused naturalists to argue for centuries that skin color was adaptive and equipped people for the climatic conditions under which they lived. Such an argument has often been countered by observations that several of these populations live in humid tropical rain forests where little sunlight reaches the ground, and these tropical peoples (Pygmies, for example) still had some of the darkest skins found anywhere. By contrast, some desert dwellers, like the !Kung of southern Africa, had skin with much less melanin. Other doubts about the correlation of skin color and latitude have been raised by arctic and subarctic peoples—Eskimos and Siberian reindeer herders, for example—who have a considerable amount of melanin though, given their environment, they would be expected to be pale like the Lapplanders. Add to this list dark-skinned Tasmanians, who lived at high latitudes (the island of Tasmania, 42 degrees south, is as far from the equator as is Boston, Massachusetts) for at least 20,000 years.

Despite these and other exceptions, there is a close positive correlation between latitude and skin light-reflectance for many populations measured; the darker the skin, the less light reflected. The objections to skin color as an adaptive trait have frequently been based on scant evidence of the degree of pigmentation (there are no measurements of Tasmanians, for example, only casual observations that they were "very dark"). There is also a considerable misunderstanding of several significant factors: the nature of solar radiation, its effect on the skin, physical geography, and the living conditions of many tropical peoples. Discussions of human pigmentation have often been purely speculative, with little reference to biochemical functions.

Ultraviolet Radiation (UVR)

Ultraviolet rays represent a portion of the sun's electromagnetic energy below the wavelength band for visible light. A large fraction of ultraviolet, in the range of 290 to 320 mμ (2,900 to 3,200 angstroms) wavelength, is absorbed by the ozone layer surrounding the earth. Little reaches ground level, but there is a sufficient amount of this energy to affect many life forms and it is this part that is of most concern. Table 5-13 lists the three components of UVR, their degree of penetration, and biological effects. These shorter wavelengths are also influenced by the angle between the sun's rays

TABLE 5-13   Solar Radiation and the Ultraviolet Spectrum

WAVELENGTH[1]	BIOLOGICAL EFFECTS[2]	PENETRATION[3]
Ultraviolet-C 190–290 mμ	Germicidal; little skin penetration	Scattered and absorbed by dust, water vapor, and ozone; little or none reaches earth's surface
Ultraviolet-B 290–320 mμ	Sunburn, cancer, tanning, and vit. D synthesis	More energy reaches earth's surface
Ultraviolet-A 320–400 mμ	Same as above but less effective; the additional influence of photolysis on some vitamins	More energy reaches earth's surface than above

[1]The units of measure of solar spectrum are given in millimicrons (mμ) which are equal to 10 angstroms.
[2]The biological effects vary according to wavelength and have greater or lesser effect on different cell structures or chemical compounds; e.g., the 290–320 range stimulates the production of melanin and also provides the energy for vitamin D synthesis from its provitamin. The higher-range UVA also has some of these effects.
[3]The penetrating power of the UV energy spectrum is a function of its wavelength; the shorter wavelengths are absorbed and scattered by more substances and little or no energy reaches the earth's surface. Likewise, the longer wavelengths penetrate the skin more deeply; e.g., at 360 mμ the penetration is twice as deep as it is at 240 mμ (see Faber, 1982).

and the earth's surface; time of day as well as season of the year causes a reduction of radiation. The sun is most intense at midday on the equator and declines with the hour. The higher the latitude, the lower the solar radiation and the greater will be the seasonal variation, as shown by the diagram of the daily UV radiation count in Minneapolis over the year (Figure 5-23). The change between mid-winter and mid-summer is about 1,800 percent. By contrast, little seasonal change occurs within the tropical zones, and these differences between tropical and temperate zones in amounts of UVR have profound biologic effects.

Human Skin and Solar Radiation

The effects of solar energy on the skin vary considerably depending on wavelength. There is a deeper penetration of the skin by energy at the near infrared range (1,000 mµ), but little ultraviolet (290–400 mµ) reaches the lower layers of the epidermis (stratum germinativum where the basal cells are most active). The thickness of the corneum, or outer layer, and melanin pigment have significant effects of blocking and scattering UVR: Darkly pigmented skin is penetrated much less deeply than fair skin. The shortest wavelength, UVC, has the least penetrating power; besides, little energy from this range reaches the earth's surface. The longer part of the ultraviolet spectrum, UVA, will reach further down into the epidermal layer, but with seemingly less biologic effect, harmful or beneficial. UVA does stimulate the melanocytes to some degree and provide energy for vitamin D synthesis. The middle range UVB, however, has the greater influence. Penetration is less and it is more readily blocked by melanin, but its biologic effects are greater,

FIGURE 5-23 Daily Total of Ultraviolet Radiation for 1974 in Minneapolis.

The record of UV measured in this North American city at 44.58° north latitude illustrates the broad range of difference between midsummer (day 185) and midwinter (day 350). (Source: From Faber, 1982. Reprinted with permission from World Health Organization, Washington, D.C.)

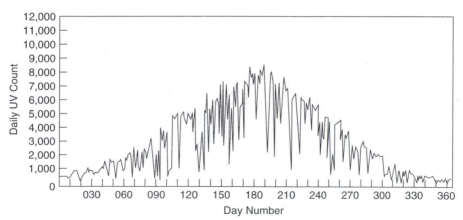

with more vitamin D synthesized and more melanin produced (Faber, 1982). These varying characteristics of UVR are important factors in our adaptation to geographic regions with variable degrees of solar radiation, as described below.

First, because we judge skin color by the visible part of the spectrum, the differences in the reflective properties of human skin should be noted. We may measure differences by beaming a quantity of light on a section of untanned skin and then measuring the amount reflected. This method gives an accurate method of detecting relative degrees of melanization. Figure 5-24 shows comparative skin-reflectance properties of Africans and Euro-Americans. The curves indicate greater reflectance by the white skin over the entire

FIGURE 5-24 Skin-Reflectance Characteristics of a Sample of American Blacks and Whites. (Redrawn; based on Barnicot, 1957.)

Average reflectance characteristics of black and white skin on the flexor surface of the forearm. Measurements made from visible light to the near-infrared range with marked absorption indicated in the white sample at approximately 5,500 angstroms (the absorption for hemoglobin).

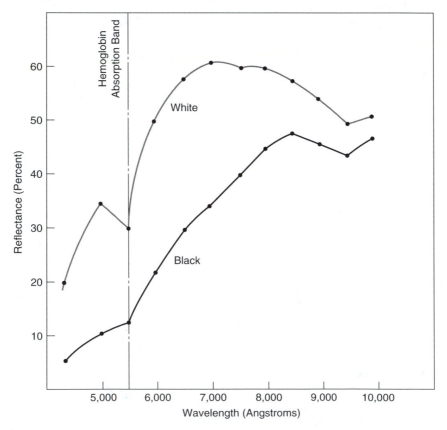

spectral range tested. These curves, however, were constructed from average values of all subjects tested and obscure ranges of reflectance variation. Figure 5-25 illustrates some of this variation of reflectance characteristics of several populations that vary in pigmentation (see also, Figure 5-21). In this study,

FIGURE 5-25 Skin-Reflectance Characteristics of Several Populations. (Source: After Walsh, R. J., "Variations of melanin pigmentation of the skin in some Asian and Pacific peoples." Copyright © 1963 by the Journal of the Royal Anthropological Institute. Reprinted by permission of the publisher.)

The mean percentage of reflectance from the foreheads of samples of several populations is indicated by the dot, and the range of plus or minus one standard deviation is indicated by the line.

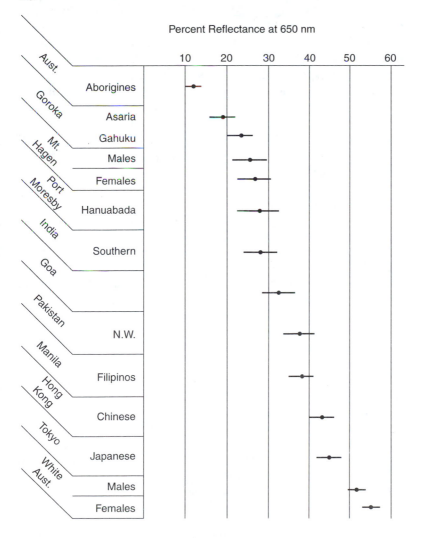

reflectance was measured at the upper end of the visible range. The whites reflected roughly 50 percent of the light, and aborigines only reflected about 10 percent; other groups showed reflectance properties between these two extremes. The two groups that recorded male and female reflectance values showed males lower on the scale.

Natural Selection and Skin Color

The simple distributional evidence of skin color is not a sufficient explanation of its adaptive advantage; consider some of the probable mechanisms that may be operating. If we regard the epidermis as a filter that reduces the amount of ultraviolet radiation penetrating the skin, we can establish the relative advantages or disadvantages of high melanin content of the skin in various environments.

First, if we consider sunburn, or the reddening of the skin, we can see many advantages enjoyed by people who naturally have dark skins or who can make melanin quickly, especially if they must work outside. Depending on the degree of burn, sunburn causes congestion of the subcutaneous capillaries, destruction of cells at several layers, and edema (collection of fluids under the skin's surface). Besides being painful, sunburn can be very dangerous. Rapid cell destruction followed by peeling of large sections of skin can open the way for infection. Another effect is the reduction in our ability to regulate body temperature, since sweat gland function is reduced to the point where internal body temperature buildup leads to heat exhaustion. Prolonged exposure to the sun can also cause permanent damage to underlying tissues. Premature wrinkling of the skin due to a destruction of the elastic collagen fibers is another effect of long-term exposure. Darkly pigmented peoples are less prone to this solar radiation damage because of the filtering effects of the melanin, and hence such people appear to "age" more slowly.

However, humans have numerous nonbiological means of protection. We can and often do use some kind of shelter or covering, but in certain climates the high temperature and humidity make clothing a disadvantage and reduce the body's capacity for heat dissipation. Skin pigmentation enables humans to be more mobile and functional in tropical sunlight, where ambient temperatures are close to normal body temperature, making heat dissipation difficult, especially when clothing is worn. An exception is seen among desert peoples like the Saharan tribes. These people live in one of the hottest regions of the world and go about with their bodies completely clothed. Their clothing is loose-fitting, however, and traps air between the skin surface and the outer garment. Perspiration is collected by the cloth and is quickly evaporated by the dry air. The garment serves both as a shield from the sun's rays and as a cooling aid through evaporation.

Overexposure can result in more permanent damage, as in the example of skin cancer, where some of the cells' DNA is altered. There are three types of skin cancer—basal cells in the lowest level of the epidermis, the flattened squamous cells near the outer layer, and malignant melanoma, a cancer of the melanocytes. The first two types are the most common of all human cancers, but have a low mortality rate since they do not metastasize and spread to other tissues. Melanoma, because it does grow and spread if not treated early, is one of the deadliest forms of all.

The incidence of these skin cancers is highest among fair-skinned persons who are exposed to the sun for prolonged periods. Persons whose occupations keep them out of doors have a greater chance of developing skin lesions, usually on the face or on the backs of the hands. The highest frequencies of skin cancers in the world are among white Australians living in Queensland—about 265 cases reported per 100,000 males and 156 per 100,000 females. The incidence among whites living in South Africa is much lower—133 per 100,000 males and 72 per 100,000 females. In contrast, British populations have a low of only 28 per 100,000 males and 15 per 100,000 females. In the United States the rate of new skin cancer cases has radically increased—up to 1,000,000 new cases per year, and some 38,000 of these are the most lethal type, malignant melanoma, that accounts for 7,000 deaths (Leffell and Brash, 1996). The relation to sunlight is clear; Tucson, Arizona, has seven times the number of new skin cancers as Minneapolis or Seattle. Even more confirmation of cancer risk is provided by the fate of thousands of albinos in Nigeria; virtually all have skin cancer or precancerous lesions by age twenty (Faber, 1982). Among the darker-skinned populations, problems related to solar radiation are minimal, and skin cancers rarely, if ever, occur. Recently, skin cancers have received more attention because of an increase during the past decade, and the number of cases are expected to rise further because of a depletion of the ozone layer that surrounds the earth, thereby allowing more UVR to penetrate the atmosphere.

The Photochemical Effects of Ultraviolet Radiation

Besides the damage caused by ultraviolet radiation (UVR), there are effects that we might call photochemical, the changes of chemical bonds when certain compounds are exposed to sunlight. Several chemicals essential for our metabolism have this sensitivity and will undergo decomposition (photolysis) under the influence of UVR. Among these sensitive chemicals are several vitamins: folic acid, riboflavin, and vitamin E. The photosensitivity of these substances has led to suggestions that dark skin may protect certain critical metabolites in the blood and dermis from the photodecomposition effects of UVR. Several experiments have shown that levels of folic acid in the blood were depressed by ultraviolet light; such was the case with patients of Scandinavian descent undergoing treatment for skin ailments by exposure to ultraviolet light. Branda and Eaton (1978) reported that folic-acid levels in such patients dropped significantly during the course of their treatment. Though no comparable study has been reported for vitamin E or riboflavin in humans, these substances are known to be photosensitive as demonstrated by laboratory experiments.

Ultraviolet radiation also has a positive photochemical effect. Vitamin D, essential for skeletal growth and absorption and transport of calcium, is synthesized by the action of UVR on a sterol compound, 7-dehydrocholesterol, an oily substance found in the lower layers of the epidermis. Because the amount required for proper maintenance of calcium levels is small (only about 300 to 400 units per day), an exposure of a small area of the body to the sun for a short period is sufficient. It has been estimated that 20 cm^2, or about the area of the skin covering a human infant's face, is sufficient. Any interference with this amount of exposure (by reduction in time, ultraviolet light, or in surface area) correspondingly diminishes the amount of vitamin D synthesized. Dark skin requires six times as long to make the same amount of the vitamin as light skin, and the time will also vary by latitude; synthesis is more rapid in the tropics and longer in the northern temperate zone. Since vitamin D is scarce in most foods except fish oils, it is usually difficult to get through dietary sources. The synthesis in the skin can then be very important when the results of a vitamin D deficiency are considered.

The effects caused by a reduction in the vitamin vary between individuals, depending on their age. Rickets, once a frequent disease in northern Europe, will develop in children deprived of vitamin D. Their rapidly growing bones will fail to mineralize properly and the weight-bearing parts of the skeleton, the legs and pelvis in particular, will become distorted and misshapen as the infant begins to walk. In its severest form, rickets can even result in death. One of the clearest examples of the course of rickets and the influence of diet and lifestyle comes from well-documented medical records of the last two centuries. Children living in crowded slums of industrial cities of eighteenth- and nineteenth-century England suffered from a high frequency of rickets. The smoke-laden air and the crowded streets with no open space and little sunlight reduced the chance of satisfying the body's requirements for the vitamin. Given the environmental influences, rickets has been called the first air-pollution disease (Loomis, 1970). Diet was an important factor also, since fresh milk and fish were expensive and scarce in the diets of factory workers. Adults did not escape this problem but suffered from osteomalacia, the adult form of poorly mineralized bone.

In addition to this example, these vitamin-D deficiency diseases have occurred in a wide variety of environments, even in the tropics. Women of some cultures suffer more frequently because of a tradition that causes them to be confined to the household from early childhood and allowed in public only if they are completely covered. The restriction on their daily activities and their required clothing reduces the amount of sunlight striking the skin to a low level. For example, Bedouin women in North Africa and the Middle

East remain inside the family's tents most of the day, and if they venture outside they must clothe themselves completely with skirts and veils. Only the small area of skin around their eyes is exposed to sunlight. This seclusion of women indoors also affects the health of infants and children. Infants in Muslim cultures and among high-caste Hindus frequently develop rickets during infancy, but many recover as young children when they are allowed to play out of doors. Females, often married at twelve years of age and then forced into the seclusion of the home and veil, frequently develop the disease again.

Rickets can also occur in modern urban populations today. For example, among the large numbers of East Indians and Pakistanis who have settled in the British Isles during the last thirty-five years, cases of rickets and osteomalacia have made their appearance. The combination of low incidence of sunlight in these northern latitudes, deeply pigmented skin, and dietary customs significantly reduces the chance of the synthesis of an adequate amount of vitamin D. The pathological results—skeletal malformations—have been reported in several clinical studies. This is similar to the experience of American black populations living in North American cities a half century ago. Before the widespread use of vitamin D supplements, rickets was suffered by many children, but most frequently among blacks.

Rickets and osteomalacia, in severe forms, can shorten life span and are most effective as selective forces among females because these diseases can lead to distortion of the pelvis. Figure 5-26 compares a normal and distorted pelvis inlet, showing the serious influence that rickets can have on female growth. Even a slight deformation of the pelvis reduces the birth canal and interferes with normal childbirth, increasing the risk of death of the mother or the fetus during childbirth. The effects of the disease can be measured by the frequency of deformed pelvis among females; only 2 percent of white women had a deformed pelvis compared with 15 percent of black women. Since the near-universal addition of vitamin D_2 to milk in the United States and most European countries, however, rickets has been

FIGURE 5-26 Outline of normal pelvic inlet (solid line) and contracted pelvic inlet due to severe childhood rickets (broken line). (From Frisancho, A. R., *Human Adaptation*, 1979. St. Louis: The C. V. Mosby Co.; modified from Eastman, N.J., *Obstetrics*, 11 ed., 1956. New York: Appleton-Century-Crofts.)

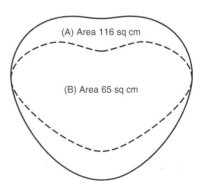

(A) Area 116 sq cm

(B) Area 65 sq cm

nearly eliminated as a childhood disease, except for some Asian migrants to northern Europe.

Despite the disadvantages of dark skin in the temperate zone, it can be advantageous to be deeply pigmented in the tropics when overexposure to ultraviolet rays could cause not only sunburn and skin cancer, but also hypervitaminosis (an overproduction of vitamin D). Too much vitamin D is harmful; as little as 2,000 IU (international units) per day synthesized or ingested over a period of time causes calcification of many soft tissues throughout the body and impairs kidney function. The toxic level may be as low as 40,000 IU for infants to 100,000 IU for adults (normal individual needs vary between 400 and 1,000 IU per day). Whole-body radiation has been estimated to produce upward of 120,000 units per hour, which is well above the toxic level (between 10,000 and 100,000 IU per day). Clothing, of course, reduces the amount of skin exposed, but the reader should remember that tropical peoples wear relatively little clothing. Besides, during the first few years, children in tropical climates seldom wear any clothing at all and during the day are much more active than adults. This would add to the degree of their exposure and hence the potential for producing toxic levels of vitamin D.

SKIN COLOR AND EVOLUTION

The preceding discussions of the harmful and helpful effects of solar radiation provide some evidence of the direct effects on human survival. Considering all those factors that relate skeletal structure, calcium metabolism, skin pigmentation, and incidence of ultraviolet radiation, we now ask: How have they affected human evolution? Is the color of *Homo sapiens* "naturally dark" and, if so, what accounts for the relative depigmentation of the Europeans and the medium pigment of Asians?

The wealth of fossil evidence accumulating today supports earlier hypotheses that *Homo sapiens* evolved in the tropics. Our immediate ancestors spread into and "permanently" occupied the northern latitudes relatively recently in time, probably not before the third interglacial period (about 120,000 years ago). At this time these prehistoric populations were probably dark-skinned and suffered the detrimental effects common to deeply pigmented peoples living in regions of low ultraviolet radiation. The selection for peoples that could thrive under such conditions—that is, relatively depigmented fair-skinned peoples—has lasted until the present century. There is evidence that the adjustment to these selective forces must have taken thousands of years. Even during the Mesolithic period, between 10,000 and 15,000 years ago, northern European populations suffered from poor mineralization. Skeletal remains from Sweden and other areas of northern Europe dating to this period show many signs of poor calcium in their teeth and bones. Likewise, evidence is seen among skeletal materials dating from medieval times.

Two things made possible the continuous survival of *Homo sapiens* in the northern latitudes. The first is the steady decline in pigmentation throughout hundreds of generations or, rather, selection favoring the survival of individuals whose genetic systems caused them to have lighter skins. The second is the increased use of fish in the diet during the past 6,000 years—particularly herring, which is rich in vitamin-D–bearing oil. Eventually, though no one knows where the practice began, a home remedy for rickets was introduced: the use of fish liver oils to cure this childhood disease. Also, there developed the practice of placing infants outside, even during the coldest months, to gain a little "fresh air and sunshine." Both of these measures have the same end results and have helped our species to sustain life and maintain large populations in northern Europe.

A discussion of the protective effects of melanin must also consider the changes of photolysis (light-caused chemical breakdown). Experiments with human and laboratory animals, noted previously, have shown that photolysis reduces folic-acid levels. If individuals live on diets marginal in folic-acid content, as many tropical populations do, then they will be particularly susceptible to a reduction in vitamin action owing to the destructive effects of the sun. Impaired growth in children and low reproductive capacity are a result of folic-acid deficiency, and would be a strong selective influence for dense pigmentation as protection against photodecomposition of this essential vitamin. A similar argument could be made for protection of riboflavin and vitamin E. The probability that melanin functions to reduce photodecomposition of certain vitamins and prevents overproduction of vitamin D argues strongly for natural selection of dark-skinned peoples in areas of intense solar radiation.

If another feature of human skin is considered, its tanning ability, then evidence can be added to that already discussed. Selection appears to have been for skin that will vary in pigmentation according to the incidence of ultraviolet. The best adapted, then, would have skin that tanned well in the summer (reducing vitamin-D synthesis as exposure to sunlight increased with the long summer days) and lightened during the winter to take all possible advantage of the weak winter sun. Europeans native to southern Europe, North Africans, and western Asian populations have skins with a higher degree of melanin content than their northern neighbors, so they tan much better—a feature that is a significant advantage in their climates.

Skin coloration happens to be much more complex and variable than is usually appreciated, and it requires far more discussion than can be given here; however, many of the interrelationships between sunlight and physiology seem clearly established. One final consideration we should note is the difference between the skin color of males and females in the same populations. Females have lighter skin, which, given their need for a more care-fully regulated calcium metabolism, makes good adaptive sense. Children are also much fairer than their parents; often the infants of dark-skinned parents are pink, and their skin steadily darkens throughout childhood. This is another factor that shows the interrelationship between the human skin pigmentation system and solar radiation, demonstrating again the selective advantages that variable skin pigmentation can confer on the human population.

EYE COLOR AND HAIR COLOR

Melanin granules also determine the various shades of eye color by the distri-bution and density of the pigment in the iris. Blue eyes occur when there is little melanin present scattered throughout the iris structure. The light reflected from the relatively depigmented upper layer is in the blue range of the visible light spectrum. So blue eyes occur most often in fair-skinned per-sons. Variations in the density of the pigment and its distribution cause a graded color series from pale blue to brown. Though eye color tends to be related to the degree of skin melanin, darker eyes do occur in individuals with fair skin. This suggests that different gene loci control the production and dis-tribution of eye pigment. The genetics of eye color has not been worked out but it is likely to be the result of several loci, which would account for the range of individual differences seen even in the same family.

Hair color is also determined by the degree of melanin present and gen-erally correlates with skin color. Most humans have darker hair, ranging from brown to black, but there appears to be an aging factor influencing hair color. Many children of European ancestry are fair-haired until adolescence, after which hair darkens. In some, there is a persistence of fair hair throughout adolescence and adult life, associated with fair skin that is especially notable in northern Europe. However, the association with fair skin is not universal; some deeply pigmented peoples have light-colored hair. In central Australia, for example, many Aborigines have blond hair as children, a feature that appears in stark contrast to their dark skin. As they reach adolescence, their hair usually darkens to match their skin, but some maintain light hair color throughout their lives. The reason for this blondness among the Aborigines of central Australia is still open to speculation and is a lively topic for discus-sion. Blondness of the Australians is apparently due to a gene or genes for the trait and not because of some European admixture, since those individuals with the blond trait have all Aboriginal characteristics, and the evidence for a lack of European genes is reinforced by carefully collected genealogies (Bird-sell, 1981). The peculiar example of the contrasts between hair and skin pig-ment raises the question of the complex inheritance of pigmentation of hair, skin, and eye color and suggests the possibility that the dark skin of Pacific peoples may be due to genes different from African populations.

HAIR FORM

When the skin of our species is compared with that of other mammals, the first distinction noticed is the near hairless, naked appearance. On closer inspection, however, the skin is not hairless; even apparently naked areas have about the same number of hair follicles as do our furrier primate relatives. Human hairs are finer, thinner in diameter, shorter, and most are relatively colorless. The distribution, density, and color of body hair, though, is subject to vast individual differences, and some ethnic groups have denser body hair than others. For example, there is a relative lack of facial hair among male Asians and Native Americans, in contrast to the heavy beards of many European males and the beards and dense body hair of the Japanese Ainu. Body hair distribution also shows significant sexual dimorphism, with females having less hair, and a near total lack of facial hair.

The hair on the head also varies considerably in length and form, from straight to wavy or curly and the spiral "peppercorn" shape. Asians have straight hair that is thicker than the wavy or curly hair of many Europeans. Frizzy or woolly hair is the form of most Africans, and the San or !Kung are noted for their short, spiral shaped hair. The adaptive significance of hair form is not understood, but it is likely that certain forms, woolly or spiral, allow for an air space between the scalp and outer edges that insulates the head from the intensity of the sun's heat in the tropics. Such an insulating mechanism would be an advantage to the !Kung hunters of Southern Africa or to Melanesians in New Guinea. As is the case with the other polygenic structures we have discussed, the distribution, form, and color of hair are inherited. The number of genes involved, though, is not known, but some inherited defects of hair structure have been reported. One rare form that is of special interest, "woolly" hair, was discovered in a large family kindred living in an isolated region of Norway. Their hair grows to only a short length before the ends break off and gives the appearance of the frizzled or woolly hair form seen in some Africans. The "woolly" hair condition is different from that of Africans, however, and is inherited as an autosomal dominant trait.

SOME CONCLUSIONS

Despite our expectations, appearances can be deceiving. Most appearances that we tend to rely on for identification are continuously variable over a broad range in any population. Further, many of these traits can change in a single generation, as in the example of body shape and size. The traits are subjected to a broad array of environmental factors that operate on the base of a number of gene-determined factors. Little is known about the inheritance mechanisms of morphology. Yet human morphological variation has been and is still used for labeling purposes. Most important, many of these complex polygenic traits follow a clinal distribution over broad geographical ranges. Human migrations, especially in historic times, and frequent interbreeding have scattered human populations widely over vast areas. It is difficult, or maybe even impossible, to define any clear-cut boundaries on the basis of a combination of these complex phenotypes. In addition to the environmental factors that have contributed to human diversity, the ways in which we have organized our social activities must be considered.

6

Distribution of Human Differences

The term *race* has been applied to units as small as local breeding populations (demes) as well as to large groups of populations occupying entire continents (geographical race). Race has also been used quite frequently to describe a cultural or political group (Jewish, Aryan, English, and so on). Another casual use of the term is shown by the phrase "the human race," which has nothing to do with biological classification. Ethnic group is more and more frequently used today as a substitute term for people presumed to be of different genetic ancestry than the majority population—as in the case of Hispanic ethnic groups in the United States. The results of such varied and inappropriate usage have misled the reader and have obscured meaningful application. Further, the inconsistent use of markers of biological data has added materially to the confusion over classification. Comparisons of populations for traits of simple inheritance yield different results than do complex traits. The geographical distribution of red-cell antigens, histocompatibility (HLA) types, and DNA polymorphisms differ markedly, and none correspond well with population boundaries based on quantitative traits like body form.

This lack of concordance of trait distribution brings up the question of how the human species may be subdivided into groups for description and study. There is no simple solution, and devising methods of division has always been difficult, particularly because many of the so-called racial differences are trivial in comparison with species differences. Genetic loci are shared by all human populations and, with rare exceptions, none are unique to any one group. It is a matter of differing frequencies of certain alleles that provide markers differentiating populations. Many genetic polymorphisms per loci vary less among the classic geographical races than among populations composing one of the races. Hence, populations of southern Africa differ significantly at several loci (Rh, GM, and HLA systems) from populations living 2,000 miles to the northwest. Such differences are also recorded among populations of other major geographic divisions. What once appeared to be a few simple subdivisions of our species turns out to be numerous large clusters of genetic heterogeneity dispersed throughout the geographic range of human occupation.

These facts of gene diversity, together with the reality of population variability, have caused several biologists to avoid or even to abandon the use of the race concept as a viable tool for the study of human diversity. Hiernaux (1964:43), for example, observes: "In my opinion, to dismember mankind into races as a convenient approximation requires such a distortion of the facts that any usefulness disappears." The facts to which Hiernaux referred are the many sources of evidence of human biological diversity, which include the several traits I discussed in the preceding chapters. With the accumulation of new genetic data over the past decades, trait diversity and distribution turns out to be much broader than formerly recognized. Further, many of these trait distributions cut across population and geographic boundaries. Some investigators still consider racial classification a useful means of studying adaptation and epidemiology because they view races as "natural units" (Polednak, 1989). Others dismiss race as but an artifact of *Homo sapiens'* past. Many believe that traits should be considered individually and not as a group or cluster unless the resulting classification, based on one character, reflects the variability of others (Livingstone, 1964:47). More and more frequently, in the past decade, the breeding population has become the unit of study.

Despite disagreement over the race concept, there is general agreement that an understanding of the distribution of human biological diversity is basic to comprehending human adaptation. Regardless of one's definition or application of the race concept, we should remember the point raised earlier: There is no reason to assume that there is now, or ever has been, a fixed number of races. I would add that there are no basic racial stocks—a misleading and confusing concept that still leads us astray. If we keep these cautions in mind, we can avoid the trap that so many nineteenth-century naturalists fell into: "If races change, how do races come to be?" This logical impasse retarded the study of human biology for many generations. In fact, we are only now beginning to appreciate the complexity of our very polytypic species, whose variability is a result of a series of interactions between the social and biological systems, as this chapter will consider.

SOME FACTORS CONTRIBUTING TO GENETIC DISTRIBUTION

Human variability as it is distributed through time and space depends on a multitude of factors. Several are the same factors that operate on any biological population and influence gene frequency throughout the generations, as described in Chapter 2. Other influences are uniquely human.[1] Humans are highly mobile and are able to manipulate the environment at will to affect successful adaptation in a variety of climates. These abilities depend not only on technological achievements but on the elaboration of complex social systems that regulate behavior and coordinate individual and group activities. Of particular importance is direction of breeding behavior—the regulation of mate choices. This is accomplished by the establishment of abstract boundaries, or mating circles, within a population.

All societies enforce some form of incest taboo that forbids or proscribes marriages between relatives of some degree, which always includes the nuclear family—parents and offspring—within this restricted category. An exception is brother–sister unions, which were favored in several ancient civilizations like the Egyptian, Hawaiian, and Incan in order to maintain the royal bloodline. But beyond the nuclear family, relationships are defined in many different ways. In the past, however, many tribal and simple agrarian cultures preferred certain types of cousin marriages. The selection of a mate from among one's uncles or aunts children was desired and helped maintain property and reinforced alliances between family lineages. This practice of marriages between relatives was also followed by several royal families of Europe over the centuries. The goal was to establish political alliances by intermarriages, usually between cousins. The Hapsburg empire of Central Europe was founded on such alliances, for example, and had the effect of uniting a good part of Europe for centuries. Later the children, grandchildren, nieces, and nephews of Queen Victoria ruled throughout Europe. This maintenance of political alliances through royal "bloodlines" worked fairly well until World War I.

For the majority of humanity, however, the tendency has been to outbreed, depending on geographic distance, economy, religion, and availability of potential mates due to population size. Marriages between cousins are forbidden in most cases but allowed in others. The restrictions and allowed exceptions are detailed and carefully codified even in nonliterate societies. Marriage regulations have been codified in the Western legal system; most state laws in the United States forbid marriages between cousins, always the first cousins, but there are fewer restrictions on second or third cousins. Exceptions are made in some states if the woman is over fifty. Also, there have

---

[1]Some primate species have been described as having social systems, boundaries, and behaviors that direct gene exchange between troops, but none as elaborate as those of humans because of our possession of language, mobility, and diversity of complex social organizations.

been laws against racial intermarriage. Until the late 1950s, many states legally prevented marriages between persons of different races. Religions also sanction some marriages and restrict others on the basis of either degrees of familial relationship or church membership. But custom, tradition, and economics have been, and in some cases remain, powerful forces in directing mate exchange; a majority of marriages in modern Western society occur between members of the same group (however defined). A study in San Francisco, California, serves to illustrate this point.[2] Of fifteen ethnic groups compared in this cosmopolitan city of 700,000, a majority of the marriages over several months in 1980 were between group members—Chinese with Chinese, Japanese with Japanese, Mexican with Mexican, and so on. Family pressure probably was one of the major reasons, but residence patterns, economic and education factors were also influential (Peach and Mitchell, 1988). This study of marriage patterns in a population of heterogeneous origins demonstrates how social forces still are effective in forming mating networks. At earlier times in our history, imagine how strong the influences of population size and group identity must have been in directing gene flow and determining the composition of the next generation.

The history of a population—how long it has lived in a given area, what selective forces have been acting on it, and what contacts it has had with other populations—helps determine the distribution of human variability. The effects of the European colonization of the world dramatize the significance of mass movements of people over the last four centuries. People carrying genomes largely adapted to conditions in a temperate zone environment now reside in tropical environments, and tropical peoples now occupy temperate environments. Over the course of these migrations, many indigenous peoples were destroyed or absorbed into a larger population network. But this describes only a short time frame of human history. Our ancestors have always moved about, and over thousands of years there have been numerous major changes of population boundaries—the prehistoric expansion of people out of the Middle East around the Mediterranean and into Europe, for example. The peopling of the Western Hemisphere from about 20,000 years ago by a series of migrations from northeastern Siberia spread populations of Asian origins into a vast area with diverse environments, founding the ancestral stock of Native Americans. The landing, about 900 years ago, of founders of modern-day Maori on the unpopulated islands of New Zealand is another case of wide dispersion of humans. Smaller-scale, more gradual changes can also occur through interpopulation contact and through the establishment of nearly isolated island populations throughout the Pacific. These changes of boundaries may occur as consequences of the pressure of overpopulation,

---

[2]Ethnic group membership in this study was defined by census records, marriage certificates, and use of surnames. This is an imperfect method, to be sure, for any genetic study, but it can suffice to demonstrate how social networks and self-identification may direct mate exchange.

new technology and exploration, or as a response to new subsistence patterns such as plant domestication, requiring more land. Whatever the causes, populations rise and fall, expand or contract over time and change the dimensions of their distribution.

If we consider these social influences on this distribution, then any grouping of human variability into some kind of a unit, no matter what we call it, may become a much more viable means of studying human diversity. The way in which we choose to group human populations depends, of course, on our purpose, and we must keep this purpose in mind when working with these groups. For example, one should not establish races or ethnic units on the basis of sociopolitical or religious criteria and then explain or interpret their existence in biological terms. The same stricture applies to groups established on the basis of geographic boundaries. The so-called natural boundaries do not prevent interpopulation contact, though distance does, of course, reduce gene flow. Likewise, sociopolitical or religious differences may influence the composition of the next generation but only to the degree that restrictions are enforced. The significance of this influence is determined by the humans involved and by their society's rules. The religious and often violent political differences in Northern Ireland, for example, have reduced or prevented interbreeding between the Catholics and Protestants, in contrast, say, to the frequent cross-religious marriages in the United States. The net effect is the establishment of two breeding populations in Northern Ireland within what could have been a homogeneous group. Similar examples can also be found in many other parts of the world where religious, economic, or political strife has resulted in a degree of isolation between groups (often referred to as ethnic groups). In their various homelands, Sunni Muslims are isolated from Shiites, Ethiopian Jews from Ashkenazim, and Koreans from Japanese, though the isolation is not complete.

There are some interesting distributions of the patterns of genetic markers or physical types around the world. If we take a single trait or several traits together, we see that many population groups vary widely from one another. The worldwide distribution of traits such as the blood groups, abnormal hemoglobins, or taste sensitivity show broad differences among populations. The same applies to a number of complex traits. These distributions are often attributed to biological factors, and biology does play an important role, especially for those traits under intense selection. The fact remains, however, that populations are socioeconomic units and have been established because of conditions other than those determined by their genomes. The combinations of genes in these populations are found there because of social, geographic, and cultural conditions that have contributed to the growth and maintenance of the biological unit, which can be defined as a breeding population. Unique gene frequencies may be found in several New Guinea populations because of their small size and geographic isolation, for example. Likewise, members of the Hutterite religious sect of North Dakota differ significantly in many genetic markers from their neighbors as a result of their decision to maintain breeding isolation. This raises the question of the nature of human populations.

BIOLOGICAL UNITS: RACES/ETHNIC GROUPS, OR BREEDING POPULATIONS

Explaining the arrangement of the varieties of organisms found in the natural world is as much a problem today as it always has been. With the newer techniques of taxonomy that use computer facilities, investigators can process thousands of items of information, many more than could naturalists of previous generations. Rather than establishing and clarifying distinct boundaries between populations, this additional information often raises new questions and casts doubts on the validity of many older, accepted taxonomic units. As noted earlier, anthropologists of the last century classified Melanesians with Africans because of similarities in skin color and hair. Such classification did not persist for long before anthropologists realized that there were numerous differences between the two groups. Over the decades many distinctive characteristics of cranial facial morphology were recorded that demonstrated that the Melanesians were more closely related to other population groupings of the Pacific region. The similarities and degrees of relatedness are summarized by Howells (1973:40) in Figure 6-1. The "distances" from some presumed common ancestor are indicated by the lengths of the branches. These, in turn, show separations of differing degrees between the contemporary peoples; the Nakanai of New Britain, a Melanesian population, are more distant from Polynesian branches than they are from peoples of New Guinea. The populations of these island groups are a diverse lot, the result of generations of "racial churning" by several migrations and mixing of neighboring groups, further varied by social forces of mate selection and genetic drift (Swindler, 1962). What the geneticists measure today in their studies of DNA polymorphisms is the result of a long process of human behavior and biological interaction. This forces any classification, no matter its basis, to be an arbitrary means of organizing the data for study, one that is subject to change.

The question is not whether the earlier or later classifications were a true, accurate description of the natural world. The former methods merely had another way of viewing biological diversity, especially through those characteristics that could be measured and compared at that time; grouping of all dark-skinned people together was as logical to the early anthropologists as the use of DNA polymorphisms is today. As other traits are considered, however, the boundaries of the first classifications break down. Since the development of genetic theory and description of DNA, life's diversity is now seen somewhat differently. Groups of organisms appear as dynamic units, many of whose identifying traits may change from generation to generation. Types or aver-

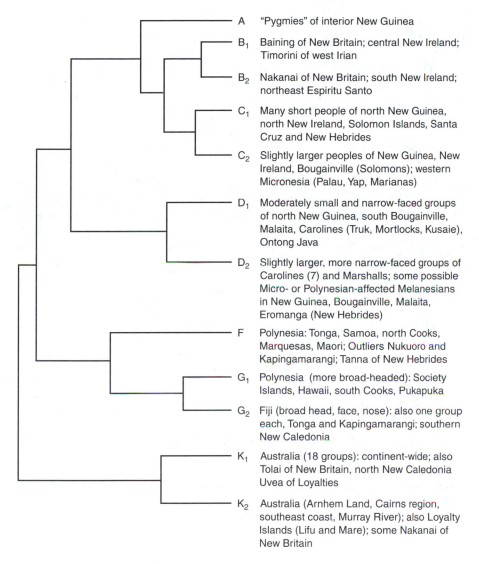

A   "Pygmies" of interior New Guinea

B_1 Baining of New Britain; central New Ireland; Timorini of west Irian

B_2 Nakanai of New Britain; south New Ireland; northeast Espiritu Santo

C_1 Many short people of north New Guinea, north New Ireland, Solomon Islands, Santa Cruz and New Hebrides

C_2 Slightly larger peoples of New Guinea, New Ireland, Bougainville (Solomons); western Micronesia (Palau, Yap, Marianas)

D_1 Moderately small and narrow-faced groups of north New Guinea, south Bougainville, Malaita, Carolines (Truk, Mortlocks, Kusaie), Ontong Java

D_2 Slightly larger, more narrow-faced groups of Carolines (7) and Marshalls; some possible Micro- or Polynesian-affected Melanesians in New Guinea, Bougainville, Malaita, Eromanga (New Hebrides)

F   Polynesia: Tonga, Samoa, north Cooks, Marquesas, Maori; Outliers Nukuoro and Kapingamarangi; Tanna of New Hebrides

G_1 Polynesia (more broad-headed): Society Islands, Hawaii, south Cooks, Pukapuka

G_2 Fiji (broad head, face, nose): also one group each, Tonga and Kapingamarangi; southern New Caledonia

K_1 Australia (18 groups): continent-wide; also Tolai of New Britain, north New Caledonia Uvea of Loyalties

K_2 Australia (Arnhem Land, Cairns region, southeast coast, Murray River); also Loyalty Islands (Lifu and Mare); some Nakanai of New Britain

FIGURE 6-1   **Relationships of Pacific Peoples by Measurement.** Comparisons of craniofacial and body measurements of 151 Pacific populations showed a clustering in three major branches: (1) Melanesian (A–D), with a subbranch of Micronesians (C_2 and D_2); (2) Polynesian (F–G); and (3) Australian (K). The degree of relationship or similarity is indicated by the length of the connecting branches in the diagram; for example, the K branches of the Australian samples are most distant from branch A of the pygmies of interior New Guinea. (Source: From Howells 1973. Reprinted by permission of George Weidenfeld and Nicolson Limited).

ages are no longer considered a sufficient means to describe groups of individuals participating in a breeding population. It is this dynamic condition that makes it extremely difficult to establish any all-inclusive taxonomic unit. The concept of basic racial stocks, or geographic races, becomes more difficult to sustain with the rise of greater knowledge of our species' genetic composition and recognition of the role played by social and environmental forces.

The problem that classification offered for biological studies was recognized early, but the labeling of people continued, and it continues to this very day. The study of human biology, especially the attempt to classify, is hampered by a disagreement over several aspects of diversity: its origin, its relation to the environment, and whether or not basic racial stocks are "real" and of great antiquity. Demographics—that is, the growth and expansion or decline of a population—is a more recent addition to the list of influences on distribution of biological diversity. Considering all of these factors it seems best to return to a fundamental statement of biological classification. Species are considered natural biological units held together by gene flow, whereas subspecies are divisions made on an arbitrary basis for a particular purpose. The subspecies (race) forms no such "natural" unit, and the composition of each or the number of subspecies described depends on the characteristics that the investigator considers important. In other words, whether or not an individual or group of individuals are identified as a particular race is determined by their possession of certain arbitrarily selected traits. More than fifty years ago, in studies of animal taxonomy, there was what was called the 75 percent rule. If 75 percent of the members of one population differed from another, then the two populations were considered to be distinct subspecies. This guideline worked more or less successfully depending on which criteria were used to assign the individuals. Another guideline was the geographical distribution of the populations and the history of contact, if any, between them.

The older rules of animal taxonomy are becoming increasingly difficult to apply, and most present-day concepts of race are founded in genetics and emphasize similarity of gene frequencies throughout populations of a geographic region. This collection, or population complex, shares a close common ancestry and has been under the influence of similar selective forces. The existence of such conditions would result in a high degree of similarity of certain genes in these populations. Recall, for example, that malarial environments have been a prime cause of the spread of abnormal hemoglobins. Then, according to many human biologists, the concept of race becomes much more useful if it is considered merely as an arbitrary grouping of populations identified for the purpose of a particular study. For example, the numerous studies today relating ethnic groups and diseases emphasize sharing of a certain genome through common descent from recent ancestors. Certain components of this genome place the individuals at risk for some disease. The higher risk of adult diabetes among Polynesians and Native Americans, or the propensity for high blood pressure among African Americans, probably has a strong genetic component. But even here, any classification must be made carefully and cautiously. The question may be raised: Which Native American group or which African American group, since each encompasses a broad, diverse genetic heritage. Arbitrary assignment of an individual to one or another group will not suffice for studies of gene and disease correlations. The means of racial/ethnic classification, the very concept, and its applicability to biomedical studies is still much debated.

The various definitions listed in the first chapter, however, cover a broad range of understanding of the race concept.[3] The definitions do share a common factor. They take into account the many racial differences that appear to relate to the geographic histories of each group. Dobzhansky (1944:252) stated: "It is recognized that most living species are more or less clearly differentiated into geographic races, each race occupying a portion of the species distribution." Many of the investigators today would likely subscribe to this definition, with the additional qualifier of gene frequency differentiation. Also, most appreciate the fluidity of boundaries due to human behavior. Few students of human diversity, however, view race as a natural unit existing in nature and awaiting discovery and classification. At least that is the case for anthropologists studying human variation, but for other professionals and for the layman it is a different matter. Race or ethnic types are labels that are too convenient to discard, and they continue to find their place as an orientation for many sociopolitical and biomedical studies, as I shall describe in the last chapter.

The importance of geography and environment has often been recognized in the definition of races and still remains significant if applied correctly. Garn (1960) used spatial distribution of human varieties as a means of establishing racial groups as he described geographical, local, and microraces. Microgeographical races and local races are smaller, less inclusive groups, comparable with the breeding populations used by many workers who study human variation. These basic units are subject to localized natural selection, and population size is also effective in causing differentiation between groups. Also the numbers and composition of local races are continually changing, with migration and interbreeding forming new ones, as experienced in Hawaii with the encounters of peoples from all parts of the world over the last 200 years. The largest, most inclusive group—the geographical race—includes many diverse local groups. The geographical race conforms most closely to the older description of basic racial stocks or major races (Australoid, American Indian, Mongoloid, Caucasoid, and Negroid). In a way, this category can be misleading, because often members of geographical races share only a few physical attributes, as in the case, cited below, of Africans who encompass at least several subdivisions in sub-Saharan populations.

---

[3]I use the word "concept" as defined in *Webster's*: "an idea of a class of objects, a general notion." Most writers do also, I believe, even though they do not state a precise meaning. Used in this way, the implication is that race is a "real" object in nature waiting to be discovered and labeled.

Except for a superficial identification of the majority of the inhabitants of a continent, "basic stock" or "geographical race" tells us little about biological diversity or the interrelationships between breeding populations or the effects of the environment, which are the dimensions of the selective forces that act on the populations. "Basic stock" does not describe gene combinations but all too often it contributes to stereotypes—the images generated when citizens of nations or regions are mentioned. That individuals seldom conform to our image is too large a disappointment to admit, a sin of which we are all guilty. Ripley's description of Races of Europe, mentioned in the first chapter, provided us with images of Europeans that tend to persist to this day, so it is important to recall an exhaustive study of human diversity within one of these "races." Hooton and Dupertius (1955) reported the results of their anthropometric study of 10,000 Irish males, residents of more than a dozen counties of Ireland. They found that few subjects fit the Irish stereotype so often used to depict one of the major "local races" of Europe. In fact, the Irish populations encompassed most of the European race types. In head form, a trait typically used to identify race in the first half of this century, they ranged in cephalic index from very narrow to very broad. Likewise in stature, the range included very short men (146 cm) to tall (202 cm); 95 percent of nearly 9,000 males were included in a range between 158–186 cm. This and other surveys of local groups using gene markers as well as anthropometric dimensions document that "geographical race" is merely a convenient label, an abstraction applied in a broad sense. To describe and study human variability, we must use a more restricted and precise grouping; otherwise, important interpopulation differences will be obscured.

Biological diversity exhibits a disrespect for classic, time-honored boundaries and stereotypes. This was recognized many years ago when Hooton (1936:512), for example, observed: "There exists no single physical criterion for distinguishing race; races are delimited by the association in human groups of multiple variations of bodily form and structure." Another consideration is that race or any such label used to identify human groups is nothing more than an informational abstraction that provides us with a research tool to investigate biological variability (Baker, 1967:21). Such labels have no more reality than any of the others that we use to identify objects we encounter in our environment.

We must consider also that human differences—especially those morphological traits often used to establish racial groups—are not as extreme or as great as generally supposed. This is most frequently seen in the case of morphological similarities that lead to the assumption that look-alikes have common ancestry, as discussed earlier. Intraracial variation is extensive in the major geographically determined races and is often overlooked. An example is the diversity found among Native Americans. Rather than matching any stereotype, they vary greatly in size and form, from tall to very short (Table 6–1). Some populations are composed of people of heavy build who are prone to

TABLE 6-1 Mean Stature of a Sample of Native American Males

TRIBE	LOCATION	STATURE (CM)
Motilon	Brazil	146.2
San Blas	Panama	149.9
Yanomama	Venezuela	153.2
Jivaro	Brazil	154.2
Maya	Yucatan	155.4
Otomi	Southern Mexico	158.0
Quechua	Peru	160.0
Hopi	Arizona	161.1
Zuni	New Mexico	161.4
Navaho	New Mexico	169.6
Aymara	Chile	161.8
Eskimo	St. Lawrence Island	165.0
Yaqui	Sonora	166.7
Papago	Arizona	168.8
Choctaw	Louisiana	171.4
Pima	Arizona	171.8
Blackfoot	North Dakota	177.4

Sources: Selected from Comas, 1960; Newman, 1953; and Eveleth and Tanner, 1976.

obesity, like the Papago of southern Arizona. In contrast are the short, slenderly built people who dwell in the tropical rain forests of Central and South America like the Yanomama of Venezuela and Brazil. Face form also covers a wide range, from broad, heavy faces to small, gracile faces with long, narrow noses; head shape varies over the range of cephalic indexes recorded for our species. Similar diversity is seen in several of the genetic markers of blood and taste sensitivity. Though Native Americans share a close common ancestry as descendants of populations who migrated from Siberia over the Bering Strait beginning approximately 15,000 to 20,000 years ago, their present-day variability should not be obscured by a broad, all-inclusive classification. This diversity among Native Americans is illustrated further by the "tree diagrams" in Figure 6-2(a, b). Figure 6-2a is a dendrogram derived from a genetic distance formula obtained from comparisons of gene frequencies at fourteen genetic loci in ten Native American groups with frequencies found in three Asian groups. This depicts the relative genetic distance between arctic peoples (North American and Siberian) and several subarctic Native American groups. Figure 6-2b is a diagram computing genetic relationships based on complex traits of dental morphology. Many of the same arctic and subarctic peoples are compared, in addition to representatives of South American populations. Both genetic distance diagrams show a greater similarity between northern Siberian and subarctic peoples of North America than with other Asian groups.

African peoples, once commonly grouped into a Negroid race, are another example of millions of people being treated incorrectly as members

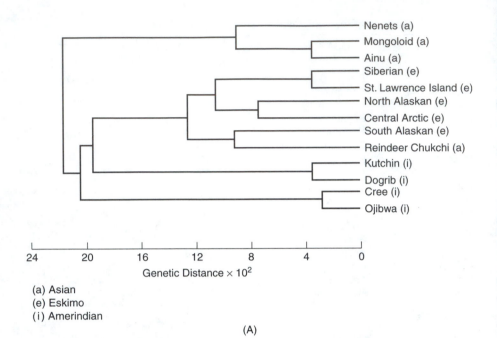

FIGURE 6-2A   **Dendrogram Showing Genetic Similarities among Asian and American Arctic and Sub-arctic Populations.** Szathmary, 1985. (Copyright © 1985 by The Journal of Pacific History, Inc. Australian National University, Canberra, Australia.)

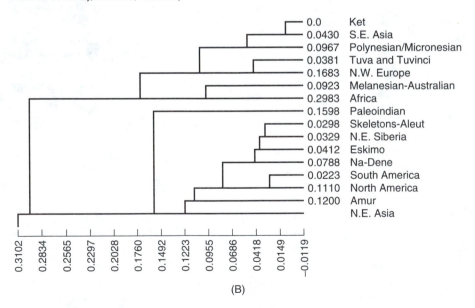

FIGURE 6-2B   **Relationships within and between Native American, Pacific, and Old World Populations.** Based on twenty-eight dental trait mean measures of divergence clustered by unweighted pair group, arithmetic averages method. Turner, 1985. (Copyright © 1985 by The Journal of Pacific History, Inc. Australian National University, Canberra, Australia.)

of a homogeneous geographical race. There are wide differences between many of the tribal or linguistic groupings, and a careful study of breeding populations is necessary. Through several studies of East African peoples, Hiernaux, a French biologist, has shown significant differences in blood groups, stature, and face form among several populations living in East Africa. Other studies during the past fifty years have also recorded broad ranges of diversity among Africans south of the Sahara, a factor that is overlooked too often in racial classification. Table 6-2 compares four physical characteristics of east-central African groups. They have been semi-isolated with little gene flow between them, so the selective forces of the individual environments have had a maximum opportunity to exert influence on each character (Hiernaux, 1966a).

The use of several genetic markers of the Rh, HLA, and Gm systems together with mtDNA and beta globin separates African populations south of the Sahara into significantly different clusters (Excoffier et al., 1987). Khoisan of southern Africa were grouped in one unit, east and west Africans in others, while all differed from Pygmies and another group, the southern Bantu (e.g., Zulu). The major African Gm haplotype (1, 17, 5) varies over a range of 50 percent among these populations. Similar ranges of diversity were reported for the Rh system (cDe, CDe, and cDE haplotypes). Both HLA-A and HLA-B gene frequencies encompassed a wide range, and analysis of ten populations established a significant difference between Khoisan, west African, and southern Bantu. What these comparisons have shown is that there are clear distinctions found in Africa, and according to Excoffier and co-workers, these distinctions agree well with linguistic divisions. These distributions of the gene frequencies are representative of a history of migrations and past contacts among Africans as well as with groups outside the continent—east Africans and Arab-Asians, for example. In addition to suggesting a history of population migrations and contacts, this record of divisions of gene markers among

TABLE 6-2   Means of Four Characters in the Mbuti Pygmies, Tutsi, and Bantu

	STATURE (CM)	NASAL INDEX	FACIAL INDEX	CEPHALIC INDEX
Mbuti Pygmies	144	103.8	78.3	77.0
Rwanda Tutsi	176	69.4	92.8	74.4
Bantu				
Wet Forest	164	94.0	81.9	76.1
Savanna	169	85.9	85.8	75.3
Arid Zone	171	85.0	89.7	74.8

Source: From Hiernaux, J. 1966. "Human biological diversity in Central Africa," *Man* 1:287–306. Courtesy of Royal Anthropological Institute of Great Britain and Ireland.

sub-Saharan peoples cautions against the use of geographic race in human biological studies.

The diversity within each of the classic geographical race divisions is clearly established whether one examines the complex morphological traits or the inherited phenotypes of the blood. In fact, Lewontin (1974) emphasized that intrapopulation diversity (the diversity among individuals) often exceeds that between populations. As he explained, 85 percent of genetic variability is among individuals within a nation or tribe. This is illustrated by his table of major genetic markers, their diversity within the species, and their proportion in populations or races (Table 6-3). Such variability has been recognized many times by human biologists and anthropologists, but it seldom prevented them from using some form of classification until recently. Since the increased use of gene markers and DNA polymorphisms, however, there has been a growing discomfort with the race concept and all of its related assumptions. Excoffier and co-workers, cited above, proceeded with caution in group identification and relied mainly on language family affinities and tribal names as ethnic identifiers.

The problems that the race concept presented to field surveys of living human populations were described in detail by Hiernaux when he began to analyze the data collected during a biological anthropology field survey in central Africa in the 1950s. He noted that, though it was customary to start a description of survey results with a classification of the groups studied, the use of existing taxonomies rather than relying on the data collected is misleading. His observation led to the question, "What do we want to classify?" The answer seems unequivocal: the gene pools of the breeding population (Hiernaux, 1966a:289). Most field studies of human diversity have followed this lead ever since.

BREEDING POPULATIONS

> The most suitable units for study are smaller local populations, groups of inter-marrying persons whether tribes, castes, or inhabitants of a particular region. (Hiernaux, 1971:40)

Earlier I defined breeding population as a group of actually or potentially interbreeding individuals. This general definition fits most sexually reproducing organisms, but *Homo sapiens*, in many ways, is unique. Our elaborate social organization and culturally directed behavior make the human breeding population a result of the interaction of multiple biological and behavioral forces. Because of human behavior, the total genome of the species is distributed in space in clustered units. Society determines which individuals will mate to produce the next generation. A complex of social customs and taboos proscribe and prescribe sexual relations and establish the basis for

TABLE 6-3   **Major Genetic Markers in *Homo sapiens***

LOCUS	ALLELE	POPULATIONS AND GENE FREQUENCIES
	SERUM PROTEINS	
Haptoglobin	Hp[1]	0.09 (Tamils)—0.92 (Lacondon)
Lipoprotein	Lp[a]	0.009 (Labrador)—0.267 (Germany)
	ENZYMES	
Red cell acid	p[a]	0.09 (Tristan da Cunha)—0.67 (Athabascan)
phosphatase	p[b]	0.33 (Athabascan)—0.91—(Tristan da Cunha)
	p[c]	0–.08 (Many)
Phosphoglucomutase	PGM$_1$	0.430 (Habbana Jews)—0.938 (Yanomama)
Adenylate kinase	AK[2]	0 (Africans)—0.130 (Amerinds-Pakistanis)
	BLOOD GROUPS	
Kidd	JK[a]	0.310 (Chinese-Dyaks)—1.000 (Eskimo)
Duffy	FY[a]	0.061 (Bantu-Chenchu)—1.000 (Eskimo)
Lewis	Le[b]	0.298 (Lapps)—0.667 (Kapinga)
Kell	K	0 (Many)—0.063 (Chenchu)
Lutheran	Lu[a]	0 (Many)—0.86 (Brazilian Amerinds)
Rh	CDe	0 (Luo)—0.960 (Papuans)
	Cde	0 (Many)—0.166 (Chenchu)
	cDE	0 (Luo)—0.308 (Dyak-Japanese)
	cdE	0 (Many)—0.174 (Ainu)
	cDe	0 (Many)—0.865 (Luo)
	cde	0 (Many)—0.456 (Basques)
ABO	A	0.07 (Toba)—0.583 (Bloods)
	B	0 (Amerinds)—0.297 (Austr.-Toda)
	O	0.509 (Oraon)—0.993 (Toda)

Source: Selected from R. C. Lewontin, 1972.

family life, as well as family lineages, clans, caste systems, and religious affiliations; these present well-established culturally defined boundaries that in turn affect the gene combination of the next generation. These boundaries are not rigid and enforcement is quite flexible, varying across generations and affected by distance and by demography.

An example of how social systems may determine gene frequency is the case of the X-linked recessive gene that causes an individual to be deficient in G6PD. In patrilocal-patrilineal societies, where males remain in the community and bring their brides from outside, many of the X-linked genes are "lost" each generation because two-thirds of the X chromosomes are provided by the females in any population. Giles showed by a mathematical model that the X-linked G6PD-deficient gene may be less frequent in a patrilocal community, because the daughters of G6PD-deficient males leave, taking the gene with them, and the women moving into the community may come from a group that lacks the recessive trait or has a lower frequency. The opposite would be true in an example of a matrilocal community in which males leave to marry outside of their community. In this case, X-linked gene frequencies would be less disturbed. Such examples show how societies' decisions can indirectly influence gene exchange, which in turn causes change in gene frequencies. It is extremely important, then, to understand the functioning of a group as a social unit when one studies their genetic composition (Giles, 1962). Another example would be population admixture through the males of a dominant society frequently impregnating females of a subordinate group. Over the centuries, European males mated with any number of females of indigenous populations in colonial areas. This process of gene exchange would influence sex-linked trait frequencies because of the unidirectional exchange of the Y chromosome.

Geographical distance is another important consideration, for it obviously limits mating choices. In prehistoric times, and even among many peoples today, distance was a major restriction to gene flow. Brierley (1970), after studying census records, noted that in rural England during the nineteenth century, a man was most likely to find his mate within 600 yards of his residence. But after the bicycle was invented, the average distance between prenuptial households jumped to 1,600 yards. If this increase in distance seems impressive, consider the mobility that has been brought about by the invention and wide use of the automobile. Even so, between 1940 and 1960, more than one-half of marriages were between persons who had lived less than one mile apart. As modern transportation has increased mobility further still, a broader exchange of genes is to be expected. Whereas formerly, small breeding units were restricted by economics, politics, or geography to a village community, today mating circles have expanded and the gene pool is much broader. In a world undergoing rapid urbanization, defining breeding populations and tracing patterns of gene flow are more difficult.

The effects that mating structures, distance, and population size have on gene frequencies are graphically illustrated by a study of modern Italian populations in the vicinity of the Parma Valley. Located in the north-central part of Italy, this region contains a combination of rural villages of various sizes and a few urban centers. In the foothills and surrounding mountains, there are several smaller, relatively isolated villages that can trace their origins back to prehistoric times. For several years, the geneticist Cavalli-Sforza carried on a thorough study of the genetic composition of these populations. The sedentary nature of the populations, the varying degree of their isolation, and the availability of marriage records from church archives made these communities an excellent source of data for the study of genetic variation (Cavalli-Sforza, 1969).

The results of the study show a close correlation between village size and gene-frequency differences. The villages in the mountains have smaller populations than those at lower elevations. This reduction in breeding population size contributes to genetic drift, which shows in the relationship between population density and the genetic variation between communities illustrated in Figure 6-3a. Those larger communities at the lower elevations show less difference. Genetic variation between villages is also influenced by the relative lack of migration. Most marriages occur between persons of the same church parish, and the next most frequent matings occur between persons within 8 kilometers (Figure 6-3b). Given these factors, many consanguinial marriages occur in the mountain communities; more special dispensations, granted by the Catholic Church for cousin marriages, are awarded to residents in these villages. As expected, the isolation, small population size, and low rate of migration limit one's choice of a mate, which is reflected in the church records.

In less developed societies, environment together with poor transportation contribute even more to population isolation. People within remote villages may have scant opportunity to intermarry with others a short distance away, even if they are members of the same tribe. The rough, hilly terrain in the west Bengal region of eastern India causes the isolation of numerous groups. One of these groups, the Pahira, provides an example of the effects of this isolation. The 1,400 people of this primitive tribe of food collectors live in small hamlets scattered over 300 square miles. They are clustered into three units or divisions. Each unit is an endogamous breeding population with lit-

FIGURE 6-3A   Variations in the Frequency of a Blood Type between Parma Valley Villages. Variations were greatest, as predicted, in the isolated upland hamlets and declined as population density increased farther down in the valley in the hill towns, on the plain, and in the city of Parma. (From Cavalli-Sforza, Luigi Luca, "Genetic Drift in an Italian Population." Copyright © 1969 by Scientific American, Inc. All rights reserved.)

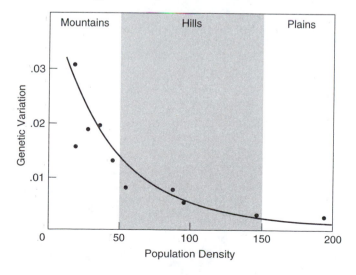

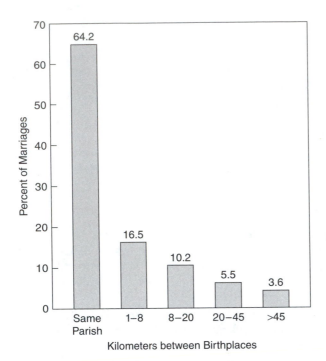

FIGURE 6-3B Distances between Prenuptial Households in Parma Valley Villages. Migration in the upper Parma Valley has been infrequent, a conclusion drawn from the fact that most marriages recorded from 1650 to 1950 in parish books united men and women who were from the same village. The number falls as the distance separating birthplaces increases. (From Cavalli-Sforza, Luigi Luca, "Genetic Drift in an Italian Population." Copyright © 1969 by Scientific American, Inc. All rights reserved.)

tle admixture of each generation. For example, considering three generations, the majority of individuals had both parents who were from the same unit. According to the Indian anthropologist Basu (1969), this village endogamy has resulted in significant differences in frequencies of the genes for the ABO blood group and taster phenotypes. Though members of the same tribe, these smaller units of hamlet clusters form distinct breeding populations. Thus, we must be extremely cautious in any statement about the gene frequencies of large groups, whether nations, states, tribes, or races.

Reports describing the gene frequency of, say, several African Bantu tribes, the Lapps, the English, or Native Americans may be completely erroneous unless the sample is taken from representatives who are from the same breeding population within the social-political unit—a difficult task but a necessary one if we are to attempt to understand the genetics of human diversity. An example is the distribution of the blood groups that have been recorded for vast numbers of people. Boyd used these traits as sorting criteria in an

attempt to differentiate races of humanity, as noted earlier, and the gene frequencies are summarized in Table 6-4. These groups cover large geographic
regions and include numerous breeding populations. The blood group genes
listed for them tend to describe or imply a homogeneity where little or none
actually exists.

TABLE 6-4 Frequencies of ABO Blood Groups

POPULATION	PLACE	NUMBER TESTED	BLOOD-GROUP FREQUENCY			
			O	*A*	*B*	*AB*
	Low A, virtually no B					
American Indians:						
Toba	Argentina	194	98.5	1.5	0.0	0.0
Sioux	South Dakota	100	91.0	7.0	2.0	.0
	Moderate A, virtually no B					
Navaho	New Mexico	359	77.7	22.5	0.0	.0
Pueblo	New Mexico:					
	Jemez, etc.	310	78.4	20.0	1.6	.0
	High A, little B					
Bloods	Montana	69	17.4	81.2	0.0	1.4
Eskimo	Baffin Land	146	55.5	43.8	.0	0.7
Australian						
Aborigines	Southern Australia	54	42.6	57.4	.0	.0
Basques	San Sebastian	91	57.2	41.7	1.1	.0
American Indians:						
Shoshone	Wyoming	60	51.6	45.0	1.6	1.6
Polynesians	Hawaii	413	36.5	60.8	2.2	0.5
	Fairly high A, some B					
English	London	422	47.9	42.4	8.3	1.4
French	Paris	1,265	39.8	42.3	11.8	6.1
Armenians	From Turkey	330	27.3	53.9	12.7	6.1
Lapps	Finland	94	33.0	52.1	12.8	2.1
Melanesians	New Guinea	500	37.6	44.4	13.2	4.8
Germans	Berlin	39,174	36.5	42.5	14.5	6.5
	High A and high B					
Welsh	North Towns	192	47.9	32.8	16.2	3.1
Italians	Sicily	540	45.9	33.4	17.3	3.4
Siamese	Bangkok	213	37.1	17.8	35.2	9.9
Finns	Hame	972	34.0	42.4	17.1	6.5
Germans	Danzig	1,888	33.1	41.6	18.0	7.3
Ukrainians	Kharkov	310	36.4	38.4	21.6	3.6
Asiatic Indians	Bengal	160	32.5	20.0	39.4	8.1

Source: From Boyd, W. C., "Genetics and the Human Race," *Science* 140:1057–1064, Table 2, 7
June 1963. Copyright © 1963 by American Association for the Advancement of Science.
Reprinted by permission of the publisher.

Population Isolates

In more complex societies with caste and class stratification, social distance can play a role in mate choice similar to that of geographic distance. Peasant–aristocracy stratification in medieval Europe tended to isolate breeding populations and cluster genetic units within smaller areas. A similar situation exists even today in Latin America between those classified as Indios (Native Americans), Mestizos, African Americans, and Euro-Americans. Though intermarriage may occur at a low level, there is considerable unidirectional mating—upper-class males mating with lower-class females. This has contributed to a high degree of admixture since the earliest colonial times, and this tendency has increased as legal and social sanctions have become less restrictive. India with its complex religious and caste systems establishes an immense social distance between groups. The higher-caste Hindus are isolated from the lower castes, and the "scheduled" or "exterior" castes are excluded by even a greater distance from any social contact. These "untouchables" have little or no chance of marrying or mating with the higher-castes, and to do so was once punished by death. Such genetic isolation has contributed to unique patterns of trait distribution over the Indian subcontinent that anthropologists and geneticists have been trying to explain for most of this century. What has made such a task even more difficult is that clear trait boundaries are difficult to define due to the sizes of these caste groups, numbering in the tens of millions. Comparisons of Hindus from two eastern states (Orissa and Andhra Pradesh) with Rajasthan in the west of India showed significant heterogeneity for several genetic markers. Differences of origins and ancient separations of these groups are reflected in their language group boundaries—Dravidian and Indo-Aryan (Tartaglia et al., 1995).

The enforcement of religious beliefs has also proved effective in isolating populations from the surrounding community even in modern U.S. society. Strict sanctions are often imposed against marrying "outsiders," and there is very little gene flow between the religious isolate and neighboring populations. The "Old Order Dunkers" of Pennsylvania provide an example of a religious enclave that has maintained a restricted mating circle over the generations since its founding.

This religious group can trace its origins to 1708 in the Rhineland area of Germany with the establishment of a sect of the German Baptist Brethren. The American colony began in 1719 when twenty-eight persons arrived in Pennsylvania. These initial colonists were joined later by others from the same Rhineland region. The New World colony flourished and grew in number until religious dissent caused the sect to split into three divisions in 1881. The smaller division retained the original beliefs and practices of the earlier settlers and became known as the Old German Baptist Brethren (or Dunkers). About 1950, there were fifty-five communities spread over the Midwest with a few in California and Florida. Three of these communities remained in the area of Pennsylvania where the colony began and where the communities were examined by a team of medical and genetic experts.

This extensive study by Glass and his co-workers (Glass et al., 1952) focused on several genetic characters, the blood groups of the ABO, Rh, and MN systems, as well as certain complex traits. Their findings showed that the Dunkers differed significantly from the average trait frequencies of the U.S. population. The Dunker isolate of 300 persons also differed significantly from populations living in those regions of Germany from which the group's ancestors had migrated. Blood type A and blood type M were much more frequent in the Dunker sample, for example. Other phenotype distinctions were observed in the population that were believed due to the small size of the effective breeding population (there were only ninety parents) and because of its isolation over the generations. Though it is difficult to document sampling error (genetic drift) in humans, this case study provided some interesting data to support population size as a factor in gene frequency change. In addition, there is the genetic composition of the colony's original founders to consider.

The Hutterite colonies of South Dakota and Canada provide further examples. A majority of the Hutterites today, about 33,000 in 300 colonies, can trace their ancestry back to 442 persons who migrated from Russia and settled in South Dakota between 1874 and 1877 (Oved, 1988). The high birth rate (an average of eight children per marriage) has caused the colonies to grow to their present size even without gaining new immigrants. The Hutterite colonies are divided into three divisions called Leutes, and there has been little interbreeding between them during the last century. This isolation of the divisions results in some unique gene frequencies when compared with North American and European populations because gene flow into the colonies from "outside" populations is near zero. As a result, the frequency of type A blood has increased, whereas type B has decreased to a low level and has even disappeared in some colonies. In addition to the RBC blood types, a recent study of the HLA system (WBC types) showed many of the HLA haplotypes common to Europeans, but the S Leut (Schmiedenleut) had high frequencies for seven HLA haplotypes that have rarely been detected among Europeans. The S Leut also differed significantly from the other two Leutes in the combination of the forty-five haplotypes recorded (Kostyu et al., 1989). This rapid growth from a few founders experienced by the Hutterites illustrates gene frequency change because of genetic drift.

Another example is the Amish of Pennsylvania, descendants of 200 founders who entered Pennsylvania between 1720 and 1770; from these few, the population grew to 45,000 in 1960. This growth from a handful of ancestors, with few immigrants added to the colony, resulted in close inbreeding through past generations, as demonstrated today by the few surnames that account for a majority of the population; 80 percent of the families in two Pennsylvania counties are accounted for by only eight surnames. Consequently, certain rare recessive genetic disorders occur in high frequency (McKusick, 1978). Further waves of migrants, about 3,000 between 1815 and 1865, led to establishment of colonies in Ohio, Indiana, and Illinois. The Amish, because of high fertility, have a population growth of 3 percent per annum, a rate exceeded only by the Hutterites. By the 1980 census there were 80,000 Amish living in twenty states and the province of Ontario, Canada.

In addition, founders or original colonists often were a select group, not a representative cross-section of the parent population from which they migrated. Hulse (1957) pointed out that a great many migrants to the British colonies in North America came from select regions of the British Isles. Also, he noted that certain physical characteristics were often possessed by these migrants that set them apart from the general population. Additional data of the uniqueness of migrant groups is provided by his study of the Italian Swiss; Hulse observed that they were generally taller and heavier than the stay-at-home group. One may suppose that such groups as the Hutterites, Dunkers, and Amish also may have descended from ancestors who were not representative of the general populations. This biased sample of migrants from a parent population can result in some unusual distributions of traits throughout future generations that sets the modern-day descendants apart. Though these factors are lumped under the term *founder's effect* or *principle*, they cover a multitude of events, some chance and some intentional. The founding group also may, by chance, have certain recessive genes that give rise to a high frequency of these alleles when the population expands. Livingstone (1969:58) noted:

> Since most of the world's populations have expanded rapidly in the last 1,000 years, much of the variability in the frequencies of lethal genes (or non-lethals for that matter) could be a consequence of the original expansion of the major populations.

Once a group is established as a breeding population, the size of the reproductive unit plays an important part in determining the composition of each succeeding generation. *Genetic Drift* or *Sewall Wright Effect* refers to chance events that alter gene frequencies in small breeding populations. The effect is accentuated because even fewer individuals contribute to the next generation. In large modern populations, one-fifth to one-sixth generally produce one-half of the next generation. In small, relatively isolated groups, the effective breeding population is even lower, and the fact that a few males father most of the children can have a profound effect on the gene fixation of each generation. Such reduced effective breeding population sizes emphasize the importance of genetic drift in the formation of genetic variation among tribes, villages, clans, or any other socially defined breeding unit.

When an investigator studies groups such as the Hutterites, Amish, or Dunkers, written records are available to guide and aid that person in establishing genealogies. For nonliterate tribes such as the Amazonian Indians in South America or tribal groups in New Guinea, however, no records exist beyond a few notes provided by travelers, anthropologists, or missionaries, which are not adequate to establish the relationships between groups definitely. Therefore, identification of these populations is made, at least initially, on the basis of language similarities. The assumption is that tribes that speak the same language or similar dialects of a language are related genetically and share close common ancestry. Often the analogy is made between the spread of language and the spread of genes, as if the processes were the same—which they are not. As noted earlier, language is not inherited but learned. Several writers, though, have dealt with language groups, families, dialects, and so on, as if they were genetically determined phenotypes and as if dialect coincided with breeding population boundaries. For some broad surveys, genetic differentiation parallels major linguistic boundaries, as in the case of a description of sub-Saharan Africa discussed above or for many Native Americans. The distribution of GM types was traced throughout North and South America and regional differences were noted (Callegari-Jacques et al., 1993). Further differences within these regions were seen when the data was grouped by language families. The Na Dene speakers (Inuit and Athapaskans of the Pacific Northwest) differed from all others. Populations of the Southwest, like the Pima and Hopi (Uto-Aztecan speakers), differed from the many tribes of Carib speakers in Central America and the Caribbean areas, and these, in turn, differed from Andean Quechua and the Yanomama of Venezuela. These studies of genetic marker distributions, however, dealt with large continent-wide populations; the data for linguistic-genetic boundary concordance is not as convincing for smaller groupings.

An example is the comparison of blood-group gene frequencies in populations of several villages of the New Guinea highlands. Livingstone showed significant differences in the gene frequencies between villages, though all spoke the same language and shared common ancestry. He cautioned that blood-group frequency and language do not correlate. These genetic differences are probably due to a combination of genetic drift and founder's effect (Livingstone, 1963:512). By contrast, in several villages on New Guinea's north coast, villagers speak seventeen different languages of the two major language groups of the region, Austronesian and non-Austronesian. There was a high correlation between language and genetic distance and each was highly correlated with gene flow (Serjeantson et al., 1983). The language-genetic correlation drops to zero if the geographic effect is removed, which considering the isolating effects of the rugged terrain, is not surprising. It reinforces the observations about the effects of genetic drift and suggests that language differences do not erect a complete barrier to marriage migration (Friedlaender, 1987).

Even the comparison of gene-frequency differences or similarities between two or more populations is not a reliable means of determining relationships or closeness of common ancestry. Though the groups may have separated into two different units only within the recent past, they still may have quite different gene frequencies. Villages of the Xavente and Yanomama, both South American tribes in the upper Amazon basin, divide into groups to establish new villages when the old settlement reaches a certain critical population size. The leaders decide who belongs to which group on the basis of family membership, and the division is usually made along family lines. The effect is to produce villages whose populations' gene frequencies differ significantly even though they are closely related. The population divergence that results from this process of population subdivision is described as the "lineal effect" by James Neel (1970:816).

Other examples of gene-frequency divergence are also offered by the Yanomama, a fierce people who until recently were continually at war with their neighbors, and village raids were often for the purpose of obtaining captive women. In one case, young women from the Makiritare tribe were brought back from a raid on a nearby village. They proved to be highly fertile over the years and produced an average of 7.3 children compared with the 3.8 average for Yanomama women. Chagnon and associates (1970) described this event as responsible for the unusually high frequency of the Diego gene among this particular group in contrast to a low frequency found in other Yanomama villages.

Polygamy may have been the preferred form of marriage in former times, and it can be an important factor influencing the composition of the next generation. In some modern groups in which this form of marriage is practiced—several South American tribes, for example—70 to 80 percent of the offspring are from polygamous unions. Because some males are able to acquire more than one wife, it is obvious that many other males have limited opportunity to reproduce; hence, the genetic contribution to succeeding generations is limited to a very few males. Some males, because of their dominant position as clan leaders or relatives of high-status individuals, contribute disproportionately to future generations. This reduces gene flow and acts much like the founder's principle in producing a certain gene combination. Polygamy may have been an important force in human evolution, especially during periods when the strongest, bravest, or best hunter was able to acquire more wives. The Eskimos, for example, were very practical in caring for widows and orphans. The surviving family of a recently deceased hunter of the band was moved into the household of the most successful hunter, whose duty it was to care for them by taking the widow as his second or third wife and the children as his own.

Chance, or "fate," and natural events or intentional acts (such as migration) play an important role in determining the growth, size, isolation, and, ultimately, gene frequency of the population. A typhoon may wipe out most of an island population, as on Puka Puka in the South Pacific, where an eighteenth-century typhoon left only seventeen survivors. These seventeen were all from the lower class in the Polynesian social structure, and persons of this class throughout Polynesia are, on the average, shorter. Shapiro (1942) explained the shorter stature of today's populations as a consequence of this chance event. Starvation and disease, too, have often decimated populations, leaving only a handful to start a new generation. Descendants often have traits or combinations of traits quite different from those expected. When studying a particular human group, the geneticist should be fully aware of its past history. Gadjusek (1964:134) noted: "The vicissitudes of history caused by social, psychological, and natural events operating on small bands have contributed greatly to the determination of the evolutionary course that has led to man." They have also added to the characteristics that set many modern human groups apart. Favorable location is another major factor in population diversity and growth; consider the eightfold increase in populations of western Europe—especially those of British origin during the past four centuries (Table 6-5).

In the case of chance events mediated by certain human actions, the founder's principle discussed earlier has been a major factor in the evolution of the human gene pool. When *Homo sapiens*, as a species, was very small in numbers during prehistoric times, the recurrence of the founder's principle would have produced much intergroup variability. The dangers of prehistoric existence probably destroyed many small groups, whereas in others a few hardy and lucky souls were able to survive and reestablish the population. As long as *Homo sapiens* remained at the nomadic hunting and gathering level, a chance fluctuation in population size because of random, natural events would cause the species to remain small. There was little possibility for the formation of large, homogeneous breeding populations.

CLINAL DISTRIBUTION OF TRAITS

Any discussion of diversity must consider another concept of human trait distribution. In addition to population clusters, gradients of biological characteristics through space occur frequently and were called *clines* by Julian Hux-

TABLE 6-5   Regional Increases of Populations (in millions)

REGION	A. D. 1	1000	1500	1650	1750	1850
Africa	16	33	46	55	61	81
China	53	66	110	140	225	435
India	35	79	105	150	175	230
Eastern Europe	5	7	20	32	48	100
Southern Europe	18	12	20	28	35	58
Western Europe	10	15	33	50	60	110
North America	1.8	3.5	6	4.5	7	34.25

ley (see Birdsell, 1993:26). They are the result of either the action of selection or of massive gene flow as in a major migration. Clinal distribution or clinal variation traces the geographical range of phenotypic or genetic characteristics of our species and assumes that they are distributed in a meaningful way, considered as a result of a regionally directed event. Clines connect a series of data points (traits, gene frequencies) on a map in much the same way as barometric pressure or temperature is plotted to depict weather fronts. The location of the sampled data is marked on a map, and then the data points of the same size are connected. These clines express traits that vary continuously or by gradual progression of some feature from one geographical region to the next. The geographical plot of the variation of skin color among the world's population is an example (refer to Figure 1-3). This map shows that the density of melanin content of the skin is highly correlated with latitude; the more northerly peoples have a lighter skin pigmentation. Likewise, Figure 6-4 traces a clinal distribution of the type B blood group frequency throughout Europe. The frequency of the allele decreases on a cline toward the west and probably is a genetic reminder of the invasions of Asian pastoral nomads into eastern and central Europe many times over the last 2,000 years. These invaders

FIGURE 6-4   Frequencies of B Allele in Europe. (From Mourant, A., *The Distribution of the Human Blood Groups*, 1954. Copyright © 1954 by Blackwell Scientific Publications, Ltd. Reprinted by permission of the publisher.)

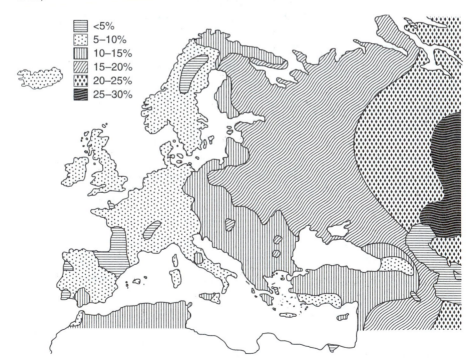

Legend:
- <5%
- 5–10%
- 10–15%
- 15–20%
- 20–25%
- 25–30%

caused by "massive" gene flow, from an area that today has populations of high type B frequency. This contributed to the founding of many of the populations of the region. Clines for other gene markers (Rh and MN) also represent this east-to-west movement but are not as clearly defined.

Taking into account genetic markers and morphological differences, geographical variability of our species is self-evident, as discussed earlier. A number of gene markers (Hb, HLA, and GM) are considered to be distributed in concordance with the selective forces of particular diseases. Some complex traits have also been considered in relationship to certain environmental features like temperature, humidity, or sunlight. To the eye of the observer, as explained earlier, there is an apparent covariation with climatic conditions. Peoples living in colder climates tend to have a larger body size. Nose form is closely related to absolute moisture content of the air (vapor pressure) and, of course, skin color is highly correlated with the quantities of solar radiation striking the earth's surface. These distributions pass through many populations as if they were entirely independent of the boundaries constructed by human mating habits. The spatial location of the populations, however, causes the formation of a gradual series of genetic or phenotypic frequencies. The construction of a line through these data points produces the cline. The fact that the location of populations forms the cline makes it difficult to explain the distribution of a single gene, though several workers have used such an approach. Most recently, gene combinations have been used to trace population distributions. The use of several genes, language families and archaeology has been applied successfully to construct population maps (Cavalli-Sforza et al., 1994) These maps produce a clinal complex that can be interpreted as population movements, gene flow, or simply the genetic distances between related groups. As such they can be used to avoid some of the pitfalls inherent in the plotting of single gene traits.

Clines represent distribution of traits over broad areas, which frequently may obscure sharp differences between adjacent populations. When there is an increased sampling of local populations, these differences are identified, and the clinal boundaries of gene frequencies must be redrawn. Figure 6-5 illustrates that as a gene-frequency distribution becomes better known, the broader, more encompassing clinal expressions break down. Compare those regions of France and Italy that list the frequencies of the B allele with those noted in the clinal distribution plotted in Figure 6-4. Note that the broad overview lists a frequency of 5–10 percent while a more comprehensive series of measures shows over 15 percent in certain Italian areas.

There are several possible explanations for clinal distributions. The most frequently offered is that clines indicate the effect of natural selection. Livingstone has suggested that clines may be due to recent advances of advantageous genes or to gene flow between populations with different equilibrium frequencies for the gene. The geographical distribution of the hemoglobin S gene, discussed in Chapter 4, describes the advance of a gene advantageous

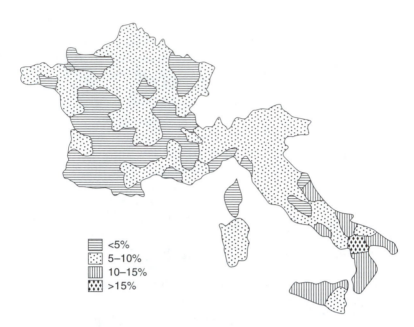

☰ <5%
∷ 5–10%
||| 10–15%
▨ >15%

FIGURE 6-5   Distribution of B Allele in France and Italy. (From Morganti, G., "Distribution of blood groups in Italy." Copyright © 1959 by Churchill. Reprinted by permission.)

to individuals confronted with malaria. This means that gene frequency follows the distribution of selective forces, but clines can also reflect the history of an exchange or flow of genes between populations. The movements of people bring about a genetic distribution often far in advance of any selective force that might be operating. The intrusion of Asians into eastern Europe, Middle Easterners into India, and the Island-hopping colonization of the Pacific all contributed to the clinal variations of the world as would have been seen before the fifteenth century European expansion.

BREEDING POPULATIONS VERSUS CLINES:
SOME CONCLUSIONS

> It has often been assumed that subspecific groupings based on the distribution of one, or at most a few characters will necessarily be concordant with the distributions of other variable characters. This, it seems, may be so for populations isolated in mountains, islands, caves or other restricted and special habitats, but is not usually the case in wider, more continuous regions. (Barnicot, 1964:198)

This quotation expresses another of the major objections to the use of geographic races as units of study. Some consider that the proper method for studying human variability is the single trait, as it is distributed across population boundaries. In contrast, others focus on the combination of characters in breeding populations. What we should be concerned with is not labeling of taxonomic units but the distribution of traits among the world's peoples and the meaning of this variation.

Several examples of this variation, at the phenotypic, genotypic, and DNA levels have been offered. Some have distributions that coincide with the distribution of certain selective forces and, in several striking examples, also with massive population movements. The presence of a cline of darkly pigmented skin in North America together with hemoglobin S (Hb^s) and a Duffy blood type (Fy^0) are due to movements of many Africans to the New World during the seventeenth and eighteenth centuries. This illustrates why contemporary populations may not provide evidence of the correlation of a gene frequency and selected force. The distribution of Rh$^-$ (cde) type in Europe and North Africa may indicate prior contact between groups living in these areas (the occupation of Spain and parts of southern Europe by North Africans during the seventh and eighth centuries). Numerous indigenous populations in the Americas today contain certain gene combinations because of their ancestors' being overrun by European colonists. The presence of several blood types and HLA markers gives evidence to this contact, just as the mtDNA sequences support Asian origins.

The clines illustrated in the various figures describe the distribution of both monogenic and polygenic traits, and there are, as previously discussed, major distinctions between them. Morphological dimensions of complex phenotypes such as skin color or body size vary continuously, and each population or group usually grades imperceptibly into neighboring groups of a region. Rarely are there sharp, clear-cut divisions and smooth geographical distributions that may be plotted. In the case of monogenetic traits, population gene frequencies can and often do change rapidly within one or two generations, as has been illustrated by the examples of island populations or small colonies. In addition, there are often steep differences between adjacent populations with a long history of occupancy but minimal mate exchange. This is illustrated by the significant differences in blood-group frequencies between four tribes in central Australia who share adjacent boundaries but yet have significant differences between them. Comparisons of one to another show differences in frequencies of ABO, MN, and Rh blood group types by as much as 60 percent. Though continent-wide, the cline of type A frequency showed a gradual decline from north to south; the effect of population boundaries is clearly demonstrated when the frequency dropped from 0.53 down to 0.13 from one tribal unit to an adjacent one (Birdsell, 1993). The probable cause of such a steep cline is the directional restriction of gene flow. Other steep changes are also recorded despite smooth directional averages for several genetic markers. Therefore, simple comparisons between trait distribution and selective forces are not always possible, since the larger overview of a distribution can often obscure significant differences. The population's size, its history, and mating patterns must be clearly defined.

Ethnic variations and their relationships to species averages are not only a matter of scale and perspective but of behavior and identity of the group under study. If we consider all those factors that cause changes in gene frequency—(1) mutation; (2) natural selection; (3) genetic drift; (4) migration or gene flow; and (5) breeding behavior—then we find that factors 1 and 2 act on certain alleles in unique ways. The first, mutation or error in DNA coding, is random and infrequent, providing the basis for all variation. Factor 2, natural selection, is determined by environmental conditions and a population's adaptation to them, and is distributed geographically, of course; and this distribution cuts across population boundaries. The other three factors, also, are important, but they are behaviorally determined and they have an intense effect on the gene frequency from generation to generation. Through society's choice, population size may be restricted for a number of generations, or an adaptive innovation may cause a rapid expansion, affecting the gene pool size. Such events will influence gene frequencies over the generations through genetic drift (factor 3). The decision to migrate or exchange mates with surrounding groups directs gene flow over time. Finally, the establishment of mating circles will direct gene exchange within a group, which may decide to limit or expand the network of mate choice. All societies do this to some extent by enforcing an incest taboo. Almost always this includes the nuclear family and extends outward to forbid the marriages of cousins, though each society has its own rules. Cousin marriages are allowed in some and forbidden in others. Often this depends on property distribution, or on the size of the pool of eligible mates.

Whatever the factors, we should recall that genes are not passed on one at a time, nor is an individual's fitness usually determined by single genes. Fitness is a compromise between the interaction of all of one's gene products and the environments encountered during one's life cycle. These are important considerations when studying clinal distributions. Gene flow is not descriptive of actual events because genes do not flow or "float around in space." They are transmitted as a group or an array by the chromosomes, and recombination of chromosomes is one of the key processes to offer variety between the generations. These several factors of behavior and basic genetics lend considerable support to the breeding population concept—that group of people participating within the same circle of matings.

The clinal approach has its strength, but only when used in conjunction with the actual basis for trait distribution through time and space—the population. The argument that one approach is more efficient as a means of studying human variation than the other is without foundation. We must consider the adaptive significance or survival value of each trait in the context of the population, and pay heed to those conditions of environment and human adaptation that contributed to an increase of our species from a few million to more than five billion people today.

7

Human Variability and Behavior

Individuals vary considerably in their behavior, as they do in many of their biological traits. One does not have to be an expert to recognize this. Just as we perceive differences in human size, shape, and color, we readily differentiate between persons on the basis of their personality traits. The behavioral differences we distinguish, however, are difficult to measure and are influenced to an extraordinary degree by cultural factors. The family, religion, and nation have profound influences that establish lifetime patterns of behavior; even the era in which we live shapes many of our responses, as any comparisons between generations in the twentieth century will show. An additional problem arises when we attempt to quantify such traits and try to draw conclusions about an individual's worth or quality or ability. All too often we seek an easy answer and rely on group membership as the key to individual evaluation. Just as with characteristics of color, size, and shape, our perceptions are based on ill-founded assumptions

The study of human behavioral diversity is further complicated not only by prejudices and misconceptions but also by the confusion of social and biological definitions of race as described earlier. For example, by the end of the last century, beliefs in racial superiority reached a peak as achievements of entire nations and civilizations throughout human history were attributed to the "superior germ plasm" of their citizens. Most frequently the Nordic race was described as the bearer of this superior germ plasm. The French aristo-crat Count Gobineau dedicated the contents of his four-volume series, "The Inequality of Races" to an attempt to prove that the Nordics, whom he described as the "bearers of the lamp of civilization," were above all other races. The rest of the species, including the bulk of Europeans, were grouped into races that were inferior. According to Gobineau, "It was the Nordic who created the high civilizations of the past and who were responsible for the for-mation of modern states" (Gobineau, in Barzun, 1965:54).

This conviction of racial superiority proved to be useful as a rationaliza-tion for the treatment of the aboriginal peoples whom Europeans encoun-tered during their world exploration and colonization. Confronted with the high mortality and declining populations that they were no doubt responsible for, the colonial government officials talked glibly of "a passing of an inferior race." The attitude was maintained after the defeat of the Maori armies in New Zealand, although these Polynesians, with their highly developed tribal government and efficient use of land, presented special problems of con-quest. The general feeling of the English colonists is summed up by one offi-cial: "Taking all things into consideration, the disappearance of the race (Maori) is scarcely subject for much regret. They are dying out in a quick, easy way, and are being supplanted by a superior race" (Belich, 1986:299). This kind of statement coming from officials virtually anywhere in the far-flung European colonies was not surprising because it expressed the general feeling of the time. Even among the medical missionaries, who were charged with tending to the physical and spiritual needs of the colonized people, there was the firm belief that the "race has run out" and, after two or three generations, only a remnant would remain to represent the people (Fenton, 1859:31). Many examples existed among peoples around the world; all non-Europeans, by definition, were incapable of higher development. Even among the Euro-peans, however, there was a scaling of biological inequality, and southern Europeans were placed lower than northern populations, and eastern Euro-peans were at the bottom of the scale. Such beliefs were common in the nine-teenth century and have persisted even into recent decades, as shown by the dominant theme of a book that revived racism in the 1970s: "It must not be forgotten that certain races of man not only never attained independently to the status of civilization, but never independently reached the intermediate phase" (Baker, 1974:528).

Such brief statements note the direction of racist writings of the last cen-tury, which sought to understand human societies in terms of heredity. Of course, today we no longer speak of "superior germ plasm" as the source of civilization, nor do we define race and national character. There is, however, a continued interest in biological determinism, or genetic determinism of behavior, which has its modern roots in the application of various tests designed to measure aptitude or intelligence. With the revival of Mendelian genetics in 1900, theories of social reform and human behavior were decidedly influenced by evidence of particulate inheritance. Since many physical characteristics were determined at conception by combinations of parental genes, it was considered probable that traits like mental ability, aggression, and social pathology were also inherited. Psychologists in the United States eagerly applied the new genetic theory to a host of social problems of the day, and the principal problem was believed to be the "flood" of immigrants entering America during the 1900s.

At the beginning of this century there was an attempt to discriminate between immigrant groups through the application of an intelligence test devised by the French psychologist Binet. Goddard, one of the first psychologists to adapt the Binet test in America, was invited by government officials in 1912 to apply the test at the Ellis Island immigrant receiving station. Goddard administered a revised Binet test and its supplements to what he called representatives of the "great mass of average immigrants." Convinced of the accuracy of his results, Goddard reported that 83 percent of the Jews, 80 percent of the Hungarians, 79 percent of the Italians, and 87 percent of the Russians were "feebleminded" and unable to deal with abstractions. The effect of these results became all too clear when Goddard reported in 1917 that the number of aliens deported because of feeblemindedness increased approximately 350 percent in 1913 and 570 percent in 1914 because of the untiring efforts of the physicians, who were inspired by the belief that mental tests could be used for detection of "undesirables" (Kamin, 1974).

The interest of authorities in the mental quality of the immigrants at the turn of the century was grounded in a firm belief that certain racial groups and even certain national groups were biologically inferior. This interest was heightened by the change in country of origin of the immigrants, which had been a worrisome problem for some time to many Americans involved in the eugenics movement dedicated to the improvement of the species. Before 1890, most immigrants came from western Europe, but by the turn of the century this source declined, and a "new immigration" began. Eastern and southern Europe were the sources of this more recent migration, all with populations of "non-Nordics." The newly devised mental tests provided a ready means of sorting out the "undesirables." The results of comparisons of test scores achieved by the new immigrants with those of U.S. citizens of Nordic descent were interpreted as a decline in immigrant intelligence, which was believed to be a grave threat to Nordic survival. Psychologists like Goddard and Brigham, a participant in the testing program of army recruits during World War I, attributed this decline directly to the change in racial origin of the immigrants. Many writers warned that steps must be taken to preserve America's "precious heritage of germ plasma," and, in 1924, steps were taken in the form of restrictive immigration laws that limited the number of immigrants according to their national origin (Cravens, 1978:228 for a review).

These restrictive immigration quotas provide another example of the notion that the superficial differences that set people apart somehow make them inferior beings or lesser humans. Such an idea is of great antiquity, as discussed in Chapter 1. Despite the thousands of pages written to present evidence to refute such misbeliefs, concepts of racial superiority and inferiority are, perhaps, as strong today as they ever were. Witness the increase in statements that attribute many aspects of human behavior to inheritance, expressing the conviction that "biological determinism" or "genetic predestination" is a reality and offers a ready explanation for many of society's problems. How much simpler to attribute these problems to "instinctive behavior" than to deal with the complex underlying causes of famine, disease, crime, and ethnic warfare. It is but a short step to conclude, then, that some ethnic groups are inferior because of their genetic complement.

The immigrants streaming through Ellis Island during the early part of this century provided a favorite target for snap judgments about inferior behavior; if their IQ did not give them away, their appearance and language would. They were smaller than the American average, some differed slightly in face form, and of course their clothing was of a different fashion. Certainly these were trivial differences, but to the scientists and immigration officials of the day they were significant. These physical and cultural differences were taken as evidence of inferiority and held up as a warning to the "superior" race (that is, Nordic) to beware of the danger of being swamped by inferior beings. This set the theme of much literature on population studies over the first decades of the century, and after a seemingly quiescent period, these ideas are being revived today. The modern-day feelings about inequality (now referred to by more subtle terms such as "ethnic differences") is dealt with from a perspective of "birth dearth" or the lower fertility rates of peoples of European origins in contrast to "others." Such fertility differences contribute to an imbalance of population growth rates and, together with the high level of legal and illegal immigration, will result in a much lower proportion of west European stock. The implied or implicit concern is that such an ethnic imbalance will contribute to social turbulence (Wattenberg, 1985:114). Though this author is discussing the changes of ethnic balances in the U.S. population, the same may be said of the United Kingdom and several countries of western Europe. This illustrates, in a contemporary context, a growing concern with cultural, ethnic, and biological differences.

There is no need at this point to review those strongly held beliefs that associate a particular form of behavior with certain racial groups. We have all heard such arguments many times. Consider, though, that if there is a wide genetic diversity within each major geographic unit (race) of the several biological traits that we have considered previously, then there should be an equally wide range of those genes that may relate to people's behavior. Simply stated, there are "bright" and "dull" people in all groups of *Homo sapiens.* Just as the distribution of easily perceived traits was not understandable by clustering them into major geographical units, so it is impossible to talk of a "racial" variation of behavior. The problem is further confused by the nature of whatever behavioral traits we identify and then treat as biological phenotypes. The complexity of human behavior does not allow simple trait definition, and it is not possible to identify separate genetic and environmental components, though this was offered as a method by the leader of the more recent revival of sociobiology, E. O. Wilson, in his book *On Human Nature*.

The uniquely human capacity of language and memory is inherited and sets us apart as a species. Once this inherited ability has been established in the newborn, the individual's mental development depends on a range of environmental stimuli for the extent and kind of knowledge acquired. These stimuli come from a range of sources, both behavioral and biological. The biological sources include those nutrients necessary for normal growth, and certain deficiencies can have profound effects if they occur at crucial periods of brain development. Substances that affect growth and metabolic rates, hormone action, and, in turn, neurotransmitters (about 2,000 chemicals) make up only a portion of biological influences. Behavioral stimuli are received from individuals with whom the infant and growing child comes into contact, and the circle of influences grows with a child's development, expanding ever outward. Given the range of the known stimuli to mental development, any attempt to categorize or classify human mental capacity into taxonomic divisions, as has been done for traits of blood or DNA, is simply beyond any reality.

The question of just how much of our behavior is determined biologically and how much by our experience is still open. Some writers claim that behavior is influenced minimally by one's inheritance in contrast to the vast changes that can be made by the environment. Others have revived the old "nature" argument used by the eugenicists of last century, who argued that a person's biological as well as behavioral makeup is determined by heredity. Few will deny, however, that there are inherited behavioral differences between individuals, and that there is probably a significant biological component underlying many of our behavioral responses. An extreme form of biological influence can be easily illustrated by the mental retardation that often accompanies several kinds of chromosome abnormalities. The Klinefelter (XXY) and Down (trisomy 21) syndromes involve mental impairment along with the physical defects that result from errors in chromosome number. But even then, environments make a large difference as improved treatment of Down's patients has demonstrated. Also, there are several possibilities for explaining certain clinically defined mental illnesses in terms of enzyme polymorphisms. The inherited diseases phenylketonuria, Tay-Sachs, and galactosemia, described in Chapter 3, all have associated effects of mental retardation. Extreme iodine deficiency is another factor, as it severely depresses thyroid function and retards growth with varying degrees of mental impairment. Cretinism is the most acute form. Beyond such pathological examples, little evidence can be offered for inheritance of mental or behavioral traits. However, there have been several studies that associate certain gene markers with some forms of pathological behavior as summarized below, but environment still remains the major causal factor.

RACE, ETHNIC GROUP, CLASS, AND BEHAVIOR

The categorizing of people according to their group membership is always a tempting exercise because it compresses the broad range of biological diversity into a few divisions and seemingly simplifies identification of a myriad of traits. The behavioral variety that appears to exist, however, is difficult, if not impossible, to attribute largely to a biological cause (the genes). Most, if not all, of the differences in lifestyle and world perception that have so puzzled observers have, at one time or another, been attributed to innate differences. That the "primitive" mind was not well developed in its reasoning powers was a frequent conclusion of western European observers when confronted with, to them, strange, exotic societies. Many of the distinctions described, though, were actually due to cultural influences, socioeconomic status, or the physical environment.

Description and comprehension of behavioral diversity is further complicated by the difficulties of measuring and identifying mental ability and behavior. Anthropologists throughout this century have demonstrated that an observer's own cultural background greatly influences his or her judgment or perception, particularly if he or she is studying an aboriginal society that lacks a written language and whose people look and/or dress quite differently from members of the observer's group. It takes many months or years to gain insight and understanding of language and culture under such conditions, and even then, most observers are only partly successful. This means that any comparisons between the "native" and "civilized" mind or national character are speculative at best and will reveal little about the inheritance of behavioral diversity.

The cultural component is responsible for a great deal of variability, and often cultures are evaluated as being modern or primitive, simple or complex. The behavior of individuals participating in a culture other than our own differs from what we have come to know as "standard" behavior. The contrasts are striking, particularly when the technology is primitive or simple, such as in the cultures of New Guinea or Australia. Rather than make a value judgment, it would be more logical and would contribute more to our understanding if each culture were considered an adaptation to the environment in which it is found. Whether it be the rigorous environment of the Australian "outback," which nurtured the culture of the Aborigines, or that of the impoverished peoples in urban ghettos, the sociocultural framework of each enables the maintenance of human society of great complexity in response to environmental challenges.

Since aboriginal populations are less available for study, the attention of social scientists has turned more frequently to minorities defined by economic class or by ethnicity. African Americans have been the object of many such studies, and the results have frequently been used in attempts to show that there is something innately inferior about this group. To the biological determinist, this would explain the higher rates of mortality, criminality, teen pregnancy, low income, high unemployment, and so on. A fact little noted by those who would explain social problems by inheritance is that minorities around the world are in a similar social position. New Zealand Maoris, gypsies in Hungary, "guest" workers in Germany, Algerians in France are among a few groups that should be mentioned because they represent a diversity of gene pools but still share the same relationship to the national majority population among which they live.

In addition to ascribing race differences to inheritance, national character has often been ascribed to inheritance in a similar way: The antipathy, the hostile acts of aggression and at times even warfare, between ethnic groups, sometimes even among close biological relatives, is said to be due to differences in genetic heritage. Darlington, a foremost human geneticist, described the centuries of conflict between the English and Irish:

> This quarrel can be understood only in terms of the profound racial difference between the Gaelic-speaking natives and the English-speaking invaders, a difference which even today, after twenty generations of limited hybridization, is still not seriously blurred.
>
> The English were sober, industrious, mechanical, calculating and ruthless; characteristics invaluable in government. The native Irish by contrast were imaginative, unpredictable and even irresponsible. Their pre-Aryan and perhaps paleolithic speech had died out only in the ninth century and they had more left of their paleolithic instincts. (Darlington, 1969: 449–450)

Thus, Darlington appeared to explain away a long and very complex sociopolitical history on the basis of persistence of "paleolithic instincts," whatever they are.

Special attention has been directed to African Americans' lower average performance on certain standardized tests, which has often been attributed to "inferior genes." There is even a belief in certain circles that "the black has a gene for 'slow learning.'" Of course, the difficulty of attempting to unravel the inheritance of learning ability of any group is compounded by the complexity of the learning processes, to say nothing of the difficulty of genetic identification of the subjects examined by these tests. Even the detection of such a gene's presence in an individual is not possible, as is also the case with many other polygenic traits that have unknown gene combinations and whose individual genes cannot be identified. About all that the many studies have shown is that, as a group, African Americans have a lower average IQ, by a few points, than the white population. Much more has been made of this small difference than the data permit, especially when discussing genes, behavior, and race or ethnic group, because no control for gene admixture is ever made. That is, the individuals of the sample grouped as black in the United States are descendants of several generations of hybridization, and the European admixture varies widely. To expect an even distribution of genes from the African founders to their descendants 400 years later is to ignore Mendel's laws and return to concepts from the days of "bloodlines" and inheritance by blending.

Where do these beliefs in biological inequality come from and why are they so frequently repeated by otherwise distinguished scientists? Well, these beliefs come from personal bias, to begin with—from the uncritical acceptance of broad generalizations reinforced by erroneous data, and sanctioned by statistical manipulation of tests designed to measure mental attributes. Writers of novels and travel books also have had an influence, one that continues even today. Such influence spreads the stereotypes of cultures, nations, and peoples. It reinforces beliefs in personal perceptions and labels. Despite overwhelming evidence to the contrary, intuitive approaches to the study of human diversity have persisted, as the following quotation illustrates:

> Nature has color-coded groups of individuals so that statistically reliable predictions of their adaptability to intellectually rewarding and effective lives can easily be made and profitably be used by the pragmatic man in the street. (Shockley, 1972:307)

What about this color coding? Are there really such simple ways by which a "pragmatic man in the street" can evaluate the quality of another human being? Is it as easy as identifying a criminal type by the size of the nose or ears, as was proposed by Lombroso a century ago? Is "innate ability" as plain as the nose on your face or the shape of your head, or are many writers today again confusing and mixing traits that bear no relationship to one another? Cranial capacity or brain size is regaining its former popularity as a measure of intelligence, "basic racial stocks" are still retained as reference points, and testing as a measure of innate differences is undergoing a resurgence (Rushton, 1992).

Ethnic Group, Classification, and Behavior

Identity of ethnic group membership may be useful for political purposes and necessary for certain government record keeping, and categorizing individuals has certainly been acceptable throughout our history. In any attempt to study trait inheritance, however, the same labels and categories do not apply. A nation's subdivision of its population relies on social and political considerations, as demonstrated by the continuing changes in the choices for self-identification by category on government forms. These are "social" classifications and bear little resemblance to the actual genetic composition of one's group. We are entering a new era of an expanded understanding of our genome, and behavioral as well as biological research should acknowledge this fact. There is no "racial behavior" any more than there is an ethnic group behavior representative of underling genetic causes.

Group classification based on some single attribute, such as geographic origin (e.g., Asian), language (e.g., Hispanic), or skin color (e.g., white versus nonwhite) ignores all other attributes and neglects to consider degree of admixture. Asians encompass thousands of populations totaling over a billion and a half people whose territory, both today and in the past, covers virtually every climate and environment on the planet. To assume that a few or thousands of individuals selected from such a large diverse group are representative is totally incorrect. The reader should not have to be reminded that "Hispanic" also is a label devoid of genetic meaning. It has gained prominent political status in the last two decades and includes people of diverse national origins. White and non-white identity is perhaps the most vague and meaningless of all. Who are included in one or the other group and how "white" or "nonwhite" does one have to be? There is considerable confusion over this seemingly simple question. Where, for example, do Hispanics fit in? The census forms allow for a person to identify as either, but does regional origin (Europe or Mexico) matter? Fernandez reviewed multiethnicity and, in trying to unravel some of the complexity of what he calls "the melting pot of La Raza," concluded that region matters: "Mexican Americans make up the second largest non-White ethnic group in the United States (1992:127)." What does the label "nonwhite" mean?

The confusion over "color," origins, and genetics is even more extensive when the ethnic group African American is considered. Their ancestry is a mixture of African and European with a contribution of Native American genes, forming, in some areas, triracial hybrids (Pollitzer, 1972). The average of European admixture is given as 25 percent, based on comparisons of fifteen polymorphic loci (Chakraborty and Kidd, 1991), but this is only an average. The range of admixture is quite broad across the United States, less in small enclaves in South Carolina and higher in large urban centers (Pollitzer, 1994). The large and widely dispersed populations of African origin in Central and South America and throughout the Caribbean add to the genetic heterogeniety of those we label African American or black. In addition, African ancestry is anything but homogeneous. African populations are as diverse as any in the world, as explained earlier, and the lineages of their New World descendants lead back to contributions from a variety of these populations. As noted in Chapter 4, slaves were imported into the Western Hemisphere from a broad geographic region. Even at a single port of entry, Charleston, South Carolina, between 1716 and 1807 the slave cargoes came from a region extending from Senegambia to Angola, a distance of about 3,000 miles.

The question of "color classification" is not answered, but this should raise doubts about its use as a meaningful genetic category. If for no other reason, criticism of studies of group differences in intelligence can be made on these grounds: The studies are often carried out on groups whose actual genetic composition is not known. Nor is the group distinguished or identified in any way as a breeding population, and its recent ancestry and history are ignored. The only concern of group identification is with the social definition of race—again highlighting the error of confusing culture and biological variables. It is one thing to discuss genetic potential, gene frequency, or inherited ability within a breeding population whose members share a large number of genes in common; it is another matter to discuss these variables in reference to a race or an ethnic group (socially, politically, or biologically defined).

Despite these problems, the claim has often been made that an admixture of European genes actually causes an increased IQ in African Americans, as if Caucasoids were a homogeneous group all possessing the same gene combinations, regardless of whether northern or southern, eastern or western Europe in origin. Such claims of effects of admixture on IQ are unfounded; data do not exist to support a contention that intelligence varies with degree of ancestry. In fact, there is no connection between the test performance of an individual and the number of that person's European ancestors. Estimates of the degree of European ancestry of 350 African-American residents of Philadelphia were made by careful analysis of blood groups and serum proteins, which is possible because, as we discussed in Chapters 4 and 6, European and African populations differ in average frequencies of certain genetic markers. This method was used instead of the usual method of asking the subjects to identify their degree of European ancestry on the basis of known white ancestors. With an estimate of their ancestry established through biochemical genetics methods, this group was given a variety of mental tests. Scarr and her associates reviewed the results and demonstrated that those persons with a high degree of African ancestry did no better and no worse than those individuals who had several European ancestors (Scarr, 1981; Scarr and Weinberg, 1978). Simply, genes did not count on test performance in this study.

Among other things, this Philadelphia study, and the twin studies described below, demonstrate that hereditary influences on behavior can only be studied when the ancestry and genetic admixture of each individual tested are known, and only when breeding-population boundaries are established can interpopulation comparisons be made. These are difficult criteria to fulfill, of course, but any study that purports to examine genotypes and the behavioral phenotypes must carefully determine population composition. Anything less produces misleading data. This is particularly true because of the confusion that still surrounds race concepts and especially the identification of an individual's group membership. Is race/ethnic group membership made by self-identification, teacher's identification, or another method, for example? These problems are often ignored even when differences in social and biological classifications are admitted, as the following quotation illustrates:

Although most of the studies of racial differences in intelligence are based on social definitions of race, it should be noted that there is usually a high correlation between the social and the biological definitions, and it is most unlikely that results of the research would be very different if the investigators had used biological rather than social criteria of race in selecting groups for comparison. (Jensen, 1971:16–17)

Jensen, a leading proponent of the racial inequality argument, knowingly mixed a social classification with a genetic one. I question his assumption that there is usually a high correlation between social and biological definitions. It has not been tested and, given the problems of admixture, self-identification, and the race concept, it is not likely to be. If he wished to argue that "American blacks" (or any group, for that matter) score lower on IQ tests than "American whites" because of some innate difference, then careful account must be taken of the genetic composition of each group. How can genetic determination be studied unless population admixture is known? What about the tests themselves? What do they, in fact, measure?

INTELLIGENCE QUOTIENT: A MEASURE OF MENTAL ABILITY?

The definition of intelligence and how it is to be determined elude us, though intelligence has become fixed in our culture as meaning "innate ability." Since Galton argued that certain tests could measure intelligence, the argument has raged on endlessly over what standardized tests actually measure. With the millions of tests administered during this century, no agreement has been reached as to what is actually tested. "Intelligence is what IQ tests measure," states one worker. "IQ tests measure learning experience," declares another. Whatever the test scores reveal about an individual's ability, the tests are widely used in our society and often place individuals within a niche in our educational system, guide employment decisions, and are used by the armed forces. Such placement has far-reaching effects on a person's intellectual development and future achievement. The test scores of an individual may vary 4 to 5 points on retesting over short intervals, but over intervals of several years, variations of 20 to 30 points are known, reinforcing the belief that tests are a measure of one's learning experience (Schiff and Lewontin, 1986:194).

Most testing procedures trace their origins to Alfred Binet, a French psychologist who developed the first usable intelligence test in 1905 (the Binet-Simon test). The purpose of the original test was to identify students with low academic aptitudes so they might be assisted by special programs. Binet was concerned with the development of therapeutic courses to aid students who had performed poorly. Tests were arranged in order of increasing difficulty, and children completed as many as they could, with their progress compared with that of other children of their age group. Binet did not attempt to describe the source of the problem of those falling below their group nor did he determine whether their poor performance was due to environmental or congenital factors. In fact, he specifically rejected those who described intelligence as a fixed quantity. Nevertheless, subsequent adaptations of Binet's test have often concluded that the results revealed the quality of inherited intelligence.

Rather than attempt to define what intelligence was, Binet took the direct approach of establishing what was "normal mental development" in his society during his time. Normal was simply the performance of a majority of children between three and thirteen years old on a series of tests. These tests were based on a collection of questions typically used in the classroom, except in the case of preschoolers. The number of items answered correctly by a child were compared to the average of correct answers for the age group. The majority range of children completing test sets was set at between 65 to 75 percent, and the lowest 25 percent with the greatest gap between their developmental and chronological ages were defined as backward. Binet, at the suggestion of a German psychologist, Stern, divided developmental or mental age (MA) by chronological age (CA) to get a quotient of mental development. The children in the majority range would have a quotient of one; those above the 75 percent level would have a quotient of greater than one, and those in the lower end of the range would be below one. The MA divided by CA was multiplied by 100 to give us an intelligence quotient or the well-known IQ. Note two things: First, the range of normals of 65–75 percent is arbitrary and based on statistical methods of the day, a fitting of the majority to a normal, or bell curve. Second, because the questions selected were those taken from material commonly taught, it is not surprising that the test performance was highly predictive of academic achievement.

The Binet-Simon test was imported to this country and became popular among American psychologists even without modification. It was first used by Goddard to test immigrants at Ellis Island, as mentioned earlier, with what was considered a great success. When American schoolchildren were tested, however, the results were poor until Lewis Terman of Stanford university adapted the test to American standards. Terman used groups of California schoolchildren and adjusted the scores of each age group so the average was 100; that is, a person performing "normally" at his or her age level would be expected to score around 100 because this was the majority score fitted to a curve described as a normal distribution. This modified form was published and distributed in 1916 as the Stanford-Binet (or IQ) test with claims that it would establish schoolchildren's intelligence and be an invaluable education tool.

The IQ test was quickly accepted and applied by teachers and American psychologists to thousands of schoolchildren. The extent of these applications went far beyond the original goals. Binet and Simon designed their test series to identify relative academic achievement and carefully avoided consideration of the results in terms of innate ability. In fact, Simon accused those who treated intelligence as a fixed quantity of having a brutal pessimism (quoted in Chase, 1977:236). Nevertheless, the pioneers of mental testing in America—Terman, Goddard, and Yerkes—readily looked to the test results as evidence of a person's inherited mental ability. Discussions of feebleminded, bright, and dull supported by IQ scores were repeated frequently in the current psychological publications. Terman's major contribution, according to his biographer, Minton (1988), was "to establish a fine gradation of measured ability so schoolchildren could be placed in educational tracks commensurate with their tested level of intelligence." This meant, in practical terms, that Terman's recommendations supported classroom segregation, since most ethnic minorities averaged lower scores. Indirectly, the testing of schoolchildren lent an aura of scientific validity to the folk beliefs of biological determinism. The "mental measuring science" was expanded even further by the approach of America's involvement in World War I.

A short time after its introduction, the modified Binet test was adapted for the testing of recruits inducted into a rapidly expanding army. Eventually nearly two million males were tested by the Alpha test (for literates) and the Beta test (for illiterates and non-English-speakers). The results of this mass testing have been described in numerous books and have generated considerable controversy, which continued more than two generations later (see Pastore, 1978). This controversy was fired by the psychologists involved in the test design, who presented the results as measures of "native" intelligence and concluded that it would be fruitless to attempt to improve the lot of the low-scoring groups. A continuing exchange of publications followed arguing over the meaning of testing procedures and "native intelligence." Briefly, many writers accepted an interpretation of the test scores that concluded that the average mental age of American adult males was fourteen. This led to the common theme that American traditions were at risk. Statements asserting that democracy was threatened because of large numbers of our citizens were of such low intellect, or that "no one of us can afford to ignore the menace of race deterioration or the evident relations of immigration to national progress and welfare" continued to appear until the eve of World War II.

Terman, defending test scores as evidence that there was a high frequency of adults of a low mental age, described the threat to the "welfare of the State" because of differences in birthrates. He warned that "the propagation of mental degenerates" must be curtailed. Such strong beliefs expressed in 1917 by a respected scientist immediately gained wide public acceptance (Block and Dworkin, 1976:348–49). The reader today, before accepting this kind of rejection of charitable attempts at assistance for the more unfortunate, should ask who the feebleminded were to whom Terman was referring. They were, of course, those who scored lowest on the IQ tests and on the army tests that were so readily employed by psychologists as a diagnostic tool of mental ability. Recall that many of the groups who scored lowest were newly arrived immigrants from eastern and southern European countries, the grandparents and great-grandparents of so many Americans living today. Their descendants occupy every profession and level of socioeconomic achievement. Their test scores are also higher!

The ready acceptance of test scores by professionals and the general public alike revealed hidden dangers to any society that based government policy on these results. Immediately, there were reactions against the conclusions and the various applications. Some writers, realizing the problems of the tests and their lack of scientific method, reacted with sharp comments laying bare some of the fallacies underlying the search for a single measure of innate human ability. Foremost among the opponents was the editorialist Walter Lippman, who observed: "The whole drift of the propaganda based on intelligence testing is to treat people with low intelligence quotients as congenitally and hopelessly inferior. The prominent testers believe that they are measuring the capacity of a human being for all time and that this capacity is fatally fixed by the child's heredity." He continued further in an exchange of letters with Terman and admitted that he was emotional in his response; "I hate the impudence of a claim that in fifty minutes you can judge and classify a human being's predestined fitness in life. I hate the abuse of a scientific method which it involved. I hate the sense of superiority which it creates and the sense of inferiority which it imposes" (see Pastore, 1978).

IQ Tests and African Americans

Throughout World War II and most of the postwar decade, the mental testing issue diminished in importance, and the environmentalists seemed to dominate the heredity–environment question that had been a battleground for a century. Equal access to quality education for all children became a central issue. This could not be achieved without school desegregation, an emotional issue that generated major opposition and resurrected the hereditarians. The acceptance of innate ability as measured by performance on standard tests regained its former scientific aura in the fight against school desegregation. The concept of racial inequality never really went away; however, some of the "races" were removed from the lists. The former inferiors—Alpine and Mediterranean types, eastern and southern Europeans—were now considered equal to the formerly superior Nordics. Further, many of these "inferior types" were now constructing and administering the new tests at all levels of the educational system. Americans of African descent were not so recognized, though after 1954 they could not be excluded or limited in educational access except on the basis of test scores.

African Americans' average test scores had placed them in the lower ranges of the army and IQ test ranges, and this fit with the racist dogma of the day. These results continued to be a prop for the legal fights to maintain separate education despite the evidence that educational expenditures and school quality largely determined test scores. Recruits from urban centers, especially in the North, scored higher on the army Alpha test than did those from rural areas; those from the southern states averaged lower in both categories. Klineberg (1935) pointed to school expenditure per pupil as the independent variable. A most embarrassing fact for the racist, and a fact generally avoided, was that African Americans who had attended schools in the northern cities scored higher than rural southern "whites." Despite this groundwork laid some two decades before, America's love affair with psychological testing was eagerly renewed, but now with many more test forms applied at all levels in our social and educational lives. The results could place us in occupational, educational, or social niches and were eagerly accepted as statements of our innate abilities.

What was said about the IQs of immigrants at the turn of the century was repeated in reference to African Americans, but with considerably more emotion. "Their intelligence is significantly lower, they lack the ability to handle abstract reasoning" (Jensen, 1969:81), and "test performance of a group improves in proportion to the admixture of Caucasoid genes" (Shockley, 1972:298) are examples of frequent statements. Such repetition of the early misapplication of test scores to another socially disadvantaged group forty years later is disheartening, especially in light of the mass of work that has gone into development of intelligence-testing programs during recent decades. We still find claims that "intelligence is inherited and relatively unchanged by the environment (education) and IQ tests are a measure of this innate ability." These claims must still be examined and refuted (Weinberg, 1989:98). Though there are many more testing procedures today, there is still no basis for the argument that performance in relation to some group average is a measure of intelligence. It is, rather, a means of classifying people by a measure of their learning experiences.

Arthur Jensen was one of those who introduced this modern version of the inappropriate use of heritability, race, and IQ. Before the American Educational Research Association meeting in 1967, Jensen launched an attack on compensatory education, which made him a famous but controversial figure. First, like many psychologists from the past, he accepted that IQ was inherited, and then he suggested that "since intelligence is largely determined genetically, we need to know the proportion of difference between blacks and whites that is genetically determined" (Hirsch, 1967:437). He treated intelligence as a trait that was possessed in unequal proportions by different "pure races." Jensen continued his criticism of the new environmentalists in a series of books and papers. In 1969 he published a paper, "How Much Can We Boost IQ and Scholastic Achievement?," which examined compensatory education programs for minority children (the Head Start program, for example). In his paper Jensen argued that IQ tests measure general ability, and individual differences in IQ were due to a high degree of genetic determination, which was the reason compensatory programs proved ineffective in overcoming the inherited differences between racial groups. Jensen's emphasis on genetic determination is surprising because, less than a decade earlier, he had presented convincing data that showed the opposite to be true. He had cited socioeconomic factors as the cause of differences in learning achievements of poor and non-poor groups (Chase, 1977:46).

Jensen compiled vast amounts of data from studies of African Americans in support of his argument. A variety of tests, including the Stanford-Binet, all placed black achievement below white. Comparison of the two groups showed the average IQ for blacks about 15 points below the average for whites. This distance between groups is an indisputable fact, but note that the range of variation is broad. Some studies report as little as 10 points or as much as 20 between the means (Figure 7-1). Also, the distribution of the IQ values of "blacks" overlaps that of "whites," but, of special importance, the means will vary depending on the study sample; comparisons of Boston schoolchildren by race yield results at variance with those reported in rural Georgia. Recall that

FIGURE 7-1 Comparison of IQ Distributions of American Black and White Elementary School Children. The distribution of American black I.Q. is taken from a sample of 1,800 children enrolled in elementary schools in five southern states. The mean of 80.7 contrasts with the 101.8 mean of a normative white sample and is the greatest difference reported. (From Kennedy, W. A., V. Van de Riet, and J. C. White, 1963. Copyright © 1963 The Society for Research in Child Development, Inc. Reprinted by permission of the publisher.)

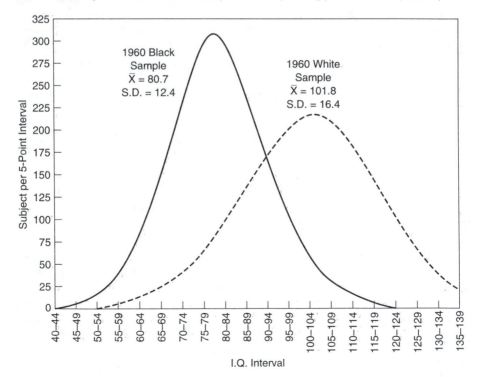

these reported differences between the two groups are very similar to those described for native-born Americans and eastern European immigrants in the 1920s. Viewing them as contrasts between regions or school districts as well as between race raises the question of significance. Is race or ethnic group a factor, or are contrasting learning environments the independent variables?

Comparisons of ethnic groups across international boundaries give results similar to those obtained in the United States. Most groups not native to or descendant from northwestern Europe scored between 10 and 20 points lower. The exceptions were subjects in Italy and European descendants in New Zealand and Australia, who performed at the mean. The rest of the sample populations were assigned IQs of about one standard deviation below the mean (100) on the basis of performance on a variety of mental tests that included the Stanford-Binet, Raven, and Catell-Culture Fair tests (Table 7-1). These results are summarized by Lynn (1978), who attempted to interpret ethnic group performance on the basis of race, the implication being that the differences were of genetic origin. He had trouble, however, explaining the high IQ of Italian subjects (mean = 100) while Spain, Greece, and Yugoslavia had the lowest for Europeans (mean = 87). The European IQ scores had a north–south gradient except for the Italian. He offered the explanation that the gradient was due to the racial composition of the population:

> If these results from Caucasoid, Iranian, and Indo-Dravidian nations are considered in the light of the racial composition of the populations, it is apparent that where the people are predominantly of northern European stock, as in Britain, northwestern Europe, the United States, Australia, and New Zealand, their mean IQs are approximately 100. (Lynn, 1978:278)

This should not be hard to explain considering that the tests were designed by and for northwestern Europeans. The differences all fall within the range reported for minorities in the United States and other countries, which is one standard deviation below the mean. Also, scores from different tests vary, as in the case of the two New Zealand Maori samples—a mean of 84 on the Otis and 94 on the Queensland tests. It should be noted in the table that Australian Aboriginal children varied in test performance depending on the closeness of their contact with European settlements. The children far removed and with little contact with Europeans scored the lowest.

What Influences IQ Test Performance?

How can this consistently lower performance of ethnic minorities around the world be explained? Some may explain away the differences in terms of genetic variation as outlined by Lynn. Many educators and psychologists, Jensen included, point out the strong role environment plays in academic achievement and IQ scores, however. Jensen (1969:60) noted that moving children from a deprived environment to an improved one can boost IQ 20

TABLE 7-1   Table of Comparisons of IQ in Several Populations

POPULATION	TEST	I.Q. SCORE
Northern Europe		
Scotland	Stanford-Binet and Terman-Merrill	100
Belgium	Cattell's Culture-Fair	104
France	Raven's Progressive Matrices	104
Southern Europe		
Italy	Raven's Progressive Matrices	100
Spain (army)	Raven's Progressive Matrices	87
Yugoslavia	Raven's Progressive Matrices	89
Greece	Wechsler Scale	89
Mid East		
Iraq	Goodenough DAM	80
Iran	Goodenough DAM	80
India		
Univ. of Calcutta	Stanford-Binet	95
Univ. of Calcutta (post-grad. students)	Raven's Progressive Matrices	75
Variety of Indian states	Raven's Progressive Matrices	81–94
Afro Americans	Shuey (81 different ones)	85
Africa		
Uganda	Raven's Progressive Matrices	88
Uganda	Terman Vocabulary and Kohs Blocks	80
Jamaica	British Intelligence	75
Jamaica	Terman Vocabulary and Kohs Blocks	low 80s
Tanzania	Raven's Progressive Matrices	88
Ghana, Jahoda	Raven's Progressive Matrices	75
South Africa	British National Foundation for Educations Research	87
South Africa—Zulu	Raven's Progressive Matrices	75
American Chinese	Stanford-Binet	97
Asians		
Japan	Wechsler Scale	106.6
Bandung, Java	Goodenough Draw-a-Man	96
Native Americans		
Eskimo	Raven's Progressive Matrices	70–80
Eskimo	Vernon—several	85
Amerinds (Canada)	Coleman—several	91–96
	Vernon—several	79

TABLE 7-1   Table of Comparisons of IQ in Several Populations (*Continued*)

POPULATION	TEST	I.Q. SCORE
Australia		
Europeans	American Otis	95
Aborigines (Victoria)	Peabody Picture Vocabulary and Illinois Psycholinguistic Ability	80
Aborigines (Queensland)	Queensland	78 in isolation 85 in close contact
Pacific		
Europeans (N. Zealand)	Otis	98.5
Maori (N. Zealand)	Otis	84
Maori (N. Zealand)	Queensland	94
Micronesia	Cattell's Culture-Fair	88
Polynesia	Pacific Infants Performance Scale	88
Southern Africa		
!Kung (Kalahari)	Maze	55

Source: Data selected and adapted from Lynn, 1978.

to 30 points. In addition, the socioeconomic status of the parents greatly affects the IQ performance of the children; also, there is a high correlation between performance and quality of education, as demonstrated by a comparison of the army Alpha tests with the state expenditure on elementary education. Adults who had resided as children in states with lower school expenditures scored lowest on the tests (Table 7-2).

Contrary to claims that compensatory education has failed to boost IQ, there are several studies that show the opposite. One of the most successful educational enrichment programs boosted IQs of a group of black preschoolers by 33 points. This project, carried out in Milwaukee by Rick Heber, an expert on mental retardation, provided a major enrichment in the lives of children born to black mothers living in the most impoverished area of the city. The program included extensive training of the mothers in simple skills and offered personal one-on-one teaching for the children from a few weeks old until six years of age. The results were astounding. This group, chosen at random from volunteers, achieved skills far beyond those achieved by the control group who were not given the special training (Loehlin et al., 1975:159–160). Likewise, another preschool enrichment program (the Abecedarian project) continued over fifteen years provided environmental stimulation for children who otherwise would have been deprived. These children gained as much as 20 IQ points over the control groups, and these gains were long-lasting, as shown by following the children through their school years (Ramey, MacPhee, and Yeates, 1982).

There have been many other demonstrations of the effects that environment has on test performance. The frequently cited Coleman report,

TABLE 7-2 Median and Mean Negro and White Army Alpha Intelligence-Test Scores and School Expenditures per Child Aged 5 to 18 Years by State

State (1)	WHITE			NEGRO			School expenditures (8)
	N (2)	Median (3)	Mean (4)	N (5)	Median (6)	Mean (7)	
Alabama	779	41.3	49.4	271	19.9	27.0	1.51
Arkansas	710	35.6	43.3	193	16.1	22.6	3.09
Florida	55	53.8	59.8	499	9.2	15.3	4.68
Georgia	762	39.3	48.3	416	10.0	17.2	2.68
Illinois	2,146	61.6	66.7	804	42.2	47.9	13.46
Indiana	1,171	56.0	62.2	269	41.5	47.6	11.75
Kansas	861	62.7	67.0	87	34.7	40.6	10.58
Kentucky	837	41.5	48.6	191	23.9	32.4	4.57
Louisiana	702	41.1	49.0	538	13.4	20.8	2.52
Maryland	616	55.3	60.2	148	22.7	30.7	8.44
Mississippi	759	37.6	43.7	773	10.2	16.8	2.63
Missouri	1,329	56.5	61.9	196	28.3	34.2	8.54
New Jersey	937	45.3	52.9	748	33.0	38.9	14.04
New York	3,300	58.4	63.7	1,188	38.6	45.3	19.22
North Carolina	702	38.2	45.9	211	16.3	22.1	1.51
Ohio	2,318	67.2	73.0	163	45.4	53.4	12.13
Oklahoma	865	43.0	50.6	98	31.4	35.9	5.50
Pennsylvania	3,280	62.0	67.1	790	34.8	40.5	12.85
South Carolina	581	45.1	51.1	334	14.2	19.2	1.93
Tennessee	710	44.0	52.0	504	29.7	35.9	2.71
Texas	1,426	43.5	50.2	854	12.2	18.2	4.38
Virginia	506	56.3	60.5	57	45.6	52.0	3.39
West Virginia	423	54.9	60.8	67	26.8	28.5	6.79
Subtotal (23 states)	25,774	49.53	56.00	9,399	26.09	32.30	6.91
District of Columbia	77	78.8	85.6	30	31.2	34.3	17.78
Total	25,851	50.75	57.23	9,429	26.43	32.39	7.36

Sources: From Spuhler and Lindzey, 1967 (copyright © 1967 by McGraw-Hill Book Co.; reprinted by permission of the publisher); data from Yerkes, 1921; and *Statistical Abstract of the United States*, 1902.

Equality of Educational Opportunity, described the results of an extensive study carried out on 650,000 schoolchildren in 4,000 public schools. The part of the report that has been frequently seized on as "proof" of racial inequality is the achievement test scores showing that "white" students scored significantly higher than "nonwhites." The application of these results as evidence to support a particular brand of racist dogma ignores the bulk of the report, which deals with the wide range of sociological factors related to the educational process and student performance. For example, the higher the socioeconomic level of the entire student body of a school, the higher the test scores of all ethnic groups (see Chase, 1977:498).

In the 1970s, a group of educational psychologists, headed by Mayeske, carefully reexamined the data published in the Coleman report. Their thorough analysis of each section isolated five significant sets of variables influencing test scores. Of these five, racial-group membership was the fourth lowest in its influence on test performance. When the scores are statistically weighted for socio-environmental differences, the average scores of the several ethnic groups show very little difference. Figure 7-2 plots the percentage of difference between these groups when each of the environmental factors is considered. When adjusted for social background the differences dropped to insignificant levels.

Health factors can also exert a major influence on test performance. Hearing defects in early childhood can lower IQ by 20 points. Premature and underweight babies have significantly lower scores at several developmental stages; at ages three to five years, for example, their IQ mean was 94.4. Multiple births are also a significant factor: Twins score 5 points lower on the average than single births, and triplets score 9 points lower (see Loehlin et al., 1975:196–229). Nutrition also affects test performance; in many studies increases of up to 10 points are reported for children placed on enriched diets provided through school lunch programs. Maternal health, as measured by prenatal nutrition, smoking, alcohol or drug abuse, and birth weights, also shows high correlations with infant and childhood development and with children's test scores during preschool and elementary school years.

What Do the Tests Measure?

Since the introduction of intelligence testing, modifications have been made to allow the testing of groups of diverse backgrounds, languages, and experiences. The search has been for a "culture-free" test—that is, a series of questions that will reveal natural ability uninfluenced by a person's past experiences. Dozen of tests have been designed since the early days of the Stanford-Binet, but to date, no culture-free test has been devised. This is not unexpected, because ability to distinguish between objects, identify words, and so forth at any age is determined by a complex of interactions between inherited qualities, development, and experiences. It should be obvious that children, regardless of their ethnic backgrounds, raised in isolated rural communities will have experiences distinct from middle-class suburban children. This was reflected by the lower scores of certain social groups tested in the 1900s. Children living today in a densely populated city ghetto have a vocabulary and language style unique to their experiences, in contrast to children raised in rural areas. Their sociocultural differences, some argue, affect IQ test performance just as in the case of the eastern European immigrants three generations ago.

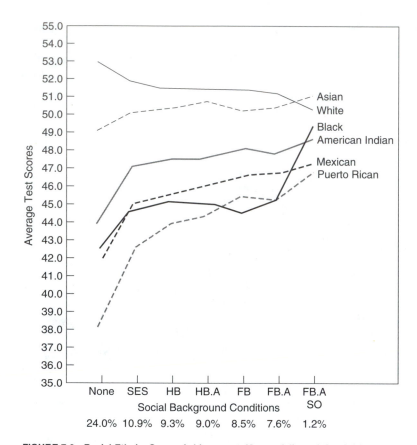

FIGURE 7-2 Racial-Ethnic Group Achievement Means Adjusted for Social Background Conditions. Percent of total difference among students in their achievement that is associated with their racial-ethnic group membership

SES = Socioeconomic status

HB = Home background; this set of variables includes both socioeconomic status and family structure

HB.A = Family attitudes about their ability to influence the course of their lives and the extent to which education benefits them

FB = Family background; educational, social, etc.

FB.A = Family background and area (of residence; regional; urban; rural; etc.)

FB.A
      = Quality and achievement-motivational mix of school attended
SO

". . . the differences among the various racial-ethnic groups in their achievement levels approach zero as more and more considerations related to differences in their respective social conditions are taken into account" (Mayeske, 1971, p. 112). (From Mayeske, 1971, U.S. Department of Health, Education and Welfare.)

Simply put, children from different social environments perform at different levels if given the same test. A case in point is the frequently used Stanford-Binet test, which was first standardized on a sampling of U.S. middle-class white children and adolescents in California. Hispanic, African-American, and Native American children performed below average on such a test. The test and its later revisions have been challenged on the basis that they are "culture bound" and handicap those of different socioeconomic backgrounds and also non-English speakers. Groups out of the "cultural mainstream" today score lower than the norm, just as eastern European immigrants did at the beginning of this century. When test content and new norms are established, scores rise accordingly, as did those of the immigrants, whose scores reflected their length of residency in the United States.

To overcome the difficulty imposed on African-American children by the Stanford-Binet, Williams, an African-American psychologist, designed the Black Intelligence Test of Cultural Homogeneity, the BITCH test (Loehlin et al., 1975:69). Questions were designed to reflect the environment and experiences of these children. The results were normed accordingly, and children who had been classed as low IQ fell well within the normal range of the BITCH test, reflecting the importance of cultural experience in measures of ability. The importance of a culturally relevant test is described from a personal perspective by Williams (1974), who related that his low scores influenced his high school counselor to discourage college and suggested that he consider a manual trade instead. Despite this discouragement he went on to earn a doctorate and achieve distinction in his profession.

Similar experiences can be cited for other minority children. In Riverside California, a sociologist was concerned with the possible mislabeling of intellectually competent people. She formed a research group and began an eight-year-long study of 644 persons selected from over 6,000 in a housing project. The results confirmed her fears of mislabeling: A majority of those adults who had been labeled "mentally retarded" because their scores had fallen below the 70-point cutoff were filling normal roles expected for their age and sex group. They were employed, raising families; over 80 percent had completed eight or more years of schooling, and 100 percent were able to care for themselves (Mercer, 1972). Given these results from such an intensive study, the fault of mislabeling probably lay with the test itself—the Wechsler Intelligence Scale for Children (WISC). On the theory that a language problem was the root cause, a Spanish-language version was used to retest children throughout California. Their median scores increased by 13 points and some of the children's scores increased by as much as 25. Wider testing across ethnic lines demonstrated that more than language was involved; over a quarter of the variances between Chicanos (Hispanics), Anglos (Euro-Americans), and Blacks (African Americans) were accounted for by sociocultural differences. It was no surprise that income, parental education, and household size headed the list of influences.

Considering these complexes of interacting factors that influence a child's variability in test performance, the tragedy is that test results are too often accepted as a measure of innate potential. The similarity between the lower scores of the immigrants fifty to eighty years ago and the lower scores of

Hispanics and African Americans today should have warned against such an acceptance. The pattern that was followed by the eastern European immigrants has shown that they and their offspring increased their IQ with residence in the United States and acculturation into American society. There is every expectation that, as more opportunities become available to ethnic minorities and there is a decrease in sociocultural differences, IQ averages will increase among these groups as it has in the past. This has already happened for many, as shown by Flynn (1984). Children in the 1970s scored an average 15 points higher than did their parents and grandparents in the 1930s. The reasons for this rise in IQ level (the Flynn Effect) have not been well established yet but they are likely to involve differences in test norms, sophistication in test taking, and a general increase in communications technology. I will leave it to the psychologists to explain why, in only two generations, there is so much gain in a score that is allegedly a measure of an innate ability. Whatever the answer turns out to be, it certainly cannot be due to genetic change.

Any genetic explanation is even more difficult when applied to ethnic minorities, who around the world score below the norm—by the magical one standard deviation. The many ethnic groups are not, as some writers continue to imply or even assert, handicapped by their genes. Such an argument rests on three faulty assumptions: first, that group classification is equivalent, or nearly so, to breeding population; second, that measurement, however made, determines some innate quality of the individual—i.e., that it is equivalent to a phenotype; third, that mental ability phenotype is largely hereditary. Of these three assumptions, the most problematic is the degree to which heredity influences intelligence, however measured.

INHERITANCE OF MENTAL ABILITY (IQ)

> While it certainly is true that I started out to study the genetics of a behavior, in the course of much thinking and experimenting over more than a decade I have come to realize that it is impossible to study the genetics of a behavior. We can study the behavior of an organism, the genetics of a population, and individual differences in the expression of some behavior by members of that population. (Hirsch, 1969:43)

Among the many polygenic traits of our species, behavioral responses or intellectual capacity are the most difficult with which to deal. Not only is little known about the genes influencing behavior, but extreme difficulty is encountered when attempts are made to identify or label the several behavioral phenotypes. The list might include pathological behaviors like alcoholism, schizophrenia, manic depression, drug addiction, and so on—diagnostic labels that are broad and vary over time and from society to society.

Witness the disagreement concerning what IQ is and the wide variation in diagnosis of mental illness or behavioral pathologies in our society. Given these factors, it is much more difficult to establish genetic relationships for behavior than for polygenic phenotypes such as skin color, face form, or stature. Because we are not concerned here with phenotypic labeling of "types" of behavior, we look only at those methods frequently employed to estimate the degree of genetic influence on the performance of standard mental tests.

Heritability of IQ

Many of the assumptions of inherited inequality, as measured by intelligence tests, are based on studies of close relatives and monozygotic (MZ) twins. The correlations of test scores of these relatives and especially of twins raised together and apart range from less than 0.2 to a high of 0.87 for MZ twins. The correlation coefficient of 0.8 has been derived from these studies and has found a prominent place in the literature discussing inherited inequality. This high correlation is interpreted as "evidence" that the genetic component influences intelligence more than environment (80 percent versus 20 percent) because correlation between subject groups is considered equivalent to heritability. The reliability of this evidence is questionable from many perspectives, but it is weak evidence of genetic influence mainly because the concept of heritability is often misunderstood and misused. The measure of the genetic component of a trait is not given by the heritability quotient, though many authors still continue to use it to support their arguments over genetic determination of behavior.

Heritability, in the broadest sense, is that proportion of variation of a trait in a population that is due to a variation of genotypes. Earlier, in Chapter 3, I described phenotype as the result of the interaction between genotype and environment, and it is useful to point out again that genes only determine a potential for response to environments. They code for proteins or regulate rates of synthesis, and the proteins, in turn, fulfill various functions that lead to some measurable trait or traits. Genes, with the special exceptions of certain pathological conditions, do not determine a phenotype directly. This results, especially in multifactorial traits, in a wide range of individual variation.

When a polygenic trait such as stature, for example, is measured in a population, there will be a mean and a range of sizes, tall and short people above or below the average. The total variation, or variance, about the mean is due to the variance in genotypes among the individuals of the population plus the variance of environments they encounter during their growth and development. In other words, the total population variation is due to both variation of genotypes and environment. This relationship can be expressed mathematically: variance in phenotype (V_p) = variance in genotypes (V_g) +

variance in environment (V_e). Heritability (H^2), then, is that proportion of variance owing to genotypic variance and can be written as follows:

$$H^2 = \frac{V_g}{V_g + V_e}$$

Phenotypes measured within a population may have a high degree of variance owing to high genetic variance; it will therefore have a high H^2. Likewise, phenotypes with low genotype variance will have low heritability. Those populations with less genotypic difference between the individuals will, thus, have a lower heritability. If the hypothetical case was considered in which all individuals were the offspring of a single fertilized egg, their genotypes would be identical copies of the original. Because there would be no genetic variance in our hypothetical population, the V_g would be zero and H^2 would then be zero. Such offspring could still have a high phenotypic variation if environmental variance was high.

Heritability then is not a measure of genetic influence on a phenotype; it is merely a measure of the total effect of the genotype variance on phenotypic variability. As described by Gregg and Sanday (1971:59): "Heritability only tells what proportion of the variance is due to genetic differences, not the extent to which a trait is determined by genetic factors." Additionally, heritability is not a constant value that tells us the degree of genetic influence on the phenotype of any single individual. As stated by Jensen (1971:13–14):

> There is no single true value of the heritability of a trait. Heritability is not a constant, but a population statistic, and it can vary according to the test used and the particular population tested.

If the example is used of a group of individuals placed on a diet that contains a carefully controlled constant amount of the amino acid phenylalanine (the $V_e = 0$), then any variance of phenylalanine blood levels (the V_p in the population) will be due to V_g or a variance in the genetic system. If later the diet is varied between members of the same group, then phenotypic variance will increase. This does not mean that the genetic contribution or the effect of the genes is any less, merely that the relative contributions of V_g and V_e will change. In neither case is the degree of genetic contribution or gene effect known. Recall the discussion or biochemical pathways in Chapter 3.

H^2 of a phenotypic variance within a population tells us nothing about the genetic component in the individual; what it does describe is the degree of variance in a population that is due to the genes under a certain set of environmental circumstances. This simple formula actually describes a method employed by animal and plant breeders long before genetic inheritance was known or understood. Farmers could selectively breed their stock by the simple logic that any variation in animals living under a stable environment (the same food, pasturage, and so on) was due to some factors of inheritance ("bloodlines") that could be passed on to the next generation. In this way, undesirable traits could be selected out and useful traits bred for. The egg producers in a flock of chickens, cows who produced the most milk, or cattle that showed the greatest weight gain could be used as breeders. The genetics were not known (and in many cases still are a mystery), but desirable effects of selective breeding could easily be seen, evaluated, and used to advantage.

Finally, heritability describes a property of populations, not of individuals, and does not distinguish the traits that they possess. H^2 is a limited piece of information that measures the degree owed to genetic variance within a given population at a particular time under specific environmental conditions. Should there be an increase in environmental variance then the heritability quotient will change. It is a population statistic just as are mortality or fertility rates, and heritability estimates derived from the variance of one population cannot be applied to another. Given the difficulty in studying the genetics of human populations, however, how is the heritability quotient derived?

Twin Studies

Hundreds of studies of monozygous or identical twins offer a source of data for estimates of heritability. The importance of these studies cannot be overstated. These individuals, conceived from a single fertilized ovum, have identical genomes. It follows, then, that any phenotypic differences are the result of environmental influences. Measurements of traits in large samples of both monozygotic (MZ) and dizygotic (DZ) twins have been made, and comparisons of the correlations have given considerable information about heritability. The data most revealing of the genetic effects comes from studies of MZ twins reared in separate households that are, presumably, different environments. Unfortunately, not many such subjects have been located and carefully studied; there have been only four such studies to date with the recent addition of the Minnesota Twin Project (Bouchard et al., 1986). Before 1974 there was another, and by far the largest study, with fifty-three twin pairs described by an English psychologist, Cyril Burt. The results of a battery of mental and achievement tests in this investigation set the standard for twin studies and provided the basis for a correlation of IQ of twin pairs of 0.771, which was cited in many papers and texts that discussed inheritance of mental ability.

Questions about Burt's results began to be raised in the early 1970s. His results were just too consistent from the data described in one study to the next as additional separated twins were identified and enrolled in the project. As the number of twin pairs increased, the correlation coefficient remained the same to the third decimal place. The possibility of data manipulation and even scientific fraud, by the outright invention of subjects, was raised. Kamin went through the laborious work of checking the data step by step and noted the statistical impossibility of the correlations remaining the same from 1951, when twenty-one pairs were described, and 1958, when the number was increased to thirty and finally to fifty-three pairs in 1964 (Kamin, 1974). Following Kamin's work, others began to examine Burt's many publications and uncovered numerous flaws, fictitious coauthors, nonexistent master's theses, and manufactured data. At that point the conclusion was inescapable: For several decades, a major fraud had been perpetrated on the scientific community (Hawkes, 1979; Hearnshaw, 1979).

The effect on educational psychology in general and on twin studies in particular would have been minimal if it had not been for the status of Burt among educational psychologists. His conclusions were quoted in many standard texts and even used as a guide to educational policies implicitly influencing the treatment of minority students, especially in their placement in academic "tracks." The exposure of the fraudulent data was a major blow to many who maintained that IQ had a high heritability and hence was largely influenced by genetics. This group soon recovered, and argued that the other twin studies supported their position that environment only minimally affected mental ability as measured by IQ tests. These arguments, however, neglected the lack of control for similarities or differences in the environments of twins raised apart. Though the Minnesota study has helped bolster a hereditarian position, the range of heritability quotients for traits other than IQ has been ignored (Table 7-3).

Despite the difficulties and doubts encountered in the separated-twin studies, correlations or similarities of phenotypes of twins offer a means of estimating heritability. Figure 7-3 shows that MZ twins raised together are most similar (correlation of 0.73 to 0.95), which compares with correlations of siblings of around 0.42. Presumably, the similarities are due to genotypes shared by related individuals. In the case of the 0.20 to 0.30 correlation between foster parent and child, similarities of IQ are due to a sharing of the home environment.

The higher correlations between the identical-twin groups are reflections of their genetic likeness and are used to establish degrees of genetic influence. Hence, a correlation of 0.95 between identical twins raised apart is taken as evidence that genes influence the trait by that much. The balance of the difference is assumed to be due to environmental variables because of their genetic identity. Therefore, the proportion of gene influence on the phenotypes is equal to the correlations between twins, or $H^2 = r_{obs}$ derived from the following formula:

$$r \text{ observed} = r \text{ genetic} \times \frac{V_g}{V_g + V_e}$$

since r genetic = 1 (there is a perfect correlation between MZ twins)

TABLE 7-3   Correlations of Identical Twins Reared Together and Apart

	MINNESOTA MZA		MZT	
	R	*PAIRS (NO.)*	*R*	*PAIRS (NO.)*
Anthropometric variables				
Fingerprint ridge count	0.97	54	0.96	274
Height	0.86	56	0.93	274
Weight	0.73	56	0.83	274
Mental ability—general factor				
WAIS IQ—full scale	0.69	48	0.88	40
WAIS IQ—verbal	0.64	48	0.88	40
WAIS IQ—performance	0.71	48	0.79	40
Raven, Mill-Hill composite	0.78	42	0.76	37
First principal component of special mental abilities	0.78	43	NA	NA
Personality variables				
Mean of 11 Multidimensional Personality Questionnaire scales	0.50	44	0.49	217
Mean of 18 California Psychological Inventory scales	0.48	38	0.49	99

MZA = monozygotic twins raised apart; MZT = monozygotic twins raised together.
Source: Data selected from Bouchard, T. J., Jr., 1990.

FIGURE 7-3   Correlation Coefficients for Intelligence Test Scores from Fifty-Two Studies. (From Erlenmeyer-Kimling, L., and L. F. Jarvik, 1963. "Genetics and Intelligence: A Review," *Science* 142:1478. Copyright © 1963 by American Association for the Advancement of Science. Reprinted by permission of the publisher.)

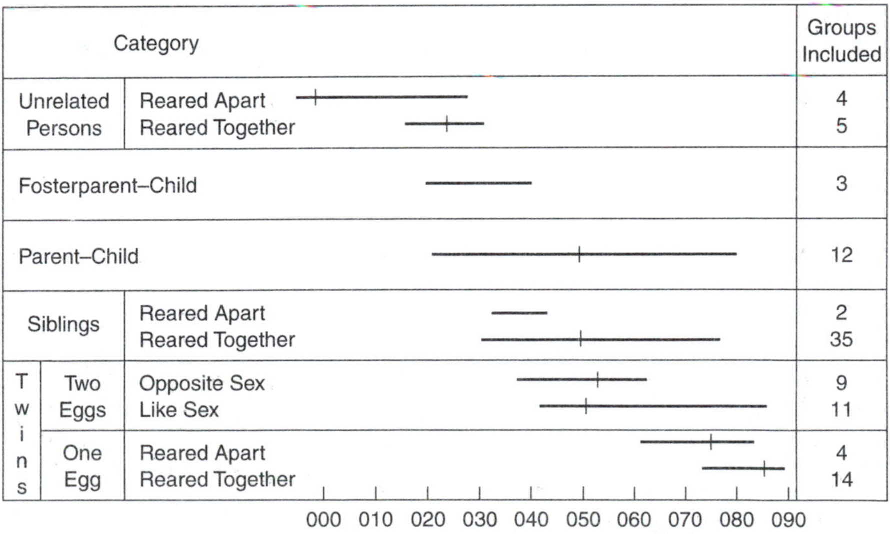

$$\text{then, } r \text{ observed} = \frac{V_g}{V_g + V_e} = H^2$$

Again, the reader is reminded that this refers to a variance observed in a "population" of twin pairs (the number of twin pairs tested) and does not express degree of genetic influence in one individual. In other words, individuals may, and often do, perform quite differently from their twin, while others earn scores close to their twins (Table 7-4). The twins raised apart are treated as separate populations, with mean and variance; the two groups are then compared for covariance (correlation).

The H^2 covers a considerable range, and this single measure depends a great deal on the selection of twins and their environments, both for MZ twins raised apart and for those raised together. The correlations that are used are based on a number of twin studies during the last fifty years, and each study has several inherent problems. First, in the case of twins reared apart (MZA), the age at time of separation varies over a wide range, from a

TABLE 7-4   Heritability Estimates in Twins Reared Apart and Together

REFERENCE	PSYCHOLOGICAL TEST VARIABLE (P)	NO. OF PAIRS (n)	INTRAPAIR CORRELA- TION (r_p)	ESTIMATES H^2
Husén (1959) year groups 1949–1952	IQ by I test	MZT 215	0.894	—
		DZT 416	0.703	—
Newman, Freeman, and Holzinger (1937)	Binet	MZS 19	0.637	0.637
	Mental Age	MZT 50	0.922	±0.136
		DZT 50	0.831	
	Binet IQ	MZS 19	0.670	0.670
		MZT 50	0.910	±0.126
		DZT 50	0.640	
	Otis score	MZT 50	0.947	—
		DZT 50	0.800	—
	Otis IQ	MZS 19	0.727	0.727
		MZT 50	0.922	±0.108
		DZT 50	0.621	
	Stanford	MZS 19	0.502	0.502
	Educat. Age	MZT 50	0.955	±0.172
		DZT 50	0.883	
Shields (1962)	Dominoes	MZS 37	0.758	0.758
	Intell. Test	MZT 34	0.735	±0.070
	Mill Hill Vocabul.	MZS 38	0.741	0.741
	scale	MZT 36	0.742	±0.073

MZS = monozygotic twins separated; MZT = monozygotic twins (brought up together); and DZT = dizygotic twins (brought up together).

Source: Adapted from Vogel and Motulsky, 1986.

few days to six years, which causes a wide variety of environmental influences on the development of the twins and in turn influences the correlations. Second, many of these studies encompass a time span of a half-century, dating back to a time when techniques and methods differed considerably from those of today. Also, the twin studies were not standardized for sex and age, both of which are influential on IQ, and improper correction for these factors will produce higher correlation values. The effects of environmental differences are indicated in Table 7-4, which also shows the relative degree of genetic influences. There are numerous other problems encountered when twin studies are attempted; even those MZ twins reared in separate households are often reared by relatives, uncles, aunts, and so forth. There are also recorded cases in which twins had maintained close contact during various stages of their childhood, even attending the same schools, which raises the probability of many shared childhood experiences before they were ever tested as participants in a twin study program (Lewontin et al., 1984).

Many of the differences or variations are even more interesting than the similarities. Twins raised apart have up to 20 points of difference, which again shows the effect of environment. In the case of adopted children there is an average gain of some 20 points over their biological mothers, and the correlation between parents and children is approximately 0.5, but bright parents usually have children with lower IQs, which is described as "regression towards the mean." These comparisons were taken a significant step further by studies of transracially adopted children (Scarr and Weinberg, 1983). The study tested parents in 101 adoptive families that had 176 adoptive children (130 were "socially" classified as black), and the families also included 143 biological children of the parents. Most adoptees (111) were younger than one year old when adopted, and 65 were adopted after their twelfth month. The homes were economically well off, and the parents scored in the bright-average range. Tests of all children were recorded; the black adopted children averaged 110 points IQ or 20 points above comparable children in the black community. The adopted black child averaged 6 points lower than the biological children in the families. Scarr and Weinberg (1983:261) interpreted these high IQ scores as an indication that genetic differences do not account for a major portion of the IQ differences between racial groups. Also, they concluded that black and interracial children reared in the "culture" of the tests perform as well as other adopted children in similar families. If all of these factors are considered, there is a basic error in the argument that lower IQs among certain ethnic or racial groups are due to "inferior" genes.

In an earlier study of genetic and environmental influences, Scarr (1971) described the results of 992 pairs of MZ twins in Philadelphia. First, and perhaps most important, was that 75 percent of the total variance on test scores of whites was due to genetic variance, whereas the proportion of genetic variance in disadvantaged black populations was less. This provided evidence for the correctness of the statement that studies of twins as a method of obtaining H^2 are not fully dependable for the general population, because twins are not a representative group.

Scarr-Salapatek (1971:1286) also tested the hypothesis that "Social class differences in phenotypic IQ are assumed to reflect primarily the mean differences in genotype distribution by social class; that is, environmental differences between social classes (and races) are seen as insignificant in determining total phenotypic variance in IQ." Scarr and Weinberg (1983) found, through extensive black and white twin comparisons, that the hypothesis was false; the environment played a more significant role in population variance. These results, together with those obtained from later studies of transracial adoptions, provide a solid base from which to reexamine the degree of genetic influence on behavior. The conclusions they reached are clear: The class, or rather the cultural environment, is of equal or greater importance to a child's development than is the genetic component.

> The implications of the differences between race and social class for intellectual achievement is that there are more likely to be genetic differences in IQ scores between social class than racial groups. (Scarr, 1981:79)

It is of interest that these two researchers reach a point where social class is given such emphasis, especially since our "racial" and ethnic labels have become more of a class designation and less of a biological one.

Class and Caste

An interesting book that deals thoroughly with the question of the effects of class and caste on IQ differences describes the relative environmental influences within and between populations; environmental influences are greater between populations than within a population (Ogbu, 1978). This is due to the fact that the two levels of comparison are not the same. Within a population, the individual differences are comparisons of biological organisms, whereas the intergroup comparisons are treating groups (castes) sociologically defined. Even the perceived differences between black and white Americans are less biological than sociological, as noted above in the discussion of transracial adoptee studies. There are, to be sure, genetic differences, but the degree covers an enormous range because of more than 300 years of interbreeding and, as shown by Scarr and Weinberg (1978), bears no relationship to the individual's test performance.

Ogbu considers the social classification of African Americans as a caste-like status and suggests that their minority position and achievements are comparable with those of other minorities—Native Americans, Mexican Americans, and Puerto Ricans. Society's expectations, the limited educational opportunities, and lower expectations of economic rewards, together with social barriers, have caused responses of "mental withdrawal," leading to a failure in educational achievement. Whether or not the reader accepts this observation, and, to be sure, the situation has changed somewhat in the last decade, the evidence of lower achievement of these minority groups is there to see. Each of these minorities scores lower on the standard tests by, interestingly enough, 15 points or one standard deviation. They also have the highest school dropout rate, the highest unemployment, the lowest income, and so on. The introduction of caste boundaries and expectations points up a further weakness of the inherited inequality arguments so often used as a simplistic explanation of group differences. It is interesting to compare again the IQ scores of several ethnic groups as listed in Table 7-1. Northwestern Europeans are at the top with the standardized score of 100, whereas all others have lower scores—many about fifteen points lower. This says more about social boundaries limiting learning experiences than about innate mental ability.

Every nation has its minorities, relegated to some caste that is, by definition, biologically inferior, and socially undesirable as well. India is famous for its elaborate caste system once codified by law and sanctioned by religious beliefs. Still maintained by custom, the castes are arranged in social stratification from Brahmin at the top, with the greatest social prestige, wealth, and political status, to a middle-group "nonpolluting caste" that performs services for the Brahmins, to the lowest-level untouchable castes that carry out the least desirable occupations of scavengers, sweepers, washermen, and other laborers. Other nations also have established social castes, perhaps not as rigid in boundaries but still an identification of a minority group, be it the "guest worker"—usually from North Africa, southern Europe, or Turkey, in France or Germany—or the historically famous gypsies, especially in central and eastern Europe. In the United States, of course, African Americans, Hispanics, and Native Americans have occupied these caste positions.

Most Asian minorities in the United States have, by and large, fared better, but in their homelands there are numerous and complex caste structures. Even in Japan, there are castelike minorities—the following statement by Nakasone, the former Japanese prime minister, notwithstanding. Nakasone, in a public speech, explained Japan's achievements by referring to the high levels of intelligence of its citizens. "Our average score is much higher than the United States. There are many Blacks, Puerto Ricans, and Mexicans in America. In consequence the average score over there is exceedingly low." Forced later to apologize for what was perceived as a racial slur, Nakasone tried to explain with the observation that Japan was a monoracial society. He added that "there are things that the Americans cannot do because of multiracial nationalities there," a statement that made matters worse.[1] On the con-

---

[1]Though these remarks by the then prime minister of Japan were later qualified and a sort of apology was published, the initial comment stated his firmly held belief in the inequality of ethnic groups (*New York Times*, 3 January 1986). Several newsmagazines published essays discussing the issues raised and were severely critical of Nakasone (*Time*, 6 October 1986; *Newsweek*, 6 October 1986).

trary, Japan does have minorities. The best recognized are the Koreans, small in number to be sure (only about 700,000) but forced by discrimination to remain on the fringes of Japanese society. A still smaller ethnic group, the Ainu descendants of the original inhabitants, have suffered considerable economic and social deprivation during the centuries. Though numbering only about 24,000 today, they too took offense at Nakasone's remarks. Another group that definitely disturbs the notion of a homogeneous society is the Burakumin, a social minority caste that has been limited, by centuries-old tradition, to undesirable occupations (sweepers, slaughterhouse workers, and so on). This social caste occupies a position in Japanese society nearly comparable with that of the untouchables of India. Though there has been intermarriage with Koreans during past generations, there has been little with the Burakumin, who rank lowest on the social scales of Japanese society; in fact, during the prewar era intermarriage was forbidden by law. The purpose of pointing out the existence of this low caste is to note that the school performance of the Burakumin children is well below the national norm; they score, on average, 15 points (one standard deviation) below the Japanese average.

Ogbu suggests that this is evidence of children's reaction to society's expectations and to a teacher's attitude toward low-caste children. He emphasized that when persons of this caste had migrated to Hawaii or the American West Coast their school performance was equal to that of the other Japanese children, since the American schoolteachers were not aware of the caste differences. The teachers simply dealt with all children of Japanese ancestry, or, for that matter, all Asians in the same way—they had high expectations of school performance. The story could be continued by relating the experiences of minority Jewish groups (Orientals, Yemenites, Ethiopians) in contact with the dominant group, the Ashkenazim, in Israel, but the contrasts are the same as related earlier. The same expectations, stereotypes, and treatment are found in Israeli society (Schiff and Lewontin, 1986).

Castes and Class: A Return to a Nineteenth-Century Perspective

While Ogbu views class and caste status as the major factors determing several measures of behavior and socioeconomic status in complex societies, several recent writers consider the opposite to be true: Groups of people become more and more assorted into classes because of inherited ability. Accordingly, in this view, a "cognitive elite" is emerging as people rise to the top in our equalitarian society because of their inherited ability, leaving behind those genetically less well endowed (Herrnstein and Murray, 1994). They see a nation (the United States) increasingly divided along lines of genetically brighter and duller people. Correlations are then made between these groups and a series of socioeconomic markers: income, education, crime rates, illegitimate births, poor parenting skills, and so on. The correlations with class are then related to average IQs and the conclusion is drawn that most of the nation's social ills emanate from the lowest of the cognitive classes. The reader should recall that there were similar discussions of class, innate ability, and societal problems 100 years ago: One's rise to the top of the social order was due to one's family lineage. Also, consider that correlations between two variables do not prove causation, especially when comparing polygenic traits developing within a complex of environmental stimuli. This caution is especially important since Herrnstein and Murray accept numerous statistically weak correlations (in the range of 0.2 to 0.4, a perfect correlation being 1.0) as indicative of cause; i.e., intelligence as the primary determiner of several social factors.[2]

These cognitive classes, so confidently derived on the basis of performance on mental tests, assumed that the tests measure a general factor or "g", a concept of mental ability defined by Spearman in 1904. Simply, there is a positive correlation of a person's performance on various mental tests. This correlation reveals a "g" factor that is presumed to be a general innate property of the human brain upon which environmental stimuli would act. Though it has enjoyed a wide popularity, the existence of "g" has not been proven and it has been roundly criticized as perhaps only a statistical artifact, or a reflection of the way multivariant data is manipulated.[3] Some psychologists accept and some reject the general intelligence concept. Given these disputes over intelligence, plus the criticisms of the tests themselves, basing a broad conclusion about innate ability on a single score for the purpose of explaining social status and behavior is questionable, to say the least. Nevertheless, IQ is offered as predictor of a range of behaviors, as in such statements as "At the lower educational levels a woman's intelligence best predicts whether she will bear an illegitimate child" (Herrnstein and Murray, 1994:167); further on the authors state that degrees of civility are correlated with IQ and that 8 points below normal is significant.

What is even more questionable is the reliance on heritability; the "proof" of genetic influence was taken by the authors from a misinterpretation of the heritability quotient. They note that various studies report H^2 ranges from 0.4 to 0.8 so they take a middle range of 0.6 as what they consider to be the degree of genetic influence on cognitive ability. This reliance on a genetic explanation ignores all of the cautions from behavioral geneticists. Genetic causes of a variety of behaviors have been sought for a long time and some successes have been recorded, but caution still remains the watchword. A behavioral geneticist, Robert Plomin, noted: "The wave of acceptance of

---

[2]Gould discusses the weak correlations as well as the misuse of statistical methods by Herrnstein and Murray. The assumptions about the meaning of multiple correlations and goodness of fit are examined (Gould, 1994).

[3]Thurstone in discussing factor analysis described the ways in which correlation results could be made to vary by rotation of the different dimensions (1940).

genetic influence on behavior is growing into a tidal wave that threatens to engulf the second message of this research: the same data provide the best evidence for the importance of environmental influence" (1989:105). This is a warning that should be heeded given the mountain of new data pouring forth from the genetic marker studies.

A complete summary and criticism of the long thesis of Herrnstein and Murray that class divisions equate to intelligence that in turn relates to behavior cannot be given here. Several books and essays have been written addressing this thesis and the various issues that arise (for example, see Jacoby and Glauberman, 1995; Fraser, 1995; and Molnar, 1996). I can, however, note some conclusions drawn by Herrnstein and Murray that are a continuum of the nineteenth-century dogma.

First, that the "wrong people" are having the most babies is implied by statements about "demographic headwinds." The authors stress that modernization has brought falling birthrates, with birthrates dropping faster for educated women. This introduces a dysgenic effect (a downward shift in ability) and affects the cognitive capital of the country. "What ever good things we can accomplish with changes in the environment would be that much more effective if they did not have to fight a demographic head wind" (Herrnstein and Murray, 1994:342). Expressing such concerns is reminiscent of Pearson's warning nearly a century ago: "England was breeding less intelligence than she had done fifty or a hundred years ago. Given the scientific fact that intelligence was inherited, the only remedy was to alter the relative fertility of the good and bad stocks in the community" (Huxley Lecture, 1903).

Second, the implication that the wrong types of immigrants are arriving on our shores is another echo of an earlier era. According to Herrnstein and Murray's interpretation, a majority of legal and illegal immigrants come from ethnic groups that score well below the "white" average (see Murray and Herrnstein, 1994:358). This comment sounds very much like some made during the battle in favor of tighter immigration restrictions in the 1900s. Discussion of the demography of intelligence goes further than repeating earlier warnings; it updates and modernizes them: The percentages of legal immigrants are broken down by ethnic group, the IQs are estimated for each group, and then these are added and an average IQ of 95 is given.

These conclusions about innate cognitive ability and group behavior are surprising, since the authors note that predictions of individual behavior cannot be made from an IQ score. They state that "Cognitive ability accounts for only a small to middling proportion of the variation among people" (Herrnstein and Murray, 1994:117). But, unfortunately, the balance of their long book is about correlations of group behavior and intelligence, and they pay little attention to the overwhelming evidence of environmental factors. Mackintosh (1986), a British psychologist, observed that IQ may have a significant heritable component, but there is little evidence that average differences between ethnic groups are genetic. He emphasized that differences in IQ between white, West Indian, Indian, and Pakistani children in Great Britain are closely correlated with their social circumstances.

Finally, the point emphasized by so many writers since IQ tests were introduced is that no one single measure can represent innate ability, and that the norms are standardized by tests administered to the majority groups and used as a standard against which all others are compared. We are dealing with a complex combination of genes when we consider mental ability, and the polygenic nature of this phenotype means that a considerable number of interactions occur between genes, gene products, and environmental stimuli. We know the location and action of the genes that enable us to distinguish or prevent us from distinguishing color, but we do not know what genes are involved in spatial orientation, reading, or math skills. It is misleading to attempt to partition the relative influence of environment and genetics in such a complex organism as *Homo sapiens*. The nature of much of our genetic system is its potential to interact with environmental stimuli. One's society provides the context and content of this stimuli. The cultural environment, the genes, and stored experience all provide a mental template that will vary from population to population and from generation to generation. It is the environment that determines whether a full range of abilities is expressed.

> It is a truism that behavior cannot be biologically inherited but must be developed and elicited under the combined influence of genetic and environmental factors. The effects of genes must be expressed through physiological action, and it has long been known that genes modify each other's effects so that only when a gene has a major and usually disruptive effect is there a one-to-one relationship between gene and character. (Scott, 1969:64)

GENETICS, INTELLIGENCE, AND THE FUTURE

Despite warnings that we face a decline in average intelligence, the opposite has occurred. Longitudinal data have shown that there has been no decline in intelligence. In fact, our generation scores higher than previous ones, and this includes minorities as well, though they still place one standard deviation below the mean. The arguments over the reasons for this gap rage on as they have throughout this century. But note that the gap is found in minorities wherever the tests have been applied; it is hard to defend the differences between a Maori minority and the New Zealand national norm on the basis of the same genetic argument made for differences recorded in the United States or among minorities in Great Britain.

The differences in measured mental ability or IQ between social groups (or racial groups) have been questioned many times and are often attributed to overall differences involving survival and lifestyles in complex industrial societies. The basis for variance in IQ may lie in discriminatory practices, economics, and language. Groups consistently scoring lower on standardized tests do not necessarily come from an "inferior" environment but from one that is distinct from the environment of the group on which the test was originally standardized. The various tests were designed as predictive devices, and as such they work very well to a limited extent in that they are predictive of academic success—but, unfortunately, people have tried to use them for other purposes. Lewontin and many others have raised the question of what these tests actually measure and—what is more important—how the results are applied (Lewontin et al., 1984). In addition, IQ tests as predictors of competence or success in a vocation after formal training have been seriously challenged (Fallows, 1989). Fallows argues that though the test scores are good predictors of academic achievement, they are poor or useless as an indication of career success. He suggests that opportunity and motivation to achieve are more important. As examples, he lists a variety of occupations and professions where the person's class standing or grades in college or training programs had little bearing on professional competence. He cites, among other examples, the success of the G.I. Bill, which supported millions of veterans in college—people who otherwise would not have had the opportunity to gain an advanced education.

Careful use of biological or social definitions of race and controlled or modified tests matter little if we simplistically assume that humans are "color coded." It is dangerous and inaccurate to assume that, if the variation of trait X in one population differs from the variation of that trait in another population, then all inherited traits differ at the same rate between the two groups. "Races" are not inferior or superior; there is no "gene for slow learning," and the genetics of whatever it is that IQ measures have yet to be determined; if it ever will be possible is another matter. The future may look bleak to some who claim a decline in IQ, but there are no data to demonstrate such a decline. On the contrary, there is every indication that environmental improvement will increase, with an expansion of the opportunities for people to realize their full potential. As Dobzhansky states:

> Correctly understood, heredity is not the "dice of destiny." It is rather a bundle of potentialities. Which part of the multitude of potentialities will be realized is for the environments, for the biography of the person, to decide. Only fanatic believers in the myth of genetic predestination can doubt that the life of every person offers numerous options, of which only a part, probably a minuscule part, is realized. (1976:160)

A personal observation as a conclusion for this chapter is in order: I would like to warn any reader to approach studies of genetics and behavior or behavioral genetics with great caution. Often, and I fear more frequently than not, the authors who describe the relationship of genetics to behavior approach the task with some bias. It is to be expected. We are, after all, the product of our experiences and training within a society and, however much we try to be objective, our conclusions are biased to some degree. The revival of the nature–nurture controversy and the development of behavioral genetics in the last decade are good examples. Too frequently, authors will accuse one another of covert or even overt racism or will refer to a political bias (for example, Marxism) and then discount the data reported or the criticisms made because of these alleged biases. Without citing specific works beyond those mentioned earlier, I would argue that we are all guilty to some degree. The major sin of writers on all sides of the question is clear but generally ignored—that is, the sin of omission. Those who write about human variability, as a group, avoid a close examination of the concept of race and its validity for the study of human variability. Nowhere are personal biases more apparent than in the taxonomy of our species. The use of racial stock, race, hybrid, or ethnic group is too frequently mixed with sociological classification, a classification based on a group's self-identification or on the labels imposed by the majority population. This casual use of stereotyping in the name of classification must stop if objectivity is to be introduced to the study of human diversity at any level, but especially in the investigation of behavioral differences and measured abilities.

8

Changing Dimensions of the Human Species

Viewed from an evolutionary perspective, our species has been extraordinarily successful in adapting and increasing its numbers. If natural selection is for reproductive success of a species, we rank among the more successful. Not only have we increased and improved our adaptation, but we have gained in the ability to alter environments to suit our needs. These environmental alterations and population increases have created a feedback system that has a profound influence on biological variability and, in turn, places limits on our adaptive responses. Human population growth, however, is determined primarily by the social system and depends on effective behavior within an environmental context (Washburn, 1964). The effectiveness of our behavior has contributed to an expansion and dispersal of *Homo sapiens* around the globe, overcoming natural obstacles, breaking down older population boundaries, and establishing new ones while, at the same time, creating new dimensions of biological diversity.

Throughout the preceding chapters I have described ways in which *Homo sapiens* varies and have considered the probable causes. Among these many causes relating to diversity is the increase in the variety of ways our species exploits natural resources. Development of technology and improved organization, for example, have aided human response to the forces of natural selection. The results have been dramatic during the past 10,000 years, the last 300 years in particular. Environments have been changed to fit human needs, but there are still many problems confronting us today. Natural selection is still operating, though, but in different forms, and it is continuing to shape the composition and diversity of human populations. The dimensions and scope of these ongoing processes require careful consideration, especially the increase in numbers of people and the burden these expanded populations place on the environment. Demographic factors of this expansion exert a major influence on worldwide distribution of gene frequencies. Epidemiology—determination and distributions of disease—is also altered in each generation as new diseases gain in population influence while older ones decline as threats to human health.

POPULATION GROWTH RATES

Two million years ago our ancestors numbered only a few hundred thousand, and from this small number our species evolved and increased until, by the time of the Neolithic (the invention of agriculture), we had reached a total of five million. This growth had been painfully slow during hundreds of thousands of years and, throughout this period, we could not be judged to have been a very successful species; in fact, many other primates far outnumbered us during these times. With the development of agriculture, however, *Homo sapiens* began to increase more rapidly. Even with this increased rate of population growth, it still took an average of 1,500 years for our species to double in number; but from A.D. 1650, when the world contained approximately five hundred million people, it took only 200 years to increase to one billion (Table 8-1). From then on the annual rate of population growth accelerated; today, our numbers

TABLE 8-1 World Population Doubling Times

YEAR	POPULATION	DOUBLING TIME (YEARS)
8000 B.C.	5,000,000[a]	1,500
A.D. 1	250,000,000[a]	1,500
1650	545,000,000[a]	200
1750	728,000,000[a]	200
1850	1,171,000,000[a]	100
1950	2,486,000,000	50
1970	3,632,000,000	35
1975	4,000,000,000	36
1990[a]	5,321,000,000	39
2000[a]	6,292,000,000	43
2020[a]	8,228,000,000	53

[a]These are estimated population sizes and doubling times in years.

Sources: Based on data from the Population Reference Bureau, 1996; and Deevey, 1960.

increase at an annual rate of 1.5 percent. About eighty-seven million new people are added each year, up from the seventy-seven million added in 1982.

Many factors have contributed to accelerated population growth since the Neolithic, and some are difficult to identify. A major influence, though, has been food—a more dependable food supply with an ability to produce and store surpluses. During much of the annual cycle, prehistoric hunters and gatherers probably had an ample food supply that, judging from studies of modern hunters, could have supported a much larger population. But seasonal changes, game population fluctuations, or a bad weather cycle would create shortages. These times of scarcity kept population numbers below the "carrying capacity" of the environment during the good times. The major achievement of the agriculturists, beginning with the Neolithic, was their ability to produce and store a surplus of food, which enabled them to survive times of scarcity between harvests. This capability helped sustain a larger average number of people than had existed before the Neolithic.[1]

Another possible factor contributing to population growth was the radical change in lifestyles brought about by agricultural subsistence. Formerly, during our nomadic hunting and gathering phase of existence, females could nurse only one child at a time; in addition, infants had to be breastfed for up to three years because of the lack of an adequate weaning food. This prolonged nursing period, plus the heavy workload and the frequent movement of camp sites, kept lean body mass high and contributed to reduced female fertility. In addition, infanticide probably played a role in keeping population growth to a minimum. There are reports that it was a common practice among recent hunting nomads to smother a newborn if the mother was still nursing the older sib (Birdsell, 1981). The mother could carry a single infant and provide sufficient breast milk, but the burden of a second infant could not be borne. The subject of infanticide and fertility among nomadic hunters is still much debated, but whatever the various causes, the result was a low fertility rate and small annual population increase for most of human existence. By contrast, a major feature of life since the earliest advent of agriculture was the establishment of semipermanent settlements, and this more sedentary life had an important effect on female fertility. The less arduous existence encountered in a sedentary village, in contrast to a nomadic hunting life, reduced the strain on females and extended their reproductive period. The average number of births per woman during her lifetime increased from an average of four (seen among the !Kung of Southern Africa in the 1960s) to six or even more, as in tropical horticultural groups today. With the advent of sedentary life, females were no longer forced to transport an infant while

---

[1]Agriculturists were more or less successful producing surpluses to carry them through the years of crop failures, but not always. Many times during the Middle Ages and even into recent centuries, two or more successive years of poor crops resulted in famine and, together with epidemics, caused high mortality rates. A recent and interesting account of these episodes in Europe details the impact of crop failures on population (Ladurie, 1988).

going about their daily round of food collecting over many miles of territory, as in former times. Also, improved infant care, proper weaning foods, and increased nutrition reduced mortality, contributing to a greater number of children reaching adolescence.

Though settled village life had certain advantages, many new problems affecting human survival were created. Greater numbers of people living in close contact over long periods polluted their environment and water. This sustained a variety of insects and microorganisms that could be readily transferred from victim to victim, causing diseases that took a heavy toll on the population and shortened life expectancy. In early agricultural periods, judging from skeletal remains, there was a high mortality among young adults and adolescents. Though comparatively improved since the days of the Paleolithic hunters, human existence was still precarious for several millennia after the introduction of agriculture. In later centuries there was an acceleration of population growth, but the contributing factors are numerous and complex and are subjects of much debate: Did a more dependable food supply contribute to an increase in numbers or did the greater number of people provide the impetus to develop improved food-producing technology (Boserup, 1981)?

During the nineteenth century we can point to improved sanitation and the control of infectious disease as major reasons for declining death rates, but in the seventeenth, eighteenth, and even the early decades of the nineteenth century, control of disease was probably not the single most important reason for growth. It is likely that increased efficiency in food production was more important. New food crops were introduced into Europe from the Americas. Plants like potatoes and corn, in particular, enabled agricultural production to increase radically because of their shorter growing season and a yield of a greater amount of calories per unit measure than the grains traditionally grown. The same amount of land planted in such crops could sustain many more people than previously possible; also, these New World crops could grow well on soils unsuited for wheat and barley, the former staple European crops. Increased food supply plus the harnessing of a new energy source, coal, brought on a new era marked by population increase and industrialization.

DEMOGRAPHIC TRANSITIONS

Toward the end of the eighteenth century, after a century of Industrial Revolution,[2] many European populations had increased as much as 133 percent, and population pressures had reached the point at which many millions from

---

[2]The term describes a rapid change in technology that occurred first in England and then in western Europe over a period of about 100 years (1760–1840). During this time, steam-powered machinery was developed and used in some of the earliest manufacturing. Driven by this new technology, the simple agrarian economy gave way to one based on manufacturing and export.

western Europe migrated to new lands. With this rapid expansion, the modern era began, and the conditions under which we live today were initiated. These modern living conditions, though varied and complex, have the capacity to change rapidly; as they change, selective forces are altered readily. Changes in natural selection, which in a previous period favored one group over another, resulted in a shift in population size and reproduction rate within a few generations. All populations of *Homo sapiens* were not affected equally, however, nor were the same selective forces present everywhere at the same time. While the technologically advanced societies were seeking new space, many, perhaps most, of the world's populations were living at pre-seventeenth-century levels. African and New World peoples were less numerous in proportion to the carrying capacity of their lands than were Asians and Europeans. Figure 8-1 shows a gain of Europeans and persons of European origins in North America of 8 percent of the total world population between A.D. 1750 and 1900, compared with only a 4 percent gain for India and China combined, whereas Africa and the Mideast showed a net decline in proportion of the total world population. Considering earlier periods, if more reliable estimates were available for the Neolithic populations in Europe and the Mideast, disproportionate population gains would likely be demonstrated. The point is, because growth is greater in some world regions than in others, some population boundaries expand, whereas others remain stable or may even contract. This change in relative sizes of geographic groups probably occurred during most of our history as a species and certainly has been and still remains a factor in this century.

FIGURE 8-1   World Regions, 1750–1950.

The populations in major world regions have grown disproportionately over the last two centuries, with Europe exceeding all others between 1750 and 1950. Even allowing for the wide range of error in these estimates, the changes in regional increases have been impressive.

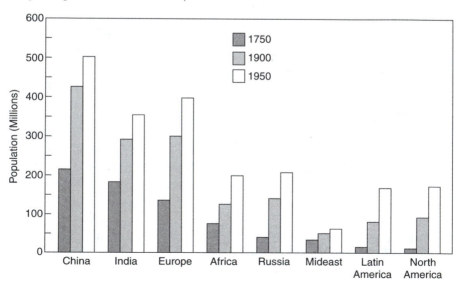

Bands of hunting nomads were much more numerous in places like Australia and the Western Hemisphere before European colonial expansion. Probably during the Neolithic they were even more numerous than many of the sedentary agriculturists. Even the !Kung, who today occupy Africa's Kalahari Desert, were probably as numerous as Europeans 10,000 years ago. Europeans have expanded and successfully occupied new areas of the world, and the few thousand !Kung have been pushed into a harsh refuge area by expanding agriculturalist and pastoral peoples within the last two thousand years—first by tribes of Bantu speakers, and more recently by Europeans (Hulse, 1955). The aboriginal peoples of Australia and North and South America have had much the same experiences. The end result of increases of the world's peoples during the last 400 years are population sizes and distributions that differ radically from those of earlier times. The hunters have all but disappeared except in a very few refuge areas, and even primitive agriculturalists are only a fraction of their former number and are rapidly diminishing as their environments and resources are destroyed. By contrast, many other peoples have sustained a phenomenal growth rate over the last few generations.

The future, if growth projections are reasonably accurate, will see an even greater change in the distribution of the world's peoples (Figure 8-2). The growth trends of two centuries ago have been reversed. Those countries

FIGURE 8-2 Regional Populations, 1975–2020.

Given the current growth rates of major world regions, the projections for the year 2020 will place Asia and Africa far ahead of the other regions. Latin American will nearly double in size in contrast to those areas that experience only slow growth (Europe, North America, and the USSR). (Data selected from Population Reference Bureau, 1990.)

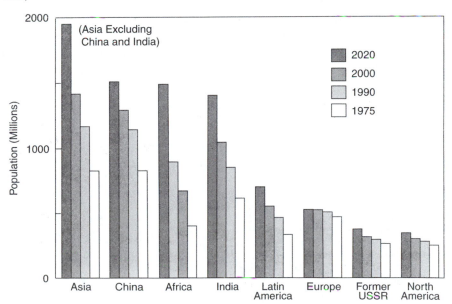

with a larger industrial base, a higher per capita income, and more techno-logical resources have a slower projected growth rate than the less developed areas of the world. The majority of the more than six billion people in the world in the year 2000 will live in these less developed countries (LDC).[3] There will be an estimated 79 percent of the world population living in the LDC, a significant increase from the 66 percent living in these regions of the world in 1950. The more developed countries (MDC) will continue to grow but very slowly, a natural increase of only about 0.1 percent per year. The LDC, though slowing from their 1975 rate of 2.1 percent, will increase their population by 1.9 percent per annum. At this rate their doubling time will be 37 years in contrast to the 114- to 500-year doubling time for North America and Europe. If China, with a rate of natural increase of 1.4 percent and a dou-bling time of 62 years, is excluded from the calculations, then the LDC dou-bling time shortens to 32 years.

The major differences between world regions in their natural popula-tion increase over the past four decades have been due to a dramatic lower-ing of death rates in the LDC. When both birth and death rates were high, a reduction in only the death rates would, of course, result in a rapid increase, as experienced by Africa, Asia, and Latin America since mid-century. Coun-tries of these regions with their rapidly growing populations are undergoing a stage of the *demographic transition*. Demographers use this term to describe a transition in the growth potential of a population. In past centuries, relatively stable populations were maintained with little or no net increase between the generations because a high birthrate was counterbalanced by a high death rate, a demographic phase one. Such populations begin to change when they enter the second phase of the demographic transition by reducing death rates through various health measures (usually associated with the introduction of modern technology and improved public health measures), while births still remain high. Then there will be a rapid natural increase (a surplus of births over deaths) that will continue until a new balance is reached. This third phase of the demographic transition is entered when birth rates begin to decline until replacement equals or barely exceeds loss, and the population approaches a zero-population-growth condition. Western European countries have reached this stage, and the United States and Canada are approaching it. A critical factor in the future will be the length of time required for the completion of this demographic transition in the less developed world. The continuously high birthrates in the LDC will cause many populations to dou-ble their size in less than a generation. Mexico, for example, has a natural

---

[3]Classification of the "more developed"(MDC) and "less developed"(LDC) regions follows that of the United Nations—that is, the MDC comprise all of Europe, North America (United States and Canada), Australia, New Zealand, and Japan. The rest of the world is regarded as LDC or, in the new terminology, developing. The LDCs vary widely in population size and their economies cover an enormous range of gross national product or per capita incomes. For exam-ple, where would China or Mexico fit?

increase of 2.2 percent, which adds more than two million new people each year to its population. If continued at this rate of growth, the population will double within 32 years.

Rapid-growth countries have younger age structures, as illustrated by the population pyramid for Mexico, where persons born between 1981 and 1996 make up 36 percent of the population, in contrast to 22 percent in the United States (a slow-growth nation). Sweden is an example of a "no-growth" nation; each age segment between birth and sixty years is nearly equal in size (Figure 8-3). These differentials of age group sizes between developed and developing countries become even broader in some large fast-grow nations; 45 percent of Nigeria's 104 million people are under fifteen years of age. The more developed countries have maintained the proportion of children under age fifteen at about 20 percent since 1950, while this age group has nearly doubled in the developing countries and may even rise further in some.

A population's age structure is an important determiner of society's present and future needs and may be measured by a *dependency ratio*. This is the ratio between the productive portion of the population, set typically between fifteen and sixty-four years, and the dependent age groups—those individuals younger than fifteen years and older than sixty-four years. The larger the dependent group, the larger will be the dependency ratio (DR). Populations in the LDC have a very high dependency ratio. Comparisons between slow-growth and rapid-growth countries show a wide difference in the DR

FIGURE 8-3   Age–Sex Population Pyramids: Rapid, Slow, and No Growth Models. (Courtesy of the Population Reference Bureau, Inc., Washngton, D.C.)

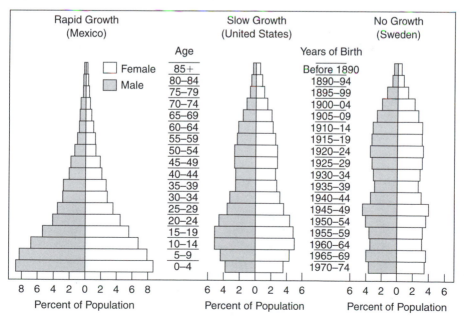

(Figure 8-4). These figures are based on estimates provided by the Population Reference Bureau but do not consider the probable use of child labor, which, of course, would reduce the size of the dependent group. Even allowing for this, the dependency ratios are high among the LDC, whose poorer economics are less able to support such a burden of dependents. Most importantly, this large proportion of children provides a potential for high reproduction rates as the children reach maturity and are a source for rapid population growth in the future.

These changes in population structure profoundly affect the economy, the environment, and the social institutions of the LDC in diverse ways. One way of gauging the impact of rapid growth on a nation's resources is to consider the structural and social dislocation created by high birthrates over short periods. Within less than a generation of rapid growth, persons of the same age cohort (born within a given time period) have to be accommodated by educational and socioeconomic systems. For example, in the United States, the group born during the "baby boom" period, considered as the period between 1946 to 1964 when the fertility rate peaked at 3.6 percent, followed the age cohort born during the Depression years, 1929 to 1941, when fertility rates were only 2.1 to 2.5 (close to replacement level). This baby boom is a seventy-five-million-person bulge in the population, which is contributing to some major stresses and sociocultural changes as they move through the life

FIGURE 8-4 Children Younger Than Fifteen Years of Age, 1950–2000. (Data selected from Population Reference Bureau, 1990.)

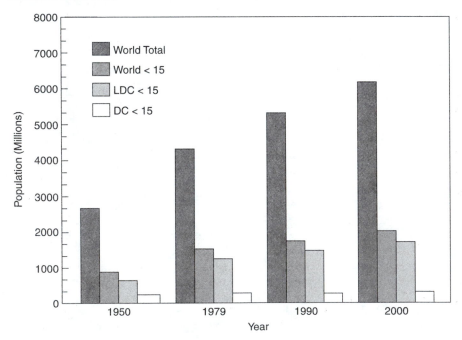

cycle. First, it was the hospitals and then the educational facilities that bore the burden as this large cohort moved through childhood and entered the next phase. College enrollments shot up, and many more persons entered the labor market in the 1970s than in previous decades. As they entered adulthood, delayed marriages and smaller families were the favored choices, so the "boomers" were followed by a smaller age cohort because of decreased birthrates (fertility below 2.1). This resulted in fewer children enrolling in elementary school, a factor that forced the closing of schools in many cities.[4] Because of the large numbers of women in their reproductive years, there was a short period of increased births despite the group's low fertility rate. This created an increase in the childhood cohort, an echo effect in the 1980s, which may be over now with the aging of the baby boom women who are leaving their prime childbearing years.

The aging of this large cohort, many of whom are now entering middle age, will place an increased burden on services for the elderly in the next few decades. This final stage in the human life cycle illustrates, as did the other stages, the impact that disproportionate age groups can have on a society. In the United States, we have witnessed and recorded some major stresses on our social system—in particular, reduced numbers of job opportunities and an increased demand for housing, education, and medical care. Magnify these problems many times and consider the effects on less developed countries. The LDCs, with between 35 and 45 percent of the total population under fifteen years of age, must find ways of meeting the needs of childhood and education, and then the economy must be expanded to offer employment as this large age cohort enters adulthood. There has been a wide variation in experience in coping with this burden, depending on the nation, its resources, government, and social institutions. Expanding industry has worked for some, while migration or seasonal labor has been more often the source of job opportunities for others.

DEMOGRAPHIC FACTORS OF POPULATION CHANGE

A significant aspect of the phenomenal population growth in this century has been the reduction in mortality rates (Table 8-2). The lowering of infant mortality, especially, has been a major contributing factor which, together with improvement in maternal care, has radically driven up fertility rates (average number of live births per female living through their reproductive years). Life expectancy has been extended, and the leading causes of death have altered. The net effect, in addition to an increase in population size, has been an alteration in the forces of natural selection acting on each generation. Indi-

---

[4]At the close of the century we are experiencing what is called the "baby boom echo" with larger numbers of school-aged children requiring the expansion of school programs.

TABLE 8-2 Population Growth Rates of Selected World Regions

	POPULATION[1] ESTIMATES				BIRTH[2] RATES		DEATH[3] RATES		NATURAL[4] INCREASE		DOUBLING[5] TIME	
	1930	1950	1972	1996	1972	1996	1972	1996	1972	1996	1972	1996
World	2,178	2,674	3,782	5,771	33	24	13	9	2.0	1.5	35	46
Major Areas												
Africa	164	222	364	732	47	41	21	13	2.6	2.8	27	25
West Africa	48	67	107	204	49	45	24	14	2.5	3.1	28	23
East Africa	46	63	103	227	47	45	22	15	2.5	2.9	28	24
North Africa	39	53	92	164	47	32	17	8	3.0	2.4	23	29
Middle Africa	21	25	38	86	44	46	24	16	2.1	2.9	33	24
South Africa	10	14	24	51	41	32	18	8	2.4	2.4	29	29
Asia	1,120	1,381	2,154	3,501	37	24	14	8	2.3	1.6	30	43
East Asia	591	684	962	1,443	29	16	12	7	1.7	1.0	41	70
Western Asia	31	44	82	176	44	32	16	7	2.8	2.4	25	29
Southern Asia	371	481	806	1,385	44	30	17	10	2.6	2.1	27	34
Southeast Asia	127	173	304	496	49	27	15	8	2.9	1.9	24	37
Western Hemisphere												
North America	134	166	233	295	17	15	9	9	1.1	0.6	63	114
Latin America	108	163	300	486	38	26	10	7	2.8	1.9	25	36
Tropical South America	55	84	160		40		10		3.0		23	
Central America	22	35	72	127	43	28	11	5	3.2	2.3	22	30
Temperate South America	19	27	41	52.4	25	20		8		1.2		58
Caribbean	12	17	27	36	33	23	11	8	2.2	1.5	32	45
South America				323		25		7		1.8		39
Europe	355	392	469	728	16	11	10	11	0.7	-0.1	99	—
Western Europe	108	123	151	181	15	11	11	10	0.5	0.1	139	716
Southern Europe	93	108	151	143	18	10	9	9	0.9	0.1	77	652
Eastern Europe	89	88	106	309	17	10	10	14	0.7	-0.4	139	—
Nothern Europe	65	73	82	94	16	13	11	11	0.9	0.2	77	445
USSR	179	180	248		17.4		8.2		0.9	0		—
Russia				147.7		9		15		-0.5		—
Oceania	10.0	12.7	20.2	29	25	19	10	7	2.0	1.1	35	60

[1] Estimates given in millions.
[2] Births/1,000.
[3] Deaths/1,000.
[4] Birthrate minus death rate.
[5] The time for population to double if rate of increase continues.

Source: Population Reference Bureau, Inc., 1996, and *Demographic Yearbook*, 1969, 1974, 1979.

viduals who, in prior times, would have died before adolescence are now surviving through their reproductive years. This shift in population fitness in all
parts of the world has had far-reaching effects on the gene pool of future populations and will contribute to an ongoing evolution. The demographic factor
with the greatest influence on population size is the infant mortality rate, an
influence well understood by every society. Infant mortality rates have varied
widely from ancient to recent times, and even slight changes had major effects
on the generations that followed.

Infant Mortality

In the United States today, 99 percent of all children born alive reach their
thirteenth birthday, compared with only 50 percent who did so 100 years ago.
This major demographic change is due primarily to a dramatic lowering of
infant mortality rates since the turn of the century followed by eradication of
many of the childhood diseases affecting preadolescents. Western European
countries have had the same experience. Table 8-3 shows comparative data on
infant mortality for selected countries. Most countries of the developed world
have brought death rates down to less than 8 per 1,000 live births, whereas less
developed countries have rates as high as 87 per 1,000. All countries listed in
this table have experienced a dramatic reduction of death rates during the
past hundred years. The greatest decreases, however, have been among the
industrialized countries.

TABLE 8-3   Infant Mortality Since 1898 of Selected Countries (per 1,000 live births)

COUNTRY	1898–1902	1918–1922	1956–1960	1972	1996
Sweden	98	65	17	11.7	4.4
Japan	155	172	36	13	4.2
Norway	88	—	20	13.8	5.2
Denmark	131	84	24	14.8	5.4
France	154	112	32	15.1	6.1
United Kingdom	152	85	23	18.4	6.2
Spain	190	158	49	27.9	7.2
United States	162	85	26	19.2	7.5
Italy	167	141	47	29.2	8.3
Hungary	204	—	—	34	11.5
Russia	—	—	81	24.4	18
Argentina	—	—	61	58	22.9
Mexico	—	—	76	69	34
Guatemala	—	—	95	92	51
Kenya	—	—	—	135	62
India	200	212	198	139	79
Nigeria	—	—	—	180	87

Source: Selected data from Population Reference Bureau, Inc., and *Demographic Yearbook*,
1979, 1996.

The United States, at the turn of the century, had an appallingly high infant mortality rate that would be comparable to that of many of the underdeveloped countries twenty years ago, but this rate has now been reduced to 7.5 per 1,000. Still, there are eighteen countries with lower infant mortality rates. All of these countries have shown a 70 to 80 percent reduction in infant deaths since the turn of the century (a graphical comparison of sixteen selected countries is shown in Figure 8-5). This reduction has been achieved through a variety of changes; improved diets, lessened female workload, better maternal care, and control of infectious diseases have all contributed. As of 1987, Sweden led the world in improvements in infant health, a fact that is reflected in Sweden's having one of the lowest infant mortality rates in the world. Because of the completeness of its health records extending back nearly two centuries, Sweden may be used as an example of what can be achieved in the field of infant health. From 250 per 1,000 infant deaths a century and a half ago, the rate was reduced to 9 per 1,000 by 1980, which was thought to be the minimum that could be achieved given the knowledge of fetal development. However, the rate has undergone a significant reduction since, and even the lower rate of 4.4 has been surpassed in Japan in 1996 with 4.2.

Sweden achieved this low level of infant death through major innovations in prenatal care and obstetrical services; a countrywide network ensures that

FIGURE 8-5 Infant Mortality of Sixteen Selected Countries. (Data from Population Reference Bureau, 1996.)

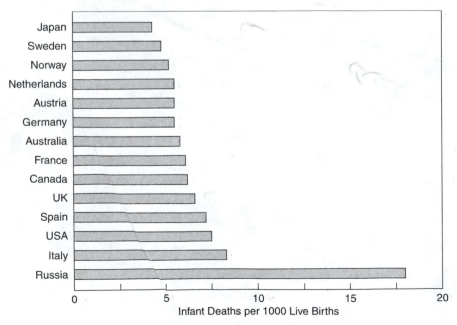

every woman is within an hour of a maternity health center, which offers free services. The Swedish experience indicates the importance of socioeconomic factors. The higher rates of mortality among those ethnic groups that occupy a lower socioeconomic position in many countries provide additional statistics that emphasize the influence of social factors. Where adequate data are available, mortality rates vary by national region; urban centers with available medical services usually have lower rates than rural areas. In the United States, for example, significant ethnic group differences have been recorded ever since health statistics have been compiled. African Americans have the highest infant mortality of any ethnic group (16.8 versus 6.9 for Euro-Americans). A variety of explanations are offered—from lack of access to medical facilities, or failure to use them, to an average younger age at first pregnancy—but whatever the causes, significant differences have been recorded throughout this century.

Maternal Health, Infant Mortality, and Natural Selection

Throughout the last few generations, as infant mortality has declined and maternal health has improved, childbirth-related deaths have been reduced drastically. Maternal death rates of 320 per 100,000 a century ago in the developed world have decreased to 10 per 100,000 today. The combined effects of lower infant and maternal mortality rates were an increase in fertility and a growth of population. Then family sizes began a decline in the industrialized countries to a point near or below replacement level today. In the less developed countries the story is somewhat different. High maternal mortality rates persist, though the rates are probably much lower than they were a few generations ago; but firm data are lacking. As shown in Table 8-4, there is a wide disparity between countries, and most have rates as high as or higher than recorded in the developed world at the turn of the century. Further improvement in prenatal care and maternity services should reduce the risks of pregnancy and contribute to a rise in fertility rates. Family planning efforts, changing traditions, and more years of formal education for women have worked in some countries to lower fertility over the past decades, and this lowering of fertility should compensate for the increased numbers of women living through their reproductive years.

Since the lowering of death rates, natural selection has continued to operate, but through a variation in birthrates and survival through the first year. The factors of maternal and infant health are radically altering the selective forces acting on the human population. A reduction of the selection against those genetic defects that contribute to early death or that affect infant susceptibility to disease will undoubtedly increase the genetic load in future populations. Likewise, improved maternity services enable many women to give birth to healthy infants when they might otherwise not have been able to because of hormonal deficiencies, poor general health, or defective pelvic structure (discussed earlier in the example of rickets influencing female

TABLE 8-4   Estimates of Maternal Mortality by Region

REGION	NUMBER OF MATERNAL DEATHS (THOUSANDS)	MATERNAL-MORTALITY RATE (PER 100,000 LIVE BIRTHS)
Africa	150	640
North	24	500
West	54	700
East	46	660
Central	18	690
Southern	8	570
Asia	308	420
West	14	340
South	230	650
Southeast	52	420
East	12	55
Latin America	34	270
Central	9	240
Caribbean	2	220
Tropical South	22	310
Temperate South	1	110
Oceania	2	100
Developing Countries	494	450
Developed Countries	6	30
World	500	390

Source: Adapted from *Population Today*, Population Reference Bureau, 1990.

growth). Also, the increasing practice of in vitro fertilization and embryo implants in the developed countries has opened up a whole new area of possibilities for reproduction by women who otherwise, because of genetically determined factors, could not have conceived and carried a fetus to term.

Fertility Differences and Population Composition

In addition to the variation in mortality rates and fertility rates between various areas of the world, there are significant differences among socioeconomic classes and ethnic groups in each country. These differences plus immigration have contributed to changes in population composition of several nations during the past three generations and are likely to continue. But alterations in total fertility rates[5] among socioeconomic classes and ethnic groups within

---

[5]The total fertility rate is the average number of births for all women living through their reproductive years.

any country are difficult to define or predict. Social statuses often shift, and fashions change as preferences for large or small families alter. The baby boom experience in the United States can serve as an example. The increase in fertility occurred mainly among middle-class women (total fertility rate went from 2.1 to 3.7), which accounted for most of the rise in number of births that produced an increase of 18.2 percent in the U.S. population between 1947 and 1964. The situation is different now, with most groups showing low fertility levels, while rates among Hispanic women have increased.

Mexican Americans, the largest group of Hispanics, lead in the number of births. The effects of this high fertility on ethnic composition and on over-all fertility rate have been traced over the last twenty years in California. The proportion of women giving birth who are identified as Hispanic increased from 20 percent to 44 percent since 1975; those classified as "non-Hispanic white" declined from 68 percent to below 38 percent, and the African-American segment decreased from 9 percent to 8 percent of total births. The remaining ethnic groups, or "others" (Asian, Pacific Islanders, Native Americans) increased their share from 3 to 10 percent (Burke, 1995). This ethnic pattern of fertility rates is followed throughout the country. The nation's total fertility rate (2.0) is exceeded by Mexican Americans (3.2), other Hispanics (2.9), and African Americans (2.5).

Immigration is also contributing to a change in the composition of the American population. Before 1960, Europe was the source of most immigrants entering the United States. Now a majority of the nearly one million legal immigrants admitted each year since 1980 are arriving from Latin American and Asian countries. Figure 8-6 illustrates this change in regional origin. Between 1951 and 1960, 52 percent came from Europe versus only 25 percent from Latin America; this ratio was nearly reversed by 1994. Asian immigrants accounted for only a small percentage in the 1950s but now enter at the rate of 37 percent of total annual immigrants. Add to this the number of illegals, mostly from Latin America, and it is easy to understand the projected changes in the ethnic composition of the country over the next half century (Figure 8-7). About one in three Americans will be members of what we call ethnic minorities, and by mid-twenty-first century the proportion will rise to one half.

This is only a part of the story regarding population composition, since immigration accounts for only 30 percent of the increase of the population in this fastest-growing of all industrialized countries. The balance is due to natural increase. The U.S. population increases at the rate of 1 percent annually compared with only 0.4 percent in Western Europe and 0.3 percent in Japan. Since fertility and immigration are higher among the ethnic minorities, it is easy, if one is a member of the majority, to fall into the trap of racial bias and deplore the changing ethnic makeup of the nation. But such anxiety should be tempered with the evidence of America's recent history. At the peak of

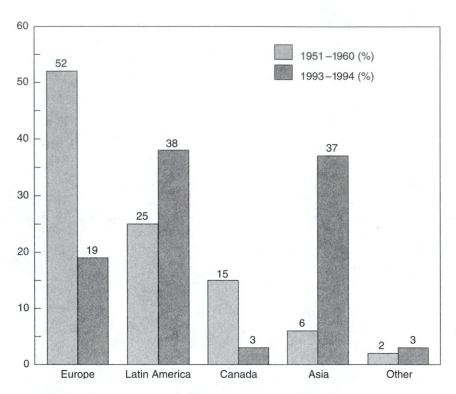

FIGURE 8-6 **Immigrants to the United States by Region of Origin.** (*Population Bulletin,* Vol. 50(4), 1996.)

immigration, between 1881 and 1920, when twenty-three million people were admitted, a cry went up regarding ethnic origins. Despite the reactions at the time by the "old" Americans toward the new wave of immigrants, no harm came to the country; rather the reverse occurred. The economy expanded and the nation prospered with the growth of population and ethnic diversity.

European Examples of Fertility Rate Differences

Socioeconomic influences on decisions to have children are even more clearly illustrated by the rapidly changing conditions in Europe in the last twenty years; the lack of housing, low family income, and high inflation rates have caused many young couples to decide against having children, resulting in significant drops in fertility rates in many countries. Several Eastern European countries have reduced their total fertility rate (TFR) below replacement level (a TFR of 2.1), but some, like Romania and Poland, maintained a replacement-level TFR until 1990 despite the hardships confronting young families. Since then, with the breakup of the Eastern European communist block, these rates have dropped to 1.3 and 1.7, respectively. The TFR for the former Soviet Union was 2.5 in 1990, which was an average for the total pop-

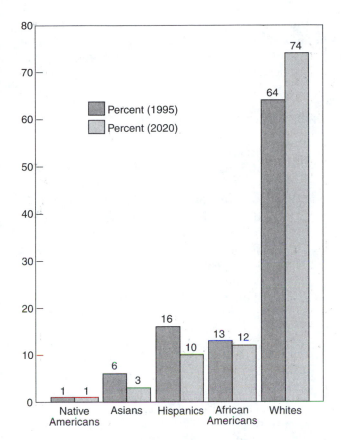

FIGURE 8-7 Changing Ethnic Composition of the United States, 1995 and 2020. (Data selected from Population Reference Bureau, 1995.)

ulation of 291 million people of diverse cultures. The religious beliefs and cultures of the central Asian republics inculcated a tradition of large families, contributing to fertility rates two to three times the Russian average. Since the separation of the republics, Russia, Belarus, and the Ukraine record some of the lowest fertility rates in the world (TFR of 1.4), while the now independent Central Asian republics have maintained their former high rates.

Harsh living conditions and poor economic prospects tend to delay marriages and keep family size low. On the other hand, improved economic circumstances can also have the same results—delayed childbearing and a reduction in completed family size. Spain and Italy have significantly improved their economic positions over the past decade but, with this improvement, critical decisions were made that affected marriages and the number of births. These decisions resulted in a TFR reduced from 2.6 to 1.2 (Spain) and from 1.9 to 1.2 (Italy) between 1980 to 1996. These examples serve to illustrate that fluctuations of population size between generations or between ethnic groups are the result of complex forces that can quickly alter demographic processes because of social or natural factors. The net effect is a wide range of differences not only among ethnic groups but between countries of the developed and less developed regions.

HEALTH, DISEASE, AND EPIDEMIOLOGICAL TRANSITION

The health dimensions of our species are undergoing some critical changes. The major plagues of the past are no longer with us to the extent they were in the sixteenth and seventeenth centuries, when periodic epidemics caused mortality surges in which 30–50 percent of a population were lost. Starting in the 1800s, we have entered a period when fewer types of infectious diseases have accounted for most illnesses and deaths each year. This change began with what may be termed an "epidemiological transition" (Omran, 1982). The first stage was marked by periodic episodes of high mortality caused by outbreaks of infectious diseases like smallpox, cholera, typhoid, plague, and a variety of acute respiratory diseases. One or another of these diseases in combination would spread throughout the poorly housed, poorly fed populations crowded into the growing cities of western Europe. The highest mortality was among infants and young children; life expectancy at birth was between twenty and forty years. Then gradual improvements in sanitation, housing, and living conditions in general reduced the impact of many of these infectious diseases and shifted the higher mortality rates to older age groups; children were now more likely to survive to adulthood. This began a second stage when average life expectancy at birth increased to fifty years.

Disease Epidemics and Selection

The scourge of epidemics throughout human history that have caused wide fluctuation in population growth gives evidence of the probability that many of our genetic polymorphisms today are the result of past natural selection. In our discussions in Chapter 3, we gave examples of the probable resistance of certain genotypes of the ABO, HLA, and GM systems to disease. Though these examples are mostly based on statistical correlations between disease and genotype, infectious diseases, which have periodically killed thousands during past millennia, should be seriously considered as probable agents of natural selection. Plague, cholera, typhus, smallpox, and typhoid, to mention a few of the major ones, have had dramatic effects on civilization throughout recorded history. Wars were won or lost, cities were abandoned, and civilizations fell because of epidemics. In past warfare, often more casualties were caused by disease than by bullets. An example is typhus, which, along with freezing weather and malnutrition, accounted for most of the deaths among Napoleon's troops in 1812 during their war with Russia. Typhoid fever killed more Union soldiers during the American Civil War than died in all of the battles fought. In fact, of the 364,000 deaths, only 140,400 were from battle wounds; the remaining 224,000 fatalities were due to disease spread through the army encampments because of poor sanitation and polluted water supplies. Aside from these episodes there were even more lethal diseases to contend with in everyday life, and some populations proved to be more susceptible than others. After the decline of the bubonic plague in Europe, smallpox, or simply the pox, was foremost as a threat to the human species, particularly among the inhabitants of the New World.

Smallpox   The invasion of the Americas by Europeans more than 400 years ago demonstrated the effect of infectious diseases on peoples who had no history of prior contact and who, therefore, had low resistance. Millions of Native Americans died—an estimated 1.5 million in Mexico alone—and smallpox is believed to have been the main cause. This deadly disease, which killed even Europeans at a rate of one out of four infected, passed from village to village, from the time of its introduction in Vera Cruz in 1507. Eventually the "pox" extended northward into what is now Arizona and New Mexico. Entire populations in the Southwest died from epidemics even before they were visited by Europeans (McNeill, 1976). Similar experiences were suffered by Native Americans in the eastern half of the continent following the establishment of European colonies in the seventeenth century. Later, in the nineteenth century, there were periodic epidemics among the populations of the Great Plains as Euro-Americans pushed westward across the Mississippi.

In modern times smallpox has been responsible for many deaths even in those populations with a long history of contact with the disease. Africa continued to suffer from recurrence of epidemics; over 100,000 cases were reported in the 1940s. The increased use of a newly developed freeze-dried vaccine that did not require refrigeration gradually reduced the number and range of these outbreaks, but they still occurred over the next decade. There were an estimated 2.5 million cases in 1967, mainly in South America, Africa, and parts of South Asia, but stringent vaccination enforcement regulations brought this number down to slightly more than 100,000 by 1972 (see Hopkins, 1983). No cases were reported for 1978, and the disease is now believed to have been eradicated entirely, but a constant watch is maintained by the World Health Organization.[6] This control of smallpox and other infectious diseases, a remarkable achievement of modern health science, should not be allowed to make us complacent, however. Eradication of smallpox is a medical milestone but there remains a continuous struggle between humans and

---

[6]The last endemic case of smallpox occurred in Somalia on 26 October, 1977. The patient, a twenty-three-year-old hospital cook, made a complete recovery. In 1980 at the Thirty-third World Health Assembly meeting in Geneva, smallpox was declared officially eradicated from the planet.

microbes, and to maintain the low death rates enjoyed during the last two generations, perpetual vigilance is necessary (DuBos, 1968). This warning is underscored by several recent experiences.

Cholera   A major cause of epidemics in the past and even today, cholera is spread by bacteria through contaminated food and water and has reappeared periodically, killing millions. Where crowded conditions exist, accompanied by poor sanitation, the population is at grave risk for infection from these bacteria. For example, 50,000 cases were reported in New York City in 1866, but there were only a few reported in 1900. The provision of clean water and improved sanitation reduced the danger of recurrence in many areas. In the same year (1900) that New York suffered only a few cases of cholera, nearly a million persons died of the disease in India. Since a major world epidemic in 1919, the disease has appeared sporadically throughout Africa and Asia. Spreading from a base in Indonesia, cholera broke out in a new epidemic in 1970, but major efforts by the World Health Organization brought it under control. Cholera has continued to decline since 1972, but it still remains a danger to world health, as witnessed by experiences in the South Pacific, where cholera had never been identified before. The disease was introduced to the island of Tarawa through bacteria carried by an unsuspecting traveler and spread quickly throughout many of the islands in the Gilbert chain (Maung, 1979). Between September and December 1977, the first cholera epidemic in South Pacific history claimed 21 victims. A total of 1,102 cases was reported, but the death toll was kept to a minimum by early diagnosis and the ready availability of modern treatment. Cholera remains a menace to human health and periodically continues its march around the world. Included in this new pandemic of 595,000 cases (as of 1995) is South America, a region spared until now.

The experiences of Peru in the first half of 1991 further illustrate the ever-present threat of cholera, in which small events can escalate into catastrophic ones under the right conditions. In that year, a ship from Asia is believed to have discharged bilge water containing the bacteria, and the organism was then picked up by the local marine life. Fishermen sold their catches of contaminated fish in the Lima markets; many of the consumers became ill and passed on the cholera bacteria into the local water and sewage systems. The lack of sanitation services and pure drinking water for more than half of the residents in the grossly overcrowded capital city of Lima hastened the spread of the disease and contributed to the first modern epidemic in South America in a century. Within a month, 23,000 cases had been reported; fortunately there were only a few hundred deaths, but the epidemic spread north. This march of cholera extended into Mexico, with a reported 16,000 cases and 137 deaths in 1995; during this same year, Peru continued to experience over 22,000 cases. Several countries of Africa also experience high rates of cholera; Nigeria reported over 12,000 cases with 10 percent mortality in

1996. These examples illustrate how a major disease from former times can reappear when conditions are right and can begin another worldwide spread in a new pandemic.

Recent Epidemiological Transitions

The health status of populations continues to undergo changes over the generations as it always has, but now the range of population differences is much broader than at any time in our history. In the developed industrialized world the major causes of death have now shifted to certain chronic diseases like cancers and diseases of the heart and circulatory system. Most populations of the developing world continue to remain in a middle transition between the infectious diseases of old and new chronic ones.

The third stage of the transition started about 1900 and was marked by significant changes in the leading causes of death. Because of preventive measures, several infectious diseases no longer plagued populations of the developed countries, though they have remained a problem in many of the developing countries. The incidence of gastrointestinal diseases, several childhood diseases, tuberculosis, and pneumonia, all once among the leading causes of death, have been reduced to insignificant levels in the United States. The major causes of death are now the chronic degenerative types of disease, such as cardiovascular disease, cancer, and respiratory disease (Table 8-5), which begin to appear during middle age. Several kinds of cancers and cardiovascular disease have steadily increased to replace tuberculosis and pneumonia as the two major causes of death. By mid-century, life expectancy had increased to sixty-five years, and there was a greater risk of dying from one of several of the chronic degenerative diseases. In the last decade, new health threats have begun to appear in the form of chronic respiratory diseases, like emphysema and bronchitis, and these are becoming significant factors in the death rates of an aging population.

Early in the transition, clean water and more efficient waste disposal, along with improved housing, contributed to a decline in infectious disease. Inoculations and early medical diagnosis and treatment were additional contributing factors, but dietary improvements have proven to be something of a mixed blessing. There are few cases of vitamin deficiencies or of malnutrition. The numbers do not even come close to experiences of the last century; the two major vitamin deficiency diseases, pellagra and rickets, have been eradicated, along with protein-energy malnutrition. The problems are now mainly of overnutrition and its consequences of obesity, diabetes, and cardiovascular problems. Overeating, especially of animal fats, and limited exercise are believed to be contributing factors to cardiovascular diseases. The American Heart Association, for example, has recommended for years that Americans reduce total caloric intake and limit fat consumption, and has bolstered its recommendation with convincing statistics that show that high cholesterol

TABLE 8-5 Average Annual Death Rates per 100,000 from Fifteen Leading Causes, United States—1900 and 1992

1900		1992	
All Causes	1,755.0	All Causes	852.9
1. Tuberculosis	201.9	1. Diseases of heart	281.4
2. Influenza and pneumonia	181.5	2. Malignant neoplasms	204.1
3. Diarrhea and enteritis	133.2	3. Cerebrovascular diseases	56.4
4. Diseases of heart	132.1	4. All accidents	34.0
5. Congenital malformations[a]	91.8	5. Chronic obstructive pulmonary disease	36.0
6. Acute and chronic nephritis	89.0	6. Pneumonia and influenza	29.7
7. Cerebral hemorrhage, embolism	75.0	7. Diabetes mellitus	19.6
8. Bronchitis and bronchopneumonia	67.6	8. Suicide	12.0
9. Cancer and other malignant tumors	63.0	9. Chronic liver disease and cirrhosis	9.6
10. Diphtheria	43.3	10. Atherosclerosis	16.1
11. Typhoid and paratyphoid	35.9	11. Nephritis, nephrotic syndrome and nephrosis	9.1
12. Cirrhosis of the liver	12.9	12. Homicide	10.0
13. Measles	12.5	13. Septicemia	19.9
14. Whooping cough	12.1	14. Certain conditions originating in the perinatal period	7.5
15. Diabetes mellitus	9.7	15. Human immunodeficiency virus infection	13.2

[a]This classification includes all diseases and malformations of early infancy contributing to deaths after the first year of life.

Source: *Statistical Abstract of the United States*, 1930 (U.S. Government Printing Office, Washington, DC; *Monthly Vital Statistics Report*, Vol. 38, No. 5, Supplement, 1995 (U.S. Dept. of Health and Human Services).

and overweight contribute to heart disease. In sum, our changing lifestyle accompanying urbanization and the rise of industrialization and its pollution, together with tobacco smoking and overeating, have contributed to an increase in cardiovascular, lung, and cancer diseases.

Just as in the comparisons of infant mortality rates discussed above, the leading causes of death also differ between the two groups of countries, the more developed (MDC) and the lesser developed (LDC). Whereas heart disease, cancer, and vascular disease head the list in the developed countries, gastroenteritis, pneumonia, and malarial diseases, aggravated by malnutrition, are the major causes of death in the lesser developed nations. World Health Organization surveys show, however, that whenever people adopt the dietary habits of the more affluent nations, certain chronic diseases increase in their effects on mortality.

Cardiovascular Diseases   In the United States cardiovascular diseases of all types account for 41 percent of mortality, and in western Europe these percentages are nearly as high. Certain developing countries are suffering an increase in coronary disease among the wealthier classes who are adopting Western lifestyles. As their incomes rise, so does their consumption of animal protein and fats together with an overabundance of total calories. The dietary influence is underscored by the experiences of several European populations during World War II. The incidence of coronary heart disease dropped to one-third of the prewar incidence in Finland and the Netherlands, but after the war, as nutrition rose back up to prewar levels, so did coronary heart disease, which reached a peak in many of the MDC in the early 1970s and then began to decline. A realization of the importance of proper diet and exercise began to influence health, and several countries began to show a dramatic decrease. The United States reduced the rate from 470 per 100,000 population in 1975 to 281 per 100,000 in 1992.

A ranking of fifty-two nations in 1987 for mortality rates from all types of cardiovascular disease showed broad differences, from a low of 119.4 per 100,000 in Guatemala to a high of 449.7 in Romania (54 percent of the deaths from all causes). Other high rates are found throughout eastern Europe. By contrast, Finland, New Zealand, Northern Ireland, and Denmark are in the mid-range of all types of cardiovascular diseases (36, 33, 39, and 18) but rank at the top for death rates from coronary heart disease (47, 46, 52, and 42). Considering only highly developed countries, Japan has the third lowest mortality rate, whereas France is the fourth lowest for all cardiovascular diseases (*World Health Statistics Annual*, 1987; see also Polednak, 1989: 67–72). These differences have generated numerous questions regarding behaviors that relate to health, as well as genetic influences. In all nations reporting health statistics by ethnic group, significant variation is seen between the groups.

In Finland, for example, a country with one of the higher coronary heart disease rates, the Saami (Lapps) have a significantly lower rate than the national average. Finns living in a region of northern Norway have higher coronary heart disease rates than Norwegians and Lapps living in the same area. Careful studies of populations in another high-rate country, New Zealand, also reveal considerable ethnic group differences. Maori, the aboriginal inhabitants, had a higher rate than those of European descent; there was even a significant difference between Maori who followed the Mormon religion and those who did not. The Mormon Maori had the lower incidence, but an interesting aspect of the study was the finding that Maori women were at higher risk from coronary heart disease than Maori men, the reverse of results from many other studies that showed males at a higher risk (Prior et al., 1986).

Coronary heart diseases, with their debilitating sequel of reduced physical activity and risk of early death, are problems confronting all people. The chance of developing heart disease increases with age, with certain lifestyles, and with some diets. In the many epidemiological studies, high-risk groups have been identified: Sex is the first distinction made—males are at greater risk than females—and the list goes on to include smoking, the use of alcohol, and overeating. A familial factor—a history of heart disease in the family—is noted as well, but whether there are gene products affecting heart disease risk is not clear, though several possibilities have been proposed. Ethnic group risk is even more difficult to define because so often minorities (frequently identified as one or another ethnic group) lead significantly different lifestyles; Maori of New Zealand, Samoans, or recent Asian immigrants in the United States are some examples (see Baker et al., 1986). During most of this century, however, attention has been directed to studies of the higher mortality and morbidity rates among African Americans because of the varying frequencies of several diseases and because of the reports of hypertension among this group.

Hypertension   On average, blood pressure tends to rise with age and with excess body weight, and is higher in males than in females, at least among populations of the developed world. Though there is no clear-cut division between normal and high blood pressure, significant differences have been reported among national groups, and between social and ethnic groups within a country. In the United States, African Americans—both males and females—have consistently higher pressures than whites. These differences have been attributed to dietary habits—the frequent and heavy use of common table salt (sodium chloride), for example—and probably genetic factors as well. It has been hypothesized that African Americans may be highly sensitive to sodium and less able to manage even moderate intakes. This hypothesis assumes their ancestors' genetic adaptation to low-sodium diets because their original homeland, West Central Africa, is a region low in available salt supplies (Wilson, 1986). This may be questioned on the grounds that there is wide variation in hypertension throughout Africa as well as a wide range of salt supplies.

A more likely explanation for hypertension in some ethnic minorities may be social. The frustration and tensions encountered in the daily lives of persons of lower socioeconomic status can add to anxiety and increased blood pressure. Attempts to link skin color (assumed to be a crude measure of African admixture) with blood pressure met with little success when corrections were made for socioeconomic level. Persons with darker skin did tend to have higher blood pressure, but only if those measured were in the lower economic and educational levels (Klag et al., 1991). African Americans as well as other minority groups around the world encounter many stressful situations in their daily lives, and there is ample physiological evidence that anxiety and tension brought about by many causes can quickly elevate blood pressure. The measurement procedure itself is often a sufficient cause of anxiety.

The stresses of modern living certainly influence us all to some degree. Populations living in isolated rural communities frequently show lower average blood pressures than their relatives living in urban areas. When aboriginal peoples move to cities and adopt Western lifestyles, one of the earliest detectable physiological responses is increased blood pressure. This relocation effect has been measured in peoples as genetically diverse as Eskimo, New Guinea highlanders, Solomon Islanders, and Australian Aborigines. In their native environments, not only is there no hypertension, but there is no increase in blood pressure with age, as is typically recorded for Europeans and persons of European ancestry. In addition, nomadic tribes of East Africa, normally with low pressure patterns, increase blood pressure when they adopt a sedentary lifestyle. The same experience is shared by numerous other tribal groups throughout Africa (Hutt and Burkitt, 1986). A feature common among these low-blood-pressure communities is a low salt intake, while diverse ethnic groups on high-salt diets show a similar history of rising blood pressure with age. The salt intake level and blood pressure relationship is not as simple as once thought, however. Other factors, such as the intake of potassium, are influential; an increase in this element in proportion to sodium lowers the "salt risk" factor.

Regardless of the causes, hypertension is a serious risk factor in cardiovascular diseases (CVD), and together with diet (the rich, high-fat, high-protein diet of developed countries) effects an increase in the mortality from these diseases. The CVD rate has been declining during the past decade in the United States, partly because of the recognition of the influence of diet and an appreciation of the need for exercise. Cardiovascular mortality, however, remains at the top of the list of leading causes of death and is often referred to as a "disease of affluence." The consumption of an excess of calories, through a refined-carbohydrate, high-fat diet, leads to a state of overnutrition and its disease sequel, as can be clearly demonstrated by the increases observed among developing countries when a segment of the population adopts a Western diet and sedentary lifestyle.

Cancer (malignant neoplasms) A variety of malignant neoplasms are grouped under the term *cancer* because they have certain characteristics in common. A malignant neoplasm is formed when a collection of cells radically change their normal functions and begin to multiply rapidly in uncontrolled growth, which eventually leads to a spreading and an overcoming of healthy tissues in other parts of the body. There are 100 varieties of this disease, classified according to the site or organ in which they originate (lung, skin, breast, prostate, colon, and so on). Certain cancers are more lethal than others, and approximately 50 percent of malignancies may prove to be fatal. The fatality rate depends a great deal on the type of neoplasm, the length of time it had grown before detection, and, of course, the treatment. The cure rate of skin cancers (basal and squamous types) is close to 100 percent, whereas it is less than 50 percent for lung cancer and for the third type of skin cancer, melanoma. About 24 percent of deaths in the United States are due to malignant neoplasms, compared with the 40 percent caused by cardiovascular disease. Though heart disease–related deaths have leveled off and have begun a decline, deaths from cancer have continued to climb; the rate increased by 6.3 percent between 1973 and 1992 (NIH Publication, 1995). There has been some success in bringing down rates of certain types of cancer but the overall rate remains high. In the developing world, cancer mortality is growing as urbanization and industrialization increase.

Causes of many cancers are still obscure—that is, the mechanisms that cause cells to become malignant are not known for certain, though there are several studies that point to a mutation in the somatic cells' DNA that energizes growth stimulation and receptor systems (Ames et al., 1995). Ionizing radiation from X-rays, nuclear power, or cosmic rays has long been known to have such mutagenic effects. In addition, persons who have been exposed to fallout from atomic testing have two to three times the national average for leukemia. Another source, ultraviolet rays from the sun, causes skin cancers, which occur most frequently in fairer-skinned persons and usually on the backs of the hands and parts of the face. Skin cancer is more likely in those fair-skinned persons whose occupations keep them outdoors a good part of the day (see Chapter 5).

In addition to these mutagens, a number of environmental risk factors have been listed for different types of malignancies. Close correlations are seen between certain diets and cancers of the stomach and colon; between alcohol and esophagus, throat, and mouth cancer; and between tobacco smoke and lung cancer. A long list of organic chemicals and substances like asbestos fibers are also implicated as causes of cancers of the lung, liver, and bladder, especially because workers exposed to them through their occupations have an extremely high incidence of certain types of cancer (lung cancer among asbestos plant workers, for example). Cancers of the lung, large intestine, and breast cause about half of all cancer deaths. Lung cancer, described by Cairns (1975:69) as "a disease of the twentieth century," is closely related to cigarette smoking; the risk of lung cancer is fifty times greater in smokers than in nonsmokers. Many health officials have pointed out that if tobacco smoking were abolished, this form of cancer would be nearly eliminated, though air pollution is considered a contributing cause. Further evidence is provided by the rising incidence of lung cancer among females, who, as a group, began to adopt the smoking habit some twenty to thirty years after the males. The rate among women was more than three times as great in 1985 as in 1950, whereas the male rate increased 2.7 times during this period but is now decreasing. Though tobacco use in much of the developed world has declined this past decade, especially in the United States, it is on the increase in many less developed countries, especially throughout Asia. China now consumes one-quarter of the world's cigarette production. Lung diseases of all types are expected to increase, while a decline is already evident in the developed countries (Lopez, 1990a).

Food habits are another likely cause of certain types of cancers. A diet high in meat and fat but low in cereals (especially unrefined) appears to be closely linked to cancer of the large intestine; a significant factor appears to be the low amount of dietary fiber in diets high in meat, fat, and refined carbohydrates. The distribution of colon cancer corresponds closely with dietary quality, and this form of cancer varies considerably between countries; the MDC have the highest incidence (Burkitt, 1971). Because of this relationship to polysaturated fats in the diet, a great deal of attention has been directed to the fat and fiber content consumed by wealthy nations. The results have reinforced the earlier observations of dietary influences (Cohen, 1987).

The most frequent cancer in women, breast cancer, has a world distribution similar to that of colon cancer in males. Because this distribution closely follows dietary quality, it is possible that some factor(s) are lost in the refined diet. Women on refined diets lacking in whole grain have higher rates of breast cancer (American women, for example). Though the evidence is not all in yet, it seems that the element selenium and vitamin E may be the factors involved, because these substances are found in abundance in many whole grains but are mostly lost during the refining process. Test results have shown the antioxidant properties of selenium and vitamin E, which work to protect cell membranes from oxidation by products of cell metabolism (Combs and Scott, 1977). The general functions of selenium in human nutrition are becoming better understood, as well as its influence on certain cancer sites (Levander, 1987). The environmental influence of diet rather than genetic factors, is supported by the example of Japanese women who migrated to Hawaii. Here, within two generations, their breast cancer rates were nearer those of Hawaiian women (80 per 100,000) than to those in Japan (11 per 100,000). However, there is a growing number of genes that have been implicated in the susceptibility for the growth of certain types of tumors.

The preceding examples plus others suggest that many cancers, perhaps 70 to 90 percent, are environmentally determined (see Cairns, 1975; Mayer, 1983; Trichopoulos et al., 1996). The data on diet, the incidence of environmental pollutants, the use of alcohol, and smoking all point to this possibility. Additional evidence is provided by a comparison of ethnic groups that have migrated and adopted the new diets of their new homelands. Japan has a very high rate of stomach cancer, but Japanese immigrants in California have significantly lower incidence. The sons of immigrants have an even lower incidence, one that is much closer to that experienced by Americans of European ancestry (Table 8-6). The high frequency of stomach cancer in Japan may be due to a diet that contains large quantities of salt fish and pickled vegetables. Other groups with similar diets also have high rates of this disease: Iceland,

TABLE 8-6   Cancer Incidence of U.S. Ethnic Groups (per 100,000 population)

ETHNIC GROUP	LUNG	BREAST (F)	STOMACH	PROSTATE (M)	COLON
EuroA	45.4	46.9	8.6	26.7	31.0
AfrA	62.5	40.2	15.4	46.1	11.7
Hispanic	34.3	54.1	15.7	—	—
Chinese (Calif.)	53.5	30.7	15.0	15.5	32.3
Chinese (Hawaian)	35.9	31.8	12.0	20.1	12.0
Japanese (Calif)	20.3	35.2	31.4	7.0	31.9
Japanese (Hawaian)	30.4	27.1	31.4	22.4	29.1

EuroA = European American; AfrA = African American

Source: Data selected from Polednak,1989.

Finland, and Norway, for example, where large quantities of dried, salted fish are eaten.

Further evidence of environmental effects on the course of the disease is offered by the increase of cancer incidence with age. Cairns described the population older than sixty years of age as the group at greatest risk. He reasoned that the longer one is exposed to carcinogenic factors, the greater the chance of developing the disease; the effects of many carcinogenic substances may not show up until twenty to forty years after exposure. With an increasing number of persons living into their eighties, a higher cancer rate is to be expected. Finally, the work environment has proved to contain many substances that are carcinogenic, but for many, the tumors will not appear until years later. Asbestos fibers, silicates in quartz dust, and polyvinyl chloride (a cause of liver cancer) lead the list of dangerous substances, which includes insecticides and organic solvents, many of which have been too recently introduced into the environment to allow us to understand their long-term biological effects fully.

Diabetes   The disease diabetes mellitus is a complex syndrome principally characterized by the inability to maintain blood sugar levels within a normal range. This condition of "glucose intolerance" has a variety of causes: the insufficiency of insulin (a pancreatic hormone regulating glucose levels), cellular insensitivity to the action of insulin, an excess of glucagon (another hormone of the pancreas), and a host of other factors—some caused by rare genetic defects of carbohydrate metabolism. The most frequent expressions of the disease are classified into two categories: type I, juvenile or insulin dependent (IDDM), and type II, an adult-onset form or non–insulin dependent (NIDDM). The juvenile or IDDM type is less frequent, has a significant genetic influence for susceptibility to certain pancreatic virus, and the symptoms appear by adolescence or young adulthood. It is controlled, principally by insulin injection. Type II, NIDDM, is the most common form afflicting world populations, and high blood glucose levels with related symptoms usually appear after forty years of age. There is a genetic component influencing susceptibility suggested by family and twin studies, but there are significant environmental influences, principally dietary, which have been identified. With major dietary and lifestyle changes in many populations, type II diabetes has increased dramatically over the past decades and continues to rise (Harris, 1990). Because it has become a significant health threat and is now one of the leading causes of death, the balance of the discussion will consider only this type of diabetes.

Once only the twenty-seventh commonest cause of death, diabetes has now reached near-epidemic proportions and is the seventh most frequent cause of death in the United States. Though medical treatment has kept the death rate from rising further, the number of diabetics has increased by 60 percent among whites and 120 percent among African Americans between 1966 and 1981. Today, there are approximately ten million cases reported in the United States, with 500,000 new cases added each year. Because a diabetic, over the years, gradually develops impaired circulation and is more prone to kidney failure, heart disease, and blindness by late middle age, the number of people involved and the cost to a population in diabetic-related illness and death is even higher than that from diabetes alone (U.S. Dept. of Health and Human Services, *Diabetes in America*, 1985).

Though there is a hereditary influence, this disease is closely linked to overnutrition; diabetes distribution has followed the spread of an affluent diet high in refined carbohydrates. In developing countries diabetes is found mainly among the wealthier classes in urban areas. For example, among the rich urban residents of India, diabetes is twice as likely to develop as among the rural poor. Further, though rare among Japanese women before the end of World War II, diabetes is now the eighth most frequent cause of death among this group. In Puerto Rico, though the general health of the population improved during the economic boom of the 1960s, diabetes rose from twelfth place to become the eighth most frequent cause of death (Eckholm, 1977).

Further evidence of the influence of Western-type[7] diets is provided by the experiences of populations like Australian Aborigines and several groups of Native Americans. The Pima and Papago of Southern Arizona are especially predisposed to diabetes in middle age; more than 60 percent of the adults aged forty-five to sixty-five were diagnosed as diabetic, which was a 50 percent increase since the epidemiological survey of 1965. Other Native American groups also have significantly higher rates than the U.S. average

---

[7]The term *Western-type diet* refers to the typical high-fat, high-protein, refined-carbohydrate diet of the more developed countries.

(up to nineteen times as high); in addition, Mexican Americans also show a high incidence of diabetes (Knowler et al., 1990). Other ethnic differences are seen among African Americans, who had twice the diabetic rate found among whites, with females of both groups showing a higher rate than the males (Harris, 1990). Among Australian Aborigines who have adopted Western diets (high in sugar and flour), the incidence of diabetes has been found to be 10 percent compared with only 2.3 percent among a European population living near the Aboriginal reserve where the study was carried out (Kirk et al., 1985).

Throughout the Pacific, similar high diabetes rates are reported for those Polynesians or Melanesians who have "urbanized" and adopted the Western diet, ceased to work as hard as they did formerly, and substantially increased their average body weight. People on the island of Nauru are a classic example of the detrimental health effects of a changing lifestyle. This small Pacific island is populated by people with one of the world's highest diabetic rates, about 42.2 percent of the adults. The disease was unknown before 1945 but, following the mining of the island's rich phosphate deposits, the population's income rose to $34,000 per capita, another world record. With this newfound wealth they radically changed their living habits, purchasing all of the available goods of the developed world from airplanes to motorcycles, and especially imported foods. The result is near-universal obesity and a record incidence of diabetes (Zimmet, 1982).

There is no single explanation for this dramatic difference between ethnic groups. There is a probability, however, that certain groups are genetically better adapted to the type of diet humans had consumed for 99 percent of the species' existence, a diet highly variable in quantity with a large mixture of complex carbohydrates. Neel (1962, 1982) offered a hypothesis he called the "thrifty genotype," which could explain the food-storage capacity of certain peoples. He noted that hunters' and gatherers' diets range from "feast to famine," with times of scarcity alternating with times of plenty, when the people gorge themselves. During these times, persons with the physiological ability to convert and store the excess food as body fat are at an advantage. The surplus food energy enables them to endure the periodic episodes of starvation. Neel proposed that their insulin-producing beta cells in the pancreas are more sensitive to stimulus, and the insulin increased rapidly and aided in this energy storage. If such persons, however, continuously consumed large quantities of refined carbohydrates during a long period, as in the case of so many people today, they would exhaust their insulin-secreting potential by middle age. They would then become unable to regulate their blood-glucose levels within physiologically acceptable limits. Another advantage of efficient energy storage was offered by Prior (1971), who suggested that Polynesians, famous for their long sea voyages in open canoes, were an example of a population who could rapidly become obese on a food surplus. This characteristic served them well in ancient times on the open ocean. Even in the tropical climate of the South Pacific, cold temperatures can be a problem when the sun goes down; the temperature drops rapidly and people in small outrigger canoes are exposed to cold winds, causing a rapid loss of body heat. Persons with thicker fatty layers were better insulated and thus protected from metabolic heat loss; such individuals would also have an excess of stored energy. Today, this predisposition for rapid weight gain, once an advantage, now contributes to a high incidence of type II diabetes.

THE DEVELOPING WORLD AND EPIDEMIOLOGICAL TRANSITIONS

The rise of these several chronic diseases, especially among people of the more developed countries, illustrates the impact of environment on human survival and, eventually, will influence the composition of the human genome. In the less developed countries (LDC) where the growing populations are undergoing a rapid change in diet and lifestyle, the epidemiological transition is not complete. Some groups of the wealthier classes have entered the final phase where the chronic diseases have risen to significant levels, but infectious diseases still remain the leading causes of morbidity and mortality for the majority in the developing world, and, hence, the major causes of deaths in the world. One-third of the 51,000,000 deaths worldwide in 1993 were due to infectious diseases, and 99 percent of these deaths occurred in the LDC. Most were caused by the "big four": acute respiratory infections, diarrheal diseases (the leading cause of death among children under five), tuberculosis, and malaria.

In the developed world, we live longer and suffer more diseases of late onset, and infectious diseases are no longer the threat to survival they were in the early 1900s. Such diseases now account for only about 1 percent of the total mortality. But as if to demonstrate that humans, wherever they live, are still at risk, several new virus strains have made periodic appearances causing high mortality. Among these have been numerous cases in Europe and the United States of Lassa, Ebola, and Marberg "fever." The course of the infections, causing high fever and severe uncontrollable hemorrhaging, is usually short, with high mortality; the first recorded outbreak of the Ebola epidemic in Zaire in 1976 claimed 90 percent of the infected victims. A more recent epidemic in 1995 quickly killed 244 people, and only quick action by the health authorities prevented its spread to Zaire's capital 100 miles away. Some outbreaks still claim as many as 90 percent of those infected. Some of these viruses appear to be maintained in a reservoir in Central Africa where periodic outbreaks occur with high mortality, but their source is not actually known. What is documented is that the viruses have been carried by infected travelers and by monkeys imported for lab experiments. A readable but very alarming book, *The Hot Zone*, by Richard Preston, describes some of these episodes of the transmission of these dangerous viruses. While the earliest outbreaks of these "hot" viruses attracted our fearful attention in the 1970s, another deadly organism had already spread around the world and was about to announce its presence as a new disease syndrome—AIDS.

The acquired immune deficiency syndrome (AIDS) was first recognized as a disease syndrome among homosexual men in the United States in 1981. These individuals were diagnosed with respiratory and other infections that did not respond to treatment. About a third of them also had a rare form of cancer, Kaposi's sarcoma. In general, they suffered from repeated opportunistic infections because of a suppressed immune system; the T cells of the lymphocytes (see Chapter 3), instead of increasing as they should, declined by as much as 50 percent when confronted by any of several infectious organisms. As the number of cases began to climb, an extensive search was made to isolate the agent that infected and gradually destroyed a major set of cells of the immune system. By 1983 the HIV (human immunodeficiency virus) was identified as the cause of AIDS, and it was being discovered in heterosexual populations in Europe, Africa, and Asia, as well as in North America. Spread by blood transfusions or blood clotting products used by hemophiliacs, and by heterosexual contact, AIDS presented the world with a newly recognized infectious disease of pandemic proportions.

The virus has a long latency period of seven to ten years before the disease symptoms appear. This had permitted the near silent spread of HIV throughout the 1980s, but the virus probably has been around much longer, since the 1950s. Though its origins are obscure, HIV is believed to have spread undetected through Zaire and Zambia in the 1970s and then into Europe and the Western Hemisphere, infecting people in Belgium, France, Haiti and the United States. Whatever its origins, the virus has been responsible for an increasing number of AIDS patients. Over 600,000 cases were reported by 1992 and the actual figure is believed to be 2.5 million, with many nations underreporting. AIDS is now the ninth leading cause of death in the United States and the number one killer of males ages 25–44; females of this age group are at just a sixth of this rate but are gaining fast (Statistical Abstract of the United States, 1995). Mortality from AIDS is much higher in sub-Saharan Africa; 1.5 million of 2.5 million deaths there in 1993 were attributed to AIDS and the rate is expected to increase, causing twice the number of deaths that would have occurred if the disease had not been present (see Jamison and Hobbs, 1994).

These mortality rates, though alarming, are small by comparison to what the future may hold, given the increasing number of people around the world infected with HIV. Midyear, 1993, there were 13 million adults and 1 million children infected, and the World Health Organization projects an increase to between 30 and 40 million by century's end. With a seemingly slow start, no region has escaped the spread of this virus. Africa leads the world at present with about a million new people infected each year, but Asia is catching up fast, with a projected 1.2 million HIV carriers by 1999. Given these large numbers and the probability that 50 percent of HIV-infected will develop the disease, AIDS mortality will skyrocket in the next century.

A New World but Old Diseases

World environments and the size and ethnic composition of the human species have been changing at an accelerated rate since the beginning of this century. Where people live and what they do has also been undergoing rapid change. Starting from a technological base established during the Industrial Revolution of the eighteenth and nineteenth centuries, all of our systems of manufacturing, communications, and transportation have risen to new levels of efficiency, encouraging mass movements of people around the globe. Improvements in agricultural technology have boosted productivity, and developments in medical science have permitted a population explosion that has ensured that there are hundreds of millions more people migrating and changing settlement patterns. In the process, there have been radical changes in human uses of space and an increased exploitation of environmental resources. These changes are too numerous to detail here, and the ecological issues involved are better addressed in specialized texts, but a few of the impacts of change on human survival have a particular influence on biological variability of the human species and will be considered.

First is the use of space that contributes to a redistribution of people, increasing population density. More and more people are migrating to expanding urban centers, especially in the the developing countries. In 1976 there were 100 cities of a million or more in each of the two major world regions (developed and less developed). Since then, world urbanization has proceeded at a growth rate of about 4.5 percent per year in the LDCs, fed by a natural population increase and by rural-to-urban migration, compared with only 0.8 percent for the developed countries. This means that, by 1990, urban populations in the LDCs totaled 1.5 billion and are projected to rise to 2.3 billion (or 45 percent of the total world population) by the year 2000, compared with the more developed countries, which are projected to remain at 0.9 billion over this same period. The scale of increase may be comprehended if we note that cities like Lagos, Nigeria; Mexico City; and Bombay, India have grown from under three million each in 1950 to nearly fifteen million by 1995. By comparison, London required over a century to grow from one to eight million residents (Ashford, 1995).

The impact of this nearly one million people per week moving into urban areas is being felt throughout the world. The lack of adequate shelter, or safe drinking water, or sanitation for a third or more of the urban populations means that the health and very survival of hundreds of millions are threatened. The crowded conditions, poor diet, and lack of basic city services place such populations at risk of epidemic diseases, both old and new. Incidence of diarrheal diseases and the others of the "big four," already high, will probably rise given the increased population densities and the polluted environments. Old diseases like typhoid, diphtheria, measles, and even typhus are already reappearing, as is cholera, spreading in a new world pandemic, and there is an occasional appearance of plague like the 1994 outbreak in India, in which 6,000 people were infected (80 percent from urban shantytowns). Early diagnosis and fast action by public health officials, aided by antibiotics and insecticides, have usually contained the epidemics and have kept mortality to lower levels than in the past. Insect vectors are developing immunity, however, to the more widely used insecticides, and many antibiotics are no longer effective in treatment of several types of infections.

Like the turning of the tide, as one writer described it, microbes that were once easily controlled by antibiotics have returned in newer, more virulent forms. Despite an announcement by the United States surgeon general in 1969 that "we can close the book on infectious diseases," several major microbes have persisted and are now an even greater threat to human health. Staphylococcus bacteria, the cause of a variety of infections of the skin, internal organs, and bone, now have several immune strains. Gonorrheal bacteria also have developed strains resistant to penicillin, and even malarial parasites have evolved varieties that resist the standard drugs used to treat the disease. These all pose problems for medical treatment, but the greatest threat is from an old disease enemy, tuberculosis.

Once a major cause of death among populations in European and American cities—in 1900 it was the number one cause of death in the United States—tuberculosis, or TB, has declined to insignificant levels in this century as improvements in housing, diet, and general health have been made. The use of antibiotics contributed to a further decline in the number of active cases of TB reported. There was a steady decrease until 1985, when the number of new cases annually began to increase, rising 18 percent from 1985 to 1991, and the number has been climbing ever since. The increase has been mainly among inner-city residents, mostly among those groups classified as "nonwhites." The homeless, drug abusers, and AIDS patients are especially at risk. A substantial number of the new cases were caused by a new drug-resistant strain of bacteria.

Most of us harbor the tuberculin bacterium but do not suffer from the symptoms of the active disease. As long as our general state of health is good and our immune system functions efficiently we are able to resist the growth and spread of the tuberculin organism. If our health declines and we are repeatedly exposed to infection, our immune system will be overchallenged and then the bacteria will seize the opportunity and multiply rapidly. This has happened in AIDS patients and other groups of individuals who, because of economic circumstances or drug abuse, suffer from failing health. When treatment is sought, one or a combination of drugs are given, but in recent years a significant number of patients have failed to respond, and physicians have recognized that there is a new TB bacterium loose in the urban population. Drugs that had been used successfully since 1948 fail to halt the progress of the disease. How widespread this multiple-drug-resistant (MDR) bacterium has become is not known but its presence in many patients has alerted health officials, who are gravely concerned about the new wave of tuberculosis. What adds to the threat is the fact that persons carrying the HIV virus are at higher risk and, because of the long dormancy period of HIV, are likely to be a source of a rising caseload of tuberculosis in the coming decades. The rise of drug-resistant strains of TB as well as of several of the other major infectious organisms set the stage for a twenty-first-century revival of epidemics of the old killers, as described by Laurie Garret in her book *The Coming Plague.*

CHANGING ENVIRONMENTS AND NATURAL SELECTION

During those recent times, just a few generations ago, when bacterial and parasitic diseases were at their peak, any gene or gene combination that reduced susceptibility would have had a marked effect on survival. The selective advantage of certain genotypes in an era of massive epidemics would have been an important factor in the biological evolution of *Homo sapiens*, particularly with rapid growth rates and major population shifts during the past few thousand years. The return of the old diseases in newer, more virulent forms adds to the complexity, but the total effect has been the alteration of combinations of disease organisms with which humans are in most frequent contact (McKeown, 1985). The well-documented recent outbreaks, summarized above, can be used to trace a significant change in our disease environment and offer insights into human adaptation.

These changing patterns of disease and mortality undoubtedly effect alteration in gene frequencies, and certain polymorphisms will be selected for or against in the future. Examination of disease influences may provide a way of interpreting population variation and selection through time. Anthropologists attempting to understand human diversity several generations in the future will likely be puzzled by the persistence of many seemingly deleterious genes, unless, of course, they understand human history and consider the alteration of environmental factors and natural selection. As described earlier, infectious diseases influence the survival of people with certain genotypes of the red blood cell antigens, the HLA types of the white blood cells, and the immunoglobulins. Differences in survival rates of heterozygotes and homozygotes for the Tay-Sachs, G6PD, and cystic fibrosis genetic disorders were also described, and, of course, the various hemoglobin variants and their relations to malarial parasites is well established. Added to these examples are large numbers of other inherited metabolic defects whose persistence is difficult to explain on the basis of natural selection. With environmental changes and population growth, however, "genetic load" is certain to vary.

Genetic Load

The usual measure of genetic load is the frequency of lethal or deleterious genes within a population. Every population's gene pool contains a quantity of alleles, either dominant or recessive, which may reduce the fitness of the carrier. As environments are altered, selective forces also change and the intensity of selection at a particular locus may be reduced. An allele that had been detrimental in the former environment may no longer reduce fitness and, in theory, the frequency of the allele would rise through the generations, increasing the "genetic load" of the populations. Today, for example, individuals with some genetic diseases can be maintained by medical treatment and will in many cases live through their reproductive years. They may even pass on the defective allele. Should their environment ever change again—for example, revert back to its original state—then selection would increase to its formerly high intensity and the homozygous recessives would then have a reduced fitness. The magnitude of a population's genetic load, however, is generally underestimated, though some gloomy appraisals of the species point out that everyone is heterozygous for many deleterious genes, and new mutations are continuously added to this load. Medical intervention enables the survival of individuals who suffer from any one of a number of types of inherited metabolic defects and congenital abnormalities. Although such treatment may not eliminate natural selection altogether, it does reduce its effects.

Congenital Defects[8]

There are a number of disorders that, in former times, would have reduced the chances of survival beyond childhood or even beyond infancy. Many defects are now correctable by medical or surgical intervention, and the individuals can survive and lead normal lives. A common disorder like cleft palate (which occurs in 1 out of 2,500 births) often resulted in an early death for the severest cases before this century, but it has been corrected by surgery for many years. A relatively minor muscular defect, pyloric stenosis—an enlargement of the muscle ring controlling the opening between the stomach and small intestine—killed most infants who had it before 1912, because food was prevented from entering the digestive tract from the stomach. Since 1912, this fairly common defect (2 out of 1,000 births) has been corrected by a minor surgical procedure. Numerous other developmental defects of the digestive tract can now be corrected by surgery. Similarly, many defects of the musculoskeletal system may be repaired: Dislocation of the hip or clubfoot are

---

[8]A defect present at birth that may be determined genetically or may be due to an external influence acting on the intrauterine environment. For example, drug addiction, alcoholism, malnutrition, and heavy metal poisoning have all been known to affect fetal development.

examples of conditions that were once significant impairments to an active, healthy life that are now treatable.

Among the greatest achievements in the correction of congenital malformations is in the treatment of heart defects. Since the development of advanced heart surgery techniques, numerous commonly occurring defects of the heart and major blood vessels that were formerly the chief cardiovascular causes of infant death can be repaired. Table 8-7 lists some of the more frequent conditions whose early diagnosis and treatment has saved the lives of thousands of infants. Patent ductus arteriosus is one of the important examples. This blood vessel shutting off some of the blood flow from the pulmonary artery to the aorta (the large artery carrying blood from the heart) during the fetal stage may remain open after birth and functioning, depriving the infant of a portion of the oxygenated blood leaving the left ventricle of the heart. Wastefully, this oxygenated blood is shifted back to the lungs without passing through the rest of the circulatory system. Such a condition places the infant at high risk, and even if the person survives, growth and physical activity are seriously impaired. This and other more critical defects are amenable to surgical correction, and this has been of great advantage to those populations where modern medicine is available. In many of the less developed countries, however, infant deaths from these and other congenital defects remain high because of the lack of medical care.

Genetic Disease

In all, there are more than 2,000 simply inherited disorders known, and several can now be successfully treated to enable the afflicted person to lead a relatively normal life. A classic example is hemophilia A, which is inherited as an X-linked recessive that causes a deficiency in the action of a globulin factor (factor VIII) and prevents the normal clotting of blood. This affliction occurs in approximately 1 in 25,000 males. Before treatment was available, it usually caused death at an early age. Through treatment with blood coagulant factors extracted from plasma, many of the hemophiliac's problems have been reduced, and life expectancy has been extended well beyond the previ-

TABLE 8-7   Examples of Congential Cardiovascular Abnormalities Amenable to Surgery in Infants[a]

Ventricular septal defect	Coarction of aorta
Atrial septal defect	Truncus arteriosis
Patent ductus arteriosus	Transposition of great arteries
Pulmonary stenosis	Tricuspid atresia
Aortic stenosis	

[a]With the rapid advances in the diagnosis and treatment of the neonate and even the fetus, many congenital deformities that formerly caused death can now be corrected. This partial listing, adapted from *The Merck Manual of Diagnosis and Therapy*, provides some examples.

ously expected eighteen years.[9] A more common genetic disease, inherited as an autosomal recessive gene, is cystic fibrosis—one of the most commonly known errors of metabolism in Caucasian populations (1 out of every 2,000 or 3,000 live births). Persons with this condition have a malfunctioning of the exocrine glands in many of their tissues (the pancreas in particular). They suffer from clogged bronchial tubes that become obstructed with an accumulation of thick mucous deposits and are prone to respiratory infections and malfunctioning of the pancreas. Before treatment was available, most people with this disease died in early childhood; now, careful management of cystic fibrosis patients has extended their life expectancy into adulthood, about the mid-thirties.

Another affliction, retinoblastoma, an inherited malignancy of the retina of the eye that appears early in childhood, will cause death if untreated. Surgical and medical treatment can now increase the chances of survival. In addition to such genetic defects, several hormone deficiencies influencing metabolic processes have also been identified, and treatments have been developed. Growth hormone deficiencies and other pituitary deficiencies can be alleviated by hormone supplements, and persons with such defects can lead normal lives and reproduce with the chance of passing on that genetic component that influenced the appearance of the defect.

The survival of individuals with these genetic diseases increases the frequency of the defective genes in future populations. The increase in gene defects, however, will not result in a "plague" overwhelming our gene pool. Most of the defects occur at low frequencies, and any increase would be a slow process over a long period of many generations.

ETHNIC GROUPS AND DISEASE

Several of these congenital abnormalities and genetic diseases occur more frequently in some populations than in others, as described earlier in Chapters 3 and 4. Certain afflictions are associated with one or more of the ethnic groups, and several of the major diseases are listed in Table 8-8. An explanation for the relative frequencies of these ailments that are at least partially influenced by genetic factors is not easy to come by. We might consider that our phenotypes are more a product of our environment than of our genes, since their expression depends on the context of environmental influences. Differences in diet, living habits, and a population's history all contribute to interpopulation variability. There are significant environmental factors affecting tumors, cardiovascular problems, diabetes, and hypertension, as examples. Further, consider the oxygen-carrying capacity of our red blood cells and

---

[9]Because the treatment requires the use of blood products, a tragic side effect has been the infection of many hemophiliacs with the human immune deficiency virus.

TABLE 8-8   Disease Incidence in Selected Ethnic Groups

ETHNIC GROUPS	RELATIVELY HIGH PREVALENCE OF THESE DISORDERS
African Black	Abnormal hemoglobin HB^s, Hb^c, thalassemia
	G6PD deficiency (African type)
	Hypertension
	Polydactyly
	Cervical cancer
	Sarcoidosis
American Indians	
Papago	Diabetes mellitus
Apache	Congenital hip dislocation
Ashkenazic Jews	Tay-Sachs disease
	Pentosuria
	Stub fingers
	Bloom's disease
	Leukemia
	Diabetes mellitus
Chinese	Thalassemia
	G6PD deficiency (Chinese type)
	Nasopharyngeal cancer
Europeans	
Northern	Phenylketonuria
	Pernicious anemia
	Cleft palate
Southern	G6PD deficiency (Mediterranean type)
	Thalassemia
Japanese	Acatalasia
	Oguchi's disease
	Cleft lip-palate
	Gastric cancer

Sources: Damon, 1962, 1971; and McKusick, 1967.

note that this capacity is also affected by a number of enzymes and not just by the hemoglobin structure itself. The high rate of diabetes among several ethnic groups in North America and the Pacific region may have other causes, as discussed earlier; one of the most likely is their adoption of a modern diet rich in refined carbohydrates. Their insulin-secreting cells, adapted through evolution to another type of diet, are ill equipped to cope with diets that require a steady maintenance of high insulin levels.

In the case of several congenital conditions, though, breeding behavior and population size have played a major role. Thus we find that among Hawaiians, for instance, clubfoot (caused by a partially penetrant dominant allele) occurs at a frequency of 68 per 10,000 births in contrast to the 11 per 10,000 in Caucasians and 6 per 10,000 in Asians. The high frequency among Hawaiians probably relates to the small size of the original founder population, in addition to a high degree of inbreeding during the earlier generations.

Examples of ethnic groups and genetic disease are illustrated by three autosomal recessive diseases—Tay-Sachs, cystic fibrosis, and PKU, which are most commonly found among Europeans or persons of European ancestry, and seldom among Asians or Africans. Even within this rather narrow distribution, there are striking differences among the several European ethnic groups. Tay-Sachs, for example, has a gene frequency of approximately 0.015 in eastern European Jews. By contrast, other Jewish populations and non-Jewish Europeans have a frequency of less than 0.001. This high frequency may be explained by the founder's effect, and also by heterozygote resistance to tuberculosis. Similar explanations have been offered for the high frequencies of PKU among western Europeans, including the possible advantage of the heterozygote (who has paler skin) in a region with an incidence of low ultraviolet radiation (McCullough, 1978). The question of the frequency of cystic fibrosis is more difficult, though the factor of the high excretion of sodium chloride by the skin through the sweat glands may hold some clues. The final explanation of the distributions of these genes will have to await further study of their biochemical influences on the general metabolism of the heterozygote.

GENETIC COUNSELING AND SELECTIVE BREEDING

With a possible rise in the genetic load of *Homo sapiens*, the eugenics question is again before us, since, at first glance, a logical course might seem to be regulation and control of mating to attempt to counteract an increase of detrimental mutants. It is fairly obvious that persons who carry a dominant gene that results in some defective development like achondrodystrophy, retinoblastoma, or Huntington's disease should consider carefully before producing children, but the case of carriers of recessive genes of low frequency is somewhat different. The chance that two persons who carry the same recessive alleles will mate is fairly remote, but the probability increases with marriages between cousins or between individuals from the same small endogamous population. In such cases, professional genetic counseling would alert the potential mates to the possibilities of producing defective offspring, particularly if defects are known to have occurred in previous generations.

Now with the newer techniques of DNA analysis, as described in Chapters 2 and 3, the chromosome and sometimes the actual locus of each gene may be identified, as has been done for many in the last five years. Much of the work on human genome mapping to date has been a stimulus for the biotech industry to develop tests to identify carriers of mutant alleles that are associated with certain diseases. There are, as of 1996, a number of tumor repressor genes (genes whose protein products affect cell division and/or DNA multiplication). Three mutant forms have been associated with breast cancer, another four with colorectal tumors, another five are implicated in melanoma and brain tumors, and there is one for retinoblastoma (Rb) whose normal form may prove to be a more general tumor suppressor (Nasmyth, 1996). Another series of reports describe genes affecting diabetes (insulin dependent type), emphysema, cystic fibrosis, Huntington's disease, and ten to twenty types of leukemia. What is overlooked in the wealth of new data about human chromosome structure is that, even with a gene's discovery, its function in human physiology is not always identified. How the mutant gene functions in a large family with a number of Huntington's disease victims is still not known. Persons express the disease symptoms differently and they may appear at an earlier or later age. Likewise for the numerous tumor-related genes; the course and onset of the tumor development varies widely. What is most important is that these tumor genes do not act in isolation (Trichopoulos et al., 1996). The environment—diet in many cases—is influential. The possession of a gene (with few exceptions) does not "cause" the disease. There is a probable predisposition under certain circumstances for a person with one of the genes for colon cancer to develop the tumor, but many do not. Many cases of colon cancer, however, occur in people without these genes.

The past decade has been a busy time for human genetics, and technology has swept us forward faster than we realize; in the process, difficult ethical issues have been raised. In fact, many of them are similar to those that confronted us at the beginning of the century as Mendelian genetics became established. Do the genes we carry predetermine our lot in life and should the carriers of certain genes, identified by physical characteristics or behaviors, be treated differently? There were no easy answers then, and what followed was a near century of controversy. Now we do not have to rely on simple visual appraisal or questionable subjective judgments, however. There are precise ways to measure and label genetic factors. But are we better off now?

One of the major results of the Human Genome project to date has been its stimulus to the biotech industry, which is designing new tests at a rapid rate. These tests, though often costly, can identify a carrier of a particular gene of interest—the BRC (breast cancer gene), for example. What does one do with this information then? Supposedly it increases the probability of getting the disease sometime in life if there is a family history, but what about those carriers of the gene without a family history of the disease? What is more important than identification of an individual case is genetic screening in general, as has been proposed. We all carry a number of mutations in our genome but continue to lead normal lives without effect, but genetic screening could turn up many of these alleles identified as influencing a predisposition to certain diseases. The mere presence of such alleles could be construed as a "pre-existing condition" and, hence, as grounds for denial of health insurance, a process that is already occurring (see Hubbard and Wald, 1993). Carriers of some alleles could also be denied employment on the general grounds that they are at a higher risk in some occupations or environments, as has been the case for carriers of the sickle cell trait described in Chapter 4. In sum, what the genetic technology has done is to open up a Pandora's box of societal troubles, while at the same time offering excellent opportunities for understanding human biological diversity. A clearer understanding of the meaning of genetic diversity is essential.

A return to the eugenics of an earlier era is impossible now with the advances in our knowledge of human heredity. We are no longer liable to confuse a dietary deficiency with "bad" genes, as was the case with people suffering from pellagra (a vitamin deficiency disease), when a whole group was stigmatized as being hereditary deficients. Nor are we liable to consider a single test score or the size of the brain a marker of intelligence, though there are some problems here because of the continued attempts to do so. We have reached a new plateau in biotechnology and we must also achieve one in the understanding of the distribution of human diversity.

ONGOING EVOLUTION AND *HOMO SAPIENS* OF THE FUTURE

We are a species whose genetic adaptations were to the conditions of an evolutionary past, mostly to a preagricultural, paleolithic form of life when population density was low and people were constantly on the move. This was the lifestyle of our species until approximately 12,000 years ago, when many *Homo sapiens* became sedentary and adopted an agricultural technology. At that time, selection began to favor new forms, helped along by increases in certain diseases, alteration in mating circles, and an increase in population sizes. Gradually, through the millennia, we have altered some of our gene frequencies. Because our environments are still changing, frequencies of certain genes will continue to alter. With an elaboration of our technologies, however, we are capable of quickly changing environments within a time span much shorter than a human generation. This factor introduces a new element into human evolution: the rapid change in selective forces, which places a heavy burden on our social systems and culture. Evolution is still very much a factor affecting our species, and "ongoing evolution" is still a reality though we have a larger hand in directing it, wittingly or unwittingly.

There will be a continuing evolution of several aspects of human physiology, probably those that relate to life in the modern, cramped, and polluted environments of a highly industrialized society. Populations of the future will be crowded into increasingly larger urban centers, especially in the less developed countries. This will increase the potential for disease transmission, not only of those organisms long familiar as causes of epidemics but also of newer and more virulent strains that are likely to appear. We have been witnessing the appearance of insects resistant to DDT, for example, which has contributed to a rise in malaria. The *falciparum* parasite, the cause of the most deadly type of malaria, is resistant to several of the antimalarial drugs, and treatment must shift to new drugs. The same holds true for numerous bacteria that are continually responding to drug treatment by developing resistant strains as described above.

The changes in dwelling space will intensify the psychological stresses of twenty-first-century society. Natural selection will probably operate more stringently on the urban dweller, subjected to noise, crowding, and foul air. These conditions place a burden on our neuroendocrine system, often stretching our psychological balance to the breaking point. The high mental-illness rate (one-fourth of all hospital admissions), the increased use of mood-altering drugs, and the rise of stress-related diseases are all part of the cost of urban living. The effect of air pollution is illustrated by the current incidence of respiratory diseases, notably bronchitis and emphysema, which have shown a steady increase over the last twenty-five years.

These stresses of living in an urban setting will likely reduce the frequency of certain genotypes and increase others. We have at least one genotype to which we can point as an example. The reports of air pollution in the cities list the increase of deaths during the worst episodes. Table 8-9 shows the significant increase in deaths from respiratory diseases during one of London's worst periods of air pollution. The elderly and persons with respiratory problems are usually the victims, and a major respiratory condition, emphysema, though rare before 1950, increases in frequency each year. A major symptom of emphysema is the loss of elasticity of the alveoli (air sacs of the lungs) and progressive reduction in pulmonary capacity. Many persons with this condition are deficient for an enzyme, alpha-1-antitrypsin, proteinase inhibitor, which has the function of neutralizing the activity of enzymes that break down proteins. Certain alleles, inherited as recessives, are less effective in their inhibitory effect. These enzymes, mainly elastase, are then free to degrade (by partial digestion) certain of the mucous membranes of the body. The tissues of the lungs are among those most sensitive and, hence, the progressive loss of elasticity appears to be greater among antitrypsin deficients.

TABLE 8-9 Registered Deaths in London Administrative County by Age: Comparison of 7-Day Period before the 1952 Episode with the 7-Day Period that Included the Episode of Air Pollution

AGE	7-DAY PERIOD PRECEDING THE EPISODE	7-DAY PERIOD INCLUDING THE EPISODE
Under 4 weeks	16	28
4 weeks to 1 year	12	26
1–14 years	10	13
15–44 years	61	99
45–64 years	237	652
65–74 years	254	717
75 years and over	355	949

Source: From Dubois, 1968.

Major environmental conditions contribute to emphysema (cigarette smoking and air pollution), but the probability of the greater susceptibility of certain genotypes is an important phenomenon to examine (Khoury et al., 1986). One could propose that, given clear air to breathe and without a smoking habit, the alpha-1-antitrypsin–deficient person would stand less risk of developing emphysema. This presents a strong argument for natural selection acting against this genotype in a modern urban setting.

Another example of selection in the future would be the narrowing of the nutritional base among many populations that have shifted to a Western diet. As food quantity becomes more of a problem with the increase of world population, less attention will be paid to quality and nutritional balance will be more difficult to obtain. Also, for years, refinement and processing have been removing many substances (trace elements and vitamins) and adding various adulterates to color and preserve our food. The cumulative effects of such processes are difficult to appreciate at this time, but already many coloring agents and preservatives have been implicated as suspected carcinogens. The removal of trace elements and vitamins may prove to be harmful as well; many of these substances have been recognized as essential for human nutrition; note the previous discussion of selenium and vitamin E. Food processing in the future will probably make greater use of such substitutes as algae and cellulose as sources of nutrients. Since our knowledge of the variation in the human digestive tract is limited, the effects on the human gene pool cannot be measured at this time.

Modern population mobility is another major factor contributing to gene-frequency changes today. Increasingly, we are becoming more urban; mating circles are ever-widening and population isolates are rapidly disappearing. A few generations ago, matings almost always occurred between persons within a limited geographic area—usually the mates' childhood residences had been within a few thousand or even hundreds of yards of each other. In much of the world this remains the case where village, class, or caste endogamy still is maintained. As industrialization and urbanization continue to increase and spread throughout the world, however, our habits and customs are breaking down, and important alterations are occurring in mating circles. Gene exchange occurs over ever-widening areas between mates of diverse ethnic origins. In the nineteenth century and throughout this century, modern transportation, and especially the automobile, have had an even more significant influence on extending population boundaries. This mobility and expansion of mating circles increases the heterozygosity of the human species and decreases the chance of producing homozygous recessives. It increases the influence of assortative mating, however, particularly the preference for mating within one's own socioeconomic group or at the same educational level, while diminishing ethnic considerations. What are called transracial marriages in the industrialized world are on the rise.

The reduced maternal mortality rate and the overall extension of the female reproductive years are also influential in changing gene frequencies. Last century the average age at menarche was 18; however, today, in many countries, it is between 12 and 13 or as low as 11 years. A later onset of menopause is usual today and age of menopause has increased from 44, the average a century ago, to 50. Thus, in many societies, the female reproductive span has been extended from a total of 27 to 36 years. More women are living through their reproductive years and many in the developing countries are marrying earlier, which, along with an increase in teen pregnancies, is significantly increasing fertility rates. Though a variety of contraceptives reduce fecundity, the increased reproductive span and lower maternal mortality rates are major contributions to the rise in fertility, particularly in underdeveloped countries.

All of these factors—the shift in selective forces, population mobility, increased reproductive span, and entirely new disease stresses—contribute to ongoing evolution of modern *Homo sapiens*. What the future holds is difficult to say, but evidence is accumulating, and more is being learned about the genetic basis for human physiological response to the environment. Human variation exists now as it has in the past, though the boundaries, as defined, keep shifting, and new ethnic groups arise while others disappear. Whether we will remain as diverse in the future, a few hundred generations hence, is not possible to predict. We do know, however, that our species is capable of numerous responses to environmental stresses, both by individual homeostatic adjustments in the short term and through genetic combination changes in the population over the long term.

Finally, we should note the prospects held out to us by developments such as recombinant DNA. Will "gene splicing" or genetic engineering enable us to direct our own evolution? We have the capability to breed those animals whose varieties are deemed most desirable and economically beneficial, but will we apply this ability to develop a species of humans that possesses all of the "ideal" attributes? Will we be able to clone or engineer human life at will and thus confront all the moral and ethical dilemmas of "playing God," as one author put it (Goodfield, 1977)? I doubt it, not just because of the technical problems presented by such a project, though they are monumental. Rather, it is the complexity of social organization required for such controlled mating or biological engineering that is overwhelming. There are many positive aspects of genetic engineering to look forward to, however. Great strides have been made in DNA research, and cells deficient in enzyme production can be treated by injection of a manufactured gene with the right code.

The first human experiment with gene replacement took place in 1990. Genetically altered lymphocytes were injected into volunteers suffering from melanoma (the deadly form of skin cancer). The goal was not to replace a gene defect but to infiltrate and destroy tumors with these altered lymphocytes, whose antibody production capacity had been increased by the new gene. Another gene modification trial was aimed at a second disease (caused by the lack of the enzyme adenosine deaminase), an inherited immune disorder in which the child lacks a crucial enzyme that normally protects the T-lymphocyte cells from toxic chemicals. The accumulation of these toxins destroys the body's immune system. Lymphocyte cells were withdrawn from two children with this defect and were altered to carry the DNA code for the missing enzyme, and then the cells were injected back into the bloodstream. The trials were successful, and the children are injected with their altered lymphocyte cells every few months (Erickson, 1992). These successful treatments, together with numerous animal experiments, prove the feasibility of gene alteration, but they were carried out on rare conditions. The difficulties of locating the correct gene and ensuring that there are no side effects from the viral transporting agent has caused scientists to proceed slowly and cautiously. Besides, in more common inherited diseases there are alternative treatments.

A more immediate application has been the synthesis of human insulin by specially programmed bacterial cell cultures. Such a process carried out in the laboratory is much less expensive than the older method of extraction of insulin from animal glands. At this time there are a dozen or more human proteins produced by bacteria with DNA altered to synthesize the desired product. Also, plant genetics will likely continue to make great achievements with new hybrids and even with bacterial control.

Even with the availability of the necessary technical means, the logistics and priorities are overwhelming in their complexity. First, each of these achievements is costly, and these costs are enormous in terms of money, resources, and trained personnel. The "payoff" or return on investment will be relatively small, in contrast to the yields for investment of resources in other areas—plant pathology, high-bred seeds, new energy sources, and so on. As the future unfolds, demands on all resources will increase radically, and priorities will likely be more and more rigidly enforced. There would probably be little support for the cost of technology required for the Human Genome project unless there were promises of rich rewards in terms of curing diseases by altering specific defective genes through gene replacement therapy, which to date has had little success; treatment of disease by diet, hormone replacement, antibiotics, or physical therapy have proven more effective. The advocates of the mapping program offer an additional justification by arguing that the description of the entire genome will tell us "what it means to be human." But "being human" depends on much more than a series of "codes" carried in the nuclei of our cells.

The effort required to locate and define a single gene defect is enormous—witness the ten-year-long effort to locate the gene for Huntington's disease. Though the chromosome has been identified, the actual locus and gene code is still not known. The maze of three billion bases distributed over the forty-six chromosomes presents more than a challenge to any genetic engineering project; it presents an almost impossible dream. Even if the technological problems of gene engineering could be overcome, in the final analysis what will keep evolutionary control out of human hands will be humans themselves.

We have yet to meet the challenges of efficient use of the environment for our billions of people, even though we have the scientific means to do so. The chief problem in dealing with growing population requirements at this point in our history lies not in our technology, but in social institutions that have failed to keep pace with technological advances. Overpopulation, pollution, and the energy crisis are all problems that were described and predicted by several writers decades ago (in a sense, some were like a latter-day Malthus). Many of their predictions proved to be all too accurate, but few, if any, societies have been able or willing to prepare for these events that engulf us at the end of this century. We cannot blame such inadequacy only on indifference or lack of foresight, but rather we must blame inertia. Our social institutions are just slow to respond, and it is this long reaction time in confronting new challenges and new technologies that hampers us as we seek to direct events and to control our fate. For example, much has been accomplished in the fields of genetics and medicine but children still die from "old-fashioned diseases" and these old diseases are returning in force. There remain broad differences in mortality rates and life expectancies experienced by populations of all countries.

Throughout this book I have described several aspects of human diversity, but our knowledge is still limited as we approach the start of a new century and the dawn of a new technological era. Many facets of human biology have yet to be explored. We need to expand our research on human variation and our collection of cellular material from populations around the world. To record the restriction DNA fragments is a major advance, but, more important, we need to change our attitude and perspective. We need to appreciate human diversity for what it is—the result of a species gene pool responding to the stresses of natural selection as modified by behavior or culture. It is not a simple matter of explaining all diversity by the action of natural selection. Other factors are involved and should be considered, such as the breeding population size, the social system, and the population's history. Extensive comparative studies must be made; contrasts should be drawn between members of breeding populations; and the reliance on large, all-encompassing taxons must be avoided. The challenges are there, the frontiers broad: Students must rise to meet these challenges with their questions.

References

ABBIE, A. A. 1967. "Book review: *The Living Races of Man*," *Current Anthrop.*, 8:113–114.

ABBIE, A. A. 1975. *Studies in Physical Anthropology*. Vols. I and II. Canberra: Australian Institute of Aboriginal Studies, RRS5.

ABBIE, A. A., and W. R. ADEY. 1953. "Pigmentation in a central Australian tribe with special reference to fair-headedness." *Am. J. Phys. Anthrop.*, 11:339–359.

AIRD, I., H. H. BENTALL, and J. A. F. ROBERTS. 1953. "A relationship between cancer of the stomach and the ABO groups." *Br. Med. J.*, 1:799–801.

ALLISON, A. C. 1954. "Protection afforded by sickle-cell trait against malarial infection." *Br. Med. J.*, 1:290–294.

ALLISON, A. C., and B. S. BLUMBERG. 1959. "Ability to taste phenylthiocarbamide among Alaskan Eskimos and other populations." *Human Bio.*, 31(4):352–359.

AMES, B. N., L. S. GOLD, and W. C. WILLETT. 1995. "The causes and prevention of cancer." *Proceedings of the National Academy of Sciences*, 92(12):5258–5265.

ANGEL, J. L. 1966. "Porotic hyperostosis anemias, malarias and marshes in prehistoric eastern Mediterranean." *Science*, 153:760–763.

ANTONARAKIS, S. E., C. D. BOEHM, G. R. SERJEANT, C. E. THESIAN, G. J. DOVER, and H. H. KAZAZIAN. 1984. "Origin of the B^S-globin gene in Blacks: The contribution of recurrent mutation or gene conversion or both." *Proceedings of the National Academy of Sciences*, 81:853–856.

ASHFORD, L. S. 1995. *New Perspectives on Population: Lessons from Cairo*. Population Bulletin 50(1). Washington, DC: Population Reference Bureau, Inc.

BAKER, J. R. 1974. *Science, Racism and Social Darwinism: A Review of Race*. London: Oxford University Press.

BAKER, P. T. 1967. "The biological race concept as a research tool." *Am. J. Phys. Anthrop.*, 27:21–25.

BAKER, P. T., J. M. HANNA, and T. S. BAKER, eds. 1986. *The Changing Samoans.* New York: Oxford University Press.

BARNICOT, N. A. 1964. "Taxonomy and variation in modern man." In *The Concept of Race,* ed. Ashley Montagu. New York: Free Press.

BARNICOT, N. A. 1957. "Human pigmentation." *Man,* 57(144):114–120.

BARZUN, J. 1965. *Race: A Study in Superstition.* New York: Harper & Row.

BASU, A. 1969. "The Pahira: A population genetical survey." *Am. J. Phys. Anthrop.,* 31:399–416.

BAYOUMI, R. A. L., N. SAHA, A. S. SALIH, A. E. BAKKAR, and G. FLATZ. 1981. "Distribution of the lactase phenotypes in the population of the Democratic Republic of The Sudan." *Hum. Genetics,* 57:279–281.

BEALS, K. L., C. L. SMITH, and S. M. DODD. 1984. "Brain size, cranial morphology, climate, and time machines." *Current Anthrop.,* 25(3):301–330.

BELICH, J. 1986. *The New Zealand Wars.* Auckland: Auckland University Press.

BERKOW, R., ed. 1977. *The Merck Manual of Diagnosis and Therapy.* Rahway, NJ: Merck, Sharpe & Dohme Research Laboratories.

BEUTLER, E. 1983. "Glucose-6-phosphate dehydrogenase deficiency." In *The Metabolic Basis of Inherited Disease,* eds. J. B. Stanbury, J. B. Wyngaarden, D. S. Fredrickson, J. Goldstein, and M. Brown. 5th ed. New York: McGraw-Hill. pp. 1629–1653.

BEUTLER, E., R. J. DERN, and C. L. FLANAGAN. 1955. "Effect of sickle-cell trait on resistance to malaria." *Br. Med. J.,* 1:1189–1191.

BIASUTTI, R. 1959. *Razze e Popoli della Terra.* 2nd ed. Torino. Unione Tipografico-Editrice Torinese.

BIERCE, A. 1978. *The Devil's Dictionary.* Owings Mills, MD: Stemmer House Publishers.

BIRDSELL, J. B. 1978. "Spacing mechanisms and adaptive behavior of Australian Aborigines." in *Population Control by Social Behavior,* eds. F. J. Ebling and D. M. Stoddart. New York: Praeger.

BIRDSELL, J. B. 1981. *Human Evolution: An Introduction to the New Physical Anthropology.* Boston: Houghton Mifflin.

BIRDSELL, J. B. 1993. *Microevolutionary Patterns in Aboriginal Australia: A Gradient Analysis of Clines.* New York: Oxford University Press.

BLOCK, N. J., and G. DWORKIN, eds. 1976. *The IQ Controversy.* New York: Pantheon, Random House.

BLUM, H. F. 1969. "Is sunlight a factor in the geographical distribution of human skin color?" *Geograph. Review,* LIX(4):557–581.

BOAS, F. 1911. *The Mind of Primitive Man.* New York: Macmillan.

BOAS, F. 1940. "The relations between physical and social anthropology." In *Race, Language and Culture.* New York: Free Press.

BODMER, J. G., L. J. KENNEDY, J. LINDSAY, and A. M. WASIK. 1987. "Applications of serology and the ethnic distribution of three locus HLA haplotypes." *Brit. Med. Bulletin,* 43(1):94–121.

BODMER, W. F., and L. CAVALLI-SFORZA. 1970. "Intelligence and race." *Scientific American,* 223(4):19–29.

BODMER, W. F., and L. L. CAVALLI-SFORZA. 1976. *Genetics, Evolution and Man.* San Francisco: W. H. Freeman.

BOSERUP, E. 1981. *Population and Technological Change: A Study of Long Term Trends.* Chicago: University of Chicago Press.

BOUCHARD, T. J., JR., D. T. LYKKEN, M. MCGUE, N. L. SEGAL, and A. TELLEGEN. 1990. "Sources of human psychological differences: The Minnesota study of twins reared apart." *Science.* 250:223–228.

BOUCHARD, T. J., JR., D. T. LYKKEN, N. L. SEGAL, and K. J. WILCOX. 1986. "Development in twins reared apart: A test of the chronogenetic hypothesis." In *Human Growth: A Multidisciplinary Review,* eds. A. Demirjian and M. Brault. London and Philadelphia: Taylor & Francis.

BOWCOCK, A. M., C. BUCCI, J. M. HEBERT, J. R. KIDD, K. K. KIDD, J. S. FRIEDLAENDER, and L. L. CAVALLI-SFORZA. 1987. "Study of 47 DNA markers in five populations from four continents." *Gene Geography,* 1:47–64.

BOWCOCK, A. M., J. M. HEBERT, J. L. MOUNTAIN, J. R. KIDD, J. ROGERS, K. K. KIDD, and L. L. CAVALLI-SFORZA. 1991. "Study of an additional 58 DNA markers in five human populations from four continents." *Gene Geography*, 5:151–173.

BOWMAN, J. E. 1977. "Genetic screening programs and public policy." *Phylon*, 38:117–142.

BOYD, W. C. 1950. *Genetics and the Races of Man.* Boston: Little, Brown.

BOYD W. C. 1963a. "Genetics and the human race." *Science*, 140:1057–1065.

BOYD, W. C. 1963b. "Four achievements of the genetical method in physical anthropology." *Am. J. Phys. Anthrop.*, 65:243–252.

BRACE, C. L. 1962. "Cultural factors in the evolution of the human dentition." In *Culture and the Evolution of Man*, ed. M. F. Ashley Montagu. New York: Oxford University Press.

BRACE, C. L., and K. D. HUNT. 1990. "A nonracial craniofacial perspective on human variation: A(Australia) to Z(Zuni)." *Am. J. Phys. Anthrop.*, 82:341–360.

BRANDA, R. F., and J. W. EATON. 1978. "Skin color and nutrient photolysis: An evolutionary hypothesis." *Science*, 201:625–626.

BRIERLEY, J. K. 1970. *A Natural History of Man.* Madison, NJ: Fairleigh Dickinson University Press.

BRUES, A. M. 1954. "Selection and polymorphism in the ABO blood groups." *Am. J. Phys. Anthrop.*, 12:559–597.

BRUES, A. M. 1963. "Stochastic tests of selection in the ABO blood groups." *Am. J. Phys. Anthrop.*, 21(3):287–300.

BRUES, A. M. 1977. *People and Races.* New York: Macmillan.

BUCHI, E. C. 1968. "Somatic groups composing the modern population of India." In *Proceedings of the Eighth International Congress of Anthropological and Ethnological Sciences.* Ueno Park, Tokyo, Japan: Science Council of Japan.

BUETTNER-JANUSCH, J. 1966. *Origins of Man.* New York: John Wiley.

BUETTNER-JANUSCH, J. 1973. *Physical Anthropology: A Perspective.* New York: John Wiley.

BURKE, B. M. 1995. "Mexican immigrants shape California's fertility future." *Population Today* (September) pp. 4–5.

BURKITT, D. F. 1971. "Epidemiology of cancer of the colon and rectum." *Cancer*, 28:3–13.

BURNHAM, S. 1985. *Black Intelligence in White Society.* Athens, GA: Social Science Press.

CAIRNS, J. 1975. "The cancer problem." *Scientific American*, 233(5):64–78.

CALLEGARI-JACQUES, S. M., F. M. SALZANO, J. CONSTANS, and P. MAURIERES. 1993. "Gm haplotype distribution in Amerindians: Relationship with geography and language." *Am. J. Phys. Anthrop.* 90:427–444.

CANN, R. L. 1987. "In search of Eve." *The Sciences*, 27:30–37.

CANN, R. L. 1988. "DNA and human origins." *Annual Review of Anthropology*, 17:127–143.

CARBONELL, V. M. 1963. "Variations in the frequency of shovel-shape incisors in different populations." In *Dental Anthropology*, ed. D. R. Brothwell. Elmsford, New York: Pergamon Press.

CARTER, T. P., and A. M. WILLEY. eds. 1986. *Genetic Disease: Screening and Management.* New York: Alan R. Liss, Inc.

CAVALLI-SFORZA, L. 1969. "Genetic drift in an Italian population." In *Readings from Scientific American—Biological Anthropology.* San Francisco, W. H. Freeman.

CAVALLI-SFORZA, L. L., ed. 1986. *African Pygmies.* New York: Academic Press.

CAVALLI-SFORZA, L. L., J. R. KIDD, K. K. KIDD, C. BUCCI, A. M. BOWCOCK, B. S. HEWLETT, and J. S. FRIEDLAENDER. 1986. "DNA markers and genetic variation in the human species." *Cold Spring Harbor Symposia on Quantitative Biology.* Vol. LI:411–417.

CAVALLI-SFORZA, L. L., P. MENOZZI, and A. PIAZZA. 1994. *The History and Geography of Human Genes.* Princeton, NJ: Princeton University Press.

CHAGNON, N. A., J. V. NEEL, L. WEITKAMP, H. GERSHOWITZ, and M. AYRES. 1970. "The influence of cultural factors on the demography and pattern of gene flow from the Makiritare to the Yanomama Indians." *Am. J. Phys. Anthrop.*, 32:339–349.

CHAKRABORTY, R., and K. K. KIDD. 1991. "The utility of DNA typing in forensic work." *Science,* 254:1735–1739.

CHAKRAVARTI, A., and R. CHAKRABORTY. 1978. "Elevated frequency of Tay-Sachs disease among Ashkenazic Jews unlikely by genetic drift alone." *Am. J. Hum. Genetics,* 30:256–261.

CHAN, V., T. K. CHAN, F. F. CHEBAB, and D. TODD. 1987. "Distribution of beta-thalassemia mutations in South China and their association with haplotypes." *Am. J. Hum. Genetics,* 41:678–685.

CHASE, A. 1977. *The Legacy of Malthus: The Social Costs of the New Scientific Racism.* New York: Knopf.

CLEGG, E. J., and J. P. GARLICK, eds. 1980. *Disease and Urbanization.* Symposia of the Society for the Study of Human Biology. Vol. XX. London: Taylor & Francis.

COHEN, L. A. 1987. "Diet and cancer." *Scientific American,* 257:42–48.

COMAS, J. 1960. *Manual of Physical Anthropology.* Springfield, IL: Charles C. Thomas.

COMBS, G. F. JR. and M. L. SCOTT. 1977. "Nutritional interrelationships of vitamin E and selenium," *Bio. Science,* 27(7):467–473.

COON, C. S. 1962. *The Origin of Races.* New York: Knopf.

COON C. S. 1965. *The Living Races of Man.* New York: Knopf.

COON, C.S., S. M. GARN, and J. B. BIRDSELL. 1950. *Races: A Study of the Problems of Race Formation in Man.* Springfield, IL: Charles C. Thomas.

COOPER, D. N., and J. SCHMIDTKE. 1986. "Diagnosis of genetic disease using recombinant DNA." *Hum. Genetics,* 73:1–11.

CRAVENS, H. 1978. *The Triumph of Evolution: American Scientists and the Heredity–Environment Controversy, 1900, 1941.* Philadelphia: University of Pennsylvania Press.

CURTIN, P D. 1969. *The Atlantic Slave Trade.* Milwaukee: University of Wisconsin Press.

DAMON, A. 1962. "Some host factors in disease: Sex, race, ethnic group, and body form." *National Med. Assoc. J.,* 54:424–431.

DAMON, A. 1965. "Stature increase among Italian-Americans: Environmental, genetic, or both?" *Am. J. Phys. Anthrop.,* 23:401–408.

DARLINGTON, C. D. 1969. *The Evolution of Man and Society.* New York: Simon & Schuster.

DAUSSET, J.W., and J. COLOMBANI. 1972. *Histocompatibility Testing 1972.* Copenhagen: Munksgaard.

DAVIS, J. M., and D. J. SVENDSGAARD. 1987. "Lead and child development." *Nature,* 329:297–300.

DEAN, G. 1963. *The Porphyrias: A Story of Inheritance and Environment.* Philadelphia: J. B. Lippincott.

DEEVEY, E. S. JR. 1960. "The human population." *Scientific American,* Vol. 203:28–36.

Demographic Yearbook. 1977. New York: United Nations.

Demographic Yearbook. 1979. New York: United Nations.

Demographic Yearbook. 1990. New York: United Nations.

Demographic Yearbook. 1995. New York: United Nations.

DE MONTELLAGNO, B. R. O. 1993. "Melanin, Afrocentricity, and pseudoscience." *Yearbook of Physical Anthropology,* 36:33–58.

DE VITA, C. J. 1996. *The United States at Mid-Decade.* Population Bulletin No. 4, Vol. 50.

DOBZHANSKY, T. 1944. "On species and races of living and fossil man." *Am. J. Phys. Anthrop.,* 2:251–265.

DOBZHANSKY, T. 1962. *Mankind Evolving: The Evolution of the Human Species.* New Haven and London: Yale University Press.

DOBZHANSKY, T. 1968. *Science and the Concept of Race.* New York: Columbia University Press.

DOBZHANSKY, T. 1971. "Race equality." In *The Biological and Social Meaning of Race,* ed. Richard H. Osborne. San Francisco: W. H. Freeman.

DOBZHANSKY, T. 1976. "The myths of genetic predestination and of tabula rasa." *Perspectives in Biology and Medicine,* 19(2):156–170.

DUBOS, R. 1968. *Man Adapting.* New Haven: Yale University Press.

DUSTER, T. 1990. *Backdoor to Eugenics.* New York: Routledge.

EATON, J. W., and J. A. GAVAN. 1965. "Sensitivity to P-T-C among primates." *Am. J. Phys. Anthrop.,* 23:381–388.

ECKHOLM, E. P. 1977. *The Picture of Health*. New York: W. W. Norton.

EDELSTEIN, S. J. 1986. *The Sickled Cell: From Myths to Molecules*. Cambridge, MA: Harvard University Press.

EDLIN, G. 1990. *Human Genetics*. Boston: Jones and Bartlett.

ENSMINGER, J. 1990. *Personal Communication*. St. Louis: Washington University.

ERHARDT, C. L. 1973. "Worldwide distribution of sickle cell disease: A consideration of available data." In *Sickle Cell Disease: Diagnosis, Management, Education and Research*, eds. H. Abramson, J. F. Bertles, and D. L. Withers. St. Louis: Mosby.

ERICKSON, D. 1992. "Genes to order." *Scientific American*, 266:112–114.

ERLENMEYER-KIMLING, L., and L. F. JARVIK. 1963. "Genetics and intelligence: A review." *Science*, 142:1477–1479.

ETKIN, N. L., and J. W. EATON. 1983. Abstract: "Blood bankers, viruses and ABO blood groups." *Am. J. Phys. Anthrop.*, 60 (2):192.

EVELETH, P. B., and J. M. TANNER. 1990. *Worldwide Variation in Human Growth*. 2nd ed. New York: Cambridge University Press.

EVELETH, P. B., and J. M. TANNER. 1976. *Worldwide Variation in Human Growth*. Cambridge: Cambridge University Press.

EXCOFFIER, L., B. PELLEGRINI, A. SANCHEZ-MAZAS, C. SIMON, and A. LANGANEY. 1987. "Genetics and history of Sub-Saharan Africa," *Yearbook of Physical Anthropology*, Vol. 30:151–194. New York: Alan Liss.

FABER, M. 1982. "Ultraviolet radiation." In *Nonionizing Radiation Protection*, ed. M. J. Suess. WHO Regional Publications European Series #10.

FACKELMANN, K. A. 1989. "Cystic fibrosis gene and protein identified." *Science News*, p. 149.

FALLOWS, J. 1989. *More Like Us*. Boston: Houghton Mifflin.

FELSENSTEIN, J. 1973. "Maximum-likelihoods estimation of evolutionary trees from continuous characters." *Am. J. Hum. Genetics*, 25:471–492.

FENTON, F. D. 1859. *Aboriginal Inhabitants of New Zealand*. Auckland: W. C. Wilson.

FERNANDEZ, C. A. 1992. "La Raza and the melting pot: A comparative look at multiethnicity." In *Racially Mixed People in America*, ed. M. P. P. Root. Newbury Park, CA: Sage. pp. 126–143.

FITZPATRICK, T. B., and K. JIMBOW. 1985. "Human skin color: Origin, variation and significance." *J. Human Evol.*, 14:43–56.

FLATZ, G., J. N. HOWELL, J. DOENCH, and S. D. FLATZ. 1982. "Distribution of physiological adult lactase phenotypes, lactose absorber and malabsorber, in Germany." *Hum. Genetics* 62:152–157.

FLYNN, J. R. 1984. "The mean IQ of Americans: massive gains 1932 to 1978." *Psychological Bulletin*, 95(1):29–51.

FOGEL, R. W., and S. L. ENGERMAN. 1984. *Time on the Cross: The Economics of American Negro Slavery*. Lanham, New York: University Press of America.

FRASER, S., ed. 1995. *The Bell Curve Wars*. New York: Basic Books.

FRAYER, D. W., M. H. WOLPOFF, A. G. THORNE, F. H. SMITH, and G. G. POPE. 1993. "Theories of modern human origins: The paleontological test." *Am. Anthrop.*, 95(1):14–50.

FRIEDLAENDER, J. S., ed. 1987. *The Solomon Islands Project: A Long-Term Study of Health, Human Biology and Culture Change*. Oxford: Oxford University Press.

FRISANCHO, A. R. 1970. "Developmental responses to high altitude hypoxia." *Am. J. Phys. Anthrop.*, 32:401–407.

FRISANCHO, A. R. 1979. *Human Adaptation: A Functional Interpretation*. St. Louis: C. V. Mosby.

FRISANCHO, A. R. 1993. *Human Adaptation and Accommodation*. Ann Arbor: University of Michigan Press.

FRISCH, R. 1988. "Fatness and fertility." *Scientific American*, 258(3): 88–95.

FRISCH, R., and R. REVELLE. 1969. "Variation in body weights and the age of the adolescent growth spurt among Latin American and Asian in relation to calorie supplies." *Human Biology*, 41:185–212.

GADJUSEK, D. C. 1964. "Factors governing the genetics of primitive human populations." *Cold Spring Harbor Symposia in Quantitative Biology*, 29:121–135.

GALTON, F. 1869. *Hereditary Genius*. Republished 1962. London: Macmillan.

GANONG, W. F. 1993. *Review of Medical Physiology*. 16th ed. Norwalk, CT: Appleton & Lange.

GARN, S. M. 1961. *Human Races*. Springfield, IL: Charles C. Thomas.

GARN, S. M., ed. 1960. *Readings on Race*. Springfield, IL: Charles C. Thomas.

GARRETT, L. 1994. *The Coming Plague*. New York: Penguin Books.

GARROD, ARCHIBALD. 1902. "Inborn errors of metabolism." *Lancet*, 2:1616–1619.

GERARD, G., D. VITRAC, J. LE PENDU, A. MULLER, and R. ORIOL. 1982. "H-deficient blood groups (Bombay) of Reunion island." *Am. J. Hum. Genetics*, 34:937–947.

GIBLETT, E. R. 1969. *Genetic Markers in Human Blood*. Philadelphia: F. A. Davis.

GILES, E. 1962. "Favism, sex-linkage, and the Indo-European kinship system." *Southwest J. Anthrop.*, 18:286–290.

GILL, P., A. J. JEFFREYS, and D. J. WERRETT. 1985. "Forensic applications of DNA fingerprints." *Nature*, 318:577.

GLASS, B. 1955. "On the unlikelihood of significant admixture of genes from the North American Indians in the present composition of the Negroes of the United States." *Am. J. Hum. Genetics*, 7(4):368–385.

GLASS, B., M. S. SACKS, E. F. JAHN, and C. HESS. 1952. "Genetic drift in a religious isolate: An analysis of the causes of variations in blood group and other gene frequencies in a small population." *American Naturalist*, 86:145–159.

GOLDSTEIN, H. 1971. "Factors influencing the height of seven year old children—Results from the National Child Development Study." *Human Biology*, 43(1):92–101.

GOODFIELD, J. 1977. *Playing God: Genetic Engineering and the Manipulation of Life*. New York: Random House.

GORING, C. 1919. *The English Convict: A Statistical Study*. Montclair, NJ: Patterson Smith.

GOULD, S. J. 1978. "Morton's ranking of races by cranial capacity." *Science*, 200:503–509.

GOULD, S. J. 1983. *The Mismeasure of Man*. New York; W. W. Norton.

GOULD, S. J. 1994. "Curveball." *The New Yorker*, Nov. 28, 1994.

GREENE, L. S. 1993. "G6PD deficiency as protection against falciparum malaria: An epidemiologic critique of population and experimental studies." *Yearbook of Physical Anthropology*, 36:153–178.

GREGG, T. G., and P. R. SANDAY. 1971. "Genetic and environmental components of differential intelligence." In *Race and Intelligence*, eds. C. L. Brace, G. R. Gamble, and J. T. Bond. Washington, D.C.: American Anthropological Association.

GUYER, M. S., and F. S. COLLINS. 1995. "How is the human genome project doing, and what have we learned so far?" *Proceedings of National Academy of Science*, 92:10841–10848.

HAKOMORI, S. I. 1986. "Glycosphingolipids." *Scientific American*, 254:44–53.

HALLER, J. S. JR. 1970. "The physician versus the Negro: Medical and anthropological concepts of race in the late nineteenth century." *Bulletin of the History of Medicine*, 44(2):154–167.

HALLER, J. S. JR. 1971. *Outcasts from Evolution: Scientific Attitudes of Racial Inferiority, 1859–1900*. Urbana: University of Illinois Press.

HAMBLY, W. D. 1940. "Craniometry of New Guinea." *Field Museum of Natural History*. Vol. XXV, No. 3.

HARRIS, H. 1980. *The Principles of Human Biochemical Genetics*. 3rd ed. Amsterdam: Elsevier/North Holland.

HARRIS, M. I. 1990. "Noninsulin-dependent diabetes mellitus in black and white Americans." *Diabetes/Metabolism Reviews*, 6(2):71–90.

HARRISON, G. 1978. *Mosquitoes, Malaria and Man: A History of the Hostilities Since 1880*. New York: E. P. Dutton.

HARRISON, G. A. 1975. Pigmentation. In *Human Variation and Natural Selection*, ed. D. F. Roberts. Symposia of the Society for the Study of Human Biology. Vol. XII, pp. 179–194. London: Taylor and Francis.

HARRISON, G. A., J. M. TANNER, D. R. PILBEAM, and P. T. BAKER. 1988. *Human Biology: An Introduction to Human Evolution, Variation, Growth, and Adaptability.* 3rd ed. New York and Tokyo: Oxford University Press.

HARRISON, G. A., J. WEINER, J. M. TANNER, and N. A. BARNICOT. 1977. *Human Biology.* 2nd ed. Oxford: Oxford University Press.

HARRISON, R., and W. MONTAGNA. 1972. *Man.* Englewood Cliffs, NJ: Prentice-Hall.

HARTL, D. L., D. FREIFELDER, and L. A. SNYDER. 1988. *Basic Genetics.* Boston: Jones and Bartlett.

HAWKES, NIGEL. 1979. "Tracing Burt's Descent to Scientific Fraud." *Science,* August 17.

HEARNSHAW, L. S. 1979. *Cyril Burt: Psychologist.* London: Hodder and Stoughton.

HERRNSTEIN, R. J., and C. MURRAY. 1994. *The Bell Curve: Intelligence and Class Structure in American Life.* New York: Free Press.

HETZEL, B. S. 1993. "The iodine deficiency disorders." In *Iodine Deficiency in Europe: A Continuing Concern,* eds. F. Delange, J. T. Gunn, and D. Glioner. New York: Plenum Press. pp. 25–31.

HIERNAUX, J. 1964. "The concept of race and the taxonomy of mankind." In *The Concept of Race,* ed. Ashley Montagu. New York: Free Press.

HIERNAUX, J. 1966a. "Peoples of Africa from 22° N to the Equator." In *The Biology of Human Adaptability,* ed. Paul T. Baker. Oxford: Clarendon Press.

HIERNAUX, J. 1966b. "Human biological diversity in Central Africa." *Man,* 1(3):287–306.

HIERNAUX, J. 1971. "Ethnic differences in growth and development." In *The Biological and Social Meaning of Race,* ed. Richard H. Osborne. San Francisco: W. H. Freeman.

HIERNAUX, J. 1977. "Long-term biological effects of human migration from the African savanna to the equatorial forest: A case study of human adaptation to a hot and wet climate." In *Population Structure and Human Variation,* ed. G. A. Harrison. New York: Cambridge University Press. pp. 187–217.

HILL, A. V. S. 1986. "The population genetics of alpha thalassemia and the malaria hypothesis." *Cold Spring Harbor Symposia on Quantitative Biology,* 489–498.

HILL, A. V. S., and J. S. WAINSCOAT. 1986. "The evolution of the alpha and beta-globin gene clusters in human populations." *Hum. Genetics,* 74:16–23.

HIRSCH, J. 1969. "Behavior genetics, or 'Experimental,' analysis: The challenge of science versus the lure of technology." In *Behavioral Genetics: Methods and Research,* eds. M. Manosevitz, G. Lindzey, and D. D. Thiessen. New York: Appleton-Century-Crofts.

HIRSCH, J., ed. 1967. *Behavior-Genetic Analysis.* New York: McGraw-Hill.

HIRSCH, N. D. M. 1926. "A study of natro-racial mental differences." *Genetic Psychology Monographs,* 1 (3 and 4).

Historical Statistics of the United States, Colonial Times to 1957. 1960. Washington, DC: U.S. Department of Commerce, Bureau of Census.

HOEKSTRA, W. G. 1975. "Biochemical function of selenium and its relation to Vitamin E." *Federation Proceedings,* 34:2083–2089.

HOOTON, E. A. 1936. "Plain statements about race." *Science,* 83:511–513.

HOOTON, E. A. 1946. *Up From the Ape.* New York: Macmillan.

HOOTON, E. A., and C. W. DUPERTUIS. 1955. *The Physical Anthropology of Ireland.* Peabody Museum of Archaeology and Ethnology. Vol. XXX, Nos. 1–2. Cambridge, MA: Harvard University.

HOPKINS, D. R. 1983. *Princes and Peasants: Smallpox in History.* Chicago: University of Chicago Press.

HOUGHTON, P. 1996. *People of the Great Ocean: Aspects of Human Biology of the Early Pacific.* Cambridge: Cambridge University Press.

HOWELL, N. 1986. "Feedbacks and buffers in relation to scarcity and abundance: Studies of hunter-gatherer populations." In *The State of Population Theory: Forward from Malthus,* eds. D. Coleman and R. Schofield. Oxford: Basil Blackwell. pp. 156–187.

HOWELLS, W. 1973. *The Pacific Islanders.* New York: Scribner's.

HUBBARD, R., and E. WALD. 1993. *Exploding the Gene Myth.* Boston: Beacon Press.

HULSE, F. S. 1955. "Technological advance and major racial stocks." *Human Bio.,* 27:184–192.

HULSE, F. S. 1957. "Some factors influencing the relative proportions of human racial stocks." *Cold Spring Harbor Symposia in Quantitative Biology*, 22:33–45.

HULSE, F. S. 1963. *The Human Species*. New York: Random House.

HULSE, F. S. 1967. "Selection for skin color among the Japanese." *Am. J. Phys. Anthrop.*, 27:143–156.

HULSE, F. S. 1971. *The Human Species*. New York: Random House.

HUTSCHNECKER, A. A. 1974. *The Drive for Power.* New York: M. Evans.

HUTT, M. S. R., and D. P. BURKITT. 1986. *The Geography of Non-Infectious Disease.* Oxford: Oxford University Press.

JACOBY, R., and N. GLAUBERMAN, eds. 1995. *The Bell Curve Debate.* New York: Times Books.

JACKSON, F. L. C. 1993. "The influence of dietary cyanogenic glycosides from cassava on human metabolic biology and microevolution." In *Tropical Forests, People and Food*, eds. C. M. Hladik et al. Paris: UNESCO and the Parthenon Publishing Group. pp. 321–338.

JAMISON, E., and F. HOBBS. 1994. *World Population Profile: 1994.* Bureau of the Census. Report WP/94. Washington, DC: U.S. Govt. Printing Office.

JEFFREYS, A. J. 1989. "Molecular biology and human evolution." In *Human Origins*, ed. J. R. Durans. Oxford: Clarendon Press. pp. 27–51.

JEFFREYS, A. J., V. WILSON, and S. L. THEIN. 1985. "Hypervariable 'minisatellite' regions in human DNA." *Nature*, 314:67–73.

JENSEN, A. R. 1969. "How much can we boost IQ and scholastic achievement?" In *Environment, Heredity, and Intelligence.* Cambridge, MA: Harvard Educational Review.

JENSEN, A. R. 1971. "Can we and should we study race differences?" In *Race and Intelligence*, eds. C. L. Brace, G. R. Gamble, and J. T. Bond. Washington, DC: American Anthropological Association.

JONES, A., and W. F. BODMER. 1974. *Our Future Inheritance: Choice or Chance.* Oxford: Oxford University Press.

JORDE, L. B., and G. M. LATHROP. 1988. "A test of the heterozygote-advantage hypothesis in cystic fibrosis carriers." *Am. J. Hum. Genetics*, 42:808–815.

KAMIN, L. J. 1974. *The Science and Politics of IQ.* Hillsdale, NJ: Erlbaum.

KAN, Y. W., and A. M. DOZY. 1978. "Polymorphism of DNA sequence adjacent to the human beta-globin structural gene: Relationship to sickle mutation." *Proceedings of the National Academy of Science*, 75:5631–5635.

KENNEDY, W. A., V. VAN DE RIET, and J. C. WHITE. 1963. *A Normative Sample of Intelligence and Achievement of Negro Elementary School Children in Southeastern United States.* Chicago: Monographs of the Society for Research on Child Development, 28, No. 6.

KEVLES, D. J. 1995. *In the Name of Eugenics.* Cambridge, MA: Harvard University Press.

KHOURY, M. J., T. H. BEATY, C. A. NEWILL, et al. 1986. "Genetic–environmental interactions in chronic airways obstruction." *International Journal Epidemiology*, 15:64–71.

KIDD, J. R., F. L. BLACK, K. M. WEISS, I. BALAZS, and K. K. KIDD. 1991. "Studies of three Amerindian populations using nuclear DNA polymorphisms." *Human Bio.*, 63(6):775–794.

KIDD, J. R., and K. K. KIDD. 1990. "Characterization of the R. Surui and Karitiana at 21 polymorphic DNA loci." *Am. J. Phys. Anthrop.*, 81(2):249 (abstract).

KIDD, K., and J. R. KIDD. 1996. "A nuclear perspective on human evolution." In *Molecular Biology and Human Evolution*, eds. A. J. Boyce and C. G. M. Mascie-Taylor. Cambridge: Cambridge University Press.

KIDD, J. R., K. K. KIDD, and K. M. WEISS. 1993. "Human genome diversity initiative." *Human Bio.*, 65(1):1–6.

KIRK, R. L., S. W. SERJEANTSON, H. KING, and P. ZIMMET. 1985. "The genetic epidemiology of diabetes mellitus." In *Diseases of Complex Etiology in Small Populations: Ethnic Differences and Research Approaches*, eds. R. Chakraborty and E. J. E. Szathmary. New York: Alan R. Liss.

KLAG, M. J., P. K. WHELTON, J. CORESH, C. E. GRIM, and L. H. KULLER, 1991. "The association of skin color with blood pressure in U.S. blacks with low socioeconomic status." *J. Am. Med. Assoc.*, 265(5):599–602.

KLINEBERG, O. 1935. *Race Differences.* New York: Harper.

KNOWLER, W. C., D. J. PETTITT, M. F. SAAD, and P. H. BENNETT. 1990. "Diabetes mellitus in the Pima Indians: Incidence, risk factors and pathogenesis." *Diabetes/Metabolism Reviews*, 6(1):1–27.

KONOTEY-AHULU, F. I. D. 1982. "Ethics of amniocentesis and selective abortion for sickle cell disease." *Lancet*, I:38–39.

KOSTYU, D. D., C. L. OBER, D. V. DAWSON, M. GHANAYEM, S. ELIAS, and A. O. MARTIN. 1989. "Genetic analysis of HLA in the U.S. Schmiedenleut Hutterites." *Am. J. Hum. Genetics*, 45:261–269.

KROEBER, A. 1917. "The superorganic." *Am. Anthropologist*, 19:163–213.

KROGMAN, W. M. 1972. *Child Growth*. Ann Arbor: University of Michigan Press.

LABIE, D., J. PAGNIER, H. WAJCMAN, M. E. FARBY, and R. L. NAGEL. 1986. "The genetic origin of the variability of the phenotypic expression of the Hb X gene." In *Genetic Variation and Its Maintenance*, eds. D. F. Roberts and G. F. De Stefano. Cambridge, MA: Cambridge University Press. pp. 149–155.

LADIMEJI, O. A. 1974. "Book Review: *Race* by John R. Baker (London: Oxford University Press)." *Race*, XVI (1):101–110.

LADURIE, E. L. 1988. *Times of Feast, Times of Famine: A History of Climate Since the Year 1000*. New York: Farrar, Straus & Giroux.

LASKER, G. W. 1973. *Physical Anthropology*. New York: Holt, Rinehart & Winston.

LEFFELL, D.J., and D. E. BRASH. 1996. "Sunlight and skin cancer." *Scientific American*, 275(1):52–59.

LERNER, M. I., and W. J. LIBBY. 1976. *Heredity, Evolution and Society*. 2nd ed. San Francisco: W. H. Freeman.

LEVANDER, O. A. 1987. "A global view of human selenium nutrition." *Annual Review of Nutrition*, 7:227–250.

LEWONTIN, R. C. 1972. "The apportionment of human diversity." In *Evolutionary Biology*, Vol. 6, eds. T. Dobzhansky, M. K. Hecht, and W. C. Steers. New York: Appleton-Century-Crofts.

LEWONTIN, R. C. 1974. *Genetic Basis of Evolutionary Change*. New York: Columbia University Press.

LEWONTIN, R. C., and D. L. HARTL. 1991. "Population genetics in forensic DNA typing." *Science* 254:1745–1750.

LEWONTIN, R. C., and D. L. HARTL. 1992. "Letters: Forensic DNA typing." *Science*, 255:1054–1055.

LEWONTIN, R. C., S. ROSE, and L. KAMIN. 1984. *Not in Our Genes*. New York: Pantheon Books.

LITTLEFIELD, A., L. LIEBERMAN, and L. T. REYNOLDS. 1982. "Redefining race: the potential demise of a concept in physical anthropology." *Current Anthrop.*, 23:641–655.

LIVINGSTONE, F. B. 1958. "Anthropological implications of sickle cell gene distribution in West Africa." *Am. Anthropologist*, 60:533–562

LIVINGSTONE, F. B. 1963. "Blood groups and ancestry: A test case from the New Guinea highlands." *Current Anthrop.*, 4:541–542.

LIVINGSTONE, F. B. 1964. "On the nonexistence of human races." In *The Concept of Race*, ed. Ashley Montagu. New York: Free Press.

LIVINGSTONE, F. B. 1967. *Abnormal Hemoglobins in Human Populations*. Chicago: Aldine.

LIVINGSTONE, F. B. 1969. "The founder effect and deleterious genes." *Am. J. Phys. Anthrop.*, 30:55–60.

LIVINGSTONE, F. B. 1973. "Data on glucose 6 phosphate dehydrogenase deficiency in human populations, 1967–1973." *Museum of Anthropology Technical Reports* (3). University of Michigan.

LIVINGSTONE, F. B. 1984. "The Duffy blood groups, vivax malaria, and malarial selection in human populations. A review." *Human Bio.*, 56:413–425.

LIVINGSTONE, F. B. 1985. *Frequencies of Hemoglobin Variants*. New York: Oxford University Press

LIVINGSTONE, F. B. 1989. "Who gave whom hemoglobin S: The use of restriction site haplotype variation for the interpretation of the evolution of the beta^s-globin gene." *Am. J. Human Biology*, II:289–302.

LOEHLIN, J. C., G. LINDZEY, and J. N. SPUHLER. 1975. *Race Differences in Intelligence*. San Francisco: W. H. Freeman.

LOGAN, W. H. G., and R. KRONFELD. 1933. "Development of the human jaws and surrounding structures from birth to the age of 15 years." *J. Am. Dent. Assoc.*, 20:379.

LOOMIS, F. W. 1970. "Rickets." *Scientific American,* 223(6):77–91.

LOPEZ, A. D. 1990a. "Causes of death: An assessment of global patterns of mortality around 1985." *World Health Statistics Quarterly,* 43(2):91–104.

LOPEZ, A. D. 1990b. "Who dies of what? A comparative analysis of mortality conditions in developed countries around 1987." *World Health Statistics Quarterly,* 43(2):105–114.

LOPEZ, A. D. 1993. "Causes of death in industrial and developing countries: Estimates for 1985–1990." In *Disease Control Priorities in Developing Countries,* eds. D. T. Jamison, W. H. Mosley, A. R. Measham, and J. L. Bobadilla. New York: Oxford University Press. pp. 35–50.

LOWREY, G. H. 1978. *Growth and Development of Children.* 7th ed. Chicago: Year Book Medical Publishers.

LUCKEISH, M. 1946. *Applications of Germicidal, Erythemal, and Infrared Energy.* Belmont, CA: Wadsworth.

LUDMAN, M. D., G. A. GRABOWSKI, J. D. GOLDBERG, and R. J. DESNICK. 1986. "Heterozygote detection and prenatal diagnosis for Tay-Sachs and Type 1 Gaucher Diseases." In *Genetic Disease: Screening and Management,* eds. T. P. Carter and A. M. Willey. New York: Alan R. Liss. pp. 19–48.

LYNN, R. 1978. "Ethnic and racial differences in intelligence. International comparisons." In *Human Variation: The Biopsychology of Age, Race, and Sex.,* eds. R. T. Osborne, C. E. Noble, and N. Weyl. New York: Academic Press.

McCOWN, T. D., and K. A. R. KENNEDY, eds. 1972. *Climbing Man's Family Tree: A Collection of Major Writings on Human Phylogeny 1699 to 1971.* Englewood Cliffs, NJ: Prentice-Hall.

McCRACKEN, R. D. 1971. "Lactase deficiency: An example of dietary evolution." *Current Anthrop.,* 12(4–5):479–500.

McCULLOUGH, J. M. 1978. "Phenylketonuria-balanced polymorphism in Europe." *J. Human Evol.,* 7(3):231–237.

McKEOWN, T. 1985. "Looking at disease in the light of human development." *World Health Forum,* 6:70–75.

MACKINTOSH, N. J. 1986. "The biology of intelligence." *Brit. Psychology,* 77:1–18.

McKUSICK, V. A. 1967. "The ethnic distribution of disease in the United States." *J. Chronic Diseases,* 20:115–118.

McKUSICK, V. A. 1978. *Mendelian Inheritance in Man.* 5th ed. Baltimore & London: John Hopkins University Press.

McKUSICK, V. A. 1986. "The gene map of *Homo sapiens:* Status and prospectus." *Cold Spring Harbor Symposia on Quantitative Biology.* LI:15–27.

McKUSICK, V. A. 1994. *Mendelian Inheritance in Man: A Catalog of Human Genes and Genetic Disorders.* Baltimore and London: Johns Hopkins Press.

McNEILL, W. H. 1976. *Plagues and Peoples.* New York: Anchor Press/Doubleday.

MANGE, A. P., and E. J. MANGE. 1990. *Genetics: Human Aspects.* 2nd ed. Sunderland, MA: Sinauer Assoc.

MARX, J. L. 1989. "The cystic fibrosis gene is found." *Science,* 245:923–925.

MATSUNAGA, E., and Y. HIRAIZUMI. 1962. "Prezygotic selection in ABO blood groups." *Science,* 135:432–434.

MATSUNAGA, E., and S. ITOH. 1958. "Blood groups and fertility in a Japanese population, with special reference to intrauterine selection due to maternal–foetal incompatibility." *Ann. Hum. Genetics,* 22:111–131.

MAUNG, T. 1979. "Cholera in the Gilberts." *World Health,* Jan.: 6–9.

MAYER, J. D. 1983. "The role of spatial analysis and geographic data in the detection of disease causation." *Social Science Medicine,* 17: 1213.

MAYESKE, G. W. 1971. *On the Explanation of Racial–Ethnic Group Differences in Achievement Test Scores.* Washington, DC: Office of Education, U.S. Department of Health, Education and Welfare.

MAYR, E. 1963. *Animal Species and Evolution.* Cambridge, MA: Belknap Press of Harvard University Press.

MAYR, E. 1982. *The Growth of Biological Thought: Diversity, Evolution, and Inheritance.* Cambridge, MA: Belknap Press of Harvard University Press.

MAYR, E. 1988. *Toward a New Philosophy of Biology.* Cambridge, MA: Belknap Press of Harvard University Press.

MEINDL, R. S. 1987. "Hypothesis: A selective advantage for cystic fibrosis." *Am. J. Phys. Anthrop.,* 74:39–45.

MERCER, J. 1972. *Labeling the Mentally Retarded.* Berkeley: University of California Press.

MERIMEE, T. J., and D. L. RIMOIN. 1986. "Growth hormone and insulin-like growth factors in the western pygmy." In *African Pygmies,* ed. L. L. Cavalli-Sforza. New York: Academic Press. pp. 167–177.

MINTON, H. L. 1988. *Lewis M. Terman: Pioneer in Psychological Testing.* New York: New York University Press.

MOLNAR, S. 1971. "Human tooth wear, tooth function and cultural variability." *Am. J. Phys. Anthrop.,* 34:175–190.

MOLNAR, S. 1996. "Book Review: *The Bell Curve: Intelligence and Class Structure in American Life.* R. J. Herrnstein & C. Murray. New York: Free Press." *Current Anthrop.,* 37:S165–S168.

MOLNAR, S., and S. C. WARD. 1977. "On the hominid masticatory complex: Biomechanical and evolutionary perspectives." *J. Human Evol.,* 6:557–568.

MONTAGU, M. F. A. 1960. *An Introduction to Physical Anthropology.* 3rd ed. Springfield, IL: Charles C. Thomas.

MONTAGU, M. F. A. 1964. "Discussion and criticism on the race concept." *Current Anthrop.,* 5:37.

MONTAGU, M. F. A. 1965. *Introduction to Physical Anthropology.* Springfield, IL: Charles C. Thomas.

MONTAGU, M. F. A. 1974. *Frontiers of Anthropology.* New York: Putnam's.

MORGANTI, G. 1959. "Distributions of blood groups in Italy." In *Medical Biology and Etruscan Origins,* eds. G. E. W. Wolstenholme and C. M. O'Connor. Ciba Foundation Symposium, Churchill, London. Boston: Little, Brown.

MORTON, N. E. 1958. "Empirical risks in consanguineous marriages: Birth weight, gestation time, and measurements of infants." *Am. J. Hum. Genetics,* 10:344–349.

MORTON, N. E. 1961. "Morbidity of children from consanguineous marriages." *Progr. Med. Genetics,* 1:261–291.

MORTON, S. G. 1839. *Crania Americana.* Philadelphia: J. Dodson.

MOURANT, A. E. 1954. *Distribution of the Human Blood Groups.* Oxford: Blackwell Scientific Publications.

MOURANT, A. W. 1983. *Blood Relations: Blood Groups and Anthropology.* New York: Oxford University Press.

MOURANT, A. E., A. C. KOPEC, and K. DOMANIEWSKA-SOBCZAK. 1978. *Blood Groups and Diseases: A Study of Associations of Diseases With Blood Groups and Other Polymorphisms.* New York: Oxford University Press.

MYEROWITZ, R., and N. G. HOGIKYAN. 1987. "A deletion involving Alu sequences in the *b* hexosaminidase—*a* chain gene of French Canadians with Tay-Sachs disease." *J. Biological Chemistry,* 262:15396–15399.

NASMYTH, K. 1996. "Another role rolls in." *Nature,* 382:28–29.

NEEL, J. V. 1962. "Diabetes mellitus; a 'thrifty' genotype rendered detrimental by progress?" *Am. J. Hum. Genetics,* 14:353–362.

NEEL, J. V. 1970. "Lessons from a 'primitive' people." *Science,* 170:815–822.

NEEL, J. V. 1982. "The thrifty genotype revisited." In *The Genetics of Diabetes Mellitus.* ed. J. Kobberling and R. Tattersall. London: Academic Press.

NEWMAN, M. 1953. "The application of ecological rules to the racial anthropology of the aboriginal New World." *Am. Anthrop.,* 55(1):311–327.

NEWMAN, M. T. 1961. "Biological adaptation of man to his environment: Heat, cold, altitude and nutrition." *Annals N.Y. Academy of Science,* 91:617–633.

NICHOLS, E. K. 1988. *Human Gene Therapy.* Cambridge, MA: Harvard University Press.

OGBU, J. U. 1978. *Minority Education and Caste: The American System in Cross-Cultural Perspective.* New York: Academic Press.

OGILVIE, M. D., B. K. CURRAN, and E. TRINKAUS. 1989. "Incidence and patterning of dental enamel hypoplasia among the Neandertals." *Am. J. Phys. Anthrop.,* 79:25–41.

OMRAN, A. R. 1982. "Epidemiologic transition." In *International Encyclopedia of Population,* ed. J. A. Ross. New York: Free Press.

OSBORN, F. 1971. "A return to the principles of natural selection." In *Natural Selection in Human Populations,* ed. Carl J. Bajema. New York: John Wiley.

OSBORNE, R. H., and F. V. DE GEORGE. 1959. *Genetic Basis of Morphological Variation.* Cambridge, MA: Harvard University Press.

OVED, Y. 1988. *Two Hundred Years of American Communes.* New Brunswick and Oxford: Transaction Books.

PAKKENBERG, H., and J. VOIGT. 1964. "Brain weight of the Danes." *Acta Anat.,* 56(4):297–307.

PASTORE, N. 1978. "The Army intelligence tests and Walter Lippman." *J. History of Behavioral Sciences,* 14:316–327.

PAULING, L., H. A. ITANO, S. J. SINGER, and I. C. WELLS. 1949. "Sickle cell anemia, a molecular disease." *Science,* 110:543–548.

PEACH, C., and J. C. MITCHELL. 1988. "Marriage distance and ethnicity." In *Human Mating Patterns,* eds. C. G. N. Mascie-Taylor and A. J. Boyce. Cambridge: Cambridge University Press. pp. 31–45.

PENROSE, L. S. 1951. "Measurement of pleiotropc effects in phenylketonuria."*Annals of Eugenics,* 16:134–141.

PETRAKIS, N. L., K. T. MOLOHON, and D. J. TEPPER. 1967. "Cerumen in American Indians: Genetic implications of sticky and dry types." *Science,* 158: 1192–1193.

PETTIGREW, T. F. 1971. "Race, mental illness and intelligence: A social psychological view." In *The Biological and Social Meaning of Race,* ed. R. H. Osborne. San Francisco: W. H. Freeman.

PIETRUSEWSKY, M. 1990. "Craniofacial variation in Australasian and Pacific populations." *Am. J. Phys. Anthrop.,* 82:319–340.

PLOMIN, R. 1989. "Environment and genes: Determinants of behavior." *Am. Psychologist,* 44(2):105–111.

POLEDNAK, A. P. 1989. *Racial and Ethnic Differences in Disease.* New York: Oxford University Press.

POLLITZER, W. S. 1958. "The negroes of Charleston (S.C.): A study of hemoglobin types, serology, and morphology." *Am. J. Phys. Anthrop.,* 16:241–263.

POLLITZER, W. S. 1972. "The physical anthropology and genetics of marginal people of the southeastern United States." *Am. Anthrop.,* 74(3):719–734.

POLLITZER, W. S. 1994. "Ethnicity and human biology." *Am. J. Human Bio.,* 6:3–11.

POLLITZER, W. S., R. M. MENEGAZ-BOCK, and J. C. HERION. 1966. "Factors in the microevolution of a triracial isolate." *Am. J Hum. Genetics,* 18(1):26–38.

POPULATION REFERENCE BUREAU. 1996. *World Population Data Sheet of the Population Reference Bureau.* Washington, DC: Population Reference Bureau.

POPULATION TODAY. 1990. Vol. 18(5).

POWARS, D. R. 1994. "Sickle cell disease in nonblack persons." *J. Am. Med. Assoc.,* 271(23):1885.

PRESTON, R. 1994. *The Hot Zone.* New York: Random House.

PRICHARD, J. C. 1826. *Researches into the Physical History of Mankind.* 2nd ed. 2 vols. London: John and Arthur Arch.

PRICHARD, J. C. 1973. *Researches into the Physical History of Man,* ed. G. W. Stocking Jr. Chicago: University of Chicago Press.

PRIOR, I. A. M. 1971. "The price of civilization." *Nutrition Today,* 6(4):2–11.

PRIOR, I. A. M., et al. 1986. "Cardiovascular epidemiological studies in New Zealand and the Pacific and the Tokelau Island migrant study." *Research Review.* Medical Research Council of New Zealand.

QUEVEDO, W. C. JR., T. B. FITZPATRICK, and K. JIMBOW. 1985. "Human skin color: origin, variation and significance." *J. Hum. Evol.,* 14:43–56.

RACE, R. R., and R. SANGER. 1975. *Blood Groups in Man*. 6th ed. Philadelphia: F. A. Davis.

RAMEY, C. T., D. MACPHEE, and K. O. YEATES. 1982. "Preventing developmental retardation: a general systems model." In *How and How Much Can Intelligence Be Increased*, eds. D. K. Detterman and R.J. Sternberg. Norwood, NJ: Ablex.

REED, T. E. 1969. "Caucasian genes in American Negroes." *Science*, 165:762–768.

RIPLEY, W. Z. 1899. *The Races of Europe*. New York: Appleton.

ROBERTS, D. F. 1978. *Climate and Human Variability*. 2nd ed. Menlo Park, CA: Cummings.

ROBERTSON, G. G. 1966. "Developmental anatomy." In *Morris Human Anatomy*, 12th ed., ed. B. J. Anson. New York: McGraw-Hill.

ROITT, I. M. 1988. *Essential Immunology*. 6th ed. Oxford: Blackwell Scientific Publications.

ROTTER, J. I., and J. M. DIAMOND. 1987. "What maintains the frequencies of human genetic diseases?" *Nature*, 329:289–290.

RUSHTON, J. P. 1992. "Cranial capacity related to sex, rank, and race in a stratified random sample of 6,325 U.S. military personnel." *Intelligence*, 16:401–413.

SAHI, T. 1978a. "Intestinal lactase polymorphisms and dairy foods." *Hum. Genetics*, Suppl. 1, 115–123.

SAHI, T. 1978b. "Intestinal lactase polymorphisms and dairy foods." International Titisee Conference. Titisee, 13–15 October 1977. *Hum. Genetics*, 50:107–143.

SALDANHA, P. H., and J. NACRUR. 1963. "Taste thresholds for phenylthiourea among Chileans," *Am. J. Phys. Anthrop.*, 21:113–120.

SALDANHA, P. H. 1958. "Taste thresholds for phenylthiourea among Japanese." *Hum. Genetics* 22:380–384.

SCARR, S. 1981. "Toward a more biological psychology." In *Science and the Question of Human Equality*, eds. M. S. Collins, I. W. D. Wainer, and T. A. Bremner. Boulder, CO: Westview.

SCARR, S., and R. A. WEINBERG. 1978. "Attitudes, interests, and IQ." *Human Nature*, 1:(4):29–36.

SCARR, S., and R. A. WEINBERG. 1983. "The Minnesota adoption studies: Genetic differences and malleability." *Child Development*, 54:260–267.

SCARR-SALAPATEK, S. 1971. "Race, social class and IQ." *Science*, 174:1285–1295.

SCHIFF, M., and R. LEWONTIN. 1986. *Education and Class: The Irrelevance of IQ Genetic Studies*. Oxford: Clarendon Press.

SCHOUR, I., and M. MASSLER. 1944. "Development and growth of teeth." In *Oral Histology and Embryology*, ed. B. Orban. St. Louis: C. V. Mosby.

SCHROEDER, W. A., and E. S. MUNGER. 1990. "Sickle cell anemia, genetic variations, and the slave trade to the United States." *Journal of African History*, 31:163–180.

SCHULL, W. J., and J. V. NEEL. 1965. *The Effects of Inbreeding on Japanese Children*. New York: Harper & Row.

SCHULTZ, A. H. 1926. "Fetal growth of man and other primates." *Quart. Rev. Biol.*, 1:493–495.

SCHWIDETZKY, I., and F. W. RÖSING. 1982. "European population of the high and late medieval period (1000–1500)—comparative statistical studies on historical physical anthropology." *Human-Biol.* Budapest 10: 39–47.

SCOTT, J. P. 1969. "Discussion." In *Science and the Concept of Race*, eds. M. Mead, T. Dobzhansky, E. Tobach, and R. E. Light. New York and London: Columbia University Press.

SEARLE, G. R. 1976. *Eugenics and Politics in Britain 1900–1914*. Leyden, The Netherlands: Noordhoff Intl. Publishing.

SERJEANTSON, S. W. 1984. "Migration and admixture in the Pacific." *J. Pacific History*, 19(3):160–171.

SERJEANTSON, S. W., R. L. KIRK, and P. B. BOOTH. 1983. "Linguistics and genetic differentiation in New Guinea." *J. Human Evol.*, 12:77–92.

SHAPIRO, H. L. 1942. "The anthropometry of Puka Puka." *Anthrop. Papers Mus. Nat. His.*, 38:141–169.

SHOCKLEY, WM. 1972. "Dysgenics, geneticity, raceology: A challenge to the intellectual responsibility of educators." *Phi Delta Kappan*, 53(5): 297–307.

SINISCALCO, M., L. L. BERNINI, G. FILIPPI, B. LATTE, P. MEERA KHAN, S. PIOMELLI, and M. RATTAZZI. 1966. "Population genetics of haemoglobin variants, thalassemia and glucose-6-phosphate dehydrogenase deficiency with particular reference to the malaria hypothesis." *Bulletin Wld. Hltd. Org.*, 34: 379–393.

SLOTKIN, J. S. 1965. *Readings in Early Anthropology.* New York: Viking Fund Publications in Anthropology, No. 40.

SMITH, T. L. 1960. *Fundamentals of Population Study.* J. P. Lippincott.

SOUTHERN, E. M. 1975. "Detection of specific sequences among DNA fragments separated by gel electrophoresis." *J. Mol. Biol.*, 98: 503–517.

SPUHLER, J. N. 1988. "Evolution of mitochondrial DNA in monkeys, apes, and humans." *Yearbook of Physical Anthropology*, 31:15–48.

SPUHLER, J. N., and G. LINDZEY. 1967. "Racial differences in behavior." In *Behavior Genetic Analysis*, ed. Jerry Hirsch. New York: McGraw–Hill.

STANTON, WM. R. 1960. *The Leopard's Spots: Scientific Attitudes Toward Race in America, 1815–59.* Chicago: University of Chicago Press.

STARKE, L., ed. 1996. *Vital Signs 1996.* New York: W. W. Norton.

Statistical Abstract of the United States. 1930. Washington, DC: U.S. Government Printing Office.

Statistical Abstract of the United States. 1995. 115th ed. Washington, DC: U.S. Government Printing Office.

STEPAN, N. 1982. *The Idea of Race in Science: Great Britain 1800–1960.* Hamden, CO: Archon Books.

STERN, C. 1973. *Principles of Human Genetics.* 3rd ed. San Francisco: W. H. Freeman.

STIGLER, S. M. 1986. *The History of Statistics: The Measurement of Uncertainty before 1900.* Cambridge, MA: Belknap Press of Harvard University Press.

STOCKING, G. W. JR., ed. 1973. *Researches into the Physical History of Man.* Chicago: University of Chicago Press.

STRINGER, C. B. 1993. New views on modern human origins. In *The Origin and Evolution of Humans and Humanness*, ed. D. T. Rasmussen. Boston: Jones and Bartlett. pp. 75–94.

SWINDLER, D. R. 1962. *The Racial Study of the West Nakanai.* University Museum, University of Pennsylvania. Museum Monographs.

SZATHMARY, E. 1985. "Peopling of North America: Clues from genetic studies." In *Out of Asia: Peopling the Americas and the Pacific*, eds. R. Kirk and E. Szathmary. The Journal of Pacific History, Inc. Australian National University, Canberra, Australia.

SZATHMARY, E. J. E. 1993. "Genetics of Aboriginal North Americans." *Evolutionary Anthrop.*, 1(6):202–220.

TANNER, J. M. 1962. *Growth at Adolescence.* Oxford: Blackwell Scientific Publications.

TANNER, J. M. 1973. "Growing up." In *Readings from Scientific American, Biological Anthropology.* San Francisco: W. H. Freeman.

TANNER, J. M. 1981. *A History of the Study of Human Growth.* Cambridge: Cambridge University Press.

TANNER, J. M. 1986. "Growth as a mirror of the condition of society: secular trends and class distinctions." In *Human Growth: A Multidisciplinary Review*, eds. A. Demirjian and M. Brault Dubue. London and Philadelphia: Taylor & Francis. pp. 3–34.

TARTAGLIA, M., R. SCACCHI, R. M. CORBO, F. POMPEI, O. RICKARDS, B. M. CIMINELLI, T. SANGATRAMANI, M. VYAS, S. DASH, and G. MODIANO. 1995. "Genetic heterogeneity among the Hindus and their relationships with the other 'Caucasoid' populations: New data on Punjab-Haryana and Rajasthan Indian states." *Am. J. Phys. Anthrop.*, 98:257–273.

TEMPLETON, A. R. 1985. "The phylogeny of the hominoid primates: A statistical analysis of the DNA hybridization data." *Mol. Biol. Evol.*, 2:420–433.

TEMPLETON, A. R. 1992. "Human origins and analysis of mitochondrial DNA sequences." *Science*, 255:737.

TEMPLETON, A. R. 1993. "The 'Eve' hypotheses: A genetic critique and reanalysis." *Am. Anthrop.*, 95(1):51–72.

THORNE, A. G., and M. H. WOLPOFF. 1992. "The multiregional evolution of humans." *Scientific American*, 266(4):76–83.

THURSTONE, L. L. 1940. "Current issues in factor analysis." *Psychological Bulletin*, 37:189–236.

TISHKOFF, S. A., E. DIETZSCH, W. SPEED, A. J. PAKTIS, J. R. KIDD, K. CHEUNG, B. BONNE-TAMIR, A. S. SANTACHIARA-BENERECETTI, P. MORAL, M. KRINGS, S. PAABO, E. WATSON, N. RISCH, T. JENKINS, and K. K. KIDD. 1996. "Global patterns of linkage disequilibrium at the CD4 locus and modern human origins." *Science*, 271:1380–1387.

TOBIAS, P. V. 1970. "Brain size, grey matter and race—fact or fiction." *Am. J. Phys. Anthrop.*, 32:3–26.

TOBIAS, P. V. 1971. *The Brain in Hominid Evolution*. New York and London: Columbia University Press.

TOBIAS, P. V. 1975. "Anthropometry among disadvantaged peoples. Studies in Southern Africa." In *Biosocial Interrelations in Population Adaptation*, eds. E. S. Watts, F. E. Johnston, and G. W. Lasker. The Hague, Paris: Mouton Publishers. pp. 287–305.

TORTORA, G. J. 1980. *Principles of Human Anatomy*. 2nd ed. New York: Harper & Row.

TRICHOPOULOS, D., F. P. LI, and D. J. HUNTER. 1996. "What causes cancer?" *Scientific American*, 275(3):80–87.

TURNER, C. G. II. 1985. "The dental search for Native American origins." In *Out of Asia: Peopling the Americas and the Pacific*, eds. R. Kirk and E. Szathmary. The Journal of Pacific History, Inc. Australian National University, Canberra, Australia.

TURNER, C. G. II. 1990. "Major features of Sundadonty and Sinodonty, including suggestions about East Asian microevolution, population history, and late Pleistocene relationships with Australian Aboriginals." *Am. J. Phys. Anthrop.*, 82:295–317.

U. S. Department of Health and Human Services. 1985. *Diabetes in America*. NIH Publication No. 85–1468.

U. S. Department of Health and Human Services. 1989. Monthly vital statistics report, Vol. 38, No. 5. Washington, DC.

U.S. Government Printing Office. 1930. Statistical abstract of the United States. Washington, DC.

VALLOIS, H. V., and P. MARQUER, 1964. "La Repartition en France des Groupes Sanguins ABO." BMSA. Vol. 6, 9th Series, No. 1. pp. 1–200.

VENTER, A. C., H. O. SMITH, and L. HOOD. 1996. "A new strategy for genome sequencing." *Nature*, 381:364–366.

VOGEL, F. 1968. "Anthropological implications of the relationship between ABO blood groups and infections." *Proceedings of the Eighth International Congress of Anthropological and Ethnological Sciences*, 1:365–370.

VOGEL, F. 1975. "ABO blood groups, the HL-A system and diseases." In *The Role of Natural Selection in Human Evolution*, ed. F. M. Salzano. New York: American Elsevier.

VOGEL, F., and A. G. MOTULSKY. 1986. *Human Genetics: Problems and Approaches*. 2nd ed. Berlin, Heidelberg, New York, Tokyo: Springer-Verlag.

VON BONIN, G. 1963. *The Evolution of the Human Brain*. Chicago: University of Chicago Press.

WADE, N. 1976. "IQ and heredity: Suspicion of fraud beclouds classic experiment." *Science*, 194:916–919.

WADE, N. 1979. "Recombinant DNA: Warming up for big payoff." *Science*, 206:663–665.

WALSH, R. J. 1963. "Variations of melanin pigmentation of the skin in some Asian and Pacific peoples." *J. Royal Anthropological Inst.*, 93, pt. 1:126–133.

WAMBAUGH, J. 1989. *The Blooding*. New York: Perigord Press.

WASHBURN, S. L. 1963. "The study of race." *Am. Anthrop.*, 65:521–531.

WASHBURN, S. L. 1964. "The study of race." In *The Concept of Race*, ed. A. Montagu. New York: Free Press of Glencoe.

WATSON, J. D. 1980. *The Double Helix: A Personal Account of the Discovery of the Structure of DNA*. New York: Norton.

WATSON, J. D. 1987. *Molecular Biology of the Gene*. 3rd ed. Menlo Park: W. A. Benjamin.

WATTENBERG, B. J. 1985. *The Birth Dearth*. New York: Pharos Books.

WEIDENREICH, FRANZ. 1947. "Facts and speculations concerning the origin of *Homo sapiens*." *Am. Anthrop.*, 49(2):135–151.

WEINBERG, R. A. 1989. "Intelligence and IQ. Landmark issues and great debates." *Am. Psychologist,* 44(2):98–104.

WEISS, K. M. 1993. *Genetic Variation and Human Disease: Principles and Evolutionary Approaches.* Cambridge: Cambridge University Press.

WILLIAMS, R. C. 1985. HLA II: "The emergence of the molecular model for the human major histocompatibility complex." *Yearbook of Physical Anthrop.,* 28:79–95.

WILLIAMS, R. J. 1956. *Biochemical Individuality.* New York: John Wiley.

WILLIAMS, R. L. 1974. "The silent mugging of the black community." *Psychology Today,* 7:pp. 32–41.

WILSON, A. C., and R. L. CANN. 1992. "The recent African genesis of humans." *Scientific American,* 266(4):68–73.

WILSON, E. O. 1978. *On Human Nature.* Cambridge, MA: Harvard University Press.

WILSON, T. W. 1986. "History of salt supplies in West Africa and blood pressures today." *Lancet,* 1:784–786.

WITKIN, H. A. et al. 1976. "Criminality in XYY and XXy men." *Science,* 193:547–555.

WITKOP, C. J. JR., W. C. QUEVEDO, JR., T. B. FITZPATRICK, and R. A. KING. 1989. "Albinism." In *The Metabolic Basis of Inherited Disease. 6th ed. Vol. II,* eds. C. R. Scriver, A. L. Beaudet, W. S. Sly and D. Valle. New York: McGraw-Hill. pp. 2905–2947.

WOLPOFF, M. H. 1996. *Human Evolution.* New York: McGraw-Hill.

WOLPOFF, M. H. 1968. "Climatic influences on the skeletal nasal aperture." *Am. J. Phys. Anthrop.,* 3:405–424.

WOOD, C. S. 1974. "Preferential feeding of anopheles gambiae mosquitoes on human subjects of blood group O: A relationship betweeen the ABO polymorphism and malaria vectors." *Human Biology,* 46(3):385–404.

WOODFIELD, D. G., L. A. SIMPSON, G. SEBER, and P. J. McINERNEY. 1987. "Blood groups and other genetic markers in New Zealand Europeans and Maoris." *Annals of Human Biology,* 14(N1):29–37.

WORLD HEALTH STATISTICS ANNUAL. 1978. Geneva.

WORLD HEALTH STATISTICS ANNUAL. 1979. Geneva.

WORLD HEALTH STATISTICS ANNUAL. 1987. Geneva.

"World Population Data Sheet," 1980. Washington, DC: Population Reference Bureau, Inc.

"World Population Data Sheet," 1990. Washington, DC: Population Reference Bureau, Inc.

"World Population Data Sheet," 1996. Washington, DC: Population Reference Bureau, Inc.

YERKES, R. M., ed. 1921. "Psychological examining in the U. S. Army." New York: *Mem. Natl. Acad. Sci.,* 15.

YINGER, N. 1990. "Focus on maternal mortality." *Population Today,* 18(5):6–7. Washington, DC: Population Reference Bureau.

YOUNG, J. B. 1971. *An Introduction to the Study of Man.* London: Oxford University Press.

ZAGO, M. A., M. S. FIGUEIREDO, and S. H. OGO. 1992. "Bantu B^s cluster haplotype predominates among Brazilian blacks." *Am. J. Phys. Anthrop.,* 88:295–298.

ZIMMET, P. 1982. "Review articles: Type 2 (non-insulin-dependent) diabetes. An epidemiological overview." *Diabetologia,* 22: 399–411.

Glossary

adaptation   response to environmental conditions by adjustments of physiological processes or behavior to improve an organism's chance of survival; may be short-term (functional), sometimes referred to as acclimatization, or a long-term response of a population's genetic variability that is affected by natural selection over several generations.

age cohorts   individuals who share a common demographic attribute; most frequently, members of the same age group.

agglutination   the clinging together of cells caused by the attraction of antibodies and antigens, as in the case of blood cells with specific antibodies.

albumin   a type of simple, soluble protein distributed throughout the tissue fluids.

allele   alternate genetic forms of the same locus.

amino acids   small organic compounds, containing the amino group, that are combined to form protein compounds.

anthropometry   the measurement of human body form.

antibodies   protein molecules in the blood serum that will react with foreign proteins and protect against invading organisms.

antigen   a substance capable of stimulating the production of an antibody; or inherited antigen forms, such as those of the red blood cell—the blood groups.

assortative mating   the preferential selection of a mate with a particular trait or attribute; most frequently seen in positive assortative mating.

autosome   all chromosomes except the sex chromosomes, X and Y.

biodeterminism   attributing certain behaviors to particular races or ethnic groups, behaviors that presumably exist because of some inherited traits.

brachycephalic   describes a short, broad-shaped head whose breadth is approximately 80 percent or more of its length.

breeding population   a group of individuals who are potentially interbreeding, who occupy a local area, and who make up a basic unit of our species.

brow ridge   the ridge of bone over the eyes.

carpals   wrist bones.

cartilage   a dense, firm, but flexible connective tissue that is the major part of most of the skeleton and that calcifies at various stages of growth.

centromere   the part of the chromosome where the chromatids are joined.

cephalic index   the ratio of the breadth to the length of the head or skull.

cerumen   the waxy substance secreted by glands in the external ear.

chiasma   crossing over of chromatids of homologous chromosomes during an early stage of meiosis.

chromatid   one of the two strands that make up the chromosome.

chromosome   the darkly staining rod-shaped structure, located in the nucleus of a cell, that is composed of DNA molecules.

clinal distribution   traces the geographical range of phenotypic or genetic characteristics of our species.

coefficient of inbreeding   the probability of like alleles from a common ancestor. The coefficient is higher, for example, in matings of first cousins (1/16) than in second cousins (1/64).

collagen   a fibrous protein that is the chief constituent part of connective tissue and bone.

congenital defect   a defective organ, system, or anatomical structure that is present at birth.

consanguineous   genetic relative; related because of a common ancestor.

cormic index   the ratio of sitting height to standing height, that shows the proportion of body height due to the head and trunk.

corneum   outer layer of the epidermis.

correlation   the degree of correspondence between two measurements.

cranial capacity   the volume of the skull; used to estimate brain volume.

craniology   a science dealing with variations in size, shape, and proportions of skulls among *Homo sapiens.*

crossover   the exchange of genetic material between homologous chromosomes when in synapse during meiosis.

culture   the learned behavioral pattern that *Homo sapiens* uses to manipulate the environment.

Darwinian fitness   states characteristic of those who produce the most offspring.

deme   *See* breeding population.

demographic transition   a transition in the growth potential of a population.

demography   the study of a population's growth, size, and composition.

deoxyribonucleic acid (DNA)   a large organic molecule composed of two intertwined strands of similar units, nucleotides; each nucleotide contains an organic base, deoxyribose sugar, and a phosphate molecule.

dependency ratio   the ratio between the economically productive portion of the population and the dependent age groups, usually taken as those under fifteen and over sixty-five years.

dermis   inner layer of skin where the blood vessels, nerves, glands, and hair follicles are located.

diaphysis   the shaft of long bones.

diploid number   the number of chromosomes in all cells except a germinal cell.

distal   referring to the direction away from the point of attachment of a limb.

DNA   *See* deoxyribonucleic acid.

dolichocephalic   describes a long, narrow head whose breadth is 75 percent or less of its length.

dominant inheritance   one allele is dominant to another and, in the heterozygote, will cause the expression of the trait.

dysgenic   those factors that reduce hereditary qualities; frequently applied to the preservation in the gene of defective traits through modern medical treatment of the affected individual; the opposite of eugenics.

effective breeding population   that proportion of the population who are in their reproductive years.

electrophoresis   a method of separating proteins by applying an electric charge to a solution of proteins.

embryo   organism during the first eight weeks of gestation of in-utero development of *Homo sapiens.*

endemic   the continuous presence of a disease in a community; often used in reference to a disease like malaria that continually infects a tropical population on a year-round basis.

endogamy   inbreeding within a certain social unit, population, or deme.

endonucleases   enzymes that break bonds at specific nucleotide sites along strands of DNA or RNA.

enzyme   a protein catalyst that causes a chemical reaction to occur in a living organism.

epidemiology   the study of the distribution and causes of a disease.

epidermis   outer layer of skin; a tissue of four layers.

epiphysis   the portion of bone that develops from secondary centers of ossification and remains separate throughout the period of bone growth; the ends of the long bones connected to the main shaft, the *diaphysis.*

erythroblastosis fetalis   the hemolytic blood disease of the newborn in which the blood cells of an Rh+ infant are destroyed by maternal antibodies from an Rh– mother.

erythrocytes   red blood cells.

ethnic group   a group of persons who share the same language and customs and who identify with certain recent origins.

eugenics   efforts to improve the human species by controlled breeding.

evolution   change in gene frequency of a population through time; descent with modification.

exogamy   matings between members of different social groups, populations, or demes; outbreeding.

exon   the segments of DNA that are transcribed into mRNA that are then translated into a polypeptide chain.

fetus   human organism from eight weeks of development until birth.

fitness   *See* Darwinian fitness.

founders' effect   establishment of a new population by a few original migrants or "founders" whose genetic composition may be an aberrant sample of the gene pool of the large population from which it migrated.

gametes   germ cells, either ova or sperm.

gamma globulin   a serum protein consisting of antibodies that act as a defense against infection.

gene   that region of the DNA molecule that contains the nucleotide sequence code for the production of a polypeptide chain relayed by a messenger RNA.

gene flow   exchange of genetic material between populations due to dispersion of gametes through interbreeding.

genetic disease   an inherited disorder, usually caused by recessive alleles but sometimes by dominants.

genetic drift   refers to chance events that alter gene frequencies in small breeding populations; the reduction in gene frequency is due to a sampling error because of a small number of matings.

genetic load   the total frequency of a population's lethal or sublethal genes that may affect an individual's growth, development, health, or chance of survival.

genotype   actual genetic composition of an organism; the pair of alleles at a locus of homologous chromosomes determined at conception.

globulins   a major group of proteins in blood plasma that include alpha, beta, and gamma globulins.

haploid   refers to the number of chromosomes in sperm or ova (twenty-three) that is one-half the number of a somatic cell (forty-six).

haplotypes   a series or combination of closely linked loci.

haptoglobin   a protein in the serum portion of blood whose function is to bind with free hemoglobin to prevent its excretion.

Hardy-Weinberg Equilibrium   a mathematical formula stating the proportions between alleles within a stable population.

hemoglobin   red respiratory protein making up more than 90 percent of the protein of a red cell and functioning to transport oxygen to the tissues of the body.

hemolysis   the bursting apart of a red blood cell, releasing its products into the blood plasma.

heritability   that proportion of variation of a trait in a population that is due to the variation of genotypes.

heterozygote   a pair of different alleles.

homeostasis   maintenance of an equilibrium of various metabolic functions in the body.
hominid   the primate family taxon that includes *Homo sapiens* and extinct ancestral forms such as the Australopithecines.
homologous   having a likeness in structure.
Homo sapiens   the human species; genus *Homo*, species *sapiens*.
homozygote   a pair of identical alleles.
hypoxia   less than normal levels of oxygen in air, blood, or tissues; also refers to a general physiological state in response to low levels of atmospheric oxygen, particularly among persons at higher elevations.
incest taboo   matings forbidden between certain classes of relatives.
intron   a noncoding region of DNA that is transcribed but excised from mature mRNA.
isolate   a population or group of populations that maintain a high degree of breeding isolation from other groups because marriages with outsiders are forbidden or restricted.
karyotype   the distinctive array of chromosomes; the size and shape of a species' chromosomes seen at metaphase of cell division.
keratin   a protein; the major constituent of the outer skin layers.
Law of Independent Assortment   two traits, simultaneously considered, will sort and recombine independently of each other; Mendel's second law.
Law of Independent Segregation   traits are transmitted as discrete units that do not blend with or contaminate each other: Mendel's first law.
linkage   two or more genes located at loci close to one another on a chromosome.
locus   a chromosome position or space for the coded unit of the gene.
mandible   the lower jaw; the bone containing the lower teeth.
matrilocal   the settlement pattern in which adult males leave to marry outside of their natal community while the females remain.
maxilla   bone of the major portion of the face; contains the teeth and upper jaw.
meiosis   process of cell division and chromosome replication in germinal cells followed by cell fission and reduction in chromosome number.
melanin   dark pigment granules of the skin and hair of animals and of structures of plants.
melanocytes   pigment cells of the skin.
menarche   the onset of menstruation; the first menstrual period.
Mendelian ratio   the ratio of genotypes of homozygote and heterozygote combinations.
mesocephalic   describes an intermediate head shape between brachycephalic (broad-headed) and dolichocephalic (long-headed).
metacarpals   the bones of the hands connecting the phalanges with the carpals (bones of the wrist).
microevolution   alteration in the frequency of occurrence of certain genes that persists throughout generations.
mitosis   cell division that occurs in somatic cells producing two identical daughter cells.
molecular clock   an estimate of the time since divergence of two related species from a common ancestor by comparison of certain molecular structures or DNA fragments.
monogenic   single gene traits as contrasted with traits determined by two or more genes (polygenic).
mutation   a change in the genetic code; a change in the sequence of base pairs of the DNA molecule.
nasal index   a ratio of the width to the length of the nose.
natal   associated with one's birth; applied to location, native or community, where one's birth took place.
natural selection   due to certain natural conditions in the environment, some individuals, because of their genetic endowment, produce more offspring who, in turn, reproduce at a higher rate than do other individuals. Through this process the less well-adapted are gradually reduced in number over the generations.
Neolithic   the "New Stone Age," a period beginning approximately 10,000 to 12,000 years ago when *Homo sapiens* began to domesticate plants and, later, animals. A major feature of the Neolithic is the sedentary lifestyle that it encouraged.
orthognathic   straight-faced; the teeth and supporting bone in the anterior part of the face lie close to a line drawn between the chin and the brow.
osteomalacia   failure of the collagen of the newly formed bone to mineralize. A similar condition in children and juveniles is referred to as *rickets*.

patrilocal   the settlement pattern in which females leave to marry outside of their natal community while the males remain.

penetrance   the frequency of expression of the phenotype; some genes are expressed less than 100 percent of the time, so they have a low penetrance.

phalanges   the long bones of the fingers and toes.

phenotype   the trait expressed as a result of the interaction of the environment and genotype.

photolysis   the destruction of chemical compounds by light; usually in reference to the ultraviolet range.

plasma   the yellowish fluid part of the blood containing nutrients, many proteins, and the red and white blood cells.

pleiotropic   genes that influence the expression of more than one trait.

polygenic   multiple genes that influence a single trait.

polymorphic   describes variability between individuals within a population.

polytypic   describes variability between populations.

porphyrins   complex pigment molecules widely dispersed in plants and animals. Examples in humans are heme (of hemoglobin), bile, and cytochrome.

prognathic   having forward protrusion of the midfacial region due primarily to large teeth and robust dental arches.

race   a geographically and culturally determined collection of individuals who share in a common gene pool and are similar in many characteristics (also referred to as a subspecies).

random mating   matings that occur without regard to genotype.

recessive inheritance   a trait determined by a pair of recessive alleles.

recombination   the formation of new combinations of linked genes by crossover between parts of homologous chromosomes during meiosis.

RFLP   restriction fragment length polymorphisms of DNA molecules produced by nucleotide specific enzymes (endonucleases).

ribonucleic acid (RNA)   a single-strand molecule of organic bases, sugars (ribose), and phosphates; used to translate the coded sequence of the DNA (RNA) or carry amino acids to the sites of protein synthesis (+RNA).

ribosomes   these small spherical structures in the cell cytoplasm are made up of proteins and RNA, and are the site for protein synthesis.

rickets   a bone disease of young children and juveniles in which their rapidly growing bones fail to mineralize properly; the bones—especially the weight-bearing ones—easily bend or may become distorted.

RNA   *See* ribonucleic acid.

sampling error   a change in gene frequencies within a population that is due to an error caused by the small size of the effective breeding population.

secular trend   a trend continuing for a long term or over a generation.

sex-linked   describes a trait determined by a gene carried on the sex chromosomes, usually the X chromosome.

sexual dimorphism   refers to the difference in form or size in males and females.

shovel-shaped incisor   incisor tooth that has thickened margins on the lingual surface (tongue side of the tooth).

somatology   the science that deals with the body, its form, and function; usually applied to comparative studies of body forms of different ethnic groups.

species   groups of interbreeding organisms reproductively isolated from other such groups.

steatopygia   an excessive accumulation of fat and probably fibrous tissue in the buttocks; particularly in evidence among females of certain ethnic groups such as the Bushmen and Hottentots of southern Africa.

subspecies   a grouping of individuals or populations that share a number of characteristics in common; frequently geographically limited.

synapsis   the pairing of homologous chromosomes during the anaphase stage of meiosis.

syndrome   the group or aggregate of symptoms associated with any disease or abnormal condition; for example, Down syndrome, a group of physical and neurological deformities appearing in a person with an extra chromosome of the twenty-first pair.

transferrins   a group of iron-binding proteins found in the serum portion of blood.

trisomy   the diploid number plus one, as in the example of a Down syndrome person with 47 chromosomes.

twins (dizygotic)   twins who are developed from a pair of fertilized ova and who are no more identical in their genotypes than sibs; also called fraternal twins.

twins (monozygotic)   twins developed from a cleavage of a single fertilized ovum; hence, they have identical genotypes; identical twins.

variance   the measure of the dispersion of values about a population mean.

zygomatic arches   cheekbones.

zygote   the fertilized egg.

Index